Nuclear, Biological and Chemical (NBC) Warfare

How to Control its Devastating Impact

Nuclear, Biological and Chemical (NBC) Warfare

How to Control its Devastating Impact

Capt. (Retd.) Komal Malik
&
B.C. Kumar

PRASHANT PUBLISHING HOUSE
DELHI-110094

Published by :
Prashant Publishing House
C-34, 28 Foota Road, Gali-3,
West Karwal Nagar, Delhi-110094.
Phone : 011-22963970, Mob. : 9810396373
e-mail.: prashantpublishinghouse@gmail.com

Nuclear, Biological and Chemical (NBC) Warfare

How to Control its Devastating Impact

First Published 2014

ISBN: 978-93-80565-47-7

PRINTED IN INDIA
Published by Mr. R.K. Jha M/s Prashant Publishing House and Published at H.S. Offset House Press, Delhi.

Preface

The book Nuclear, Biological and Chemical Warfare provides a thoughtful and comprehensive analysis of the historical motives for acquiring and possibly using-nuclear, biological and chemical weapons.

Nuclear warfare (sometimes atomic warfare or thermonuclear warfare) is a military conflict or political strategy in which nuclear weaponry is used to inflict damage on the enemy. Compared to conventional warfare, nuclear warfare can be vastly more destructive in range and extent of damage, and in a much shorter time frame. A major nuclear exchange would have long-term effects, primarily from the fallout released, and could also lead to a "nuclear winter" that could last for decades, centuries, or even millennia after the initial attack. Some analysts claim that with this potential nuclear winter side-effect of a nuclear war almost every human on Earth could starve to death, While other analysts, that dismiss the nuclear winter hypothesis, calculate that with nuclear weapon stockpiles at Cold War highs, in a surprise countervalue global nuclear war, megadeaths to billions of casualties would have resulted but billions of people would nevertheless have survived the global thermonuclear war.

Biological warfare (BW)—also known as germ warfare—is the use of biological toxinsor infectious agents such as bacteria, viruses, smallpox, and fungi with intent to kill or incapacitate humans, animals or plants as an act of war. Biological weapons (often termed "bio-weapons", "biological threat agents", or "bio-agents") are living organisms or replicating entities (viruses, which are not universally considered "alive") that reproduce or replicate within their host victims. Entomological (insect) warfare is also considered a type of biological weapon.

This type of warfare is distinct from nuclear warfare and chemical warfare, which together make up NBC, the military acronym for nuclear, biological, and chemical (warfare or weapons), all of which are considered "weapons of mass destruction" (WMDs). None of these fall under the term conventional weaponswhich are primarily effective due to their destructive potential.

Rapid detection and quantification of a CW/BW attack on a water supply is difficult at best. Unlike aerial delivery, a CW/BW attack via water won't be heralded by incoming missiles or bombs and concomitant weapons detonation. Dumping a thermos of concentrated anthrax spores into a clear well won't garner much attention. The first evidence of attack is likely to be a flood of sick or dying at the emergency room. By the time water is recognized as the source, identification and quantification of the agent could take days if not weeks. To further complicate force protection, the adversary could tailor the effect based on his objective, using chemicals or fast acting pathogens for a quick kill, or slower incubating pathogens for delayed effects.

Among the Weapons of Mass Destruction, chemical warfare (CW) is probably one of the most brutal created by mankind in comparison with biological and nuclear warfare. Chemical weapons are inexpensive and are relatively easy to produce, even by small terrorist groups, to create mass casualties with small quantities. The characteristics of various CW agents, general information relevant to current physical as well as medical protection methods, detection equipment available and decontamination techniques. A brief note on Chemical Weapons Convention is also provided.

Nuclear power reactors contain an enormous amount of radioactive material. Much attention has been focused on the possibility that reactor containment systems might fail, leading to escape of radioactivity and the possible death of up to tens of thousands of people. The meltdown and dispersal of a portion of the core of a nuclear power reactor could readily result from attack on a nuclear power plant by conventional or nuclear weapons which disabled cooling and other control systems. Even more devastating, though, would be the result of direct hit by a nuclear weapon on a nuclear power reactor, with the nuclear reactor's radioactive inventory being directly incorporated into the fireball of the nuclear explosion. This inventory would then be incorporated into the fallout cloud from the explosion.

This book will provide some of the tools for students to research the area of chemical and biological warfare and, given that opportunity, to make their own judgments of the facts and opinions of many different agencies.

—Editor

Contents

1

Introduction

USE OF NUCLEAR, BIOLOGICAL OR CHEMICAL WEAPONS: INTERNATIONAL LAW AND POLICY

Use of Nuclear Weapons

Today there is no comprehensive and universal prohibition on the use of nuclear weapons in either customary or conventional international law.

Nonetheless, on 8 July 1996 the International Court of Justice, the principal judicial organ of the United Nations, gave an Advisory Opinion about the *Legality of the threat or use of nuclear weapons.*

The 14 judges of the Court examined current treaty law, customary rules and State practice with regard to nuclear weapons and, based on their analysis, concluded unanimously that the principles and rules of international humanitarian law apply to the use of nuclear weapons. They added that the use of nuclear weapons would generally be contrary to the principles and rules of international humanitarian law.

Use of Biological and Chemical Weapons

According to customary international humanitarian law which is binding on all States and on all parties to an armed conflict, the use of biological and chemical weapons is prohibited.

This norm is based on the ancient taboo against the use in war of " plague and poison ", which has been passed down for generations in diverse cultures. It was most recently codified in the 1925 Geneva Protocol and subsequently in the 1972 Biological Weapons Convention and in the 1993 Chemical Weapons Convention. The great majority of States are parties to these three treaties. The prohibitions based on these texts cover not only the use, but also the development, production and stockpiling of biological and chemical weapons. It should be emphasized that in situations of armed conflict this absolute prohibition applies to all biological and chemical agents, whether labelled " lethal " or " non-lethal ". For example, even the use of riot control agents which is permitted for domestic riot control purposes is prohibited in situations of armed conflict.

RESOLUTIONS ADOPTED BY INTERNATIONAL CONFERENCES

In response to the development of nuclear, biological and chemical weapons, the Movement repeatedly expressed its concerns about such weapons in various resolutions adopted by several International Conferences of the Red Cross and Red Crescent.

The resolutions called for preventive action with regard to the threat to the civilian population and to humanity at large posed by nuclear, biological and chemical weapons. They urged Governments to agree, within the framework of general disarmament, on a plan for the international control of atomic energy that would ensure the prohibition of nuclear weapons. They also urged Governments to conclude as rapidly as possible an agreement banning the production and stockpiling of chemical and biological weapons to complement the ban on use in the 1925 Geneva Protocol.

Recent International Conferences of the Red Cross and Red Crescent have not focused on the issue of nuclear, biological and chemical weapons in part due to the fact that the humanitarian problems caused by conventional weapons such as anti-personnel landmines, blinding laser weapons, the availability of small arms and explosive remnants of war, needed to be urgently addressed.

NUCLEAR, BIOLOGICAL AND CHEMICAL WEAPONS

Nuclear Weapons

One year ago the ICRC reviewed its policy statement on nuclear weapons in particular to take account of the 1996 Advisory Opinion of the International Court of Justice (ICJ). While basing its legal opinion on the existing international law and the ICJ Advisory Opinion, the ICRC, as an humanitarian organisation, also takes a position based on broader ethical and humanitarian considerations. Its position is presented here:

- The principles and rules of international humanitarian law, and in particular the principles of distinction and proportionality and the prohibition on causing superfluous injury or unnecessary suffering, apply to the use of nuclear weapons. The ICRC finds it difficult to envisage how the use of nuclear weapons could be compatible with the principles and rules of international humanitarian law.
- In view of the unique characteristics of nuclear weapons, the ICRC calls on States to ensure that these weapons are not used, irrespective of whether they consider them to be lawful or not. Nuclear weapons are characterized in particular by their destructive power, the unspeakable suffering caused by their use, the fact that it is extremely difficult to bring aid to victims, the fact that it is impossible to control their effects in space and time, the risk of escalation and proliferation which any use of nuclear weapons necessarily involves, and the dangers which such weapons entail for the environment, future generations and the survival of humanity.
- The ICRC furthermore calls on States to take every appropriate measure to limit the risk of the proliferation of nuclear weapons and to effectively combat any trade in substances or components liable to promote such proliferation.
- Finally, the ICRC calls on States to pursue negotiations with a view to achieving a complete prohibition on nuclear weapons as well as the elimination of such weapons, as they have undertaken to do.

Biological and Chemical Weapons

As early as February 1918, deeply concerned by the increasing use of chemical weapons in World War I, the ICRC issued an impassioned appeal *International Bulletin of the Red Cross Societies* , N° 194, April 1918, pp. 185-187 (in French only) or on ICRC's website. stating that if warfare by poison were accepted " we can only see ahead a struggle which will exceed in barbarity anything which history has known so far".

It protested " with all the force at [its] command against such warfare, which can only be called criminal. " This appeal is still valid today. Because of their potential to cause horrific forms of suffering and the difficulties of protecting civilian populations, the ICRC continues to consider the use of biological and chemical weapons to be abhorrent. The use of such weapons would contravene existing international treaties and many of the fundamental norms of international humanitarian law.

On 25 September 2002, the ICRC launched an Appeal on Biotechnology, Weapons and Humanity to promote consideration of the risks, rules and responsibilities related to advances in biotechnology which may lead to their hostile use to cause poisoning and deliberate disease.

The ICRC appealed to all political and military authorities to strengthen their commitment to the international humanitarian law norms which prohibit the hostile uses of biological agents, and to work together to subject potentially dangerous biotechnology to effective controls. All States were urged to ensure faithful implementation of the relevant treaties related to biological and chemical weapons and to adopt stringent national legislation in order to ensure that the legal norms prohibiting biological and chemical warfare are known and respected.

The ICRC also called on the scientific and medical communities, industry and civil society in general to ensure that potentially dangerous biological knowledge and agents be subject to effective controls.

Finally the Appeal urges States to adopt in 2003 at a high political level an international Declaration on " Biotechnology, Weapons and Humanity " containing a renewed commitment to existing norms and specific commitments to future preventive action.

BIOLOGICAL/CHEMICAL WEAPONRY

"Biological warfare is the intentional use of disease-causing microorganisms or other entities that can replicate themselves (e.g., viruses, infectious nucleic acids and prions) against humans, animals or plants for hostile purposes. It may also involve the use of toxins: poisonous substances produced by living organisms...plants...and animals.

If they are utilized for warfare purpose, the synthetically manufactured counterparts of these toxins are biological weapons."

Delivery of such substances can be as easy as sending it via mail, as in the anthrax example, or as sophisticated as mounting a chemical warhead onto a missile.

Other possible means of delivery include introducing a substance to a water supply or through air dispersal in the form of gas.

As far back as the 6th century BC, warring nations have been involved with the use of biological weaponry. Despite its long history, it is perhaps best to look at more recent events.

- With the better understanding of disease in the 20th century, various forms of chemical and biological weaponry emerged. For example, during World War I, poisonous gases were used in addition to anthrax applications by German operatives.
- Even more recently, radical groups have implemented various chemical agents with the intent of mass destruction. For example, in addition to the anthrax threat, in March of 1995, a nerve gas called sarin was released in a subway system of Japan.

In such cases, it is clear that the endangerment of human life is wrong. However, stopping such activity is becoming increasingly more difficult with the continued development of chemical and biological weaponry by rogue parties and states.

LEGAL ISSUES: THE CHEMICAL WEAPONS CONVENTION

In 1992, in order to curb the proliferation of chemical and biological war agents, members of the United Nations agreed upon the text of the Convention on the Prohibition of the Development, Production, Stockpiling and Use of Chemical Weapons and on Their Destruction — more simply, the Chemical Weapons Convention (CWC). It is, most simply put, an extension of the Geneva Protocol of 1925 and the Biological and Toxin Weapons Convention of 1972 (BTWC).

- The Geneva Protocol called for the prohibition of the use of chemical and biological weapons in war.
- The BTWC outlawed biological and toxin weapons altogether and required their destruction.
- What the CWC added was more specific information regarding actual chemicals as well as provisions for assistance if chemical weapons are used on a cooperating state.

The CWC and like-minded protocols have given an outline for cooperating states to follow. However, it is difficult to contend with groups who do not adhere to the CWC. Because the development and use of biological weapons continue throughout rogue states, the question arises on how to deal with the situation. Under the guidelines of the CWC, cooperating nations such as the United States are not allowed to develop, produce, or use chemical weapons. As such, the use of weapons by a cooperating state should not be an issue. In order to deal with the possible use of toxins against a nation under the CWC, research for vaccines is allowed.

A Code of Ethics

Most people and nations agree that the use of biological or chemical weapons is unethical and morally wrong. So why are such weapons produced? One significant reason is that most biotechnology is dual-use, that is, it has both peaceful and harmful purposes. The same technology that gives us genetically engineered medicine can also give us military weapons.

A 2001 research study illustrates the dual-use dilemma:

In an effort to develop a contraceptive vaccine for purposes of pest control, scientists inadvertently created a potential bioweapon. Early this year, Australian researchers hypothesized that introducing a gene that creates large amounts of interleukin-4 (IL-4) into mice would stimulate antibodies against mouse eggs and render the animals infertile. IL-4 occurs naturally in the body, but an overabundance triggers an immune response. The researchers working on this study needed a vehicle to get the new gene incorporated into the mouse DNA. The scientists chose a benign mousepox virus as their vector and, to their surprise, the virus killed all of the mice in the study. IL-4 suppressed the immune system, making it unable to fight the mousepox virus. With no defensive launched by the immune system the virus was 100 percent lethal. The virus was significantly lethal even in mice vaccinated against this particular strain of mousepox. Mousepox is a virus equivalent to human smallpox. "It would be safe to assume that if some idiot did put human IL-4 into human smallpox they'd increase the lethality quite dramatically," said Ronald J. Jackson in the Jan. 10, 2001 issue of the New Scientist. *Jackson is one of the researchers on the Australian study.*

When the conventions to ban such weapons were formulated, the world did not think these weapons had major military uses. Now, recent terrorist and scientific developments require stronger measures. For example:

- Especially controversial is the Human Genome Diversity Project, begun in 1993 to study the genetic variation across different human populations. The project could contribute to the understanding of human genetics and the improvement of human health. However, some critics of the project fear the information may be used to create weapons to target a particular racial or ethnic group. Although many researchers conclude that ethnic biological warfare is not a practical possibility today, they nevertheless caution that it cannot be ruled out in the future.
- Weapons targeting specific varieties of plants and animals are a real possibility today. In regions where monoculture (large acreage of genetically-identical crops) is the norm, such weapons could destroy a nation's agricultural output.

One of the proposals put forth by some nations, including the U.S., is to institutionalize a code of ethics for scientists working with potentially dangerous pathogens and toxins. Scientists would be required to foresee potential dangerous applications of their work and to either discontinue the research or redirect their work.

In 2002, the Stockholm International Peace Research Institute (SIPRI) conducted an online survey (English-only sites) of how many scientific organizations worldwide had a code of ethics. The Institute discovered a code of ethics for the following:

- 11% of 71 international scientific organizations
- 12% of 267 national or regional scientific organizations

Ethics is about recognizing that there are some things we cannot and will not support or do. Codes of ethics have been around for a long time in the sciences. Perhaps the best-known one is the doctor's Hippocratic Oath, which states "I will neither give a deadly drug to anybody if asked for it, nor will I make a suggestion to this effect." The Stimson Center, a security think-tank organization, offers some of the reasons why ethics codes in the sciences are not well established:

- codes are not particularly well publicized
- science students are not sufficiently educated in such codes at universities
- codes that are already in place vary in form from good to poor among scientific organizations

Another consideration for a code that prohibits scientists from working on dangerous substances with potential military applications — How can scientists know in advance the outcome of their experiments or all future applications of their work? Einstein had no idea that his work would lead to the atomic bomb.

In addition to ethical codes, there are other ways to increase ethical awareness:

- inclusion of ethical content and decision-making instruction in scientific curricula
- online ethical resources
- ethical awareness campaigns conducted by professional science organizations
- workshops for industry, academia, and scientists on the interface between research and business ethics
- ongoing discussion in scientific journals and the mainstream press
- accountability mechanisms and public oversight of research
- provision of confidential ethical mentoring services
- protection for whistle-blowers.

With the current evolution of potential threats, the issue of biological and chemical weaponry is a very important one. Ethical issues regarding war in general are a paper in and of itself.

The use of weapons comes down to whether or not it is morally acceptable and ethically responsible to do harm to another person. And essentially, the destruction of human life is unacceptable in most areas of the world. Just like nuclear weapons, the potential for mass destruction using biological/ toxin weapons is too great a threat.

The CWC is right in imposing its guidelines. However, because the threat of biotechnological attacks exist, it is also important to develop and implement a global scientific code of conduct to curb the proliferation of such weaponry. One organization, the Federation of American Scientists (FAS), believes that the education of young scientists is an important step in the elimination of weapons of mass destruction. FAS would like to see first-year science graduate students taking at least one course on the essentials of treaties, laws, regulations, and other programs designed to control biological warfare. This, FAS believes, would "raise the ethical consciousness of bioscientists, increase their awareness of the potential for hostile or dangerous exploitation of biotechnology, and persuade them of their responsibility to take action whenever possible to prevent it."

2

Nuclear Warfare

Nuclear warfare (sometimes atomic warfare or thermonuclear warfare) is a military conflict or political strategy in which nuclear weaponry is used to inflict damage on the enemy. Compared to conventional warfare, nuclear warfare can be vastly more destructive in range and extent of damage, and in a much shorter time frame. A major nuclear exchange would have long-term effects, primarily from the fallout released, and could also lead to a "nuclear winter" that could last for decades, centuries, or even millennia after the initial attack. Some analysts claim that with this potential nuclear winter side-effect of a nuclear war almost every human on Earth could starve to death, While other analysts, that dismiss the nuclear winter hypothesis, calculate that with nuclear weapon stockpiles at Cold War highs, in a surprise countervalue global nuclear war, megadeaths to billions of casualties would have resulted but billions of people would nevertheless have survived the global thermonuclear war.

Only two nuclear weapons have been used in the course of warfare, both by the United States near the end of World War II. On August 6, 1945, a uranium gun-type device (code name "Little Boy") was detonated over the Japanese city of Hiroshima. Three days later, on August 9, a plutonium implosion-type device (code name "Fat Man") was detonated over Nagasaki, Japan. These two bombings resulted in the deaths of approximately 200,000 people from acute injuries sustained in the detonations.

After World War II, nuclear weapons were also developed by the Soviet Union (1949), theUnited Kingdom (1952), France (1960), and the People's Republic of China (1964), which contributed to the state of conflict and extreme tension that became known as the Cold War. In 1974, India, and in 1998, Pakistan, two countries that were openly hostile toward each other, developed nuclear weapons. Israel (1960s) and North Korea (2006) are also thought to have developed stocks of nuclear weapons, but their governments have never admitted to having nuclear weapons. South Africa also manufactured several complete nuclear weapons in the 1980s, but subsequently became the first country to voluntarily destroy their domestically made weapons stocks and abandon further production (1990s).

Nuclear weapons have been detonated on over two thousand occasions for testing purposes and demonstrations.

After the collapse of the Soviet Union in 1991 and the resultant end of the Cold War, the threat of a major nuclear war between the two nuclear superpowers was generally thought to have declined. Since then, concern over nuclear weapons has shifted to the prevention of localized nuclear conflicts resulting from nuclear proliferation, and the threat of nuclear terrorism.

TYPES OF NUCLEAR WARFARE

The possibility of using nuclear weapons in war is usually divided into two subgroups, each with different effects and potentially fought with different types of nuclear armaments.

The first, a *limited nuclear war* (sometimes *attack* or *exchange*), refers to a small-scale use of nuclear weapons by two (or more) belligerents. A "limited nuclear war" could include targeting military facilities - either as an attempt to pre-emptively cripple the enemy's ability to attack as a defensive measure, or as a prelude to an invasion by conventional forces, as an offensive measure. This term could apply to *any* small-scale use of nuclear weapons that may involve military or civilian targets (or both).

The second, a *full-scale nuclear war*, could consist of large numbers of nuclear weapons used in an attack aimed at an entire country, including military, economic, and civilian targets. Such an attack would almost certainly destroy the entire economic, social, and military infrastructure of the target nation, and would probably have a devastating effect on Earth's biosphere.

Some Cold War strategists such as Henry Kissinger argued that a limited nuclear war *could* be possible between two heavily armed superpowers (such as the United States and the Soviet

Union). Some predict, however, that a limited war could potentially "escalate" into a full-scale nuclear war. Others have called limited nuclear war "global nuclear holocaust in slow motion" - arguing that once such a war took place, others would be sure to follow over a period of decades, effectively rendering the planet uninhabitable in the same way that a "full-scale nuclear war" between superpowers would, only taking a much longer (and arguably more agonizing) path to the same result.

Even the most optimistic predictions of the effects of a major nuclear exchange foresee the death of many millions of victims within a very short period of time. More pessimistic predictions argue that a full-scale nuclear war could potentially bring about the extinction of the human race, or at least its *near* extinction, with only a relatively small number of survivors (mainly in remote areas) and a reduced quality of life and life expectancy for centuries afterward.

However such exaggerated pessimistic predictions, assuming total war with nuclear arsenals atCold war highs, have not been without considerable criticism. Such a horrific catastrophe as global nuclear warfare would almost certainly cause permanent damage to most complex life on the planet, its ecosystems, and the global climate - particularly if predictions about the production of a nuclear winter are accurate, it would also change the balance of global power, with countries such as Australia, New Zealand, China, Argentina and Brazil predicted to become world superpowers if the Cold war ever turned hot.

A study presented at the annual meeting of the American Geophysical Union in December 2006 asserted that even a small-scale regional nuclear war could produce as many direct fatalities as all of World War II and disrupt the global climate for a decade or more.

In a regional nuclear conflict scenario in which two opposing nations in the subtropics each used 50 Hiroshima-sized nuclear weapons (c. 15 kiloton each) on major population centres, the researchers predicted fatalities ranging from 2.6 million to 16.7 million per country. Also, they estimated that as much as five million tons of soot could be released, producing a cooling of several degrees over large areas of North America and Eurasia (including most of the grain-growing regions). The cooling would last for years and could be "catastrophic", according to the researchers.

Either a limited or full-scale nuclear exchange could occur during an *accidental nuclear war*, in which the use of nuclear weapons is triggered unintentionally.

Postulated triggers for this scenario have included malfunctioning early warning devices and/or targeting computers, deliberate malfeasance by rogue military commanders, consequences of an accidental straying of warplanes into enemy airspace, reactions to unannounced missile tests during tense diplomatic periods, reactions to military exercises, mistranslated or misscommunicated messages, and others.

A number of these scenarios actually occurred during the Cold War, though none resulted in the use of nuclear weapons. Many such scenarios have been depicted in popular culture, such as in the 1962 novel *Fail-Safe (released* as a film in 1964), and the film *Dr. Strangelove or: How I Learned to Stop Worrying and Love the Bomb*, also released in 1964.

HISTORY

Atomic Bombings of Hiroshima and Nagasaki

During the final stages of World War II in 1945, the United States conducted two atomic bombings against the Japanese cities of Hiroshima and Nagasaki, the first on August 6, 1945, and the second on August 9, 1945. These two events are the only use of nuclear weapons in war to date.

For six months before the atomic bombings, the United States intensely firebombed 67 Japanese cities. Together with the United Kingdom and the Republic of China, the United States called for the unconditional surrender of Japan in the Potsdam Declaration issued July 26, 1945. The Japanese government ignored this ultimatum. By executive order of President Harry S. Truman, the U.S. employed the uranium-type nuclear weapon code named "Little Boy" on the city of Hiroshima on Monday, August 6, 1945, followed three days later by the detonation of the plutonium-type weapon code named "Fat Man" over the city of Nagasaki on August 9.

Within the first two to four months after the bombings, acute effects killed 90,000–166,000 people in Hiroshima and 60,000–80,000 in Nagasaki, with roughly half of the deaths in each city occurring in the first 24 hours. The Hiroshima prefectural health department estimates that - of the people who died on the day of the detonation - 60% died from flash or flame burns, 30% from falling or flying debris, and 10% from other causes. During the following months, large numbers died from the chronic effects of burns, radiation sickness, and other injuries, compounded by illnesses. In a U.S. estimate of the total immediate and short-term causes of death, 15–20% died from radiation sickness, 20–30% from flash burns, and 50–60% from other injuries, compounded by illnesses. In both cities, most of the dead were civilians.

Six days after the detonation over Nagasaki, on August 15, 1945, Japan announced its surrender to the Allied Powers, signing the Instrument of Surrender on September 2, 1945, officially ending the Pacific War and, therefore, World War II, as Germany had already signed its Instrument of Surrender on May 7, 1945, ending the war in Europe. The two atomic bombings led, in part, to post-war Japan's adopting of the Three Non-Nuclear Principles, which forbade the nation from developing nuclear armaments. The role of the bombings in the surrender of Japan, the ethical justification of the US for using them, as well as their strategic importance, is still hotly debated.

Immediately after the Japan Bombings

Immediately after the atomic bombings of Japan, the status of atomic weapons in international and military relations was unclear. Presumably, the United States hoped atomic weapons could offset the Soviet Union's larger conventional ground forces in Eastern Europe, and possibly be used to pressure Soviet leader Joseph Stalin into making concessions. Under Stalin, the Soviet Union pursued its own atomic capabilities through a combination of scientific research and espionage directed against the American program. The Soviets believed that the Americans, with their limited nuclear arsenal, were unlikely to engage in any new world wars, while the Americans were not confident they could prevent a Soviet takeover of Europe, despite their atomic advantage.

Within the United States the authority to produce and develop nuclear weapons was removed from military control and put instead under the civilian control of the United States Atomic Energy Commission. This decision reflected an understanding that nuclear weapons had unique risks and benefits that were separate from other military technology known at the time.

For several years after World War II, the United States developed and maintained a strategic force based on the Convair B-36 bomber that would be able to attack any potential enemy from bomber bases in the United States. It deployed atomic bombs around the world for potential use in conflicts. Over a period of a few years, many in the American defence community became increasingly convinced of the invincibility of the United States to a nuclear attack. Indeed, it became generally believed that the threat of nuclear war would deter any strike against the United States.

Many proposals were suggested to put all American nuclear weapons under international control (by the newly formed United Nations, for example) as an effort to deter both their usage and an arms race. However, no terms could be arrived at that would be agreed upon by both the United States and the Soviet Union.

On August 29, 1949, the Soviet Union tested its first nuclear weapon at Semipalatinsk inKazakhstan. Scientists in the United States from the Manhattan Project had warned that, in time, the Soviet Union would certainly develop nuclear capabilities of its own. Nevertheless, the effect upon military thinking and planning in the United States was dramatic, primarily because American military strategists had not anticipated the Soviets would "catch up" so soon. However, at this time, they had not discovered that the Soviets had conducted significant nuclear espionage of the project from spies at Los Alamos, the most significant of which was done by the theoretical physicist Klaus Fuchs. The first Soviet bomb was more or less a deliberate copy of the Fat Manplutonium device.

With the monopoly over nuclear technology broken, worldwide nuclear proliferation accelerated. The United Kingdom tested its first independent atomic bomb in 1952, followed by France in 1960 and then China in 1964. While much smaller than the arsenals of the United States and the Soviet Union, Western Europe's nuclear reserves were nevertheless a significant factor in strategic planning during the Cold War. A top-secret White Paper, compiled by the Royal Air Force and produced for the British Government in 1959, estimated that British atomic bombers were capable of destroying key cities and military targets in the Soviet Union, with an estimated 16 million deaths in the Soviet Union (half of whom were estimated to be killed on impact and the rest fatally injured) *before* bomber aircraft from the U.S. Strategic Air Command reached their targets.

After the successful Trinity (test) July 16, 1945, which was the very first nuclear detonation, the manhattan project lead manager J. Robert Oppenheimer recalled:

We knew the world would not be the same. A few people laughed, a few people cried, most people were silent. I remembered the line from the Hindu scripture the *Bhagavad Gita*. Vishnu is trying to persuade the prince that he should do his duty and to impress him takes on his multiarmed form and says, "Now, I am become Death, the destroyer of worlds." I suppose we all thought that one way or another." —J. Robert Oppenheimer, The Decision To Drop The Bomb

The 1950s

Although the Soviet Union had nuclear weapon capabilities in the beginning of the Cold War, the United States still had an advantage in terms of bombers and weapons. In any exchange of hostilities, the United States would have been capable of bombing the Soviet Union, whereas the Soviet Union would have more difficulty carrying out the reverse mission.

The widespread introduction of jet-powered interceptor aircraft upset this imbalance somewhat by reducing the effectiveness of the American bomber fleet. In 1949 Curtis LeMay was placed in command of the Strategic Air Command and instituted a program to update the bomber fleet to one that was all-jet. During the early 1950s the B-47 and B-52 were introduced, providing the ability to bomb the Soviet Union more easily. Before the development of a capable strategic missile force in the Soviet Union, much of the war-fighting doctrine held by western nations revolved around using a large number of smaller nuclear weapons used in a tactical role. It is debatable whether such use could be considered "limited" however, because it was believed that the United States would use their own strategic weapons (mainly bombers at the time) should the Soviet Union deploy any kind of nuclear weapon against civilian targets. Douglas MacArthur, an American general, was fired by President Harry Truman, partially because he persistently requested permission to use his own discretion in deciding whether to use atomic weapons on the People's Republic of China in 1951 during the Korean War.Mao Zedong,

China's communist leader, gave the impression that he would welcome a nuclear war with the capitalists because it would annihilate what he viewed as their "imperialist" system.

Let us imagine how many people would die if war breaks out. There are 2.7 billion people in the world, and a third could be lost. If it is a little higher it could be half... I say that if the worst came to the worst and one-half dies, there will still be one-half left, but imperialism would be razed to the ground and the whole world would become socialist. After a few years there would be 2.7 billion people again. — Mao Zedong, 1957

Several scares about the increasing ability of the Soviet Union's strategic bomber forces surfaced during the 1950s. The defensive response by the United States was to deploy a fairly strong "layered defence" consisting of interceptor aircraft and anti-aircraft missiles, like the Nike, and guns, like the Skysweeper, near larger cities. However, this was a small response compared to the construction of a huge fleet of nuclear bombers. The principalnuclear strategy was to massively penetrate the Soviet Union. Because such a large area could not be defended against this overwhelming attack in any credible way, the Soviet Union would lose any exchange.

This logic became ingrained in American nuclear doctrine and persisted for much of the duration of the Cold War. As long as the strategic American nuclear forces could overwhelm their Soviet counterparts, a Soviet preemptive strike could be averted. Moreover, the Soviet Union could not afford to build any reasonable counterforce, as the economic output of the United States was far larger than that of the Soviets, and they would be unable to achieve "nuclear parity".

Soviet nuclear doctrine, however, did not match American nuclear doctrine. Soviet military planners assumed they can win the nuclear war. Therefore, they *expected* a large-scale nuclear exchange, followed by a "conventional war" which itself would involve heavy use of tactical nuclear weapons. American doctrine rather assumed that Soviet doctrine was similar, with the *mutual* in Mutually Assured Destruction necessarily requiring that the other side see things in much the same way, rather than believing - as the Soviets did - that they could fight a large-scale, "combined nuclear and conventional" war.

In accordance with their doctrine, the Soviet Union conducted large-scale military exercises to explore the possibility of defensive and offensive warfare during a nuclear war. The exercise, under the code name of "Snowball", involved the detonation of a nuclear bomb about twice as powerful as that which fell on Nagasaki and an army of approximately 45,000 soldiers on maneuvers through the hypocenter immediately after the blast. The exercise was conducted on September 14, 1954, under command of Marshal Georgy Zhukov to the north of Totskoye village in Orenburg Oblast, Russia.

A revolution in nuclear strategic thought occurred with the introduction of the intercontinental ballistic missile (ICBM), which the Soviet Union first successfully tested in August 1957. In order to deliver a warhead to a target, a missile was much faster and more cost-effective than a bomber, and enjoyed a higher survivability due to the enormous difficulty of interception of the ICBMs (due to their high altitude and extreme speed). The Soviet Union could now afford to achieve nuclear parity with the United States in terms of raw numbers, although for a time, they appeared to have chosen not to.

Photos of Soviet missile sites set off a wave of panic in the U.S. military, something the launch of Sputnik would do for the American public a few months later. Politicians, notably then-U.S. Senator John F. Kennedy suggested that a "missile gap" existed between the Soviet Union and the United States. The US military gave missile development programs the highest national priority, and several spy aircraft and reconnaissance satellites were designed and deployed to observe Soviet progress.

Early ICBMs and bombers were relatively inaccurate, which led to the concept of countervalue strikes — attacks directly on the enemy population, which would theoretically lead to a collapse of the enemy's will to fight. During the Cold War, the Soviet Union invested in extensive protected civilian infrastructure, such as large "nuclear-proof" bunkers and non-perishable food stores. By comparison, smaller scale civil defence programs were instituted in the United States starting in the 1950s, where schools and other public buildings had basements stocked with non-perishable food supplies, canned water, first aid, and dosimeter and Geiger counter radiation-measuring devices. Many of the locations were given "Fallout Shelter" designation signs. Also, CONELRAD Radio information systems were adopted, whereby the commercial radio sector would broadcast on two AM frequencies in the event of a Civil Defence

(CD) emergency. These two frequencies-640 and 1240 marked with small CD triangles on the tuning dial can still be seen on 1950s-vintage radios on online auction sites and museums. Also, the occasional backyard fallout shelter was built by private individuals.

1960s

An extensive, complicated, and worrisome situation developed in 1962, in what is called the Cuban Missile Crisis. The Soviet Union placed medium-range ballistic missiles 90 miles (140 km) from the United States - a move considered by many as a direct response to American Jupiter missiles placed in Turkey. After intense negotiations, the Soviets ended up removing the missiles from Cuba and decided to institute a massive weapons-building program of their own. In exchange, the United States dismantled its launch sites in Turkey, although this was done secretly and not publicly revealed for over two decades. Khrushchevdid not even reveal this part of the agreement when he came under fire by political opponents for mishandling the crisis.

By the late 1960s, the number of ICBMs and warheads was so high on both sides that it was believed that both the United States and the Soviet Union were capable of completely destroying the infrastructure and a large proportion of the population of the other country. Thus, by some western game theorists, a balance of power system known as mutually assured destruction (or *MAD*) came into being. It was thought that any full-scale exchange between the powers would not result in an outright winner, with at best one side emerging the pyrrhic victor, and thus both sides were deterred from risking the initiation of a direct confrontation, instead being forced to engage in lower intensity proxy wars.

During this decade the Peoples Republic of China began to build subterranean infrastructure such as the Underground Project 131following the Sino-Soviet split.

One drawback of the MAD doctrine was the possibility of a nuclear war occurring without either side intentionally striking first. Warning system\Early Warning Systems (EWS) were notoriously error-prone. For example, on 78 occasions in 1979 alone, a "missile display conference" was called to evaluate detections that were "potentially threatening to the North American continent". Some of these were trivial errors and were spotted quickly, but several went to more serious levels. On September 26, 1983, Stanislav Petrov received convincing indications of an American first strike launch against the Soviet Union, but positively identified the warning as a false alarm. Though it is unclear what role Petrov's actions played in preventing a nuclear war during this incident, he has been honoured by the United Nations for his actions.

Similar incidents happened many times in the United States, due to failed computer chips, misidentifications of large flights of geese, test programs, and bureaucratic failures to notify early warning military personnel of legitimate launches of test or weather missiles. For many years, the U.S. Air Force's strategic bombers were kept airborne on a daily rotating basis "around the clock", until the number and severity of accidents, the 1968 Thule Air Base B-52 crash in particular, persuaded policymakers it was not worthwhile.

1970s

By the late 1970s, people in both the United States and the Soviet Union, along with the rest of the world, had been living with the concept of mutual assured destruction (MAD) for about a decade, and it became deeply ingrained into the psyche and popular culture of those countries. Such an exchange would have killed many millions of individuals directly, and possibly induced a nuclear winter if enough soot from firestorms reached the stratosphere, which was believed to have the potential to decrease post war agriculture yields, and with that lead to the death of a large portion of humanity and - potentially - the collapse of global civilization. On May 18, 1974, India conducted its first nuclear test in the Pokhran test range. The name of the operation was Smiling Buddha, and India termed the test as a "peaceful nuclear explosion".

According to the 1980 United Nations report *General and Complete Disarmament: Comprehensive Study on Nuclear Weapons: Report of the Secretary-General*, it was estimated that there were a total of about 40,000 nuclear warheads in existence at that time, with a potential combined explosive yield of approximately 13,000 megatons.

By comparison, when the volcano Mount Tambora erupted in 1815 - turning 1816 into the Year Without A Summer due to the levels of global dimming sulfate aerosols and ash expelled - it exploded with a force of roughly 1,000 megatons, however it must be noted that comparisons with supervolcanos are more misleading than helpful due to the different aerosols released, the likely air burst fuzing height of nuclear weapons and the globally scattered location of these potential nuclear detonations all being in contrast to the singular and subterranean nature of a supervolcanic eruption. Nonetheless, many people believe that a full-scale nuclear war would result in the extinction of the human species, though not all analysts agree on the assumptions required for these models.

The idea that any nuclear conflict would eventually escalate was a challenge for military strategists. This challenge was particularly severe for the United States and its NATO allies because it was believed (until the 1970s) that a Soviet tank invasion of Western Europewould quickly overwhelm NATO conventional forces, leading to the necessity of the West escalating to the use of tactical nuclear weapons, one of which was the W-70.

This strategy had one major (and possibly critical) flaw, which was soon realised by military analysts but highly underplayed by the U.S. military: conventional NATO forces in the European theatre of war were far outnumbered by similar Soviet and Warsaw Pact forces, and it was assumed that in case of a major Soviet attack (commonly envisioned as the "Red tanks rolling towards the North Sea" scenario) that NATO - in the face of quick conventional defeat - would soon have no other choice but to resort to tactical nuclear strikes against these forces. Most analysts agreed that once the first nuclear exchange had occurred, escalation to global nuclear war would likely become inevitable.

The 1980s

In the late 1970s and, particularly, during the early 1980s under U.S. President Ronald Reagan, the United States renewed its commitment to a more powerful military, which required a large increase in spending on U.S. military programs. These programs, which were originally part of the defence budget of U.S. President Jimmy Carter, included spending on conventional and nuclear weapons systems. Under Reagan, defensive systems like the Strategic Defence Initiative became emphasized as well.

Another major shift in nuclear doctrine was the development and the improvement of the submarine-launched, nuclear-armed, ballistic missile, or SLBM. It was hailed by many military theorists as a weapon that would make nuclear war less likely. SLBMs - which can move with "stealth" (greatly lessened detectibility) virtually anywhere in the world - give a nation a "second strike" capability (i.e. after absorbing a "first strike"). Before the advent of the SLBM, thinkers feared that a nation might be tempted to initiate a first strike if it felt confident that such a strike would incapacitate the nuclear arsenal of its enemy, making retaliation impossible. With the advent of SLBMs, no nation could be certain that a first strike would incapacitate its enemy's entire nuclear arsenal. To the contrary, it would have to fear a (near certain) retaliatory second strike from SLBMs. Thus, a first strike was a much less of feasible (or desirable) option, and a (deliberately initiated) nuclear war was thought to be less likely to start.

However, it was soon realized that submarines could "sneak up" close to enemy coastlines and decrease the "warning time" (the time between detection of the missile launch and the impact of the missile) from as much as half an hour to possibly under three minutes. This effect was especially significant to the United States, Britain and China, whose capitals all lay within 100 miles (160 km) of their coasts. Moscow was much more secure from this type of threat, due to its considerable distance from the sea. This greatly increased the credibility of a "surprise first strike" by one faction and (theoretically) made it possible to knock out or disrupt the chain of command of a target nation before any counterstrike could be ordered (known as a "decapitation strike"). It strengthened the notion that a nuclear war could possibly be "won" - resulting not only in greatly increased tensions and increasing calls for fail-deadly control systems, but also in a dramatic increase in military spending. The submarines and their missile systems were very expensive, and one fully equipped nuclear-powered and nuclear-armed missile submarine could cost more than the entire GNP of a developing country. It was also calculated, however, that the greatest cost came in the development of *both* sea- and land-based anti-submarine defenses and in improving and strengthening the "chain of command", and as a result, military spending skyrocketed.

South Africa developed a nuclear weapon capability during the 1970s and early 1980s. It was operational for a brief period before being dismantled in the early 1990s.

On Sept. 1, 1983, Korean Air Lines Flight 007 was shot down by Soviet jet fighters. On the 26th, a Soviet early warning station under the command of Stanislav Petrov falsely detected 5 inbound intercontinental ballistic missiles from the US. Petrov correctly assessed the situation as a false alarm, and hence did not report his finding to his superiors. It is quite possible that his actions prevented "World War III", as the Soviet policy at that time was immediate nuclear response upon discovering inbound ballistic missiles.

The world came unusually close to nuclear war - although perhaps not as close as during the Cuban Missile Crisis - when the Soviet Union thought that the NATO military exercise Able Archer 83 was a ruse or "cover up" to begin a nuclear first strike. The Soviets responded by raising readiness and preparing their nuclear arsenal for immediate use. Soviet fears of an attack ceased once the exercise concluded without incident.

Post–Cold War

Although the dissolution of the Soviet Union ended the Cold War and greatly reduced tensions between the United States and the Russian Federation, the Soviet Union's formal successor state, both countries remained in a "nuclear stand-off" due to the continuing presence of a very large number of deliverable nuclear warheads on both sides. Additionally, the end of the Cold War led the United States to become increasingly concerned with the development of nuclear technology by other nations outside of the former Soviet Union. In 1995, a branch of the U.S. Strategic Command produced an outline of forward-thinking strategies in the document "Essentials of Post–Cold War Deterrence".

As an effect of the 9/11 attacks on the USA, American forces immediately increased their readiness to the highest level in 28 years, closing the blast doors of the NORAD's Cheyenne Mountain Operations Center for the first time due to a non-exercise event. But unlike similar increases during the Cold War, Russia immediately decided to stand down a large military exercise in the Arctic region, in order to minimize the risk of incidents, rather than following suit.

The former chair of the United Nations disarmament committee stated that there are more than 16,000 strategic and tactical nuclear weapons ready for deployment and another 14,000 in storage, with the U.S. having nearly 7,000 ready for use and 3,000 in storage, and Russia having about 8,500 ready for use and 11,000 in storage. In addition, China is thought to possess about 400 nuclear weapons, Britain about 200, France about 350, India about 80-100, and Pakistan 100-110. North Korea is confirmed as having nuclear weapons, though it is not known how many, with most estimates between 1 and 10. Israel is also widely believed to possess usable nuclear weapons. NATO has stationed about 480 American nuclear weapons in Belgium, the Netherlands, Italy, Germany, and Turkey, and several other nations are thought to be in pursuit of an arsenal of their own.

A key development in nuclear warfare throughout the 2000s and early 2010s is the proliferation of nuclear weapons to the developing world, with India and Pakistan both publicly testing several nuclear devices, and North Korea conducting an underground nuclear test on October 9, 2006. The U.S. Geological Survey measured a 4.2 magnitude earthquake in the area where the North Korean test is said to have occurred. A further test was announced by the North Korean government on May 25, 2009. Iran, meanwhile, has embarked on a nuclear program which - while officially for civilian purposes - has come under close scrutiny by the United Nations and many individual states.

Recent studies undertaken by the CIA cite the enduring India-Pakistan conflict as the one "flash point" most likely to escalate into a nuclear war. During the Kargil War in 1999, Pakistan came close to using its nuclear weapons in case the conventional military situation underwent further deterioration. Pakistan's foreign minister had even warned that it would "use any weapon in our arsenal", hinting at a nuclear strike against India. The statement was condemned by the international community, with Pakistan denying it later on. This conflict remains the only war (of any sort) between two declared nuclear powers. The 2001-2002 India-Pakistan standoffagain stoked fears of nuclear war between the two countries. Despite these very serious and relatively recent threats, relations between India and Pakistan have been improving somewhat over the last few years. A bus line directly linking Indian- and Pakistani-administered Kashmir has recently been established. However, with the November 26, 2008 Mumbai terror attacks, India currently will not rule out war with Pakistan.

Another potential geopolitical issue which is considered particularly worrisome by military analysts is a possible conflict between theUnited States and the People's Republic of China over Taiwan. Although economic forces are thought to have decreased somewhat the possibility of a military conflict, there remains worry about the increasing military buildup of China (China is rapidly increasing their naval capacity), and that any move toward Taiwan independence could potentially spin out of control.

Israel is thought to possess somewhere between one hundred and four hundred nuclear warheads. It has been asserted that the submarines which Israel received from Germany have been adapted to carry missiles with nuclear warheads, so as to give Israel asecond strike capability. Israel has been involved in wars with its neighbours in the Middle East (and with other "non-state actors") on numerous prior occasions, and its small geographic size and population could mean that, in the event of future wars, the Israeli military might have very little time to react to an invasion or other major threat. Such a situation could escalate to nuclear warfare very quickly in some scenarios.

In the Persian Gulf, Iran appears to many observers to be in the process of developing a nuclear weapon, which has greatly heightened fears of a nuclear conflict and arms races in the Middle East—either with Israel or with one or more Arab states (a "Shia-Sunni" conflict).

On March 7, 2013, North Korea threatened the United States with a pre-emptive nuclear strike. On April 9, North Korea urged foreigners to leave South Korea, stating that both countries were on the verge of nuclear war. On April 12, North Korea stated that a nuclear war was unavoidable. The country declared Japan as its first target.

Sub-strategic Use

The above examples envisage nuclear warfare at a strategic level, i.e. total war. However, nuclear powers have the ability to undertake more limited engagements.

"Sub-strategic use" includes the use of either "low-yield" tactical nuclear weapons, or of variable yield strategic nuclear weapons in a very limited role, as compared to battlefield exchanges of larger-yield strategic nuclear weapons. This was described by the UK Parliamentary Defence Select Committee as "the launch of one or a limited number of missiles against an adversary as a means of conveying a political message, warning or demonstration of resolve". It is believed that all current nuclear weapons states possess tactical nuclear weapons, with the exception of the United Kingdom, which decommissioned its tactical warheads in 1998. However, the UK does possess scalable-yield strategic warheads, and this technology tends to blur the difference between "strategic", "sub-strategic", and "tactical" use or weapons. American, French and British nuclear submarines are believed to carry at least *some* missiles with these types of high-tech warheads for this purpose - potentially allowing a strike as low as one kiloton (or less) against a single target. Only the People's Republic of China and the Republic of India have declarative, unqualified, unconditional "no first use" nuclear weapons policies.

Commodore Tim Hare, former Director of Nuclear Policy at the British Ministry of Defence, has described "sub-strategic use" as offering the Government "an extra option in the escalatory process before it goes for an all-out strategic strike which would deliver unacceptable damage". However, this sub-strategic capacity has been criticized as potentially increasing the "acceptability" of using nuclear weapons. The related consideration of new generations of limited-yield nuclear weapons by the United States (i.e. "bunker busters") has also alarmed anti-nuclear groups, who believe it will make the use of nuclear weapons "more acceptable" or likely.

Also of note is that the United States adopted a policy in 1996 of allowing the targeting of its nuclear weapons at non-state actors ("terrorists") armed with weapons of mass destruction.

NUCLEAR TERRORISM

Nuclear terrorism by non-state organizations or actors (even individuals) is a largely unknown and understudied factor in nuclear deterrence thinking, as states possessing nuclear weapons are susceptible to retaliation in kind, while sub- or trans-state actors may be less so. The collapse of the Soviet Union has given rise to the possibility that former Soviet nuclear weapons might become available on the black market (so-called 'loose nukes'). While no warheads are known to have been mislaid, it has been alleged that at least some very small or suitcase-size bombs might be unaccounted for.

A number of other concerns have been expressed about the security of nuclear weapons in other, newer nuclear powers with relatively less stable governments, such as Pakistan, but in each case, the fears have been addressed to some extent by statements and evidence provided by those nations, as well as cooperative programs between nations. Worry remains, however, in many circles that a relative decrease in security of nuclear weapons has emerged in recent years, and that terrorists or others may attempt to exert control over (or use) nuclear weapons, militarily applicable technology, or nuclear materials and fuel.

Another possible nuclear terrorism threat are devices designed to disperse radioactive materials over a large area using conventional explosives, called dirty bombs. The detonation of a "dirty bomb" would not cause a nuclear explosion, nor would it release enough radiation to kill or injure a lot of people. However, it could cause severe disruption and require potentially very costly decontamination procedures and increased spending on security measures.

Survival

The predictions of the effects of a major countervalue nuclear exchange include millions of city dweller deaths within a short period of time. Some predictions argue that a full-scale nuclear war could eventually bring about the extinction of the human race; however such pessimistic predictions, assuming total war with nuclear arsenals at Cold war highs, have not been without considerable criticism. Nonetheless, a number of Cold War publications advocate preparations that can allegedly be taken in order to allow the majority of civilians to survive even a total nuclear war. Among the most famous of these is the aptly named Nuclear War Survival Skills.

To avoid injury and death from a nuclear weapons heat flash and blast effects, the two most far ranging prompt effects of nuclear weapons, schoolchildren were taught to duck and cover by the early cold war film of the same name. Such advice is once again being given in case of nuclear terrorist attacks.

Prussian blue, or "Radiogardase", is stockpiled in the US, along with potassium iodide and DPTA as pharmaceuticals useful in treating internal exposure to harmful radioisotopes in fallout.

Publications on adapting to a changing diet and supplying nutritional food sources following a nuclear war, with particular focus on agricultural radioecology, include *Nutrition in the postattack environment* by the RAND corporation.

Many countries maintain plans for continuity of government following a nuclear attack or similar disasters.

The Soviet government believed they could win, not only a strategic nuclear war, which they planned to absorb with their extensive Civil Defence schemes and infrastructure dispersal, but also win the conventional war that they predicted would follow after their strategic nuclear arsenal had been depleted.

A number of other countries around the world have taken significant efforts to maximize their survival prospects in the event of large calamities, both natural and manmade. For example, metro stations in Pyongyang, North Korea, were constructed 110 metres (360 ft) below ground, and were designed to serve as nuclear shelters in the event of war, with each station entrance built with thick steel blast doors. While examples of privately funded fallout shelters are the Ark Two Shelter in Ontario, Canada, one of the best known privately constructed autonomous shelters, with a focus on post-war networking and reconstruction. In Switzerland, the majority of homes have an underground blast and fallout shelter. The country has an overcapacity of such shelters and can accommodate slightly more than the nation's population size.

3

Proliferation of Nuclear Weapons: Opportunities for Control and Abolition

Controlling the proliferation of nuclear weapons is one of the major challenges we face as a global society. Given that public health is "what we, as a society, do collectively to ensure the conditions in which people can be healthy," controlling the proliferation of nuclear weapons—and ultimately abolishing them—must be a major global health priority. The threat posed by the proliferation of nuclear weapons has 3 major aspects:

1. The development of the capability for producing or acquiring nuclear weapons by countries that do not currently have nuclear weapons (horizontal proliferation).
2. The increase of weapon stockpiles by countries that currently have nuclear weapons, the improvement of technical sophistication or reliability of these weapons, and the development of new weapons, such as "mini-nukes" or battlefield nuclear weapons (vertical proliferation).
3. The acquisition of nuclear weapons or the materials and knowledge by individuals or nonstate entities, often termed "terrorists," to produce nuclear weapons (another form of horizontal proliferation).

Another important component of the nuclear proliferation issue involves delivery mechanisms. In order to pose a nuclear threat, nations or other entities not only need these weapons but also need missiles or other methods for delivering them.

Controlling proliferation of nuclear weapons involves national governments, intergovernmental organizations, and nongovernmental (civil-society) organizations. Governments thus far have attempted to control the proliferation of nuclear weapons through bilateral and multilateral treaties. Intergovernmental bodies, such as the United Nations, the International Atomic Energy Agency, and the International Court of Justice (World Court), have also attempted to control proliferation. Nongovernmental organizations—including professional organizations, such as the Federation of American Scientists, the International Physicians for the Prevention of Nuclear War (IPPNW), and Physicians for Social Responsibility (IPPNW's US affiliate)—have worked to control proliferation through education, information dissemination, and advocacy aimed at governments and governmental organizations. An increasing number of individuals and organizations, including senior US statesmen, believe that the only way to address the danger of nuclear weapons is to eliminate them entirely.

HISTORICAL EVOLUTION OF NUCLEAR WEAPONS

In 1939, Albert Einstein and Leo Szilard warned of developments in Nazi Germany and urged President Franklin D. Roosevelt to begin a research program on nuclear fission for military use. The Manhattan Project was established in 1941 to develop, produce, and test the first "atomic bombs," and J. Robert Oppenheimer was appointed director. On July 16, 1945, the first "atomic bomb" was tested at Alamogordo, NM, and on August 6 and 9 of the same year, US military aircraft dropped atomic bombs on Hiroshima and Nagasaki, Japan. These bombs, based on nuclear fission, each had an explosive power equivalent to about 20 000 tons (20 kilotons) of TNT. Together, they caused the immediate deaths of approximately 200 000 people and the subsequent deaths of thousands more from blast and thermal injuries, radiation sickness, and malignancies.

Despite opposition by Oppenheimer and other physicists, President Harry Truman ordered development work on bombs based on nuclear fusion—termed "thermonuclear weapons," "hydrogen bombs," or "H-bombs"—in 1951. The work was performed under the direction of Edward Teller, who had urged the development of a fusion weapon while working on the Manhattan Project. The first hydrogen bomb test took place in 1952 at Eniwetok Atoll in the Marshall Islands.

The blast had an explosive power equivalent to 10 400 000 tons (10.4 megatons) of TNT—500 times greater than the power of each of the bombs dropped on Hiroshima and Nagasaki. In 1953, the Soviet Union, which had exploded its first fission bomb in 1949, exploded its first fusion bomb. In 1961, the Soviet Union detonated a fusion bomb with a yield equivalent to 50 megatons of TNT—over 2000 times greater than the yield of the Hiroshima and Nagasaki bombs and greater than the total destructive power of all the bombs and explosives used in World War II. The development of these weapons led to the initiation of a worldwide movement for nuclear disarmament.

After the release of information on the physical effects of thermonuclear weapons and testimony before a Congressional committee about the effects of a possible thermonuclear attack on the United States, a group of Boston physicians analyzed the medical consequences of such an attack. Their papers, published in the *New England Journal of Medicine*, led in 1962 to the formation of Physicians for Social Responsibility in the United States and in 1980 to the establishment of IPPNW, a worldwide federation of national medical organizations. IPPNW received the Nobel Prize for Peace in 1985 in recognition of its work in easing tensions that threatened nuclear war between the United States and the Soviet Union.

PROLIFERATION OF NUCLEAR WEAPONS

Horizontal Proliferation

The United States and the Soviet Union remained the only states with nuclear weapons until 1952, when the United States provided nuclear weapons to the United Kingdom. Other nations then began to acquire nuclear weapons: France, China, and, it is believed, Israel. South Africa initiated, but later terminated, a nuclear weapons program. India and Pakistan each conducted explosive tests of nuclear weapons in 1998. In 2003, The Democratic People's Republic of Korea (North Korea) unilaterally withdrew from the Nuclear Non-Proliferation Treaty (NPT) and expelled the international inspectors who had been monitoring its stockpile of fissile materials. Despite attempts by a 6-nation group to get North Korea to end its development of nuclear weapons, North Korea announced in 2006 that it had the capability to construct nuclear weapons and apparently tested one. In the same year, North Korea unsuccessfully tested several ballistic missiles capable of carrying nuclear war-heads, and the United Nations Security Council unanimously adopted a resolution demanding that it suspend its missile program and banned all UN member states from (1) selling material or technology for missiles or weapons of mass destruction to North Korea, and (2) receiving missiles, banned weapons, or related technology from North Korea. North Korea immediately rejected the Security Council's decision. In July 2007 North Korea agreed to permanent disabling of a nuclear reactor complex at Yongbyon.

In 2003, Iran, which is a member of the NPT, had begun to build a uranium-enrichment facility that could have the capability to produce uranium suitable for use in nuclear weapons. In mid-2006, a 6-nation group presented Iran with a set of proposals that called for a halt in uranium enrichment in return for economic and diplomatic incentives and warned that if Iran failed to respond, they would refer the case to the UN Security Council. Iran continues to insist that its enrichment plans are purely for civilian use. Although analysts believe Iran is still some years away from building nuclear weapons, there is concern that the United States may stage a military attack on Iran's nuclear capabilities.

Vertical Proliferation

Several of the nations with nuclear weapons have worked to develop new types of nuclear weapons and to improve and maintain existing ones.

The Bush administration is pursuing development of a range of new war-heads under the Reliable Replacement Warhead program and is implementing plans for a complete renewal of nuclear weapons complex infrastructure. The United States has proposed development of new nuclear weapons, such as small tactical nuclear weapons ("mini-nukes"), but Congress has blocked funding for these projects.

The United Kingdom is planning to invest £1 billion to update its Atomic Weapons Establishment at Aldermaston and to maintain its Trident warhead stockpile. The British Parliament may be asked to replace 1 or more of its 4 Trident submarines, each of which can carry 48-kiloton nuclear warheads. Russia has also announced plans to maintain or improve its nuclear arsenals, and Pakistan may be expanding its nuclear program.

Acquisition by Individuals or Nonstate Entities

Individuals or nonstate entities may attempt to acquire nuclear weapons or the materials and know-how to produce them.

There is considerable dispute over the use of the term *terrorism*, which many believe should include actions intended to produce terror by nation-states ("state terrorism") as well as by nonstate entities. But we will use the terms *terrorism* and *terrorist*, as they are commonly used, to refer only to nonstate entities. Concerns have been raised about the potential acquisition of nuclear weapons by nonstate entities from nation-states that possess these weapons. The Nunn-Lugar Cooperative Threat Reduction Program, designed to lessen the possibility that nuclear weapons could be obtained from Russia, has been only partially successful. In addition, there is concern about the possibility that nonstate entities will obtain fissile materials and the technical capability for producing nuclear weapons, and about the possibility of those entities making so-called dirty bombs—explosive or incendiary weapons purposely contaminated with radioactive materials. Although dirty bombs are defined as radiological rather than nuclear weapons, they could nonetheless create widespread radioactive contamination and instill great fear in the general population.

Controlling the Proliferation of Nuclear Weapons

Many of the physicists who worked on the Manhattan Project urged that the ready-for-use atomic bombs be detonated as a dramatic demonstration on an uninhabited island rather than on Japanese cities. After the bombs fell on Hiroshima and Nagasaki, these physicists and others, through the Federation of American Scientists and the*Bulletin of the Atomic Scientists*, worked to prevent proliferation and to urge the destruction of existing stockpiles. Work to end nuclear proliferation by other civil-society organizations, including IPPNW and its affiliates in 60 countries, has been heightened through the production of further reports on the health and environmental consequences of nuclear weapons use.

Another concern is the possibility of the accidental firing of nuclear missiles in response to false warnings of a nuclear attack. There have been close calls, in which nuclear missiles—many of which are on hair-trigger alert—were being prepared for launch on the basis of faulty reports of incoming missiles.

Limited Nuclear Test Ban Treaty

During the Cold War, both the United States and Soviet Union sought to deter each other from the use of nuclear weapons, through a policy known as mutual assured destruction (MAD). The first international agreement that attempted to control the testing of nuclear weapons, the 1963 Limited Nuclear Test Ban Treaty (LTBT), was signed by the United States, the United Kingdom, and the Soviet Union.

It prohibited nuclear test explosions in the atmosphere, in space, or underseas. The LTBT was initiated by President John F. Kennedy when evidence was presented of fallout of radioisotopes after each atmospheric nuclear test. In 1997, the National Cancer Institute published a study on the risk of the development of thyroid cancer from the iodine-131 fallout from the nearly 100 atmospheric nuclear bomb tests during the 1950s and the 1960s.

It was estimated that 17 200 new cases of thyroid cancer would develop annually in the United States. Nuclear weapons tests have continued since the LTBT has been ratified and implemented; but tests have been conducted underground or by simulation.

Anti-Ballistic Missile Systems Treaty

In 1972, the Treaty on the Limitation of Anti-Ballistic Missile Systems (ABM Treaty) between the United States and Soviet Union was signed in Moscow. It was ratified by the US Senate and went into effect soon afterward. The United States and the Soviet Union signed a protocol to the treaty, which went into force in 1976, that reduced the number of ABM deployment areas from 2 to 1—deployed either around each party's national capital area or at a deployment area of a single intercontinental ballistic missile. The Soviet Union deployed an ABM system around Moscow, but the United States elected not to deploy an ABM system.

The United States withdrew from the treaty in 2002 in order to permit work on a national missile defence system, work that had been prohibited by the treaty. After the United States withdrew from the treaty, it announced plans to deploy interceptor missiles in Poland and a radar system for missile defence in the Czech Republic. Then, Russia tested a new multiple-warhead intercontinental ballistic missile and a new cruise missile with a range of up to 500 kilometers. Although the President of Russia, Vladimir Putin, and other officials have called the treaty outdated, they have not said that Russia would opt out of it.

Treaty on the Non-Proliferation of Nuclear Weapons

In 1968, the Treaty on the Non-Proliferation of Nuclear Weapons, also referred to as the NPT, was first signed. It obligates the 5 original nuclear-weapon states (the United States, the Soviet Union, the United Kingdom, France, and China) not to transfer nuclear weapons, other nuclear explosive devices, or their technology to any non–nuclear-weapons state.

Non–nuclear-weapons states that are parties to the NPT undertake an avoidance of acquisition or production of nuclear weapons or nuclear explosive devices, in return for acquisition of nuclear technologies for peaceful activities, such as power generation, and for protection by the nuclear-weapon states.

They are required also to accept safeguards to detect diversions of nuclear materials from peaceful activities to the production of nuclear weapons or other nuclear explosive devices.

The NPT went into effect in 1970. In 1992, China and France acceded to it. In 1996, Belarus joined Ukraine and Kazakhstan in removing and transferring to the Russian Federation the last of the remaining former Soviet nuclear weapons located within their territories, and each of these nations has become a party to the NPT, as a non–nuclear-weapon state.

The NPT is the most widely-accepted arms control agreement. Cuba, Israel, India, and Pakistan were the only major nations that were not parties to the NPT, until North Korea unilaterally withdrew—a withdrawal that was not recognized by the other 187 parties. India and Pakistan acquired nuclear weapons capability during the 1990s while remaining outside the NPT. Israel is said to retain a significant nuclear weapons capability also outside the NPT.

The Bush administration, in 2005, signed an agreement with India to provide assistance in the development of nuclear energy for civilian use. Some analysts contend that the agreement will undermine the NPT, which India has not joined, by providing benefits that are currently reserved for parties to the NPT. The US Congress approved the agreement in late 2006.

International Court of Justice Advisory Opinion

Under the NPT, the nuclear-weapons states assumed an obligation to pursue negotiations for nuclear disarmament. In 1996, the International Court of Justice handed down an Advisory Opinion on the request made by the General Assembly of the United Nations and by the World Health Organization for an opinion on the legality of the use or threat of use by a state of nuclear weapons in armed conflict.

In a split decision, the Court stated that "in view of the current state of International Law, and of the elements of fact at its disposal, the Court cannot conclude definitively whether the threat or use of nuclear weapons would be lawful or unlawful in an extreme circumstance of self-defence, in which the very survival of a State would be a stake." But the Court ruled unanimously that "there exists an obligation to pursue in good faith and bring to a conclusion negotiations leading to nuclear disarmament in all its aspects under strict and effective international control."

Model Nuclear Weapons Convention

In 1997, the United Nations General Assembly called for negotiations leading to the conclusion of a Nuclear Weapons Convention. That same year, the Lawyers' Committee on Nuclear Policy (part of the International Association of Lawyers Against Nuclear Arms, IALANA), the International Network of Engineers and Scientists for Global Responsibility, and IPPNW released the Model Nuclear Weapons Convention at the United Nations as part of an international campaign to stimulate the commencement of negotiations on an international treaty to abolish nuclear weapons. Abolition 2000, an international network of over 700 organizations, supports the approval and implementation of such a treaty.

The Model Nuclear Weapons Convention would prohibit the development, testing, production, stockpiling, transfer, use, and threat of use of nuclear weapons. States possessing nuclear weapons would be required to destroy their arsenals according to a series of phases over 15 years. The convention would also prohibit the production of weapons-usable fissile material and require delivery vehicles to be destroyed or converted to make them incapable of nuclear uses. The proposed convention outlines a series of 5 phases for the elimination of nuclear weapons: taking nuclear weapons off alert, removing weapons from deployment, removing nuclear warheads from their delivery vehicles, disabling the warheads, removing and disfiguring the plutonium "pits" needed for nuclear weapons and placing the fissile material under international control. In the initial phases, the United States and Russia would be required to make the deepest cuts in their nuclear arsenals.

THE CURRENT SITUATION

There are approximately 27 000 nuclear warheads worldwide, with an explosive force equivalent to 10 billion tons of TNT—almost 2 tons for every human being. The warheads produce a force more powerful than 200 000 of the bombs dropped on Hiroshima. About 2000 to 3000 of these warheads are mounted on missiles that are on hair-trigger alert for "launch on warning"; that is, they are ready to be launched on a few minutes' notice. About 10 000 are inactive, i.e., they are not currently mounted as war-heads on missiles or ready to be dropped from airplanes. Both the active and inactive weapons and stockpiles of plutonium and highly enriched uranium, from which nuclear weapons could be constructed, remain in nations' stockpiles.

The Bush administration is pursuing development of new warheads and a complete renewal of the US nuclear weapons complex infrastructure. The US policy, as elaborated in the National Security Strategy of 2002, undermines the NPT and all arms-control accords by asserting that nuclear weapons and other weapons of mass destruction are only dangerous if in the hands of so-called dangerous people. This policy, therefore, rejects a general nonproliferation standard. The administration has rejected 40 years of bipartisan nonproliferation and arms-control policy in favour of a policy of "counterproliferation," thereby doing serious damage to global efforts to contain the spread of nuclear weapons and move toward their elimination. Its counterproliferation policy and military doctrine allows for the use of nuclear weapons to bring about the nuclear disarmament of an enemy state.

The lack of disarmament progress, with nuclear weapons retaining a central role in the defence and security strategies of nuclear-weapon states, has impeded efforts to prevent proliferation and provides an excuse for those who seek to acquire nuclear weapons in contravention of their obligations under the NPT and other international treaties.

At a conference in 2006 organized by IPPNW, Abolition 2000 Europe, IALANA, and the International Peace Bureau—to mark the 10th anniversary of the advisory opinion on nuclear weapons issued by the International Court of Justice—attendees noted the lack of progress toward implementation of the unanimous opinion of the court on the obligation "to pursue in good faith and bring to a conclusion negotiations leading to nuclear disarmament." The conference urged that the UN General Assembly, which had together with the World Health Organization requested the advisory opinion from the court in 1996, be asked to return to the court with evidence that little progress had been made in response to the court opinion and with a request for a new advisory opinion that would clarify the meaning of "good faith" negotiations and of bringing them to a conclusion.

PUBLIC HEALTH PRACTICE

The contributions of public health workers to the prevention of war, and specifically to the control of nuclear proliferation, have taken a wide variety of forms and have been published in a wide variety of venues. Some contributions cover a wide spectrum of public health activities to prevent war. Some are specific to nuclear weapons abolition. Some deal with blocking production of fissionable material that might be used in nuclear weapons. Some deal with the perceptions of local residents about the risks of nuclear weapons production. Some, the most risky for public health care workers, deal with activities of health workers working in war zones to seek to prevent the continuation of war. Overall, the contributions of public health workers to disarmament and peace have been extremely important.

In many ways, the dangers posed by the proliferation of nuclear weapons are greater now than ever before. Although these issues may seem distant from the day-to-day practice of public health in a state or local health department, healthcare institution, or academic public health practice environment, there is much that public health workers can do to address the challenges posed by the proliferation of nuclear weapons. Public health workers can educate colleagues, policymakers, and the general public about these issues and disseminate information to them. They can advocate for stronger national and international policies to control the proliferation of nuclear weapons. They can help strengthen public health preparedness in their local areas in the event of a dirty bomb attack. And, through their membership and participation in professional, advocacy, and other nongovernmental organizations, they can play important roles in helping to stop the spread of nuclear weapons and, ultimately, to eliminate these weapons.

NUCLEAR WEAPON

A nuclear weapon is an explosive device that derives its destructive force from nuclear reactions, either fission or a combination of fission and fusion. Both reactions release vast quantities of energy from relatively small amounts of matter. The first fission ("atomic") bombtest released the same amount of energy as approximately 20,000 tons of TNT. The firstthermonuclear ("hydrogen") bomb test released the same amount of energy as approximately 10,000,000 tons of TNT.

A thermonuclear weapon weighing little more than 2,400 pounds (1,100 kg) can produce an explosive force comparable to the detonation of more than 1.2 million tons (1.1 million tonnes) of TNT. Thus, even a small nuclear device no larger than traditional bombs can devastate an entire city by blast, fire, and radiation. Nuclear weapons are consideredweapons of mass destruction, and their use and control have been a major focus of international relations policy since their debut.

Two nuclear weapons have been used in the course of warfare, both times by the United States near the end of World War II. On 6 August 1945, a uranium gun-type fission bombcode-named "Little Boy" was detonated over the Japanese city of Hiroshima. Three days later, on 9 August, a plutonium implosion-type fission bomb code-named "Fat Man" was exploded over Nagasaki, Japan. These two bombings resulted in the deaths of approximately 200,000 people—mostly civilians—from acute injuries sustained from the explosions. The role of the bombings in Japan's surrender, and their ethical status, remain the subject of scholarly and popular debate.

Since the bombings of Hiroshima and Nagasaki, nuclear weapons have been detonated on over two thousand occasions for testing purposes and demonstrations. Only a few nationspossess such weapons or are suspected of seeking them. The only countries known to have detonated nuclear weapons—and that acknowledge possessing such weapons—are (chronologically by date of first test) the United States, the

Soviet Union (succeeded as a nuclear power by Russia), the United Kingdom, France, the People's Republic of China, India, Pakistan, and North Korea. Israel is also widely believed to possess nuclear weapons, though it does not acknowledge having them. One state, South Africa, fabricated nuclear weapons in the past, but as its apartheid regime was coming to an end it disassembled its arsenal, acceded to the Nuclear Non-Proliferation Treaty, and accepted full-scope international safeguards. The Federation of American Scientists estimates there are more than 17,000 nuclear warheads in the world as of 2012, with around 4,300 of them considered "operational", ready for use.

TYPES

There are two basic types of nuclear weapons: those that derive the majority of their energy from nuclear fission reactions alone, and those that use fission reactions to begin nuclear fusion reactions that produce a large amount of the total energy output.

Fission Weapons

All existing nuclear weapons derive some of their explosive energy from nuclear fission reactions. Weapons whose explosive output is exclusively from fission reactions are commonly referred to as atomic bombs or atom bombs (abbreviated as A-bombs). This has long been noted as something of a misnomer, as their energy comes from the nucleus of the atom, just as it does with fusion weapons.

In fission weapons, a mass of fissile material (enriched uranium or plutonium) is assembled into a supercritical mass—the amount of material needed to start an exponentially growing nuclear chain reaction—either by shooting one piece of sub-critical material into another (the "gun" method) or by compressing a sub-critical sphere of material using chemical explosives to many times its original density (the "implosion" method). The latter approach is considered more sophisticated than the former and only the latter approach can be used if the fissile material is plutonium.

A major challenge in all nuclear weapon designs is to ensure that a significant fraction of the fuel is consumed before the weapon destroys itself. The amount of energy released by fission bombs can range from the equivalent of just under a ton of TNT, to upwards of 500,000 tons (500 kilotons) of TNT. All fission reactions necessarily generate fission products, the radioactive remains of the atomic nuclei split by the fission reactions. Many fission products are either highly radioactive (but short-lived) or moderately radioactive (but long-lived), and as such are a serious form of radioactive contamination if not fully contained. Fission products are the principal radioactive component of nuclear fallout.

The most commonly used fissile materials for nuclear weapons applications have been uranium-235 and plutonium-239. Less commonly used has been uranium-233. Neptunium-237 and some isotopes of americium may be usable for nuclear explosives as well, but it is not clear that this has ever been implemented, and even their plausible use in nuclear weapons is a matter of scientific dispute.

Fusion Weapons

The other basic type of nuclear weapon produces a large proportion of its energy in nuclear fusion reactions. Such fusion weapons are generally referred to as thermonuclear weapons or more colloquially as hydrogen bombs (abbreviated as H-bombs), as they rely on fusion reactions between isotopes of hydrogen (deuterium and tritium). All such weapons derive a significant portion, and sometimes a majority, of their energy from fission. This is because a fission weapon is required as a "trigger" for the fusion reactions, and the fusion reactions can themselves trigger additional fission reactions.

Only six countries—United States, Russia, United Kingdom, People's Republic of China, France and India—have conducted thermonuclear weapon tests. (Whether India has detonated a "true", multi-staged thermonuclear weapon is controversial.) Thermonuclear weapons are considered much more difficult to successfully design and execute than primitive fission weapons. Almost all of the nuclear weapons deployed today use the thermonuclear design because it is more efficient.

Thermonuclear bombs work by using the energy of a fission bomb to compress and heat fusion fuel. In the Teller-Ulam design, which accounts for all multi-megaton yield hydrogen bombs, this is accomplished by placing a fission bomb and fusion fuel (tritium, deuterium, orlithium deuteride) in proximity within a special, radiation-reflecting container. When the fission bomb is detonated, gamma rays and X-rays emitted first compress the fusion fuel, then heat it to thermonuclear temperatures. The ensuing fusion reaction creates enormous numbers of high-speed neutrons, which can then induce fission in materials not normally prone to it, such as depleted uranium. Each of these components is known as a "stage", with the fission bomb as the "primary" and the fusion capsule as the "secondary". In large, megaton-range hydrogen bombs, about half of the yield comes from the final fissioning of depleted uranium.

Virtually all thermonuclear weapons deployed today use the "two-stage" design described above, but it is possible to add additional fusion stages—each stage igniting a larger amount of fusion fuel in the next stage. This technique can be used to construct thermonuclear weapons of arbitrarily large yield, in contrast to fission bombs, which are limited in their explosive force. The largest nuclear weapon ever detonated—the Tsar Bomba of the USSR, which released an energy equivalent of over 50 million tons (50 megatons) of TNT—was a three-stage weapon. Most thermonuclear weapons are considerably smaller than this, due to practical constraints from missile warhead space and weight requirements.

Fusion reactions do not create fission products, and thus contribute far less to the creation of nuclear fallout than fission reactions, but because all thermonuclear weapons contain at least one fission stage, and many high-yield thermonuclear devices have a final fission stage, thermonuclear weapons can generate at least as much nuclear fallout as fission-only weapons.

Other Types

There are other types of nuclear weapons as well. For example, a boosted fission weapon is a fission bomb that increases its explosive yield through a small amount of fusion reactions, but it is not a fusion bomb. In the boosted bomb, the neutrons produced by the fusion reactions serve primarily to increase the efficiency of the fission bomb.

Some weapons are designed for special purposes; a neutron bomb is a thermonuclear weapon that yields a relatively small explosion but a relatively large amount of neutron radiation; such a device could theoretically be used to cause massive casualties while leaving infrastructure mostly intact and creating a minimal amount of fallout. The detonation of any nuclear weapon is accompanied by a blast of neutron radiation. Surrounding a nuclear weapon with suitable materials (such as cobalt orgold) creates a weapon known as a salted bomb. This device can produce exceptionally large quantities of radioactive contamination.

Research has been done into the possibility of pure fusion bombs: nuclear weapons that consist of fusion reactions without requiring a fission bomb to initiate them. Such a device might provide a simpler path to thermonuclear weapons than one that required development of fission weapons first, and pure fusion weapons would create significantly less nuclear fallout than other thermonuclear weapons, because they would not disperse fission products. In 1998, the United States Department of Energy divulged that the United States had, "...made a substantial investment" in the past to develop pure fusion weapons, but that, "The U.S. does not have and is not developing a pure fusion weapon", and that, "No credible design for a pure fusion weapon resulted from the DOE investment".

Most variation in nuclear weapon design is for the purpose of achieving different yields for different situations, and in manipulating design elements to attempt to minimize weapon size.

Antimatter, which consists of particles resembling ordinary matter particles in most of their properties but having opposite electric charge, has been considered as a trigger mechanism for nuclear weapons. A major obstacle is the difficulty of producing antimatter in large enough quantities, and there is no evidence that it is feasible beyond the military domain. However, the U.S. Air Force funded studies of the physics of antimatter in the Cold War, and began considering its possible use in weapons, not just as a trigger, but as the explosive itself. A fourth generation nuclear weapon design is related to, and relies upon, the same principle as Antimatter-catalyzed nuclear pulse propulsion.

WEAPONS DELIVERY

Nuclear weapons delivery—the technology and systems used to bring a nuclear weapon to its target—is an important aspect of nuclear weapons relating both tonuclear weapon design and nuclear strategy. Additionally, development and maintenance of delivery options is among the most resource-intensive aspects of a nuclear weapons program: according to one estimate, deployment costs accounted for 57% of the total financial resources spent by the United States in relation to nuclear weapons since 1940.

Historically the first method of delivery, and the method used in the two nuclear weapons used in warfare, was as a gravity bomb, dropped from bomber aircraft. This is usually the first method that countries developed, as it does not place many restrictions on the size of the weapon and *weapon miniaturization* requires considerable weapons design knowledge. It does, however, limit attack range, response time to an impending attack, and the number of weapons that a country can field at the same time. With the advent of miniaturization, nuclear bombs can be delivered by both strategic bombers and tactical fighter-bombers, allowing an air force to use its current fleet with little or no modification. This method may still be considered the primary means of nuclear weapons delivery; the majority of U.S. nuclear warheads, for example, are free-fall gravity bombs, namely the B61.

More preferable from a strategic point of view is a nuclear weapon mounted onto a missile, which can use a ballistic trajectory to deliver the warhead over the horizon. Although even short-range missiles allow for a faster and less vulnerable attack, the development of long-range intercontinental ballistic missiles (ICBMs) and submarine-launched ballistic missiles (SLBMs) has given some nations the ability to plausibly deliver missiles anywhere on the globe with a high likelihood of success.

More advanced systems, such as multiple independently targetable reentry vehicles (MIRVs), can launch multiple warheads at different targets from one missile, reducing the chance of a successful missile defence. Today, missiles are most common among systems designed for delivery of nuclear weapons. Making a warhead small enough to fit onto a missile, though, can be difficult.

Tactical weapons have involved the most variety of delivery types, including not only gravity bombs and missiles but also artillery shells, land mines, and nuclear depth charges andtorpedoes for anti-submarine warfare. An atomic mortar was also tested at one time by the United States. Small, two-man portable tactical weapons (somewhat misleadingly referred to as suitcase bombs), such as the Special Atomic Demolition Munition, have been developed, although the difficulty of combining sufficient yield with portability limits their military utility.

NUCLEAR STRATEGY

Nuclear warfare strategy is a set of policies that deal with preventing or fighting a nuclear war. The policy of trying to prevent an attack by a nuclear weapon from another country by threatening nuclear retaliation is known as the strategy of nuclear deterrence. The goal in deterrence is to always maintain a second strike capability (the ability of a country to respond to a nuclear attack with one of its own) and potentially to strive for first strike status (the ability to completely destroy an enemy's nuclear forces before they could retaliate). During the Cold War, policy and military theorists in nuclear-enabled countries worked out models of what sorts of policies could prevent one from ever being attacked by a nuclear weapon, and developed weapon game theory models that create the greatest and most stable deterrence conditions.

Different forms of nuclear weapons delivery allow for different types of nuclear strategies. The goals of any strategy are generally to make it difficult for an enemy to launch a pre-emptive strike against the weapon system and difficult to defend against the delivery of the weapon during a potential conflict. Sometimes this has meant keeping the weapon locations hidden, such as deploying them on submarines or land mobile transporter erector launchers whose locations are very hard for an enemy to track, and other times, this means protecting them by burying them in hardened missile silo bunkers.

Other components of nuclear strategies have included using missile defence (to destroy the missiles before they land) or implementation of civil defence measures (using early-warning systems to evacuate citizens to safe areas before an attack).

Note that weapons designed to threaten large populations, or to generally deter attacks are known as *strategic weapons*. Weapons designed for use on a battlefield in military situations are called *tactical weapons*.

There are critics of the very idea of nuclear strategy for waging nuclear war who have suggested that a nuclear war between two nuclear powers would result in mutual annihilation. From this point of view, the significance of nuclear weapons is purely to deter war because any nuclear war would immediately escalate out of mutual distrust and fear, resulting in mutually assured destruction. This threat of national, if not global, destruction has been a strong motivation for anti-nuclear weapons activism.

Critics from the peace movement and within the military establishment have questioned the usefulness of such weapons in the current military climate. According to an advisory opinion issued by the International Court of Justice in 1996, the use of (or threat of use of) such weapons would generally be contrary to the rules of international law applicable in armed conflict, but the court did not reach an opinion as to whether or not the threat or use would be lawful in specific extreme circumstances such as if the survival of the state were at stake.

Another deterrence position in nuclear strategy is that nuclear proliferation can be desirable. This view argues that, unlike conventional weapons, nuclear weapons successfully deter all-out war between states, and they succeeded in doing this during the Cold Warbetween the U.S. and the Soviet Union. In the late 1950s and early 1960s, Gen. Pierre Marie Gallois of France, an adviser to Charles DeGaulle, argued in books like *The Balance of Terror: Strategy for the Nuclear Age* (1961) that mere possession of a nuclear arsenal, what the French called the *force de frappe*, was enough to ensure deterrence, and thus concluded that the spread of nuclear weapons could increase international stability. Some very prominent neo-realist scholars, such as the late Kenneth Waltz, formerly a Political Science at UC Berkeley and Adjunct Senior Research Scholar at Columbia University, and John Mearsheimer of University of Chicago, have also argued along the lines of Gallois. Specifically, these scholars have advocated some forms of nuclear proliferation, arguing that it would decrease the likelihood of total war, especially in troubled regions of the world where there exists a unipolar nuclear weapon state. Aside from the public opinion that opposes proliferation in any form, there are two schools of thought on the matter: those, like Mearsheimer, who favour selective proliferation, and those of Kenneth Waltz, who was somewhat more non-interventionist.

The threat of potentially suicidal terrorists possessing nuclear weapons (a form of nuclear terrorism) complicates the decision process. The prospect of mutually assured destruction may not deter an enemy who expects to die in the confrontation.

Further, if the initial act is from a stateless terrorist instead of a sovereign nation, there is no fixed nation or fixed military targets to retaliate against. It has been argued by the New York Times, especially after the September 11, 2001 attacks, that this complication is the sign of the next age of nuclear strategy, distinct from the relative stability of the Cold War. In 1996, the United States adopted a policy of allowing the targeting of its nuclear weapons at terrorists armed with weapons of mass destruction.

Robert Gallucci, president of the John D. and Catherine T. MacArthur Foundation, argues that although traditional deterrence is not an effective approach toward terrorist groups bent on causing a nuclear catastrophe, Gallucci believes that "the United States should instead consider a policy of expanded deterrence, which focuses not solely on the would-be nuclear terrorists but on those states that may deliberately transfer or inadvertently lead nuclear weapons and materials to them. By threatening retaliation against those states, the United States may be able to deter that which it cannot physically prevent.".

Graham Allison makes a similar case, arguing that the key to expanded deterrence is coming up with ways of tracing nuclear material to the country that forged the fissile material. "After a nuclear bomb detonates, nuclear forensics cops would collect debris samples and send them to a laboratory for radiological analysis. By identifying unique attributes of the fissile material, including its impurities and contaminants, one could trace the path back to its origin." The process is analogous to identifying a criminal by fingerprints. "The goal would be twofold: first, to deter leaders of nuclear states from selling weapons to terrorists by holding them accountable for any use of their own weapons; second, to give leader every incentive to tightly secure their nuclear weapons and materials."

GOVERNANCE, CONTROL, AND LAW

Because of the immense military power they can confer, the political control of nuclear weapons has been a key issue for as long as they have existed; in most countries the use of nuclear force can only be authorized by the head of government or head of state.

In the late 1940s, lack of mutual trust was preventing the United States and the Soviet Union from making ground towards international arms control agreements. The Russell–Einstein Manifesto was issued in London on July 9, 1955 by Bertrand Russell in the midst of the Cold War. It highlighted the dangers posed by nuclear weapons and called for world leaders to seek peaceful resolutions to international conflict. The signatories included eleven pre-eminent intellectuals and scientists, including Albert Einstein, who signed it just days before his death on April 18, 1955. A few days after the release, philanthropist Cyrus S. Eatonoffered to sponsor a conference—called for in the manifesto—in Pugwash, Nova Scotia, Eaton's birthplace. This conference was to be the first of the Pugwash Conferences on Science and World Affairs, held in July 1957.

By the 1960s steps were being taken to limit both the proliferation of nuclear weapons to other countries and the environmental effects of nuclear testing. The Partial Test Ban Treaty (1963) restricted all nuclear testing tounderground nuclear testing, to prevent contamination from nuclear fallout, whereas the Nuclear Non-Proliferation Treaty (1968) attempted to place restrictions on the types of activities signatories could participate in, with the goal of allowing the transference of non-military nuclear technology to member countries without fear of proliferation.

In 1957, the International Atomic Energy Agency (IAEA) was established under the mandate of the United Nations to encourage development of peaceful applications for nuclear technology, provide international safeguards against its misuse, and facilitate the application of safety measures in its use. In 1996, many nations signed the Comprehensive Test Ban Treaty, which prohibits all testing of nuclear weapons. A testing ban imposes a significant hindrance to nuclear arms development by any complying country.The Treaty requires the ratification by 44 specific states before it can go into force; as of 2012, the ratification of eight of these states is still required.

Additional treaties and agreements have governed nuclear weapons stockpiles between the countries with the two largest stockpiles, the United States and the Soviet Union, and later between the United States and Russia. These include treaties such as SALT II (never ratified), START I (expired), INF, START II (never ratified), SORT, and New START, as well as non-binding agreements such as SALT Iand the Presidential Nuclear Initiatives of 1991. Even when they did not enter into force, these agreements helped limit and later reduce the numbers and types of nuclear weapons between the United States and the Soviet Union/Russia.

Nuclear weapons have also been opposed by agreements between countries. Many nations have been declared Nuclear-Weapon-Free Zones, areas where nuclear weapons production and deployment are prohibited, through the use of treaties. The Treaty of Tlatelolco(1967) prohibited any production or deployment of nuclear weapons in Latin America and the Caribbean, and the Treaty of Pelindaba(1964) prohibits nuclear weapons in many African countries. As recently as 2006 a Central Asian Nuclear Weapon Free Zone was established amongst the former Soviet republics of Central Asia prohibiting nuclear weapons.

In the middle of 1996, the International Court of Justice, the highest court of the United Nations, issued an Advisory Opinion concerned with the "Legality of the Threat or Use of Nuclear Weapons". The court ruled that the use or threat of use of nuclear weapons would violate various articles of international law, including the Geneva Conventions, the Hague Conventions, the UN Charter, and the Universal Declaration of Human Rights. In view of the unique, destructive characteristics of nuclear weapons, the International Committee of the Red Cross calls on States to ensure that these weapons are never used, irrespective of whether they consider them lawful or not.

Additionally, there have been other, specific actions meant to discourage countries from developing nuclear arms. In the wake of the tests by India and Pakistan in 1998, economic sanctions were (temporarily) levied against both countries, though neither were signatories with the Nuclear Non-Proliferation Treaty. One of the stated *casus belli* for the initiation of the 2003 Iraq War was an accusation by the United States that Iraq was actively pursuing nuclear arms (though this was soon discovered not to be the case as the program had been discontinued). In 1981, Israel had bombed a nuclear reactor being constructed in Osirak, Iraq, in what it called an attempt to halt Iraq's previous nuclear arms ambitions; in 2007, Israel bombed another reactor being constructed in Syria.

In 2013, Mark Diesendorf says that governments of France, India, North Korea, Pakistan, UK, and South Africa have used nuclear power and/or research reactors to assist nuclear weapons development or to contribute to their supplies of nuclear explosives from military reactors.

Disarmament

Nuclear disarmament refers to both the act of reducing or eliminating nuclear weapons and to the end state of a nuclear-free world, in which nuclear weapons are completely eliminated.

Beginning with the 1963 Partial Test Ban Treaty and continuing through the 1996 Comprehensive Test Ban Treaty, there have been many treaties to limit or reduce nuclear weapons testing and stockpiles. The 1968 Nuclear Non-Proliferation Treaty has as one of its explicit conditions that all signatories must "pursue negotiations in good faith" towards the long-term goal of "complete disarmament". The nuclear weapon states have largely treated that aspect of the agreement as "decorative" and without force.

Only one country—South Africa—has ever fully renounced nuclear weapons they had independently developed. The former Soviet republics of Belarus, Kazakhstan, and Ukrainereturned Soviet nuclear arms stationed in their countries to Russia after the collapse of the USSR.

Proponents of nuclear disarmament say that it would lessen the probability of nuclear war occurring, especially accidentally. Critics of nuclear disarmament say that it would undermine the present nuclear peace and deterrence and would lead to increased global instability. Various American elder statesmen, who were in office during the Cold War period, have recently been advocating the elimination of nuclear weapons. These officials include Henry Kissinger, George Shultz, Sam Nunn, and William Perry.

In January 2010, Lawrence M. Krauss stated that "no issue carries more importance to the long-term health and security of humanity than the effort to reduce, and perhaps one day, rid the world of nuclear weapons". In the years after the end of the Cold War, there have been numerous campaigns to urge the abolition of nuclear weapons, such as that organized by the Global Zero movement, and the goal of a "world without nuclear weapons" was advocated by United States President Barack Obama in an April 2009 speech in Prague. A CNN poll from April 2010 indicated that the American public was nearly evenly split on the issue.

Some analysts have argued that nuclear weapons have made the world relatively safer, with peace through deterrence and through the stability–instability paradox, including in south Asia. Kenneth Waltz has argued that nuclear weapons have helped keep an uneasy peace, and further nuclear weapon proliferation might even help avoid the large scale conventional wars that were so common prior to their invention at the end of World War II.

But former Secretary Henry Kissinger says there is a new danger, which cannot be addressed by deterrence: "The classical notion of deterrence was that there was some consequences before which aggressors and evildoers would recoil.

In a world of suicide bombers, that calculation doesn't operate in any comparable way". George Shultz has said, "If you think of the people who are doing suicide attacks, and people like that get a nuclear weapon, they are almost by definition not deterrable".

United Nations

The UN Office for Disarmament Affairs (UNODA) is a department of the United Nations Secretariat established in January 1998 as part of the United Nations Secretary-General Kofi Annan's plan to reform the UN as presented in his report to the General Assembly in July 1997. Its goal is to promote nuclear disarmament and non-proliferation and the strengthening of the disarmament regimes in respect to other weapons of mass destruction, chemical and biological weapons.

It also promotes disarmament efforts in the area of conventional weapons, especially land mines and small arms, which are often the weapons of choice in contemporary conflicts.

CONTROVERSY

Ethics

Even before the first nuclear weapons had been developed, scientists involved with the Manhattan Project were divided over the use of the weapon. The role of the two atomic bombings of the country in Japan's surrender and the U.S.'s ethical justification for them has been the subject of scholarly and popular debate for decades. The question of whether nations should have nuclear weapons, or test them, has been continually and nearly universally controversial.

Notable nuclear weapons accidents:

- February 13, 1950: a Convair B-36B crashed in northern British Columbia after jettisoning a Mark IV atomic bomb. This was the first such nuclear weapon loss in history.
- 7 June 1960: the 1960 Fort Dix IM-99 accident destroyed a Boeing CIM-10 Bomarc nuclear missile and shelter and contaminated the BOMARC Missile Accident Site in New Jersey.
- 24 January 1961: the 1961 Goldsboro B-52 crash occurred near Goldsboro, North Carolina. A B-52 Stratofortress carrying two Mark 39 nuclear bombs broke up in mid-air, dropping its nuclear payload in the process.
- 1965 Philippine Sea A-4 crash, where a Skyhawk attack aircraft with a nuclear weapon fell into the sea. The pilot, the aircraft, and the B43 nuclear bomb were never recovered. It was not until the 1980s that the Pentagon revealed the loss of the one-megaton bomb.
- January 17, 1966: the 1966 Palomares B-52 crash occurred when a B-52G bomber of the USAF collided with a KC-135 tankerduring mid-air refuelling off the coast of Spain. The KC-135 was completely destroyed when its fuel load ignited, killing all four crew members. The B-52G broke apart, killing three of the seven crew members aboard. Of the four Mk28 type hydrogen bombs the B-52G carried, three were found on land near Almería, Spain. The non-nuclear explosives in two of the weapons detonated upon impact with the ground, resulting in the contamination of a 2-square-kilometer (490-acre) (0.78 square mile) area by radioactiveplutonium. The fourth, which fell into the Mediterranean Sea, was recovered intact after a 2½-month-long search.
- January 21, 1968: the 1968 Thule Air Base B-52 crash involved a United States Air Force (USAF) B-52 bomber. The aircraft was carrying four hydrogen bombs when a cabin fire forced the crew to abandon the aircraft. Six crew members ejected safely, but one who did not have an ejection seat was killed while trying to bail out. The bomber crashed onto sea ice in Greenland, causing the nuclear payload to rupture and disperse, which resulted in widespread radioactive contamination.

Nuclear Fallout

Over 500 atmospheric nuclear weapons tests were conducted at various sites around the world from 1945 to 1980. Radioactive falloutfrom nuclear weapons testing was first drawn to public attention in 1954 when the Castle Bravo hydrogen bomb test at the Pacific Proving Grounds contaminated the crew and catch of the Japanese fishing boat *Lucky Dragon*. One of the fishermen died in Japan seven months later, and the fear of contaminated tuna led to a temporary boycotting of the popular staple in Japan.

The incident caused widespread concern around the world, especially regarding the effects of nuclear fallout and atmospheric nuclear testing, and "provided a decisive impetus for the emergence of the anti-nuclear weapons movement in many countries".

As public awareness and concern mounted over the possible health hazards associated with exposure to the nuclear fallout, various studies were done to assess the extent of the hazard. A Centres for Disease Control and Prevention/ National Cancer Institute study claims that fallout from atmospheric nuclear tests would lead to perhaps 11,000 excess deaths amongst people alive during atmospheric testing in the United States from all forms of cancer, including leukemia, from 1951 to well into the 21st century. As of March 2009, the U.S. is the only nation that compensates nuclear test victims. Since the Radiation Exposure Compensation Act of 1990, more than $1.38 billion in compensation has been approved. The money is going to people who took part in the tests, notably at the Nevada Test Site, and to others exposed to the radiation..

Public Opposition

Peace movements emerged in Japan and in 1954 they converged to form a unified "Japanese Council Against Atomic and Hydrogen Bombs". Japanese opposition to nuclear weapons tests in the Pacific Ocean was widespread, and "an estimated 35 million signatures were collected on petitions calling for bans on nuclear weapons".

In the United Kingdom, the first Aldermaston March organised by the Campaign for Nuclear Disarmament(CND) took place at Easter 1958, when, according to the CND, several thousand people marched for four days from Trafalgar Square, London, to the Atomic Weapons Research Establishment close to Aldermaston in Berkshire, England, to demonstrate their opposition to nuclear weapons. The Aldermaston marches continued into the late 1960s when tens of thousands of people took part in the four-day marches.

In 1959, a letter in the *Bulletin of Atomic Scientists* was the start of a successful campaign to stop the Atomic Energy Commission dumping radioactive waste in the sea 19 kilometres from Boston. In 1962, Linus Pauling won the Nobel Peace Prize for his work to stop the atmospheric testing of nuclear weapons, and the "Ban the Bomb" movement spread. In 1963, many countries ratified the Partial Test Ban Treaty prohibiting atmospheric nuclear testing. Radioactive fallout became less of an issue and the anti-nuclear weapons movement went into decline for some years. A resurgence of interest occurred amid European and American fears of nuclear war in the 1980s.

COSTS AND TECHNOLOGY SPIN-OFFS

According to an audit by the Brookings Institution, between 1940 and 1996, the U.S. spent $8.75 trillion in present day terms on nuclear weapons programs. 57 percent of which was spent on building nuclear weapons delivery systems. 6.3 percent of the total, $549 billion in present day terms, was spent on Environmental remediation and nuclear waste management, for example cleaning up the Hanford site, and 7 percent of the total, $615 billion was spent on making nuclear weapons themselves.

NON-WEAPONS USES

Civil Engineering and Energy Production

Apart from their use as weapons, nuclear explosives have been tested and used for variousnon-military uses. These have included large-scale earth moving and the creation of artificial bays. Due to the inability of the physicists to reduce the fission fraction of small, approximately 1 kiloton, yield nuclear devices that would have been required for many civil engineering projects, when long term health and clean-up costs from fission products were included in the cost, there was virtually no economic advantage over conventional explosives, except for potentially the very largest of projects.

At the peak of the Atomic Age, the United States Federal government initiated Operation Plowshare, involving "peaceful nuclear explosions". The United States Atomic Energy Commission chairman announced that the Plowshares project was intended to "highlight the peaceful applications of nuclear explosive devices and thereby create a climate of world opinion that is more favourable to weapons development and tests". The Operation Plowshare program included 27 nuclear tests designed towards investigating these non-weapons uses from 1961 through 1973.

The Qattara Depression Project, as developed by Professor Friedrich Bassler who during his appointment to the West German ministry of economics in 1968 put forth a plan to create a Saharan lake and hydroelectric power station by blasting a tunnel between the Mediterranean sea and the Qattara Depression in Egypt, an area that lies below sea level. The core problem of the entire project was the water supply to the depression. Calculations by Bassler showed that digging a canal or tunnel would be too expensive, therefore Bassler determined that the use of nuclear explosive devices, to excavate the canal or tunnel, would be the most economical. The Egyptian government declined to pursue the idea.

The Soviet Union's Nuclear Explosions for the National Economy was a program in the Soviet Union that investigated non-weapons uses of nuclear explosions. These included one 30 kiloton explosion being used to close the Uzbekistani *Urtabulak* gas well in 1966 that had been blowing since 1963, and a few months later a 47 kiloton explosive was used to seal a higher pressure blowout at the nearby *Pamuk* gas field.

The public records for devices that produced the highest proportion of their yield via fusion-only reactions are possibly the Soviet peaceful nuclear explosions of the 1970s, with 98% of their 15 kiloton explosive yield being derived from fusion reactions, a total fission fraction of 0.3 kilotons in a 15 kt device.

The repeated detonation of nuclear devices underground in salt domes, in a somewhat analogous manner to the explosions that power a car internal combustion engine (in that it would be a heat engine) has also been proposed as a means of fusion power, in what is termed PACER. Other investigated uses for peaceful nuclear explosions were underground detonations to stimulate, by a process analogous to fracking, the flow of petroleum and natural gas in tight formations, this was most developed in the Soviet Union, with an increase in the production of many well heads being reported.

Physics

The discovery and synthesis of new chemical elements by nuclear transmutation, and their production in the necessary quantities to allow the studying of their properties, was carried out in nuclear explosive device testing. For example, the discovery of the short lived einsteinium and fermium, both created under the intense neutron flux environment within thermonuclear explosions, followed the first Teller-Ulam thermonuclear device test - Ivy Mike. The rapid capture of so many neutrons required in the synthesis of einsteinium would provide the needed direct experimental confirmation of the so-called r-process, the multiple neutron absorptions needed to explain the cosmic nucleosynthesis (production) of all heavy chemical elements heavier than nickel on the periodic table, in supernova explosions, before beta decay, with the r-process explaining the existence of many stable elements in the universe.

In 2008 the worldwide presence of new isotopes from atmospheric testing beginning in the 1950s was developed into a reliable way of detecting art forgeries, as all paintings created after that period may contain traces of caesium-137 and strontium-90, isotopes that did not exist in nature before 1945. Fission products like Cs-137 and Sr-90 did occur in nature prior to 1945, being produced in the natural nuclear fission reactor at Oklo, but almost all traces of them had long since decayed away before the rise of even the earliest known human painting.

Both climatology and particularly aerosol science, a subfield of atmospheric science, were largely created to answer the question of how far and wide fallout would travel. Similar to radioactive tracersused in hydrology and materials testing, fallout and the neutron activation of nitrogen gas served as a radioactive tracer that was used to measure and then help model global circulations in the atmosphere by following the movements of fallout aerosols.

After the Van Allen Belts surrounding Earth were published about in 1958, James Van Allen suggested that a nuclear detonation would be one way of probing the magnetic phenomenon, data obtained from the August 1958 Project Argus test shots, a high altitude nuclear explosion investigation, were vital to the early understanding of Earth's magnetosphere.

Soviet nuclear physicist and Nobel peace prize recipient Andrei Sakharov also proposed the idea that earthquakes could be mitigated and particle accelerators could be made by utilizing nuclear explosions, with the latter created by connecting a nuclear explosive device with another of his inventions, the explosively pumped flux compression generator, to accelerate protons to collide with each other to probe their inner workings, an endeavour that is presently done at much lower energy levels with non-explosive superconducting magnetsin CERN. Sakharov suggested to replace the copper coil in his MK generators by a bigsuperconductor solenoid to magnetically compress and focus underground nuclear explosions into a shaped charge effect. He theorized this could focus 10^{23} positively chargedprotons per second on a 1 mm^2 surface, then envisaged making two such beams collide in the form of a supercollider.

Underground nuclear explosive data from peaceful nuclear explosion test shots have been used to investigate the composition of Earth's mantle, analogous to the exploration geophysics practice of mineral prospecting with chemical explosives in "deep seismic sounding" reflection seismology.

Project A119, proposed in the 1960s, which as Apollo scientist Gary Latham explained, would have been the detonating of a "smallish" nuclear device on the Moon in order to facilitate research into its geologic make-up. Analogous in concept to the comparatively low yield explosion created by the water prospecting (LCROSS) Lunar Crater Observation and Sensing Satellite mission, which launched in 2009 and released the "Centaur" kinetic energy impactor, an impactor with a mass of 2,305 kg (5,081 lb), and an impact velocity of about 9,000 km/h (5,600 mph), releasing the kinetic energy equivalent of detonating approximately 2 tons of TNT (8.86 GJ).

Propulsion Use

Although likely never achieving orbit due to aerodynamic drag, the first macroscopic object to obtain Earth orbital velocity was a "manhole cover" propelled by the detonation of test shot Pascal-B, beforesputnik obtained orbital velocity, and also successfully became the first satellite, in October 1957. The use of a subterranean shaft and nuclear device to propel an object to escape velocity has since been termed a "thunder well".

The direct use of nuclear explosives, by using the impact of propellant plasma from a nuclear shaped charge acting on a pusher plate, has also been seriously studied as a potential propulsion mechanism for space travel.

Edward Teller, in the United States, proposed the use of a nuclear detonation to power an explosively pumped *soft* X-ray laser as a component of a ballistic missile defence shield, this would destroy missile components by transferring momentum to the vehicles surface by laser ablation. This ablation process is one of the damage mechanisms of a laser weapon, but it is also the basis of pulsed laser propulsion for spacecraft.

Ground flight testing by Professor Leik Myrabo, using a non-nuclear, conventionally powered pulsed laser test-bed, successfully lifted a lightcraft 72 meters in altitude by a method similar to ablative laser propulsion in 2000. A powerful solar system based *soft* X-ray, to ultraviolet, laser system has been calculated to be capable of propelling an interstellar spacecraft, by the light sail principle, to 11% of the speed of light. In 1972 it was also calculated that a 1 Terawatt, 1-km diameter x-ray laser with 1 angstrom wavelength impinging on a 1-km diameter sail, could propel a spacecraft to Alpha Centauri in 10 years.

ASTEROID IMPACT AVOIDANCE

A proposed means of averting an asteroid impacting with Earth, assuming low lead times between detection and Earth impact, is to detonate one, or a series, of nuclear explosive devices, on, in, or in a stand-off proximity orientation with the asteroid, with the latter method occurring far enough away from the incoming threat to prevent the potential fracturing of thenear-Earth object, but still close enough to generate a high thrust laser ablation effect.

A 2007 NASA analysis of impact avoidance strategies using various technologies stated: Nuclear stand-off explosions are assessed to be 10-100 times more effective than the non-nuclear alternatives analyzed in this study. Other techniques involving the surfaceor subsurface use of nuclear explosives may be more efficient, but they run an increased risk of fracturing the target near-Earth object. They also carry higher development and operations risks.

Analysis of the uncertainty involved in nuclear device asteroid deflection shows that the ability to protect the planet does not imply the ability to also target the planet, which is the case with all non-nuclear alternatives, such as the controversial gravity tractor technology. A nuclear explosion that changed an asteroid's velocity by 10 m/s (±20%) would be adequate to push it out of an Earth-impacting orbit. However, if the uncertainty of the velocity change is more than a few plus or minus percent, there would be no chance of directing the asteroid to a particular target. However, if the need arises to use nuclear explosive devices to prevent an asteroid impact event, it may face the legal issue that presently the United Nations Committee on the Peaceful Uses of Outer Space, and the 1996 Comprehensive Nuclear-Test-Ban Treaty technically ban nuclear weapons in space.

HISTORY OF NUCLEAR WEAPONS

Nuclear weapons possess enormous destructive power derived from nuclear fission or combined fission and fusion reactions. Starting with scientific breakthroughs made during the 1930s, the United States, the United Kingdom and Canada collaborated during World War II in what was called the Manhattan Project to counter the suspected Nazi German atomic bomb project. In August 1945 two fission bombs were dropped on Japan ending the Pacific War. The Soviet Union started development shortly thereafter with their own atomic bomb project, and not long after that both countries developed even more powerful fusion weapons known as "hydrogen bombs."

PHYSICS AND POLITICS IN THE 1930S AND 1940s

In the first decades of the 20th century, physics was revolutionised with developments in the understanding of the nature of atoms. In 1898, Pierre and Marie Curie discovered that pitchblende, an ore of uranium, contained a substance—which they named radium—that emitted large amounts of radioactivity. Ernest Rutherford and Frederick Soddy identified that atoms were breaking down and turning into different elements. Hopes were raised among scientists and laymen that the elements around us could contain tremendous amounts of unseen energy, waiting to be harnessed.

H. G. Wells was inspired to write about atomic weapons in a 1914 novel, *The World Set Free*, which appeared shortly before the First World War. In a 1924 article, Winston Churchillspeculated about the possible military implications: "Might not a bomb no bigger than an orange be found to possess a secret power to destroy a whole block of buildings—nay to concentrate the force of a thousand tons of cordite and blast a township at a stroke?"

In January 1933, Adolf Hitler was elected Chancellor of Germany and it quickly became unsafe for Jewish scientists to remain in the country. Leó Szilárd fled to London where he proposed, and in 1934 patented, the idea of a nuclear chain reaction via neutrons. The patent also introduced the term critical mass to describe the minimum amount of material required to sustain the chain reaction and its potential to cause an explosion. (British patent 630,726.) He subsequently assigned the patent to the British Admiralty so that it could be covered by the Official Secrets Act. In a very real sense, Szilárd was the father of the atomic bomb academically. Also in 1934, Irène and Frédéric Joliot-Curie discovered that artificial radioactivity could be induced in stable elements by bombarding them with alpha particles; Enrico Fermireported similar results when bombarding uranium with neutrons.

In December 1938, Otto Hahn and Fritz Strassmann sent a manuscript to *Naturwissenschaften reporting* that they had detected the element barium after bombarding uranium with neutrons. Lise Meitner and her nephew Otto Robert Frisch correctly interpreted these results as being due to the splitting of the uranium atom. (Frisch confirmed this experimentally on January 13, 1939.) They gave the process the name "fission" because of its similarity to the splitting of a cell into two new cells. Even before it was published, news of Meitner's and Frisch's interpretation crossed the Atlantic. Scientists at Columbia University decided to replicate the experiment and on January 25, 1939, conducted the first nuclear fission experiment in the United States in the basement of Pupin Hall. The following year, they identified the active component of uranium as being the rare isotope uranium-235.

Uranium appears in nature primarily in two isotopes: uranium-238 and uranium-235. When the nucleus of uranium-235 absorbs a neutron, it undergoes nuclear fission, releasing energy and, on average, 2.5 neutrons. Because uranium-235 releases more neutrons than it absorbs, it can support a chain reaction and so is described as fissile. Uranium-238, on the other hand, is not fissile as it does not normally undergo fission when it absorbs a neutron. By the time Nazi Germany invaded Poland in 1939, beginning World War II, many of Europe's top scientists had already fled the imminent conflict. Physicists on both sides were well aware of the possibility of utilizing nuclear fission as a weapon, but no one was quite sure how it could be done. In August 1939, concerned that Germany might have its own project to develop fission-based weapons, Albert Einstein signed a letter to U.S. President Franklin D. Roosevelt warning him of the threat.

Roosevelt responded by setting up the Uranium Committee under Lyman James Briggs but, with little initial funding ($6,000), progress was slow. It was not until the Japanese attack on Pearl Harbor in December, 1941, that the U.S. decided to commit the necessary resources.

Organized research first began in Britain as part of the Tube Alloys project. The Maud Committee was set up following the work of Frisch and Rudolf Peierls who calculated uranium-235's critical mass and found it to be much smaller than previously thought which meant that a deliverable bomb should be possible. In the February 1940 Frisch–Peierls memorandum they stated that: "The energy liberated in the explosion of such a super-bomb...will, for an instant, produce a temperature comparable to that of the interior of the sun. The blast from such an explosion would destroy life in a wide area. The size of this area is difficult to estimate, but it will probably cover the centre of a big city."

Edgar Sengier, a director of Shinkolobwe Mine which produced by far the highest quality uranium ore in the world, had become aware of uranium's possible use in a bomb. In late 1940, fearful of its seizure by the Germans, he shipped the mine's entire stockpile of ore to a warehouse on Staten Island.

For 18 months British research outpaced the American but by mid-1942, it became apparent that the industrial effort required was beyond Britain's already stretched wartime economy. In September 1942, General Leslie Groves was appointed to lead the U.S. project which became known as the Manhattan Project. Two of his first acts were to obtain authorization to assign the highest priority AAA rating on necessary procurements, and to put in train the purchase of all 1,250 tons of the Shinkolobwe ore. The Tube Alloys project was quickly overtaken by the U.S. effort and after Roosevelt and Churchill signed the Quebec Agreement in 1943, it was relocated and amalgamated into the Manhattan Project.

FROM LOS ALAMOS TO HIROSHIMA

With a scientific team led by J. Robert Oppenheimer, the Manhattan project brought together some of the top scientific minds of the day, including many exiles from Europe, with the production power of American industry for the goal of producing fission-based explosive devices before Germany. Britain and the U.S. agreed to pool their resources and information for the project, but the other Allied power, the Soviet Union (USSR), was not informed. The U.S. made an unprecedented investment in the project which at the time was the largest industrial enterprise ever seen, spread across more than 30 sites in the U.S. and Canada. Scientific development was centralized in a secret laboratory at Los Alamos.

For a fission weapon to operate, there must be sufficient fissile material to support a chain reaction, a critical mass. To separate the fissile uranium-235 isotope from the non-fissile uranium-238, two methods were developed which took advantage of the fact that uranium-238 has a slightly greater atomic mass: electromagnetic separation and gaseous diffusion. Another secret site was erected at rural Oak Ridge, Tennessee, for the large-scale production and purification of the rare isotope, which required considerable investment. At the time, K-25, one of the Oak Ridge facilities, was the world's largest factory under one roof. The Oak Ridge site employed tens of thousands of people at its peak, most of whom had no idea what they were working on.

Although uranium-238 cannot be used for the initial stage of an atomic bomb, when it absorbs a neutron, it becomes uranium-239 which decaysinto neptunium-239, and finally the relatively stable plutonium-239, an element that does not exist naturally on Earth, but is fissile like uranium-235. After Fermi achieved the world's first sustained and controlled nuclear chain reaction with the creation of the first atomic pile, massive reactors were secretly constructed at what is now known as Hanford Site to transform uranium-238 into plutonium for a bomb.

The simplest form of nuclear weapon is a gun-type fission weapon, where a sub-critical mass would be shot at another sub-critical mass. The result would be a super-critical mass and an uncontrolled chain reaction that would create the desired explosion. The weapons envisaged in 1942 were the two gun-type weapons, Little Boy (uranium) and Thin Man (plutonium), and theFat Man plutonium implosion bomb.

In early 1943 Oppenheimer determined that two projects should proceed forwards: the Thin Man project (plutonium gun) and the Fat Man project (plutonium implosion). The plutonium gun was to receive the bulk of the research effort, as it was the project with the most uncertainty involved. It was assumed that the uranium gun-type bomb could then be adapted from it.

In December 1943 the British mission of 19 scientists arrived in Los Alamos. Hans Bethebecame head of the Theoretical Division.

In April 1944 it was found by Emilio Segrè that the plutonium-239 produced by the Hanford reactors had too high a level of background neutron radiation, and underwent spontaneous fission to a very small extent, due to the unexpected presence of plutonium-240 impurities. If such plutonium were used in a gun-type design, the chain reaction would start in the split second before the critical mass was fully assembled, blowing the weapon apart with a much lower yield than expected, in what is known as a fizzle.

As a result, development of Fat Man was given high priority. Chemical explosives were used to implode a sub-critical sphere of plutonium, thus increasing its density and making it into a critical mass. The difficulties with implosion centered on the problem of making the chemical explosives deliver a perfectly uniform shock wave upon the plutonium sphere— if it were even slightly asymmetric, the weapon would fizzle. This problem was solved by the use of explosive lenses which would focus the blast waves inside the imploding sphere, akin to the way in which an optical lens focuses light rays.

After D-Day, General Groves ordered a team of scientists to follow eastward-moving victorious Allied troops into Europe to assess the status of the German nuclear program (and to prevent the westward-moving Russians from gaining any materials or scientific manpower). They concluded that, while Germany had an atomic bomb program headed by Werner Heisenberg, the government had not made a significant investment in the project, and it had been nowhere near success.

Historians claim to have found a rough schematic showing a Nazi nuclear bomb. In March 1945, a German scientific team was directed by the physicist Kurt Diebner to develop a primitive nuclear device in Ohrdruf, Thuringia. Last ditch research was conducted in an experimental nuclear reactor at Haigerloch.

On April 12, after Roosevelt's death, Vice-President Harry S. Truman assumed the presidency. At the time of the unconditional surrender of Germany on May 8, 1945, the Manhattan Project was still months away from producing a working weapon.

Because of the difficulties in making a working plutonium bomb, it was decided that there should be a test of the weapon. On July 16, 1945, in the desert north of Alamogordo, New Mexico, the first nuclear test took place, code-named "Trinity", using a device nicknamed "the gadget." The test, a plutonium implosion type device, released energy equivalent to 19 kilotons of TNT, far more powerful than any weapon ever used before. The news of the test's success was rushed to Truman at the Potsdam Conference, where Churchill was briefed and Joseph Stalin was informed of the new weapon. On July 26, the Potsdam Declaration was issued containing an ultimatum for Japan: either surrender or suffer "complete and utter destruction", although nuclear weapons were not mentioned. After hearing arguments from scientists and military officers over the possible uses of the weapons against Japan (though some recommended using them as demonstrations in unpopulated areas, most recommended using them against built up targets, a euphemistic term for populated cities), Truman ordered the use of the weapons on Japanese cities, hoping it would send a strong message that would end in the capitulation of the Japanese leadership and avoid a lengthy invasion of the islands. On May 10–11, 1945, the Target Committee at Los Alamos, led by Oppenheimer, recommended Kyoto, Hiroshima, Yokohama, and the arsenal at Kokura as possible targets. Concerns about Kyoto's cultural heritage led to it being replaced by Nagasaki.

On August 6, 1945, a uranium-based weapon, Little Boy, was detonated above the Japanese city of Hiroshima. Three days later, a plutonium-based weapon, Fat Man, was detonated above the city of Nagasaki. The atomic bombs killed at least one hundred thousand Japanese outright, most of them civilians, with the heat, radiation, and blast effects. Many tens of thousands would later die of radiation sicknessand related cancers. Truman promised a "rain of ruin" if Japan did not surrender immediately, threatening to systematically eliminate their ability to wage war. On August 15, Emperor Hirohito announced Japan's surrender.

SOVIET ATOMIC BOMB PROJECT

The Soviet Union was not invited to share in the new weapons developed by the United States and the other Allies. During the war, information had been pouring in from a number of volunteer spies involved with the Manhattan Project (known in Soviet cables under the code-name of*Enormoz*), and the Soviet nuclear physicist Igor Kurchatov was carefully watching the Allied weapons development. It came as no surprise to Stalin when Truman had informed him at the Potsdam conference that he had a "powerful new weapon." Truman was shocked at Stalin's lack of interest.

The Soviet spies in the U.S. project were all volunteers and none were Russians. One of the most valuable, Klaus Fuchs, was a German émigré theoretical physicist who had been part of the early British nuclear efforts and the UK mission to Los Alamos. Fuchs had been intimately involved in the development of the implosion weapon, and passed on detailed cross-sections of the Trinity device to his Soviet contacts. Other Los Alamos spies—none of whom knew each other—included Theodore Hall and David Greenglass. The information was kept but not acted upon, as Russia was still too busy fighting the war in Europe to devote resources to this new project.

In the years immediately after World War II, the issue of who should control atomic weapons became a major international point of contention. Many of the Los Alamos scientists who had built the bomb began to call for "international control of atomic energy," often calling for either control by transnational organizations or the purposeful distribution of weapons information to all superpowers, but due to a deep distrust of the intentions of the Soviet Union, both in postwar Europe and in general, the policy-makers of the United States worked to attempt to secure an American nuclear monopoly.

A half-hearted plan for international control was proposed at the newly formed United Nations by Bernard Baruch (The Baruch Plan), but it was clear both to American commentators—and to the Soviets—that it was an attempt primarily to stymie Russian nuclear efforts. The Soviets vetoed the plan, effectively ending any immediate postwar negotiations on atomic energy, and made overtures towards banning the use of atomic weapons in general.

The Soviets had put their full industrial might and manpower into the development of their own atomic weapons. The initial problem for the Soviets was primarily one of resources—they had not scouted out uranium resources in the Soviet Union and the U.S. had made deals to monopolise the largest known (and high purity) reserves in the Belgian Congo. The USSR used penal labour to mine the old deposits in Czechoslovakia—now an area under their control—and searched for other domestic deposits (which were eventually found).

Two days after the bombing of Nagasaki, the U.S. government released an official technical history of the Manhattan Project, authored by Princeton physicist Henry DeWolf Smyth, known colloquially as the Smyth Report. The sanitized summary of the wartime effort focused primarily on the production facilities and scale of investment, written in part to justify the wartime expenditure to the American public.

The Soviet program, under the suspicious watch of former NKVD chief Lavrenty Beria (a participant and victor in Stalin's Great Purge of the 1930s), would use the Report as a blueprint, seeking to duplicate as much as possible the American effort. The "secret cities" used for the Soviet equivalents of Hanford and Oak Ridge literally vanished from the maps for decades to come.

At the Soviet equivalent of Los Alamos, Arzamas-16, physicist Yuli Khariton led the scientific effort to develop the weapon. Beria distrusted his scientists, however, and he distrusted the carefully collected espionage information. As such, Beria assigned multiple teams of scientists to the same task without informing each team of the other's existence. If they arrived at different conclusions, Beria would bring them together for the first time and have them debate with their newfound counterparts. Beria used the espionage information as a way to double-check the progress of his scientists, and in his effort for duplication of the American project even rejected more efficient bomb designs in favour of ones that more closely mimicked the tried-and-true Fat Man bomb used by the U.S. against Nagasaki. Working under a stubborn and scientifically ignorant administrator, the Soviet scientists struggled on. On

August 29, 1949, the effort brought its results, when the USSR tested its first fission bomb, dubbed "Joe-1" by the U.S., years ahead of American predictions. The news of the first Soviet bomb was announced to the world first by the United States, which had detected the nuclear fallout it generated from its test site in Kazakhstan.

The loss of the American monopoly on nuclear weapons marked the first tit-for-tat of the nuclear arms race. The response in the U.S. was one of apprehension, fear, and scapegoating, which would lead eventually into the Red-baiting tactics of McCarthyism. Yet recent information from unclassified Venona intercepts and the opening of the KGB archives after the fall of the Soviet Union show that the USSR had useful spies that helped their program, although none were identified by McCarthy. Before this, though, President Truman announced a decision to begin a crash program that would develop a far more powerful weapon than those the U.S. used against Japan: the hydrogen bomb.

AMERICAN DEVELOPMENTS AFTER WORLD WAR II

In 1946 Congress established the civilian Atomic Energy Commission (AEC) to take over the development of nuclear weapons from the military, and to develop nuclear power. The AEC made use of many private companies in processing uranium and thorium and in other urgent tasks related to the development of bombs. Many of these companies had very lax safety measures and employees were sometimes exposed to radiation levels far above what was allowed then or now. In 1974, the Formerly Utilized Sites Remedial Action Program (FUSRAP) of the Army Corps of Engineers was set up to deal with contaminated sites left over from these operations.

THE FIRST THERMONUCLEAR WEAPONS

The notion of using a fission weapon to ignite a process of nuclear fusion can be dated back to 1942. At the first major theoretical conference on the development of an atomic bomb hosted by J. Robert Oppenheimer at the University of California, Berkeley, participant Edward Teller directed the majority of the discussion towards Enrico Fermi's idea of a "Super" bomb that would use the same reactions that powered the Sun itself.

It was thought at the time that a fission weapon would be quite simple to develop and that perhaps work on a hydrogen bomb (thermonuclear weapon) would be possible to complete before the end of the Second World War. However, in reality the problem of a regular atomic bomb was large enough to preoccupy the scientists for the next few years, much less the more speculative "Super" bomb. Only Teller continued working on the project—against the will of project leaders Oppenheimer and Hans Bethe.

After the atomic bombings of Japan, many scientists at Los Alamos rebelled against the notion of creating a weapon thousands of times more powerful than the first atomic bombs. For the scientists the question was in part technical—the weapon design was still quite uncertain and unworkable—and in part moral: such a weapon, they argued, could only be used against large civilian populations, and could thus only be used as a weapon of genocide. Many scientists, such as Bethe, urged that the United States should not develop such weapons and set an example towards the Soviet Union. Promoters of the weapon, including Teller, Ernest Lawrence, and Luis Alvarez, argued that such a development was inevitable, and to deny such protection to the people of the United States—especially when the Soviet Union was likely to create such a weapon themselves—was itself an immoral and unwise act.

Oppenheimer, who was now head of the General Advisory Committee of the successor to the Manhattan Project, the Atomic Energy Commission, presided over a recommendation against the development of the weapon. The reasons were in part because the success of the technology seemed limited at the time (and not worth the investment of resources to confirm whether this was so), and because Oppenheimer believed that the atomic forces of the United States would be more effective if they consisted of many large fission weapons (of which multiple bombs could be dropped on the same targets) rather than the large and unwieldy super bombs, for which there was a relatively limited number of targets of sufficient size to warrant such a development.

Furthermore, were such weapons developed by both the U.S. and the USSR, they would be more effectively used against the U.S. than by it, as the U.S. had far more regions of dense industrial and civilian activity as targets for large weapons than the Soviet Union.

In the end, President Truman made the final decision, looking for a proper response to the first Soviet atomic bomb test in 1949. On January 31, 1950, Truman announced a crash program to develop the hydrogen (fusion) bomb. At this point, however, the exact mechanism was still not known: the classical hydrogen bomb, whereby the *heat* of the fission bomb would be used to ignite the fusion material, seemed highly unworkable. However, an insight by Los Alamos mathematician Stanislaw Ulam showed that the fission bomb and the fusion fuel could be in separate parts of the bomb, and that*radiation* of the fission bomb could first work in a way to *compress* the fusion material before igniting it. Teller pushed the notion further, and used the results of the boosted-fission "George" test (a boosted-fission device using a small amount of fusion fuel to boost the yield of a fission bomb) to confirm the fusion of heavy hydrogen elements before preparing for their first true multi-stage, Teller-Ulam hydrogen bomb test. Many scientists initially against the weapon, such as Oppenheimer and Bethe, changed their previous opinions, seeing the development as being unstoppable.

The first fusion bomb was tested by the United States in *Operation Ivy* on November 1, 1952, on Elugelab Island in the Enewetak (or Eniwetok) Atoll of the Marshall Islands, code-named "Mike." Mike used liquid deuterium as its fusion fuel and a large fission weapon as its trigger. The device was a prototype design and not a deliverable weapon: standing over 20 ft (6 m) high and weighing at least 140,000 lb (64 t) (its refrigeration equipment added an additional 24,000 lb (11,000 kg) as well), it could not have been dropped from even the largest planes.

Its explosion yielded energy equivalent to 10.4 megatons of TNT—over 450 times the power of the bomb dropped onto Nagasaki— and obliterated Elugelab, leaving an underwater crater 6240 ft (1.9 km) wide and 164 ft (50 m) deep where the island had once been. Truman had initially tried to create a media blackout about the test—hoping it would not become an issue in the upcoming presidential election—but on January 7, 1953, Truman announced the development of the hydrogen bomb to the world as hints and speculations of it were already beginning to emerge in the press.

Not to be outdone, the Soviet Union exploded its first thermonuclear device, designed by the physicist Andrei Sakharov, on August 12, 1953, labeled "Joe-4" by the West.

This created concern within the U.S. government and military, because, unlike Mike, the Soviet device was a deliverable weapon, which the U.S. did not yet have. This first device though was arguably not a true hydrogen bomb, and could only reach explosive yields in the hundreds of kilotons (never reaching the megaton range of a staged weapon). Still, it was a powerful propaganda tool for the Soviet Union, and the technical differences were fairly oblique to the American public and politicians.

Following the Mike blast by less than a year, Joe-4 seemed to validate claims that the bombs were inevitable and vindicate those who had supported the development of the fusion program. Coming during the height of McCarthyism, the effect was pronounced on the security hearings in early 1954, which revoked former Los Alamos director Robert Oppenheimer's security clearance on the grounds that he was unreliable, had not supported the American hydrogen bomb program, and had made long-standing left-wing ties in the 1930s. Edward Teller participated in the hearing as the only major scientist to testify against Oppenheimer, resulting in his virtual expulsion from the physics community.

On March 1, 1954, the U.S. detonated its first practical thermonuclear weapon (which used isotopes of lithium as its fusion fuel), known as the "Shrimp" device of the Castle Bravo test, at Bikini Atoll, Marshall Islands. The device yielded 15 megatons, more than twice its expected yield, and became the worst radiological disaster in U.S. history. The combination of the unexpectedly large blast and poor weather conditions caused a cloud of radioactive nuclear fallout to contaminate over 7,000 square miles (18,000 km). 239 Marshall Island natives and 28 Americans were exposed to significant amounts of radiation, resulting in elevated levels of cancer and birth defectsin the years to come.

The crew of the Japanese tuna-fishing boat *Lucky Dragon 5*, who had been fishing just outside the exclusion zone, returned to port suffering from radiation sickness and skin burns. Efforts were made to recover the contaminated fish but at least two large tuna were probably sold and eaten. A further 75 tons of tuna caught between March and December were found to be unfit for human consumption. When a crew member died and the full results of the contamination were made public by the

U.S., Japanese concerns were reignited about the hazards of radiation.

The hydrogen bomb age had a profound effect on the thoughts of nuclear war in the popular and military mind. With only fission bombs, nuclear war was something that possibly could be limited. Dropped by planes and only able to destroy the most built up areas of major cities, it was possible for many to look at fission bombs as a technological extension of large-scale conventional bombing—such as the extensive firebombing against Japan and Germany during World War II). Proponents brushed aside as grave exaggeration claims that such weapons could lead to worldwide death or harm.

Even in the decades before fission weapons, there had been speculation about the possibility for human beings to end all life on the planet, either by accident or purposeful maliciousness—but technology had not provided the capacity for such action. The great power of hydrogen bombs made world-wide annihilation possible. The Castle Bravo incident itself raised a number of questions about the survivability of a nuclear war. Government scientists in both the U.S. and the USSR had insisted that fusion weapons, unlike fission weapons, were cleaner, as fusion reactions did not produce the dangerously radioactive by-products of fission reactions.

While technically true, this hid a more gruesome point: the last stage of a multi-staged hydrogen bomb often used the neutrons produced by the fusion reactions to induce fissioning in a jacket of natural uranium, and provided around half of the yield of the device itself. This fission stage made fusion weapons considerably more dirty than they were made out to be. This was evident in the towering cloud of deadly fallout that followed the *Bravo* test. When the Soviet Union tested its first megaton device in 1955, the possibility of a *limited*nuclear war seemed even more remote in the public and political mind. Even cities and countries that were not direct targets would suffer fallout contamination. Extremely harmful fission products would disperse via normal weather patterns and embed in soil and water around the planet.

Speculation began to run towards what fallout and dust from a full-scale nuclear exchange would do to the world as a whole, rather than just cities and countries directly involved. In this way, the fate of the world was now tied to the fate of the bomb-wielding superpowers.

DETERRENCE AND BRINKMANSHIP

Throughout the 1950s and the early 1960s the U.S. and the USSR both endeavored, in a tit-for-tat approach, to prevent the other power from acquiring nuclear supremacy. This had massive political and cultural effects during theCold War.

The first atomic bombs dropped on Hiroshima and Nagasaki were large, custom-made devices, requiring highly trained personnel for their arming and deployment. They could be dropped only from the largest bomber planes—at the time the B-29 Superfortress—and each plane could only carry a single bomb in its hold. The first hydrogen bombs were similarly massive and complicated. This ratio of one plane to one bomb was still fairly impressive in comparison with conventional, non-nuclear weapons, but against other nuclear-armed countries it was considered a grave danger. In the immediate postwar years, the U.S. expended much effort on making the bombs "G.I.-proof"—capable of being used and deployed by members of the U.S. Army, rather than Nobel Prize–winning scientists. In the 1950s, the U.S. undertook a nuclear testing program to improve the nuclear arsenal.

Starting in 1951, the Nevada Test Site (in the Nevada desert) became the primary location for all U.S. nuclear testing (in the USSR, Semipalatinsk Test Site in Kazakhstan served a similar role). Tests were divided into two primary categories: "weapons related" (verifying that a new weapon worked or looking at exactly how it worked) and "weapons effects" (looking at how weapons behaved under various conditions or how structures behaved when subjected to weapons).

In the beginning, almost all nuclear tests were either atmospheric (conducted above ground, in the atmosphere) or underwater (such as some of the tests done in the Marshall Islands). Testing was used as a sign of both national and technological strength, but also raised questions about the safety of the tests, which released nuclear fallout into the atmosphere (most dramatically with the Castle Bravo test in 1954, but in more limited amounts with almost all atmospheric nuclear testing).

Because testing was seen as a sign of technological development (the ability to design usable weapons without some form of testing was considered dubious), halts on testing were often called for as stand-ins for halts in the nuclear arms race itself, and many prominent scientists and statesmen lobbied for a ban on nuclear testing. In 1958, the U.S., USSR, and the United Kingdom (a new nuclear power) declared a temporary testing moratorium for both political and health reasons, but by 1961 the Soviet Union had broken the moratorium and both the USSR and the U.S. began testing with great frequency.

As a show of political strength, the Soviet Union tested the largest-ever nuclear weapon in October 1961, the massive Tsar Bomba, which was tested in a reduced state with a yield of around 50 megatons—in its full state it was estimated to have been around 100 Mt.

The weapon was largely impractical for actual military use, but was hot enough to induce third-degree burns at a distance of 62 mi (100 km) away. In its full, dirty, design it would have increased the amount of worldwide fallout since 1945 by 25%.

In 1963, all nuclear and many non-nuclear states signed the Limited Test Ban Treaty, pledging to refrain from testing nuclear weapons in the atmosphere, underwater, or in outer space. The treaty permitted underground tests.

Most tests were considerably more modest, and worked for direct technical purposes as well as their potential political overtones. Weapons improvements took on two primary forms. One was an increase in efficiency and power, and within only a few years fission bombs were developed that were many times more powerful than the ones created during World War II. The other was a program of miniaturization, reducing the size of the nuclear weapons.

Smaller bombs meant that bombers could carry more of them, and also that they could be carried on the new generation of rockets in development in the 1950s and 1960s. U.S. rocket science received a large boost in the postwar years, largely with the help of engineers acquired from the Nazi rocketry program. These included scientists such as Wernher von Braun, who had helped design the V-2 rockets the Nazis launched across the English Channel. An American program, Project Paperclip, had endeavored to move German scientists into American hands (and away from Soviet hands) and put them to work for the U.S.

WEAPONS IMPROVEMENT

Early nuclear-tipped rockets—such as the MGR-1 Honest John, first deployed by the U.S. in 1953—were surface-to-surface missiles with relatively short ranges (around 15 mi/25 km maximum) and yields around twice the size of the first fission weapons. The limited range meant they could only be used in certain types of military situations. U.S. rockets could not, for example, threaten Moscow with an immediate strike, and could only be used as tactical weapons (that is, for small-scale military situations).

Strategic weapons—weapons that could threaten an entire country—relied, for the time being, on long-range bombers that could penetrate deep into enemy territory. In the U.S., this requirement led, in 1946, to creation of the Strategic Air Command—a system of bombers headed by General Curtis LeMay (who previously presided over the firebombing of Japan during WWII). In operations like Chrome Dome, SAC kept nuclear-armed planes in the air 24 hours a day, ready for an order to attack Moscow.

These technological possibilities enabled nuclear strategy to develop a logic considerably different than previous military thinking allowed. Because the threat of nuclear warfare was so awful, it was first thought that it might make any war of the future impossible.

PresidentDwight D. Eisenhower's doctrine of "massive retaliation" in the early years of the Cold War was a message to the USSR, saying that if the Red Army attempted to invade the parts of Europe not given to the Eastern bloc during the Potsdam Conference (such as West Germany), nuclear weapons would be used against the Soviet troops and potentially the Soviet leaders.

With the development of more rapid-response technologies (such as rockets and long-range bombers), this policy began to shift. If the Soviet Union also had nuclear weapons and a policy of "massive retaliation" was carried out, it was reasoned, then any Soviet forces not killed in the initial attack, or launched while the attack was ongoing, would be able to serve their own form of nuclear retaliation against the U.S. Recognizing that this was an undesirable outcome, military officers and game theorists at the RAND think tank developed a nuclear warfare strategy that was eventually called Mutually Assured Destruction (MAD).

MAD divided potential nuclear war into two stages: *first strike* and *second strike*. First strike meant the first use of nuclear weapons by one nuclear-equipped nation against another nuclear-equipped nation. If the attacking nation did not prevent the attacked nation from a nuclear response, the attacked nation would respond with a second strike against the attacking nation. In this situation, whether the U.S. first attacked the USSR or the USSR first attacked the U.S., the end result would be that both nations would be damaged to the point of utter social collapse.

According to game theory, because starting a nuclear war was suicidal, no logical country would shoot first. However, if a country could launch a first strike that utterly destroyed the target country's ability to respond, that might give that country the confidence to initiate a nuclear war. The object of a country operating by the MAD doctrine is to deny the opposing country this first strike capability.

MAD played on two seemingly opposed modes of thought: cold logic and emotional fear. The English phrase MAD was often known by, "nuclear deterrence," was translated by the French as "dissuasion," and "terrorization" by the Russians. This apparent paradox of nuclear war was summed up by British Prime Minister Winston Churchill as "the worse things get, the better they are"—the greater the threat of mutual destruction, the safer the world would be.

This philosophy made a number of technological and political demands on participating nations. For one thing, it said that it should always be assumed that an enemy nation may be trying to acquire first strike capability, which must always be avoided. In American politics this translated into demands to avoid "bomber gaps" and "missile gaps" where the Soviet Union could potentially outshoot the Americans. It also encouraged the production of thousands of nuclear weapons by both the U.S. and the USSR, far more than needed to simply destroy the major civilian and military infrastructures of the opposing country. These policies and strategies were satirized in the 1964 Stanley Kubrick film Dr. Strangelove, in which the Soviets, unable to keep up with the US's first strike capability, instead plan for MAD by building a Doomsday Machine, and thus, after a (literally) mad US General orders a nuclear attack on the USSR, the end of the world is brought about.

The policy also encouraged the development of the first early warning systems. Conventional war, even at its fastest, was fought over days and weeks. With long-range bombers, from the start of a nuclear attack to its conclusion was mere hours. Rockets could reduce a conflict to minutes. Planners reasoned that conventional command and control systems could not adequately react to a nuclear attack, so great lengths were taken to develop computer systems that could look for enemy attacks and direct rapid responses.

The U.S., poured massive funding into development of SAGE, a system that could track and intercept enemy bomber aircraft using information from remote radar stations. It was the first computer system to feature real-time processing, multiplexing, and display devices. It was the first general computing machine, and a direct predecessor of modern computers.

EMERGENCE OF THE ANTI-NUCLEAR MOVEMENT

The atomic bombings of Hiroshima and Nagasaki and the end of World War II quickly followed the 1945 Trinity nuclear test, and the Little Boy device was detonated over the Japanese city of Hiroshima on 6 August 1945. Exploding with a yield equivalent to 12,500 tonnes of TNT, the blast and thermal wave of the bomb destroyed nearly 50,000 buildings and killed approximately 75,000 people. Subsequently, the world's nuclear weapons stockpiles grew.

Operation Crossroads was a series of nuclear weapon tests conducted by the United States at Bikini Atoll in the Pacific Ocean in the summer of 1946. Its purpose was to test the effect of nuclear weapons on naval ships. To prepare the Bikini atoll for the nuclear tests, Bikini's native residents were evicted from their homes and resettled on smaller, uninhabited islands where they were unable to sustain themselves.

National leaders debated the impact of nuclear weapons on domestic and foreign policy. Also involved in the debate about nuclear weapons policy was the scientific community, through professional associations such as the Federation of Atomic Scientists and the Pugwash Conference on Science and World Affairs.

Radioactive fallout from nuclear weapons testing was first drawn to public attention in 1954 when a Hydrogen bomb test in the Pacific contaminated the crew of the Japanese fishing boat *Lucky Dragon*. One of the fishermen died in Japan seven months later. The incident caused widespread concern around the world and "provided a decisive impetus for the emergence of the anti-nuclear weapons movement in many countries". The anti-nuclear weapons movement grew rapidly because for many people the atomic bomb "encapsulated the very worst direction in which society was moving".

Peace movements emerged in Japan and in 1954 they converged to form a unified "Japanese Council Against Atomic and Hydrogen Bombs". Japanese opposition to the Pacific nuclear weapons tests was widespread, and "an estimated 35 million signatures were collected on petitions calling for bans on nuclear weapons". The Russell–Einstein Manifesto was issued in London on July 9, 1955 by Bertrand Russell in the midst of the Cold War. It highlighted the dangers posed by nuclear weapons and called for world leaders to seek peaceful resolutions to international conflict. The signatories included eleven pre-eminent intellectuals and scientists, including Albert Einstein, who signed it just days before his death on April 18, 1955. A few days after the release, philanthropist Cyrus S. Eaton offered to sponsor a conference—called for in the manifesto—in Pugwash, Nova Scotia, Eaton's birthplace. This conference was to be the first of the Pugwash Conferences on Science and World Affairs, held in July 1957.

In the United Kingdom, the first Aldermaston March organised by the Campaign for Nuclear Disarmament took place at Easter 1958, when several thousand people marched for four days from Trafalgar Square, London, to the Atomic Weapons Research Establishmentclose to Aldermaston in Berkshire, England, to demonstrate their opposition to nuclear weapons. The Aldermaston marches continued into the late 1960s when tens of thousands of people took part in the four-day marches.

In 1959, a letter in the *Bulletin of Atomic Scientists* was the start of a successful campaign to stop the Atomic Energy Commission dumping radioactive waste in the sea 19 kilometres from Boston. On November 1, 1961, at the height of the Cold War, about 50,000 women brought together by Women Strike for Peace marched in 60 cities in the United States to demonstrate against nuclear weapons. It was the largest national women's peace protest of the 20th century.

In 1958, Linus Pauling and his wife presented the United Nations with the petition signed by more than 11,000 scientists calling for an end to nuclear-weapon testing. The "Baby Tooth Survey," headed by Dr Louise Reiss, demonstrated conclusively in 1961 that above-ground nuclear testing posed significant public health risks in the form of radioactive fallout spread primarily via milk from cows that had ingested contaminated grass. Public pressure and the research results subsequently led to a moratorium on above-ground nuclear weapons testing, followed by the Partial Test Ban Treaty, signed in 1963 by John F. Kennedy and Nikita Khrushchev.

CUBAN MISSILE CRISIS

Bombers and short-range rockets were not reliable: planes could be shot down, and earlier nuclear missiles could cover only a limited range— for example, the first Soviet rockets' range limited them to targets in Europe. However, by the 1960s, both the United States and the Soviet Union had developed intercontinental ballistic missiles, which could be launched from extremely remote areas far away from their target.

They had also developed submarine-launched ballistic missiles, which had less range but could be launched from submarines very close to the target without any radar warning. This made any national protection from nuclear missiles increasingly impractical.

The military realities made for a precarious diplomatic situation. The international politics of brinkmanship led leaders to exclaim their willingness to participate in a nuclear war rather than concede any advantage to their opponents, feeding public fears that their generation may be the last. Civil defence programs undertaken by both superpowers, exemplified by the construction of fallout shelters and urging civilians about the survivability of nuclear war, did little to ease public concerns.

The climax of brinksmanship came in early 1962, when an American U-2 spy plane photographed a series of launch sites for medium-range ballistic missiles being constructed on the island of Cuba, just off the coast of the southern United States, beginning what became known as the Cuban Missile Crisis. The U.S. administration of John F. Kennedy concluded that the Soviet Union, then led by Nikita Khrushchev, was planning to station Russian nuclear missiles on the island, which was under the control of communist Fidel Castro. On October 22, Kennedy announced the discoveries in a televised address. He announced a naval blockade around Cuba that would turn back Soviet nuclear shipments, and warned that the military was prepared "for any eventualities." The missiles had 2,400 mile (4,000 km) range, and would allow the Soviet Union to quickly destroy many major American cities on the Eastern Seaboard if a nuclear war began.

The leaders of the two superpowers stood nose to nose, seemingly poised over the beginnings of a third world war. Khrushchev's ambitions for putting the weapons on the island were motivated in part by the fact that the U.S. had stationed similar weapons in Britain, Italy, and nearby Turkey, and had previously attempted to sponsor an invasion of Cuba the year before in the failed Bay of Pigs Invasion. On October 26, Khrushchev sent a message to Kennedy offering to withdraw all missiles if Kennedy committed to a policy of no future invasions of Cuba. Khrushchev worded the threat of assured destruction eloquently:

"You and I should not now pull on the ends of the rope in which you have tied a knot of war, because the harder you and I pull, the tighter the knot will become. And a time may come when this knot is tied so tight that the person who tied it is no longer capable of untying it, and then the knot will have to be cut. What that would mean I need not explain to you, because you yourself understand perfectly what dreaded forces our two countries possess."

A day later, however, the Russians sent another message, this time demanding that the U.S. remove its missiles from Turkey before any missiles were withdrawn from Cuba. On the same day, a U-2 plane was shot down over Cuba and another almost intercepted over Russia, as Soviet merchant ships neared the quarantine zone. Kennedy responded by accepting the first deal publicly, and sending his brother Robert to the Soviet embassy to accept the second deal privately. On October 28, the Soviet ships stopped at the quarantine line and, after some hesitation, turned back towards the Soviet Union. Khrushchev announced that he had ordered the removal of all missiles in Cuba, and U.S. Secretary of State Dean Rusk was moved to comment, "We went eyeball to eyeball, and the other fellow just blinked."

The Crisis was later seen as the closest the U.S. and the USSR ever came to nuclear war and had been narrowly averted by last-minute compromise by both superpowers. Fears of communication difficulties led to the instalment of the first hotline, a direct link between the superpowers that allowed them to more easily discuss future military activities and political maneuverings. It had been made clear that missiles, bombers, submarines, and computerized firing systems made escalating any situation to Armageddon far more easy than anybody desired.

After stepping so close to the brink, both the U.S. and the USSR worked to reduce their nuclear tensions in the years immediately following. The most immediate culmination of this work was the signing of the Partial Test Ban Treaty in 1963, in which the U.S. and USSR agreed to no longer test nuclear weapons in the atmosphere, underwater, or in outer space. Testing underground continued, allowing for further weapons development, but the worldwide fallout risks were purposefully reduced, and the era of using massive nuclear tests as a form of saber-rattling ended.

In December 1979, NATO decided to deploy cruise and Pershing II missiles in Western Europe in response to Soviet deployment of intermediate range mobile missiles, and in the early 1980s, a "dangerous Soviet-US nuclear confrontation" arose. In New York on June 12, 1982, one million people gathered to protest about nuclear weapons, and to support the second UN Special Session on Disarmament. As the nuclear abolitionist movement grew, there were many protests at the Nevada Test Site. For example, on February 6, 1987, nearly 2,000 demonstrators, including six members of Congress, protested against nuclear weapons testing and more than 400 people were arrested. Four of the significant groups organizing this renewal of anti-nuclear activism were Greenpeace, The American Peace Test, The Western Shoshone, and Nevada Desert Experience.

There have been at least four major false alarms, the most recent in 1995, that resulted in the activation of nuclear attack early warning protocols. They include the accidental loading of a training tape into the American early-warning computers; a computer chip failure that appeared to show a random number of attacking missiles; a rare alignment of the Sun, the U.S. missile fields and a Russian early-warning satellite that caused it to confuse high-altitude clouds with missile launches; the launch of a Norwegian research rocketresulted in President Yeltsin activating his nuclear briefcase for the first time.

INITIAL PROLIFERATION

In the fifties and sixties, three more countries joined the "nuclear club." The United Kingdom had been an integral part of the Manhattan Project following the Quebec Agreement in 1943. The passing of the McMahon Act by the United States in 1946 unilaterally broke this partnership and prevented the passage of any further information to the United Kingdom. The British Government, under Clement Attlee, determined that a British Bomb was essential. Because of British involvement in the Manhattan Project, Britain had extensive knowledge in some areas, but not in others.

An improved version of 'Fat Man' was developed, and on 26 February 1952, Prime Minister Winston Churchill announced that the United Kingdom also had an atomic bomb and a successful test took place on 3 October 1952. At first these were free-fall bombs, intended for use by the V Force of jet bombers. A Vickers Valiant dropped the first UK nuclear weapon on 11 October 1956 at Maralinga, South Australia. Later came a missile, Blue Steel, intended for carriage by the V Force bombers, and then the Blue Streak medium-range ballistic missile (later canceled). Anglo-American cooperation on nuclear weapons was restored by the 1958 US-UK Mutual Defence Agreement. As a result of this and the Polaris Sales Agreement, the United Kingdom has bought United States designs for submarine missiles and fitted its own warheads. It retains full independent control over the use of the missiles. It no longer possesses any free-fall bombs.

France had been heavily involved in nuclear research before World War II through the work of the Joliot-Curies. This was discontinued after the war because of the instability of the Fourth Republic and lack of finances. However, in the 1950s, France launched a civil nuclear research program, which produced plutonium as a byproduct.

In 1956, France formed a secret Committee for the Military Applications of Atomic Energy and a development program for delivery vehicles. With the return of Charles de Gaulle to the French presidency in 1958, final decisions to build a bomb were made, which led to a successful test in 1960. Since then, France has developed and maintained its own nuclear deterrent independent of NATO.

In 1951, China and the Soviet Union signed an agreement whereby China supplied uranium ore in exchange for technical assistance in producing nuclear weapons. In 1953, China established a research program under the guise of civilian nuclear energy. Throughout the 1950s the Soviet Union provided large amounts of equipment. But as the relations between the two countries worsened the Soviets reduced the amount of assistance and, in 1959, refused to donate a bomb for copying purposes. Despite this, the Chinese made rapid progress and tested an atomic bomb on October 16, 1964, at Lop Nur. They tested a nuclear missile on October 25, 1966, and a hydrogen bomb on June 14, 1967.

Chinese nuclear warheads were produced from 1968 and thermonuclear warheads from 1974. It is also thought that Chinese warheads have been successfully miniaturised from 2200 kg to 700 kg through the use of designs obtained by espionage from the United States. The current number of weapons is unknown owing to strict secrecy, but it is thought that up to 2000 warheads may have been produced, though far fewer may be available for use. China is the only nuclear weapons state to have guaranteed the non-first use of nuclear weapons.

COLD WAR

After World War II, the balance of power between the Eastern and Western blocs and the fear of global destruction prevented the further military use of atomic bombs.

This fear was even a central part of Cold War strategy, referred to as the doctrine of Mutually Assured Destruction. So important was this balance to international political stability that a treaty, the Anti-Ballistic Missile Treaty (or ABM treaty), was signed by the U.S. and the USSR in 1972 to curtail the development of defenses against nuclear weapons and the ballistic missiles that carry them. This doctrine resulted in a large increase in the number of nuclear weapons, as each side sought to ensure it possessed the firepower to destroy the opposition in all possible scenarios.

Early delivery systems for nuclear devices were primarily bombers like the United States B-29 Superfortress and Convair B-36, and later the B-52 Stratofortress. Ballistic missile systems, based on Wernher von Braun's World War II designs (specifically the V-2 rocket), were developed by both United States and Soviet Union teams (in the case of the U.S., effort was directed by the German scientists and engineers although the Soviet Union also made extensive use of captured German scientists, engineers, and technical data).

These systems were used to launch satellites, such as Sputnik, and to propel the Space Race, but they were primarily developed to create Intercontinental Ballistic Missiles (ICBMs) that could deliver nuclear weapons anywhere on the globe. Development of these systems continued throughout the Cold War—though plans and treaties, beginning with the Strategic Arms Limitation Treaty (SALT I), restricted deployment of these systems until, after the fall of the Soviet Union, system development essentially halted, and many weapons were disabled and destroyed.

There have been a number of potential nuclear disasters. Following air accidents U.S. nuclear weapons have been lost near Atlantic City, New Jersey (1957); Savannah, Georgia(1958); Goldsboro, North Carolina (1961); off the coast of Okinawa (1965); in the sea near Palomares, Spain (1966); and near Thule, Greenland (1968). Most of the lost weapons were recovered, the Spanish device after three months' effort by the DSV Alvin and DSV Aluminaut.

The Soviet Union was less forthcoming about such incidents, but the environmental group Greenpeace believes that there are around forty non-U.S. nuclear devices that have been lost and not recovered, compared to eleven lost by America, mostly in submarine disasters. The U.S. has tried to recover Soviet devices, notably in the 1974 Operation Jennifer using the specialist salvage vessel *Hughes Glomar Explorer*. On January 27, 1967, more than 60 nations signed the Outer Space Treaty, banning nuclear weapons in space.

The end of the Cold War failed to end the threat of nuclear weapon use, although global fears of nuclear war reduced substantially. In a major move of symbolic de-escalation, Boris Yeltsin, on January 26, 1992, announced that Russia planned to stop targeting United States cities with nuclear weapons.

Cost

The designing, testing, producing, deploying, and defending against nuclear weapons is one of the largest expenditures for the nations which possess nuclear weapons. In the United States during the Cold War years, between "one quarter to one third of all military spending since World War II [was] devoted to nuclear weapons and their infrastructure." According to a retrospective Brookings Institute study published in 1998 by the Nuclear Weapons Cost Study Committee (formed in 1993 by the W. Alton Jones Foundation), the total expenditures for U.S. nuclear weapons from 1940 to 1998 was $5.5 trillion in 1996 Dollars. The total public debt at the end of fiscal year 1998 was $5,478,189,000,000 in 1998 Dollars or $5.3 trillion in 1996 Dollars. The *entire public debt* in 1998 was therefore equal to the cost of research, development, and deployment of U.S. nuclear weapons and nuclear weapons-related programs during the Cold War.

SECOND NUCLEAR AGE

The *second nuclear age* can be regarded as proliferation of nuclear weapons among lesser powers and for reasons other than the American-Soviet-Chinese rivalry.

India embarked relatively early on a program aimed at nuclear weapons capability, but apparently accelerated this after border war with China in 1962. India's first atomic-test explosion was in 1974 with *Smiling Buddha*, which it described as a "peaceful nuclear explosion."

After the collapse of Eastern Military High Command and the disintegration of Pakistan as a result of the 1971 Winter war, Bhutto of Pakistan launched scientific research on nuclear weapons. The Indian test caused Pakistan to spur its programme, and the ISIconducted successful espionage operations in the Netherlands, while also developing the programme indigenously. India tested fission and perhaps fusion devices in 1998, and Pakistan successfully tested fission devices that same year, raising concerns that they would use nuclear weapons on each other.

All of the former Soviet bloc countries with nuclear weapons (Belarus, Ukraine, and Kazakhstan) returned their warheads to Russia by 1996.

South Africa also had an active program to develop uranium-based nuclear weapons, but dismantled its nuclear weapon program in the 1990s. Experts do not believe it actually tested such a weapon, though it later claimed it constructed several crude devices that it eventually dismantled. In the late 1970s American spy satellites detected a "brief, intense, double flash of light near the southern tip of Africa." Known as the Vela Incident, it was speculated to have been a South African or possibly Israeli nuclear weapons test, though some feel that it may have been caused by natural events or a detector malfunction.

Israel is widely believed to possess an arsenal of up to several hundred nuclear warheads, but this has never been officially confirmed or denied (though the existence of their Dimona nuclear facility was confirmed by Mordechai Vanunu in 1986).

In January 2004, Dr A. Q. Khan of Pakistan's programme confessed to having been a key mover in "proliferation activities", seen as part of an international proliferation network of materials, knowledge, and machines from Pakistan to Libya, Iran, and North Korea.

North Korea announced in 2003 that it also had several nuclear explosives though it has not been confirmed and the validity of this has been a subject of scrutiny amongst weapons experts. The first claimed detonation of a nuclear weapon by the Democratic People's Republic of Korea was the 2006 North Korean nuclear test, conducted on October 9, 2006. On May 25, 2009, North Korea continued nuclear testing, violating United Nations Security Council Resolution 1718. A third test was conducted on 13 February 2013.

In Iran, Ayatollah Ali Khamenei issued a fatwa forbidding the production, stockpiling and use of nuclear weapons on August 9, 2005. The full text of the fatwa was released in an official statement at the meeting of the International Atomic Energy Agency (IAEA) in Vienna. Despite this, however, there is mounting concern in many nations about Iran's refusal to halt its nuclear power program, which many (including some members of the US government) fear is a cover for weapons development.

NUCLEAR WEAPONS IN THE TWENTY-FIRST CENTURY

Nuclear weapons played a pivotal role in international security during the latter half of the twentieth century. Despite rapid increases in communications, transportation, and weapons technology, there has been no large-scale strategic conflict since the Second World War. Nuclear weapons, as the most destructive instruments ever invented, had a stabilizing effect on superpower relations by making any conflict unacceptably costly. However, geopolitical change and the evolution of military technology suggest that the composition of our nuclear forces and our strategy for their employment may be different in the twenty-first century. The time is right for a fundamental rethinking of our expectations and requirements for these unique weapons.

Nuclear weapons are one component of an integrated defence strategy that includes diplomacy and conventional forces. The principal role of nuclear weapons was and continues to be that of deterring any potential adversaries from an attack on America or our vital interests. This role is expected to continue for as long as nuclear weapons hold the appellation of ýýsupreme" instruments of military force. However, this does not mean that their role in military planning will not change at all. Changes in the geopolitical environment and the inexorable advance of military technology here and abroad suggest that the position of nuclear weapons in national security policy will evolve with time. Given the unique destructive power of nuclear weapons, it is essential that this evolution be planned, to the extent possible, with due consideration of the integration of strategic nuclear forces into a consistent and comprehensive policy for national security.

Even with the dramatic changes that have occurred in the world during the past decade, nuclear warplanning today is similar in many respects to what it was during the Cold War. The Single Integrated Operational Plan (SIOP) is focused on a massive counterattack strategy that aims to eliminate the ability of an adversary to inflict further damage to American interests. Nuclear weapons provide an assured retaliatory capability to convince any adversary that aggression or coercion would be met with a response that would be certain, overwhelming, and devastating. It is often, but not universally, thought that nuclear weapons would be used only in extremis, when the nation is in the gravest danger. While there has been some discussion of "single weapon" strikes against isolated targets, such as sites of weapons of mass destruction, most of the attention in nuclear strategy has been and is directed toward large-scale engagements. This may not be true in the future.

The advance of conventional weapons technology may result in the ability of conventional weapons to perform some of the missions currently assigned to nuclear weapons. For example, take the case of a road mobile ballistic missile. If one knows the location of such a target and if one can place a conventional weapon on that target with meter-scale accuracy, then it can be destroyed without a nuclear weapon. On the other hand, if one does not know the location of the target to within many kilometers then even a nuclear weapon may not destroy it. The key parameters required for target destruction are intelligence and precision delivery, not the explosive force of the weapon. However, even if a weapon is precisely delivered to the correct target point, countermeasures as simple as steel netting, boulder fields, or decoys complicate reliance on conventional weapons with limited radii of destruction.

The role of nuclear weaponry as the ultimate deterrent to aggression and the ultimate destructive force in combat will likely lead to the retention of at least some nuclear forces for decades to come. However, the composition of our nuclear arsenal may undergo significant modification to respond to changing conditions, changing military needs, and changes in our confidence in our ability to maintain credible nuclear forces without nuclear testing or large-scale weapons production. Options for precision delivery of nuclear weapons may reduce the requirement for high yield. Lower yield weapons could be produced as modifications of existing weapons designs, or they could employ more rugged and simpler designs that might be developed and maintained with high confidence without nuclear testing and with a smaller nuclear weapons complex than we envision is required to maintain our current nuclear forces.

To the role that nuclear weapons might play in the twenty-first century, starting about 2020. A twenty-year horizon was chosen because over this time scale it is possible to make reasonable projections of technology and some assumptions about the probable threat situation. It takes about twenty years for substantially new weapons technologies to be developed and fielded into dependable military systems.

Since this is true for other countries as well as the United States, one can project the development of potential adversarial capabilities to some degree. Of course, changes in governments could occur quickly compared to this time scale, but the technology that would be employed against the United States would proceed more slowly. This chapter focuses on state-to-state defence and does not explicitly consider terrorism or the rapid evolution of entirely new state threats. It is unlikely that an emergent power would be able to develop the technology necessary to confront the United States on a time scale faster than two decades without some obvious indicators that would enable our technological or diplomatic response.

Why is this an important issue now? Current plans call for the deployment of the "next generation" of strategic forces in about 2020, including replacements for intercontinental ballistic missiles (ICBMs), the Ohio-class ballistic missile submarine, and perhaps even the venerable B52 bomber. This strategic modernization will be expensive, and it is not too soon to begin the debate over what kinds of strategic forces are needed to meet future needs.

It takes at least a decade to deploy a new technology, and if research and development are required, additional time may be needed. For such a key component of national defence, it is not sufficient to merely demonstrate that new systems work. There must be sufficient time to shake out the inevitable problems associated with new systems so as to make them dependable beyond reasonable doubt of our own government and the governments of potential adversaries. Time must also be allowed for the negotiation of treaties or other international agreements that support the new force structure and that preclude the marginalization of our forces by either a massive breakout or any other action that would reduce the effectiveness of our forces. Finally, the twentieth century repeatedly demonstrated that sweeping geopolitical changes occur on a short time scale compared to our ability to respond with new technologies or doctrines. It is imperative to consider the widest range of potential options before a crisis develops and to maintain a sufficiently robust research and development base to enable a response at that time.

The development of naval air power during the 1930s is a prime example of the need to evaluate the role of new technologies well before any anticipated engagement. The development of radar and ballistic missiles during the 1940s is an example of technologies developed during a conflict using preexisting foundations of research and technology. Some investment in thinking about future strategic forces now could reap significant dividends in the future.

Planning for future strategic defence is a highly complex affair that requires the consideration of many possible contingencies. This chapter is not intended to be a complete analysis of such a complex topic. Rather, its purpose is to stimulate thinking about changes in the international environment and technology that might be expected to influence the makeup of our strategic warfighting capability.

In order to set the stage, I first present a brief overview of the geopolitical situation that might reasonably be expected to influence defence strategy in 2020. The weapons technology might be available to the United States and other countries. Some force structures, including weapons and supporting infrastructure, that might satisfy future defence needs. The chapter concludes with a summary and suggestions for further work.

THE INTERNATIONAL SITUATION IN THE TWENTY-FIRST CENTURY

Before one can rationally future defence needs, it is necessary to know what one is defending against. The past decade has demonstrated the difficulty and danger of predicting the geopolitical future, but there are some forecasts that can be made with reasonable confidence.

Strategic Threats to U.S. National Security in the Twenty-First Century

Future national security threats to the United States might be divided into three major categories: major power conflicts, especially those involving Russia and China; regional conflicts, including potential nuclear states such as Iran, Iraq, or North Korea; and conflicts involving terrorist groups and other nonstate organizations. Only the first two major categories will be considered here, since it is arguable whether there is any role for strategic nuclear forces in dealing with terrorism and substate threats. However, strategic conflicts can be sparked by terrorist acts, as was the case in the First World War and other conflicts.

Russia — During the past 200 years European Russia has sustained a series of catastrophes including the invasion of Napoleon, the Crimean War, the First World War, the Revolution, the Second World War, and now the transition from a communist state to something else. In each case the country recovered within a generation. Even after the Second World War, when the country was essentially in ruins, it came back to launch Sputnik within twelve years. While one cannot predict what will happen in a country so volatile as Russia, it is not unreasonable to assume that it will endeavour to return to a conventional military power while continuing to rely on a significant nuclear capability. It is clear from Russia's investment in conventional military technology that it wishes to reassert its status in this area and to continue a lucrative business in the international arms trade.

China — China's international aims are in development, but their long stated intention to "reunify" Taiwan into the mainland and their territorial moves in the South China Sea indicate that they plan to play a broader role on the international stage. China has a small nuclear arsenal but one capable of inflicting unacceptable damage on American territory and interests. It is unclear at present what, if any, impact alleged Chinese nuclear espionage will have on the modernization of its nuclear arsenal. However, it is worth noting that China has several nuclear weapons systems in the advanced development stage including a new cruise missile, which presumably can carry a nuclear warhead, and new land-launched and sea-launched ballistic missiles. Road mobile nuclear capable missiles add a degree of survivability to China's limited nuclear arsenal. The desire to develop an operational ballistic missile submarine is another suggestion that China is concerned about the survivability of its nuclear forces and perhaps is a comment on its future goals of power projection outside of the immediate Pacific area.

Other Countries ýÿ The nuclear tests of India and Pakistan again demonstrate that countries will act in their own perceived national interests, sometimes in direct opposition to the wishes of the United States or to previous treaty commitments or arrangements. Continued tensions in South Asia, including Sino-Indian tensions, bear close monitoring, but they may not directly involve the United States. The Middle East will continue to be a problem area due to the misalignment of ethnic, cultural, and national borders. The prospects for Arab or Islamic unification do not appear imminent at present, but historically this unification has relied on a charismatic leader, whose advent is difficult to predict. Continued problems in the Balkans and elsewhere in the world may tax American and allied conventional capabilities, but such conflicts are not expected to assume a nuclear dimension in the foreseeable future. North Korea is presumed to have at least some nuclear capability and has demonstrated remarkable progress in ballistic missile technology, despite its perilous economic condition. Japan and South Korea look upon North Korea's nuclear ambitions with concern and could pursue their own nuclear programs if they felt uncertainty in the American nuclear umbrella. Similar concerns could apply to Taiwan in light of recent statements made by the People's Republic of China.

Nuclear engagement scenarios are not necessarily binary. Third countries may feel compelled to intervene in disputes between nuclear states or in conflicts involving weapons of mass destruction that could spill over into their territory or interests. For example, China may feel a need to act in a nuclear exchange between India and Pakistan. Similarly, Israel may feel a need to act in a major conflict of its neighbours that involved weapons of mass destruction.

FOREIGN WEAPONS TECHNOLOGY IN THE TWENTY-FIRST CENTURY

Trends evident today suggest that by 2020 many countries in the world will have access to several important technologies.

- Weapons of mass destruction: India and Pakistan graphically demonstrated the ability of midlevel technology states to construct or obtain nuclear weapons. Chemical and biological weapons are assumed to be within the reach of many countries today.
- Long-range ballistic missile technology: It is apparent that countries like North Korea, Iran, India, Pakistan, and other countries have or will soon have the capability to project force at intercontinental distances. The developing international marketplace in these technologies may make long-range missiles available to almost any country that has the money and the basic

technical capability to acquire and use them. Although such missiles may lack the precision of current U.S. weapons, they might be entirely adequate for the delivery of weapons of mass destruction.

- Space imaging: Commercial services already provide high-resolution images from space. The technical capability to provide these images in real time to customers around the world should be expected to develop. Whether international agreements will be enacted to prevent collection against sensitive sites remains to be seen. At some point, Third World countries will have the capability to launch their own intelligence satellites or will pay others to launch them, thus bypassing the need for commercial services.
- Russian weapons technology: Despite its economic troubles, Russia is committing significant resources to the research and development of advanced conventional weapons. Part of the reason for this is certainly to provide a credible defence of Russia and its vital interests. However, Russia also sees a lucrative international arms market that appreciates the low cost and operational simplicity of its weapons. One might expect more countries to have access to "last generation" but quite capable Russian military technology including missiles, air defenses, submarines, tanks, and other systems.
- Advanced communications and computer technology: The spread of communications and computer technology will serve as a force multiplier for a growing number of countries. The ability to effectively employ a small number of electronic weapons against a technologically and/or numerically superior enemy is a cost-effective force-levelling tactic.

The United States will enjoy superiority in conventional and nuclear weapons as long as adequate investments are made in research and development and in the deployment of the resulting weapons systems. However, we should expect other countries to employ many of our ideas in their own defence strategy including the simple copying of our technology and doctrines, or the use of our technology to develop weapons systems of their own. They may also attempt to exploit weaknesses in our advanced technology through means such as electromagnetic weapons, chemical and/or biological weapons, and other "asymmetric means."

U.S. DEFENCE TECHNOLOGIES IN THE TWENTY-FIRST CENTURY

Conventional Military Technology

Advances in military technology have been much discussed in the literature and are said to be leading toward a revolution in military affairs. Relevant to the present discussion, there are several advances in conventional weapons technology that deserve mention.

- Advanced precision munitions: It is already possible for cruise missiles to deliver payloads to targets hundreds of miles from their launch point with few meter accuracy. High precision for intercontinental missiles, either land- or sea-launched, is also possible. Given that ballistic missile reentry vehicles arrive on target with velocities of thousands of meters per second, it is not necessary to have explosive payloads to destroy some classes of targets.
- Advanced real-time imagery and data fusion: Data collection from satellites and from unmanned forward platforms will enable real-time remote battle management, including the direction of precision munitions to distant, even mobile, targets.
- Antiballistic missile technology will mature if the appropriate investment is made, enabling some defence against limited missile attacks. Analogous defenses could be developed against cruise missiles and aircraft, although these threats are in many ways a tougher problem due to the greater number of potential entry points and the availability of stealth technology.
- Information warfare may develop in such a fashion to enable the United States to interdict enemy command, control, and communications.

There has been much discussion of other advanced conventional technologies including unmanned aircraft, sensor technology, beam weapons, and so on. In this chapter we will focus on those technologies that could have a strategic impact and that are related to the changing role of nuclear weapons.

The importance of considering future defence against ballistic missiles, cruise missiles, and aircraft cannot be overestimated. The inexorable advance of technology will eventually make such defenses feasible and will put them within the grasp of any country that wishes to have them. Such is the case now with reasonably sophisticated air defenses.

Long range strategic planners must at least consider the return of a traditional "armour /antiarmor" competition even for strategic forces. Stealth technologies, advanced countermeasures, and new technologies will affect these trades but will not change the fundamental ability of defence technologies to influence strategic thinking.

Nuclear Weapons—Related Technology

Nuclear weapons pack incredible destructive force into a small, deliverable package. In addition to their psychological deterrent value, they are the only current means of holding at risk several classes of targets.

- Mobile targets, such as road mobile and rail mobile missiles
- Fixed moderately hard targets, such as missile silos
- Distributed targets, such as airfields or naval bases
- Hard targets, such as deeply buried command structures
- Superhard targets, such as facilities located beneath mountains

Conventional weapons might be able to address some of the missions currently assigned to nuclear weapons, but not all of them. Some targets, like missile silos and command and control structures, are sufficiently hard that no conventional weapon will have the energy to defeat them.

Other targets, such as airfields and naval bases, are sufficiently dispersed that a massive amount of conventional explosives would be required for their destruction. Even though conventional weapons could damage or destroy such targets, they could do so today only over an extended time frame and with the use of limited resources that may be required in other theatres of operation.

Future conventional weapons designs may change this, but there are still limits on the amount of damage that can be caused with a given quantity of high explosive. For these and other reasons, nuclear weapons are expected to continue to play a role in strategic doctrine, independent of their role as a psychological deterrent to aggression. The United States employs a counterforce strategy that targets military assets that could inflict damage to our national interests. We do not threaten cities or populations as in a countervalue policy, although there is an implicit threat of doing so that is a potent element of the deterrent calculus. American nuclear weapons systems are designed to hold specific classes of targets at risk, using the minimum explosive forces necessary to accomplish the mission. However, a sizable factor governing the explosive force required to defeat a target of given hardness is the precision with which weapons can be delivered. The evolution of accurate delivery systems could change engagement strategies for nuclear weapons, in some cases reducing the required yield or even eliminating the need for an explosion at all.

Once again, the use of conventional weapons presumes a level of detailed information on the location and characteristics of the target that has so far eluded military planners. A reliance on precision conventional munitions for some strategic missions presumes a major investment in intelligence collection and analysis tools, including accurate means of assessing target damage following an attack. This is particularly important for strategic targets such as mobile missiles or weapons of mass destruction that could, if they survive, inflict significant damage.

Advances in military technology may change the makeup and use of our strategic forces in several ways.

- Some important classes of targets, such as mobile missiles, might be effectively dealt with by long-range precision conventional weapons. One can envision submarine-launched ballistic missiles (SLBMs) and intercontinental ballistic missiles (ICBMs), loaded with such precision weapons, which could be directed by real-time intelligence to targets anywhere on the planet within 30 minutes. Maneuvering reentry vehicles could enable these weapons to follow and destroy moving targets.
- A 5-kiloton (kt) nuclear explosive detonated on a 30-foot-thick missile silo door will vaporize that door, destroying the missile inside. With precision delivery many hard targets might be able to be defeated with nuclear explosives having lower yield than we might currently employ. Such lower-yield weapons could use

simpler and/or more robust designs than we have in our current arsenal. Simpler, more robust designs, in turn, might allow the nuclear arsenal to be maintained with a smaller maintenance and production complex than is required to support the sophisticated, highly optimized weapons in our stockpile. As in the case of advanced conventional weapons, the use of lower-yield nuclear weapons against hardened targets could be made problematic through the use of relatively simple countermeasures. In the example of a silo door, shielding could be used to separate the blast from the door area, reducing the effectiveness of the weapon.

- Widely dispersed targets require energy (yield) for assured destruction. Several dispersed lower-yield weapons will produce the same effect as a single higher-yield weapon. Using multiple weapons on a single target assumes that fratricide effects can be dealt with in planning multiple nuclear bursts in a single target area. Such an approach also requires a larger number of weapons, a factor that would be more challenging if deep cuts in weapons numbers are negotiated. A benefit of lower-yield weapons is that the collateral damage sustained by the near-target area may be reduced, an important factor in attacks near urban areas.
- Some very hard targets require high yield to destroy them. No application of conventional explosives or even lower-yield nuclear explosives will destroy such targets, which might include hardened structures buried beneath hundreds of feet of earth or rock. For such purposes it might be desirable to retain a small number of higher-yield nuclear weapons in the arsenal as deterrents against enemy confidence in the survival of such targets.
- Superhard targets, such as those found under certain Russian mountains, may not be able to be defeated reliably by even high-yield nuclear weapons. In this case, one might use a different strategy such as "functional defeat" in which power, communications, or other vital functions are eliminated or denied without the physical destruction of the main target. Alternately, one might use negotiations to eliminate a target, bargaining away a limited set of special targets for concessions on our part.

These proposals are a departure from conventional thinking on nuclear issues. For example, our ability to negotiate away superhard targets would be very difficult at best. Others, such as the ability of precision advanced conventional munitions to hold at risk mobile and other soft-point targets, are more realistic and require only projections of current technology. In the latter case, a challenge may come from arms control concerns of other countries that see their own nuclear forces made marginal. Also, potential adversaries may use "asymmetric means" to counter our advanced technology.

An important consideration in thinking about lower-yield nuclear forces for most of our strategic nuclear requirements is that such weapons could be much simpler than our current highly optimized nuclear designs. Given sufficient throw-weight on our missiles, we could use gun-assembled or other simple, rugged designs that might be maintained with high confidence without nuclear testing. Such designs would require a significantly smaller industrial plant for their maintenance than our current forces. If based on uranium weapons designs, a much smaller plutonium infrastructure would be required. Other technologies specific to high-yield nuclear weapons could be placed in a standby mode rather than a production mode. Finally, simpler weapons might be maintained with higher confidence for longer periods by a weapons staff that has little or no direct experience with nuclear testing. However, should the country elect to follow such a path it will still be necessary to retain expertise in more sophisticated nuclear designs as a hedge against changing conditions in the future.

There is an additional, nontechnical, consideration that will influence future nuclear policy. Given current and projected scientific capabilities, it is difficult or impossible to confidently field a new, highly optimized, nuclear warhead design without nuclear testing. For this and other reasons, the United States intends to maintain its existing nuclear designs into the indefinite future. This is a fundamental change in how we maintain our arsenal. Recent concerns about espionage in the weapons program raise questions about our ability to keep weapons designs secret over many decades. Some in the intelligence community contend that a fixed target, such as our nuclear designs, will be compromised by a determined adversary given sufficient time. Information about our designs could provide important guidance to countries that wish to improve their own nuclear arsenals. Such information would also be advantageous to countries attempting to optimize some future ballistic missile defence system of their own for use against our systems. Finally, it could assist potential adversaries in deploying their strategic forces in a manner designed to make it difficult for us to assure their destruction.

Planners need to consider what we will do when, and not if, the details of our nuclear forces become known by a potential adversary. There are several paths that could be employed here, including disinformation, counterintelligence, etc. One path that has been proven to work has been to change our forces on a regular basis in response to evolving military requirements and technology options. The certification of substantially new nuclear weapons designs is difficult or impossible to do with high confidence without underground nuclear testing. However, the United States has a large archive of previously tested designs that might be fielded with reasonable confidence to meet evolving military needs. In addition, the current stockpile has significant flexibility for modification for new requirements. Such flexibility was most recently evidenced by the modification of the B61 bomb to provide earth-penetrating capability. A move toward a mixed force of long-range conventional and lower-yield nuclear weapons with improved accuracy would be another means of meeting this need. Such decisions need not be exclusive. It may be wisest to employ multiple technologies, both nuclear and nonnuclear, to create a robust future strategic posture.

STRATEGIC FORCES TO MEET FUTURE DEFENCE NEEDS

Planning strategic forces is a highly complicated affair that must include technical, geopolitical, and military considerations. A full analysis is not attempted here. The purpose of this section is to suggest some broad options that can be used as starting points for more detailed treatment. Although this section concentrates on strategic forces, it is worth noting that several countries possess potent "nonstrategic" nuclear forces that are designed for tactical engagements. Nonstrategic forces include nuclear artillery shells, atomic demolition munitions, short-range missiles, and air-delivered bombs. While such weapons are typically lower in yield than most strategic bombs and warheads, they are still nuclear explosives with destructive power vastly greater than conventional weapons. One might expect the division between "tactical" and "strategic" weapons to blur in the future, especially if significant reductions in strategic arsenals occur.

Status Quo

Nuclear weapons represent the ultimate defence of the nation, a deterrent against any and all potential adversaries. Combined with diplomacy and conventional military capabilities, nuclear weapons have helped to avoid a large-scale conflict between leading world powers for over fifty years. This is an astonishing achievement given the acceleration in communications and transportation that took place during this time. When the Cold War ended, the U.S. nuclear stockpile consisted of a set of highly optimized warheads and bombs on highly reliable missiles and aircraft. These weapons systems were designed primarily to counter the massive Soviet threat. They were and are the most advanced of their kind in the world. Current plans call for them to be retained essentially indefinitely. There are several good reasons for this.

- These weapons are safe, reliable, and meet performance requirements.
- We have nuclear test data that support our understanding of their operation.
- New warheads of comparable capability are difficult or impossible to field without nuclear testing.
- They can be modified in many ways to respond to changing military requirements, as was done when the B61 bomb was modified to give it an earth-penetrating capability.

This scenario maintains a triad of ICBMs, SLBMs, and bombers. More than one type of weapon is maintained in each leg of the triad to provide backup capability should one weapon type encounter a problem. This strategy served us well during the Cold War. Given the rapidity with which the geopolitical situation can change, there is merit in following a prudent and conservative path for future nuclear forces.

There are several potential disadvantages to maintaining the existing stockpile indefinitely. Over time such highly optimized systems may be less well suited to military requirements. Refurbishment and other changes will be made to aging warheads and bombs, changes that might be difficult to certify without nuclear testing. Also, the cost of maintaining these weapons is high for both DoD and DOE. In the case of DOE, an extensive infrastructure of laboratories and plants is required for the Stockpile Stewardship program, including a new manufacturing capability for plutonium pits. Finally, the current stockpile may not be credible against some set of potential adversaries. For example, if a national emergency were to develop that involved the imminent use of weapons of mass destruction against American interests, would an adversary consider our threat of a multiwarhead attack by the Peacekeeper ICBM or a Trident SLBM as overkill and hence not a realistic threat? Such a reliance on high-yield strategic weapons could lead to "self-deterrence," a limitation on strategic options, and consequently a lessening of the stabilizing effect of nuclear weapons.

Reduced Stockpile of Existing Designs

This scenario assumes that arms control initiatives have make it advantageous to the United States to greatly reduce our stockpile of existing nuclear weapons. It is similar to Scenario 1 with lower force levels. One can debate the merit of eliminating one arm of the strategic triad or the nonstrategic (i.e. tactical) nuclear forces under such circumstances, depending on the depth of the reductions. Cost savings associated with reduced numbers are not directly proportional to the number of weapons since a significant infrastructure is required to support any type of modern nuclear design. The cost advantage would be in the size of the required production plant and not in the diversity of technical capabilities that are required.

At very low stockpile numbers it may be useful to explicitly consider a "flexible stockpile" strategy that takes advantage of the flexibility inherent in current nuclear weapon designs. The United States could have a mixed force of weapons based upon current types suitably modified to meet evolving military needs. Special consideration might be given to maneuvering reentry vehicles that can deal effectively with enemy defenses. One could consider tailored output weapons for special applications such as those that produce an enhanced electromagnetic pulse for the disabling of electronics or those that produce enhanced radiation for the destruction of chemical or biological weapons with minimum collateral damage. (There is serious doubt in the nuclear weapons community as to whether such systems could be introduced into the stockpile without additional nuclear testing.) Careful consideration must be given to single-point failure in a reduced stockpile. For example, the use of a common missile or a common warhead for ICBMs and SLBMs would save money but would introduce a potential single-point failure in the majority of strategic forces.

In selecting weapons that would be maintained in a smaller force structure, consideration might be given to those that are the most rugged, the easiest and cheapest to maintain, and the most flexible. Highly optimized weapons may be more efficient, but efficiency can come at the cost of complexity of maintenance. Without nuclear testing, small changes caused by natural aging or required component replacements will introduce some uncertainty into the stockpile, uncertainty that must be figured into military strategy. Understanding such uncertainty is especially important if the number of weapons types is reduced, admitting the possibility of single-point failure of a large part of the force. It may be advisable to view ruggedness and ease of maintenance as principal criteria for the selection of the types and distribution of weapons within a reduced stockpile. Given the uncertainty of future military needs, the ability of a weapon to be maintained, modified, and/or certified without nuclear testing may also be an important element in the decision process.

Mixed Conventional and Nuclear Strategic Forces

Reasonable assumptions about the development of advanced conventional munitions leads to a scenario where the strategic workload is carried by a combination of nuclear and nonnuclear forces. It is possible to envision nonnuclear components to each of the arms of the strategic triad. Using conventional ICBMs and SLBMs, or their projected replacements, one could design reentry warheads to achieve high accuracy. These warheads would contain "smart" guidance systems that would receive intelligence handoffs from satellites or other sources before and/or during flight. Such systems would know that a target exists in a general area, be aware of its potential movement and signatures, and be able to home in on it. Given the kinetic energy of a reentering warhead, it might not be necessary for the system to contain high explosives. Hitting the target might be sufficient to destroy it. Similar warheads could be developed for cruise missiles that could be launched from bombers, submarines, or surface warships. In the case of cruise missiles, the lower velocity of delivery would require a high-explosive warhead.

A nonnuclear long-range weapon would be especially useful against limited numbers of time-urgent weapons of mass destruction targets such as biological weapons warheads that were in preparation for use against U.S. forces. Long-range nonnuclear weapons would enable such targets to be destroyed without causing the United States to be the first to employ nuclear weapons in a conflict. The use of nonnuclear strategic weapons against Russia, China, or other nuclear states would require care, since the appearance of such a weapon on long-range sensors might be indistinguishable from a nuclear attack by the United States.

A word of caution is needed on the use of precision munitions for high-value strategic targeting: The Kosovo conflict demonstrated very clearly that just the ability to place a weapon on the designated aim point is not enough to ensure mission success. Inaccurate target coordinates provided to pilots sometimes resulted in weapons being delivered very precisely to the wrong spot. Effective utilization of precision munitions demand that a premium be placed on the collection and the analysis of target information. This includes postattack damage assessments that determine the need for follow-on attacks and the ability of the adversary to use its weapons for offense or defence.

The nuclear component in this scenario could take one of several forms. First, one could employ a small number of existing weapons designs to retain a traditional counterforce deterrent strategy. Second, one could modify existing designs to reduce their yield, relying on precision delivery to help achieve military objectives.

n this case one could use existing reentry warheads or develop new ones with the precision guidance necessary to destroy moderately-hard-point targets with low yield. Third, one could design and deploy a new set of nuclear weapons that do not require nuclear testing to be certified. Such weapons might be, but do not need to be, based on simple gun-assembled uranium designs that do not require a plutonium infrastructure and that do not require the same sophistication in nuclear weapons science and engineering as our current stockpile. However, nothing comes for free, and one must recognize that such simple weapons have important, perhaps fatal, tactical limitations that would preclude their use in some engagement scenarios. Also, such simple devices would be based on a very limited nuclear test database and would require extensive and expensive flight testing to assure that they could be delivered with the required precision. Fourth, one could consider a combination of new or modified low-yield warheads and some existing higher-yield designs to be retained against the possibility of unexpected developments in adversaries' defenses or of the need to hold very hard targets at risk. In this case one would need to retain much of the infrastructure of the current stockpile to ensure the continued performance of these highly optimized weapons. Savings could be achieved in the size of the plant complex required to remanufacture components and complete weapons.

Prospects for Wholly Nonnuclear Strategic Forces

It is almost impossible to conceive of technological and political developments that would enable the United States to meet its defence needs in 2020 without nuclear weapons. There are several reasons for this. First, nuclear weapons continue to play a vital role in deterring other countries from launching significant military strikes against America, our allies, or our vital interests. The real threat of not just military defeat but national annihilation is a potent deterrent now and should be expected to remain so for at least the next few decades. Second, it does not appear possible with current or projected technology to assure ourselves that there are no—and never will be any nuclear weapons in the hands of potential adversaries. Given the unique destructive power of nuclear weapons, an asymmetry of this kind should be unacceptable to American military planners. Third, the development of antiballistic missile defence is encouraging, but the assumption that a leak-proof shield can be fielded by 2020 is debatable. Fourth, some targets will not be able to be held at risk by any type of conventional weapon because of their extreme hardness. Fifth, the ability of an adversary to deliver a nuclear weapon by aircraft, cruise missile, naval vessel, or by clandestine insertion into this country are additional concerns beyond the long-range ballistic missile threat. Lacking the ability to deter such threats and to respond in kind would open up the country to blackmail.

It is critical in any discussion of strategic forces to consider the overall stability provided by technology and policy. Such calculations have become considerably more complex in the multipolar world that is expected to persist at least over the time scale addressed in this chapter.

The future is unpredictable, but we can count on it to be dynamic. Strategic thinking must be flexible and must consider the evolution of several possible futures, each of which has branches that are contingent on the geopolitical situation and technological capabilities here and abroad. Countries will respond to technology and policy developments in the United States and elsewhere. We must be careful that any changes to our strategic position make the overall situation better and not worse.

Russia has already promised that it will use "asymmetric means" to counter advanced U.S. technology. Official Chinese publications indicate that China will likely follow a similar strategy. The capabilities of their own research and development complex should not be underestimated. While Russia cannot yet match the United States in the most sophisticated technology, it has shown a remarkable ability to achieve military objectives through cleverness and sometimes through brute force. Finally, the development of advanced conventional strategic weapons could push the Russians to an even greater reliance on high-yield nuclear weapons. Rather than an evolution toward some fixed strategy, strategic thinking should be done along a flexible time line that recognizes changes in the world and in military technology. What may work at one time may not work at another time when the situation has substantially changed.

One "asymmetric" counter to advanced technology is cyber-warfare, including non-explosive weapons that could disable or render ineffective advanced conventional or even nuclear munitions. Precision kill requires sophisticated electronics, and electronics can be affected by various means such as radio frequency or microwave weapons. Russia's electromagnetic weapons program is perhaps the most advanced in the world, and at least some of this technology has been shared with China. Given the uncertainty in future advanced weapons technology, the United States may wish to retain some higher-yield nuclear weapons as hedges against the development of potent point or area defenses. The development of antisatellite weapons would create a similar complication to the United States if we were to rely on advanced conventional weapons that require precise targeting information to be effective.

Arms control initiatives will play an important role in the planning of future strategic forces. Proposed deep reductions in nuclear stockpiles may be a motivation for using conventional weapons as part of the strategic weapons mix. Such a decision will strongly depend on whether warheads or launchers are the counted quantity. If nuclear warheads and not delivery vehicles are the counted quantity, then existing or new launchers can be equipped with advanced conventional warheads. If missiles and aircraft are the counted quantity, we will need to be careful about treaties that allow only one warhead, nuclear or conventional, on a missile. Maintaining an effective deterrent requires a minimum number of nuclear weapons, and the dilution of our forces with conventional weapons could drive us from a counterforce strategy (military targets) to a countervalue strategy (cities) with attendant ethical and perhaps legal problems.

Arms control agreements can assist in strategic planning by restricting certain classes of weapons or targets. If, in some scenario, our weapons are particularly susceptible to nuclear interceptors, then we may wish to negotiate the elimination of nuclear interceptors in return for some other concession. If we are unable to destroy one or more targets by any weapon in our arsenal, we may want to attempt to negotiate away the target in return for assurances that we will not construct similarly hard targets in the United States. Such negotiations are by nature complex because they involve giving up different commodities on each side. However, the advantages of reduced reliance on nuclear weapons, with their large radii of destruction, might be an incentive. Also, the development of new conventional strategic weapons, the use of which might be incorporated into nonnuclear war planning and that will not necessarily lead to national destruction, should be considered with care.

One of the features of nuclear weapons is that they are so destructive that their use is reserved for only the most extreme cases. Making strategic weapons more "usable" could start the

United States on a path of escalation that could exacerbate and not reduce the potential for war.

Conversely, lowering the threshold for using nuclear weapons in response to a strategic situation could raise the level of care with which countries interact. This points to the need for a detailed stability analysis to be performed as a prelude to any arms control negotiations. Such an analysis must explicitly include the balance of nuclear forces, the state and projected future of ballistic missile defenses, and the ability of advanced conventional weapons to perform missions formerly assigned to nuclear weapons. The weapons research and development programs of potential adversaries will provide input to this analysis by providing pointers to future defence capabilities. And, of course, any analysis of future strategic weapons needs must necessarily consider the possible geopolitical situation that will be present at the time of their deployment. Finally, the distinction between tactical and strategic nuclear weapons will fade for small stockpiles. Both types of weapons must be included in negotiations for overall stability to be maintained.

Another important consideration in planning future strategic forces is cost. Nuclear weapons systems are sometimes considered expensive to maintain due to their complexity, their unique characteristics, and the lack of private industry support of some components of their infrastructure. In fact, nuclear weapons are cheaper to develop and to maintain than very large conventional force structures. This was the reason why NATO chose to rely on nuclear weapons as a principal part of its defence against the massive Soviet conventional threat in Europe. Nuclear weapons are considered expensive today because they are primarily strategic in nature and we are in the midst of a ÿÿstrategic pause" that has lessened the perceived need for strategic weapons.

For the DoD, costs include operations, maintenance, and the development of next generation capabilities that will replace current systems upon their obsolescence. For the DOE, costs include the operation of the weapons laboratories and production plants and the material costs associated with weapons refurbishment. To first order, the cost of maintaining the DOE nuclear weapons complex is independent of the number of weapons in the stockpile. Some capability in uranium, plutonium, and other special materials is required. Scientific capabilities must be maintained, especially in those classified areas unique to nuclear weapons, to enable informed decisions to be made on weapons aging, component replacements, and future modifications. Tritium has some variable cost, as it must be produced to support some fixed number of weapons. Plutonium pit production can be maintained at a small rate at Los Alamos, but any stockpile above about one thousand weapons will require the construction of a new large production plant to replace the Rocky Flats facility, which ceased production in 1989. Should the country go to a precision low-yield nuclear force that is based on uranium rather than plutonium, the cost of the large pit-production facility could be avoided, and the remaining high-yield weapons that did employ plutonium pits could be supported by a modified Los Alamos plutonium facility.

The end of the Cold War, the evolution of new regional threats to international security, and the stated desire of many countries to reduce or eliminate their nuclear arsenals suggest that the time is right for a fundamental rethinking of the role of nuclear weapons in national security. Nuclear weapons, as the most destructive instruments yet invented, must be considered as part of a coordinated national security program that employs diplomacy, arms control initiatives, and conventional forces to optimize stability and peace in the world.

Technology assessments suggest that advanced conventional weapons delivered by ballistic or cruise missiles could defeat many targets that are presently targeted by nuclear weapons. Precision delivery of nuclear weapons would enable some classes of hard targets to be defeated with much lower yields than are currently employed. Some number of current nuclear weapons designs might be retained in order to address very hard targets or for traditional deterrent roles. Simple, rugged nuclear weapons designs that might be maintained at relatively low cost and without the need for nuclear testing might be a part of such a strategy.

Nuclear weapons cannot be uninvented. Nor can we assume that their role in strategic deterrence will never change. Prudent thought given to the role of nuclear weapons in the twenty-first century will reap handsome dividends for the national security of the United States and for the stability of the whole world.

4

Biological Warfare

Biological warfare (BW)—also known as germ warfare—is the use of biological toxinsor infectious agents such as bacteria, viruses, smallpox, and fungi with intent to kill or incapacitate humans, animals or plants as an act of war. Biological weapons (often termed "bio-weapons", "biological threat agents", or "bio-agents") are living organisms or replicating entities (viruses, which are not universally considered "alive") that reproduce or replicate within their host victims. Entomological (insect) warfare is also considered a type of biological weapon.

This type of warfare is distinct from nuclear warfare and chemical warfare, which together make up NBC, the military acronym for nuclear, biological, and chemical (warfare or weapons), all of which are considered "weapons of mass destruction" (WMDs). None of these fall under the term conventional weaponswhich are primarily effective due to their destructive potential.

Biological weapons may be employed in various ways to gain a strategic or tactical advantage over the enemy, either by threats or by actual deployments. Like some of the chemical weapons, biological weapons may also be useful as area denial weapons. These agents may be lethal or non-lethal, and may be targeted against a single individual, a group of people, or even an entire population. They may be developed, acquired, stockpiled or deployed by nation states or by non-national groups. In the latter case, or if a nation-state uses it clandestinely, it may also be considered bioterrorism.

There is an overlap between BW and chemical warfare, as the use of toxins produced by living organisms is considered under the provisions of both the Biological Weapons Convention and the Chemical Weapons Convention. Toxins and psychochemical weapons are often referred to as *midspectrum agents*. Unlike bioweapons, these midspectrum agents do not reproduce in their host and are typically characterized by shorter incubation periods.

OVERVIEW

Offensive biological warfare, including mass production, stockpiling and use of biological weapons, was outlawed by the 1972 Biological Weapons Convention (BWC). The rationale behind this treaty, which has been ratified or acceded to by 165 countries as of 2011, is to prevent a biological attack which could conceivably result in large numbers of civilian casualties and cause severe disruption toeconomic and societal infrastructure. Many countries, including signatories of the BWC, currently pursue research into the defence or protection against BW, which is not prohibited by the BWC.

A nation or group that can pose a credible threat of mass casualty has the ability to alter the terms on which other nations or groups interact with it. Biological weapons allow for the potential to create a level of destruction and loss of life far in excess of nuclear, chemical or conventional weapons, relative to their mass and cost of development and storage. Therefore, biological agents may be useful as strategic deterrents in addition to their utility as offensive weapons on the battlefield.

As a tactical weapon for military use, a significant problem with a BW attack is that it would take days to be effective, and therefore might not immediately stop an opposing force. Some biological agents (smallpox, pneumonic plague) have the capability of person-to-person transmission via aerosolized respiratory droplets. This feature can be undesirable, as the agent(s) may be transmitted by this mechanism to unintended populations, including neutral or even friendly forces. While containment of BW is less of a concern for certain criminal or terrorist organizations, it remains a significant concern for the military and civilian populations of virtually all nations.

HISTORY

Rudimentary forms of biological warfare have been practiced since antiquity. During the 6th century BC, the Assyrians poisoned enemy wells with a fungus that would render the enemy delirious. In 1346, the bodies of Mongol warriors of the Golden Horde who had died of plague were thrown over the walls of the besieged Crimean city of Kaffa. It has been speculated that this operation may have been responsible for the advent of the Black Deathin Europe. The British Army used smallpox in New South Wales in 1789, having used it as a weapon earlier when they gave contaminated blankets to the Lenape duringPontiac's War (1763–66) and sent infected civilians with smallpox to the Continental Armyduring the American Revolutionary War.

The advent of the germ theory and advances in bacteriology brought a new level of sophistication to the theoretical use of bio-agents in war. Biological sabotage—in the form of anthrax and glanders—was undertaken on behalf of the Imperial German government during World War I (1914–1918), with indifferent results. The Geneva Protocol of 1925 prohibited the use of chemical weapons and biological weapons.

Interwar period and WWII

With the onset of WWII, the Ministry of Supply in the United Kingdom established a BW programme at Porton Down, headed by the microbiologist Paul Fildes. The research was championed by Winston Churchill and soontularemia, anthrax, brucellosis, and botulism toxins had been effectively weaponized. In particular, Gruinard Island in Scotland, during a series of extensive tests was contaminated with anthrax for the next 48 years. Although the UK never offensively used the biological weapons it developed on its own, its program was the first to successfully weaponize a variety of deadly pathogens and bring them into industrial production.

When the USA entered the war, mounting British pressure for the creation of a similar research program for an Allied pooling of resources, led to the creation of a large industrial complex at Fort Detrick, Maryland in 1942 under the direction of George W. Merck. The biological and chemical weapons developed during that period were tested at the Dugway Proving Grounds in Utah. Soon there were facilities for the mass production of anthrax spores, brucellosis, and botulism toxins, although the war was over before these weapons could be of much operational use.

The most notorious program of the period was run by the secret Imperial Japanese Army Unit 731during the war, based at Pingfan in Manchuria and commanded by Lieutenant General Shirô Ishii. This unit did research on BW, conducted often fatal human experiments on prisoners, and produced biological weapons for combat use. Although the Japanese effort lacked the technological sophistication of the American or British programs, it far outstripped them in its widespread application and indiscriminate brutality. Biological weapons were used against both Chinese soldiers and civilians in several military campaigns. In 1940, the Imperial Japanese Army Air Force bombed Ningbo with ceramic bombs full of fleas carrying the bubonic plague. Many of these operations were ineffective due to inefficient delivery systems, although up to 400,000 people may have died.

Postwar Period

Considerable research into BW was undertaken throughout the Cold War by the US, UK and USSR, and probably other major nations as well, although it is generally believed that such weapons were never used. In Britain, the 1950s saw the weaponization of plague, brucellosis, tularemia and laterequine encephalomyelitis and vaccinia viruses, but the programme was unilaterally cancelled in 1956. The United States Army Biological Warfare Laboratories weaponized anthrax, tularemia, brucellosis, Q-fever and others.

In 1969, the UK and the Warsaw Pact, separately, introduced proposals to the UN to ban biological weapons, and US President Richard Nixon terminated production of biological weapons, allowing only scientific research for defensive measures. The Biological and Toxin Weapons Convention was signed by the US, UK, USSR and other nations, as a ban on "development, production and stockpiling of microbes or their poisonous products except in amounts necessary for protective and peaceful research" in 1972. However, the Soviet Union continued research and production of massive offensive biological weapons in a program called Biopreparat, despite having signed the convention. By 2011, 165 countries had signed the treaty and none are proven—though nine are still suspected—to possess offensive BW programs.

MODERN BW OPERATIONS

Offensive

It has been argued that rational people would never use biological weapons offensively. The argument is that biological weapons cannot be controlled: the weapon could backfire and harm the army on the offensive, perhaps having even worse effects than on the target. An agent like smallpox or other airborne viruses would almost certainly spread worldwide and ultimately infect the user's home country. However, this argument does not necessarily apply to bacteria. For example, anthrax can easily be controlled and even created in a garden shed. Also, using microbial methods, bacteria can be suitably modified to be effective in only a narrow environmental range, the range of the target that distinctly differs from the army on the offensive. Thus only the target might be affected adversely. The weapon may be further used to bog down an advancing army making them more vulnerable to counterattack by the defending force.

Anti-personnel

Ideal characteristics of a biological agent to be used as a weapon against humans are highinfectivity, high virulence, non-availability of vaccines, and availability of an effective and efficient delivery system. Stability of the weaponized agent (ability of the agent to retain its infectivity and virulence after a prolonged period of storage) may also be desirable, particularly for military applications, and the ease of creating one is often considered. Control of the spread of the agent may be another desired characteristic. The primary difficulty is not the production of the biological agent, as many biological agents used in weapons can often be manufactured relatively quickly, cheaply and easily. Rather, it is the weaponization, storage and delivery in an effective vehicle to a vulnerable target that pose significant problems.

For example, Bacillus anthracis is considered an effective agent for several reasons. First, it forms hardy spores, perfect for dispersal aerosols. Second, this organism is not considered transmissible from person to person, and thus rarely if ever causes secondary infections. A pulmonary anthrax infection starts with ordinary influenza-like symptoms and progresses to a lethal hemorrhagic mediastinitis within 3–7 days, with a fatality rate that is 90% or higher in untreated patients. Finally, friendly personnel can be protected with suitable antibiotics.

A large-scale attack using anthrax would require the creation of aerosol particles of 1.5 to 5 μm: larger particles would not reach the lower respiratory tract, while smaller particles would be exhaled back out into the atmosphere. At this size, conductive powders tend to aggregate because of electrostatic charges, hindering dispersion. So the material must be treated to insulate and neutralize the charges. The weaponized agent must be resistant to degradation by rain and ultraviolet radiation from sunlight, while retaining the ability to efficiently infect the human lung. There are other technological difficulties as well, chiefly relating to storage of the weaponized agent.

Agents considered for weaponization, or known to be weaponized, include bacteria such as *Bacillus anthracis*, *Brucella spp.*, *Burkholderia mallei*, *Burkholderia pseudomallei*, *Chlamydophila psittaci*, *Coxiella burnetii*, *Francisella tularensis*, some of the Rickettsiaceae (especially *Rickettsia prowazekii* and *Rickettsia rickettsii*), *Shigella spp.*, *Vibrio cholerae*, and *Yersinia pestis*. Many viral agents have been studied and/or weaponized, including some of the Bunyaviridae (especially Rift Valley fever virus), Ebolavirus, many of the Flaviviridae (especially Japanese encephalitis virus), Machupo virus, Marburg virus, Variola virus, and Yellow fever virus. Fungal agents that have been studied include *Coccidioides spp.*.

Toxins that can be used as weapons include ricin, staphylococcal enterotoxin B, botulinum toxin, saxitoxin, and many mycotoxins. These toxins and the organisms that produce them are sometimes referred to as select agents. In the United States, their possession, use, and transfer are regulated by the Centres for Disease Control and Prevention's Select Agent Program.

The former US biological warfare program categorized its weaponized anti-personnel bio-agents as either Lethal Agents (*Bacillus anthracis*, *Francisella tularensis*, Botulinum toxin) or Incapacitating Agents (*Brucella suis*, *Coxiella burnetii*, Venezuelan equine encephalitis virus, Staphylococcal enterotoxin B).

ANTI-AGRICULTURE

Anti-crop/anti-vegetation/anti-fisheries

The United States developed an anti-crop capability during the Cold War that used plant diseases (bioherbicides, or mycoherbicides) for destroying enemy agriculture. Biological weapons also target fisheries as well as water-based vegetation.

It was believed that destruction of enemy agriculture on a strategic scale could thwart Sino-Soviet aggression in a general war. Diseases such as wheat blast and rice blast were weaponized in aerial spray tanks and cluster bombs for delivery to enemy watersheds in agricultural regions to initiate epiphytotics (epidemics among plants). When the United States renounced its offensive biological warfare program in 1969 and 1970, the vast majority of its biological arsenal was composed of these plant diseases. Enterotoxins and Mycotoxins were not affected by Nixon's order.

Though herbicides are chemicals, they are often grouped with biological warfare and chemical warfare because they may work in a similar manner as biotoxins or bioregulators. The Army Biological Laboratory tested each agent and the Army's Technical Escort Unitwas responsible for transport of all chemical, biological, radiological (nuclear) materials. Scorched earth tactics or destroying livestock and farmland were carried out in the Vietnam war (cf. Agent Orange) and Eelam War in Sri Lanka.

Biological warfare can also specifically target plants to destroy crops or defoliate vegetation. The United States and Britain discovered plant growth regulators (i.e., herbicides) during the Second World War, and initiated a herbicidal warfare program that was eventually used in Malaya and Vietnam in counterinsurgency operations.

Anti-livestock

In 1980s Soviet Ministry of Agriculture had successfully developed variants of foot-and-mouth disease, and rinderpest against cows, African swine fever for pigs, and psittacosis to kill chicken. These agents were prepared to spray them down from tanks attached to airplanes over hundreds of miles. The secret program was code-named "Ecology".

Attacking animals is another area of biological warfare intended to eliminate animal resources for transportation and food. In the First World War, German agents were arrested attempting to inoculate draft animals with anthrax, and they were believed to be responsible for outbreaks of glanders in horses and mules. The British tainted small feed cakes with anthrax in the Second World War as a potential means of attacking German cattle for food denial, but never employed the weapon. In the 1950s, the United States had a field trial withhog cholera. During the Mau Mau Uprising in 1952, the poisonous latex of the African milk bush was used to kill cattle. Unconnected with inter-human wars, humans have deliberately introduced the rabbit disease Myxomatosis, originating in South America, to Australia and Europe, with the intention of reducing the rabbit population – which had devastating but temporary results, with wild rabbit populations reduced to a fraction of their former size but survivors developing immunity and increasing again.

Entomological Warfare

Entomological warfare (EW) is a type of biological warfare that uses insects to attack the enemy. The concept has existed for centuries and research and development have continued into the modern era. EW has been used in battle by Japan and several other nations have developed and been accused of using an entomological warfare program. EW may employ insects in a direct attack or as vectors to deliver a biological agent, such as plague. Essentially, EW exists in three varieties. One type of EW involves infecting insects with apathogen and then dispersing the insects over target areas. The insects then act as a vector, infecting any person or animal they might bite. Another type of EW is a direct insect attack against crops; the insect may not be infected with any pathogen but instead represents a threat to agriculture. The final method uses uninfected insects, such as bees, wasps, etc., to directly attack the enemy.

Defensive

Research and Development into Medical Counter-measures

In 2010 at The Meeting of the States Parties to the Convention on the Prohibition of the Development, Production and Stockpiling of Bacteriological (Biological) and Toxin Weapons and Their Destruction in Geneva the sanitary epidemiological reconnaissance was suggested as well-tested means for enhancing the monitoring of infections and parasitic agents, for practical implementation of theInternational Health Regulations (2005). The aim was to prevent and minimize the consequences of natural outbreaks of dangerous infectious diseases as well as the threat of alleged use of biological weapons against BTWC States Parties.

Role of Public Health and Disease Surveillance

It is important to note that all classical and modern biological weapons organisms are animal diseases, the only exception being smallpox. Thus, in any use of biological weapons, it is highly likely that animals will become ill either simultaneously with, or perhaps earlier than humans.

Indeed, in the largest biological weapons accident known– the anthrax outbreak in Sverdlovsk (now Yekaterinburg) in the Soviet Union in 1979, sheep became ill with anthrax as far as 200 kilometers from the release point of the organism from a military facility in the southeastern portion of the city.

Thus, a robust surveillance system involving human clinicians and veterinarians may identify a bioweapons attack early in the course of an epidemic, permitting the prophylaxis of disease in the vast majority of people (and/or animals) exposed but not yet ill.

For example in the case of anthrax, it is likely that by 24–36 hours after an attack, some small percentage of individuals (those with compromised immune system or who had received a large dose of the organism due to proximity to the release point) will become ill with classical symptoms and signs (including a virtually unique chest X-ray finding, often recognized by public health officials if they receive timely reports). By making these data available to local public health officials in real time, most models of anthrax epidemics indicate that more than 80% of an exposed population can receive antibiotic treatment before becoming symptomatic, and thus avoid the moderately high mortality of the disease.

Common Epidemiologic clues that may signal biological attack :

- Large numbers of ill persons with a similar disease or syndrome.
- Unusual illness in a population.
- Higher morbidity and mortality in association with a common disease or syndrome or failure of such patients to respond to usual therapy.
- Single case of disease caused by an uncommon agent (i.e. small pox, viral hemorrhagic fever, pulmonary anthrax).
- Several unusual or unexplained diseases coexisting in the same patient without any other explanation.

- Disease with an unusual geographic or seasonal distribution (i.e. influenza in the summer).
- Illness that is unusual (or atypical) for a given population or age group such as an outbreak of measles-like rash in adults.
- Unusual disease presentation such as pulmonary instead of cutaneous anthrax.
- Similar genetic type among agents isolated from distinct sources at different times or locations.
- Unusual, atypical, genetically engineered, or antiquated strain of an agent or antibiotic resistance pattern.
- Stable endemic disease with an unexplained increase in incidence (i.e. plague).
- Simultaneous clusters of similar illness in non-contiguous areas, domestic or foreign.
- Atypical disease transmission through aerosols, food, or water, which suggests deliberate sabotage.
- Ill persons who seek treatment at about the same time.
- No illness in persons who are not exposed to common ventilation systems when illness is seen in persons in close proximity who have a common ventilation system.
- Unusual pattern of death or illness among animals, that precedes or accompanies illness or death in humans.

Identification of Bioweapons

The goal of biodefense is to integrate the sustained efforts of the national and homeland security, medical, public health, intelligence, diplomatic, and law enforcement communities.

Health care providers and public health officers are among the first lines of defence. In some countries private, local, and provincial (state) capabilities are being augmented by and coordinated with federal assets, to provide layered defenses against biological weapons attacks. During the first Gulf War the United Nations activated a biological and chemical response team, Task Force Scorpio, to respond to any potential use of weapons of mass destruction on civilians.

The traditional approach toward protecting agriculture, food, and water: focusing on the natural or unintentional introduction of a disease is being strengthened by focused efforts to address current and anticipated future biological weapons threats that may be deliberate, multiple, and repetitive. The growing threat of biowarfare agents and bioterrorism has led to the development of specific field tools that perform on-the-spot analysis and identification of encountered suspect materials. One such technology, being developed by researchers from the Lawrence Livermore National Laboratory (LLNL), employs a "sandwich immunoassay", in which fluorescent dye-labeled antibodies aimed at specific pathogens are attached to silver and gold nanowires. In the Netherlands, the company TNO has designed Bioaerosol Single Particle Recognition eQuipment (BiosparQ). This system would be implemented into the national response plan for bioweapons attacks in the Netherlands. Researchers at Ben Gurion University in Israel are developing a different device called the BioPen, essentially a "Lab-in-a-Pen", which can detect known biological agents in under 20 minutes using an adaptation of the ELISA, a similar widely employed immunological technique, that in this case incorporates fiber optics.

Synthetic BW

Theoretically, novel approaches in biotechnology, such as synthetic biology could be used in the future to design novel types of biological warfare agents. Special attention has to be laid on future experiments (of concern) that:

1. Would demonstrate how to render a vaccine ineffective;
2. Would confer resistance to therapeutically useful antibiotics or antiviral agents;
3. Would enhance the virulence of a pathogen or render a nonpathogen virulent;
4. Would increase transmissibility of a pathogen;
5. Would alter the host range of a pathogen;
6. Would enable the evasion of diagnostic/detection tools;
7. Would enable the weaponization of a biological agent or toxin

Most of the biosecurity concerns in synthetic biology, however, focused on the role of DNA synthesis and the risk of producing genetic material of lethal viruses (e.g. 1918 Spanish flu, polio) in the lab.

HISTORY OF BIOLOGICAL WARFARE

Various types of biological warfare (BW) have been practiced repeatedly throughout history. This has included the use of biological agents (microbes and plants) as well as the biotoxins, including venoms, derived from them.

Before the 20th century, the use of biological agents took three major forms:

- Deliberate contamination of food and water with poisonous or contagious material
- Use of microbes, biological toxins, animals, or plants (living or dead) in a weapon system
- Use of biologically inoculated fabrics and persons

In the 20th century, sophisticated bacteriological and virological techniques allowed the production of significant stockpiles of weaponized bio-agents:

- Bacterial agents: Anthrax, Brucella, Tularemia, etc.
- Viral agents: Smallpox, Viral hemorrhagic fevers, etc.
- Toxins: Botulinum, Ricin, etc.

ANTIQUITY

The earliest documented incident of the intention to use biological weapons is recorded in Hittite texts of 1500–1200 BC, in which victims of tularemia were driven into enemy lands, causing an epidemic. Although the Assyrians knew of ergot, a parasitic fungus of rye which produces ergotism when ingested, there is no evidence that they poisoned enemy wells with the fungus, as has been claimed. According to Homer's epic poems about the legendary Trojan War, the *Iliad* and the *Odyssey*, spears and arrows were tipped with poison. During the First Sacred War in Greece, in about 590 BC, Athens and the Amphictionic League poisoned the water supply of the besieged town of Kirrha (near Delphi) with the toxic plant hellebore. During the 4th century BC Scythian archers tipped their arrow tips with snake venom, human blood, and animal feces to cause wounds to become infected.

In a naval battle against King Eumenes of Pergamon in 184 BC, Hannibal of Carthage had clay pots filled with venomous snakes and instructed his sailors to throw them onto the decks of enemy ships. The Roman commander Manius Aquillius poisoned the wells of besieged enemy cities in about 130 BC. In about AD 198, the Parthian city of Hatra (near Mosul, Iraq) repulsed the Roman army led bySeptimius Severus by hurling clay pots filled with live scorpions at them.

There are numerous other instances of the use of plant toxins, venoms, and other poisonous substances to create biological weapons in antiquity.

MIDDLE AGES

The Mongol Empire established commercial and political connections between the Eastern and Western areas of the world, through the most mobile army ever seen. The armies, composed of the most rapidly moving travelers who had ever moved between the steppes of East Asia (where bubonic plague was and remains endemic among small rodents), managed to keep the chain of infection without a break until they reached, and infected, peoples and rodents who had never encountered it. The ensuing Black Death may have killed roughly a third of the population of Europe in the next decades, changing the course of Asian and European history.

During the Middle Ages, victims of the bubonic plague were used for biological attacks, often by flinging fomites such as infected corpses and excrement over castle walls using catapults. In 1346, during the siege of Kafa (now Feodossia, Ukraine) the attacking Tartar Forces which were subjugated by the Mongol empire under Genghis Khan, used the bodies of Mongol warriors of the Golden Horde who had died of plague, as weapons. An outbreak of plague followed and the defending forces retreated, followed by the conquest of the city by the Mongols. It has been speculated that this operation may have been responsible for the advent of the Black Death in Europe. At the time, the attackers thought that the stench was enough to kill them, though it was the disease that was deadly.

At the siege of Thun-l'Évêque in 1340, during the Hundred Years' War, the attackers catapulted decomposing animals into the besieged area.

In 1422, during the siege of Karlstein Castle in Bohemia, Hussite attackers used catapults to throw dead (but not plague-infected) bodies and 2000 carriage-loads of dung over the walls.

The last known incident of using plague corpses for biological warfare occurred in 1710, when Russian forces attacked the Swedes by flinging plague-infected corpses over the city walls of Reval (Tallinn). However, during the 1785 siege of La Calle, Tunisian forces flung diseased clothing into the city.

English Longbowmen usually did not draw their arrows from a quiver, rather, they stuck their arrows into the ground in front of them. This allowed them to nock the arrows faster and the dirt and soil was likely to stick the arrowheads, thus making the wounds much more likely to become infected.

18TH CENTURY

North America

The Native American population was devastated after contact with the Old World due to the introduction of several fatal infectious diseases, notably smallpox. These diseases can be traced to Eurasia where people had long lived with them and developed some immunological ability to survive their presence. Without similarly long ancestral exposure, indigenous Americans were immunologically naive and therefore extremely vulnerable.

There are two documented instances of biological warfare by the British against North American Indians during Pontiac's Rebellion(1763–66). In the first, during a parley at Fort Pitt on June 24, 1763, Captain Simeon Ecuyer gave representatives of the besieging Delawares two blankets and a handkerchief that had been exposed to smallpox, hoping to spread the disease to the Natives in order to end the siege. William Trent, the militia commander, left records that clearly indicated that the purpose of giving the blankets was "to Convey the Smallpox to the Indians."

British commander Lord Jeffrey Amherst and Swiss-British officer Colonel Henry Bouquet discussed the topic separately in the course of the same conflict; there exists correspondence referencing the idea of giving smallpox-infected blankets to enemy Indians. It cited four letters from June 29, July 13, 16 and 26th, 1763. Excerpts: Amherst wrote on July 16, 1763, *"P.S. You will Do well to try to Inocculate the Indians by means of Blankets, as well as to try Every other method that can serve to Extirpate this Execrable Race. I should be very glad your Scheme for Hunting them Down by Dogs could take Effect,..."* Bouquet replied on July 26, 1763, *"I received yesterday your Excellency's letters of 16th with their Inclosures. The signal for Indian Messengers, and all your directions will be observed."* Smallpox is highly infectious and does not require contaminated blankets to spread uncontrollably, and — together withmeasles, influenza, chicken pox, and so on — had been doing so since the arrival of Europeans and their animals. Trade and combat also provided ample opportunity for transmission of the disease.

New South Wales

Australian aborigines (Kooris) have always maintained that

the British deliberately spread smallpox in 1789, but this possibility has only been raised by historians from the 1980s when Dr Noel Butlin suggested; "there are some possibilities that... disease could have been used deliberately as an exterminating agent".

In 1997, David Day claimed there "remains considerable circumstantial evidence to suggest that officers other than Phillip, or perhaps convicts or soldiers ... deliberately spread smallpox among aborigines" and in 2000 Dr John Lambert argued that "strong circumstantial evidence suggests the smallpox epidemic which ravaged Aborigines in 1789, may have resulted from deliberate infection".

Judy Campbell argued in 2002 that it is highly improbable that the First Fleet was the source of the epidemic as "smallpox had not occurred in any members of the First Fleet"; the only possible source of infection from the Fleet being exposure to variolous matter imported for the purposes of inoculation against smallpox. Campbell argued that, while there has been considerable speculation about a hypothetical exposure to the First Fleet's variolous matter, there was no evidence that Aboriginal people were ever actually exposed to it. She pointed to regular contact between fishing fleets from the Indonesia archipelago, where smallpox was endemic, and Aboriginal people in Australia's North as a more likely source for the introduction of smallpox. She notes that while these fishermen are generally referred to as 'Macassans', referring to the port of Macassar on the island of Sulawesi from which most of the fishermen originated, "some travelled from islands as distant as New Guinea". She noted that there is little disagreement that the smallpox epidemic of the 1860s was contracted from Macassan fishermen and spread through the Aboriginal population via their traditional social, kinship and trading networks. She argued that the 1789-90 epidemic followed the same pattern.

These claims are controversial as it is argued that any smallpox virus brought to New South Wales probably would have been sterilised by heat and humidity encountered during the voyage of the First Fleet from England and incapable of biological warfare. However, in 2007, Christopher Warren demonstrated that the British smallpox may have been still viable. Since then some scholars have argued that the British committed biological warfare in 1789 near their new convict settlement at Port Jackson. In 2013 Warren reviewed the issue and argued that smallpox did not spread across Australia before 1824 and showed that there was no smallpox at Macassar that could have caused the outbreak at Sydney. Warren, however, did not address the issue of persons who joined the Macassan fleet from other islands and from parts of Sulawesi other than the port of Macassar. Warren concluded that the British were "the most likely candidates to have released smallpox" near Sydney Cove in 1789. Warren proposed that the British had no choice as they were confronted with dire circumstances when, among other factors, they ran out of ammunition for their muskets. Warren also uses native oral tradition and the archaeology of native graves to analyse the cause and effect of the spread of smallpox in 1789.

Prior to the publication of Warren's article (2013), John Carmody argued that the epidemic was an outbreak of chickenpox which took a drastic toll on an Aboriginal population without immunological resistance. With regard to smallpox, Dr Carmody said: "There is absolutely no evidence to support any of the theories and some of them are fanciful and far-fetched.." Warren covered the chickenpox theory at endnote 3 of *Smallpox at Sydney Cove - Who, When, Why?*.

20TH CENTURY

By the turn of the 20th century, advances in microbiology had made thinking about "germ warfare" part of the *zeitgeist*. Jack London, in his short story "'Yah! Yah! Yah!'" (1909), described a punitive European expedition to a South Pacific island deliberately exposing thePolynesian population to measles, of which many of them died. While much of the material for London's *South Sea Tales* is derived from his personal experience in the region, it is not known whether this particular incident is historical. London went on to write a science fiction tale, "The Unparalleled Invasion" (1910), in which the Western nations wipe out all of China with a biological attack.

First World War

During the First World War (1914–1918), the Empire of Germany made some early attempts at biological warfare. Using diplomatic pouches and couriers, the German General Staff supplied small teams of saboteurs in the Russian Duchy of Finland, and in the then-neutral countries of Romania, the

United States, and Argentina. In Finland, saboteurs mounted on reindeer placed ampoules of anthrax in stables of Russian horses in 1916. Anthrax was also supplied to the German military attaché in Bucharest, as was glanders, which was employed against livestock destined for Allied service. German intelligence officer and US citizen Dr. Anton Casimir Dilger established a secret lab in the basement of his sister's home in Chevy Chase, Maryland, that produced glanders which was used to infect livestock in ports and inland collection points including, at least, Newport News, Norfolk, Baltimore, and New York, and probably St. Louis and Covington, Kentucky. In Argentina, German agents also employed glanders in the port of Buenos Aires and also tried to ruin wheat harvests with a destructive fungus.

The Geneva Protocol of 1925 prohibited the use of chemical weapons and biological weapons, but said nothing about experimentation, production, storage, or transfer; later treaties did cover these aspects. Twentieth-century advances in microbiology enabled the first pure-culture biological agents to be developed by World War II.

Interwar Period and WWII

In the interwar period, little research was done in BW in both the UK and the US at first. In Britain the preoccupation was mainly in withstanding the anticipated conventional bombing attacks that would be unleashed in the event of war with Germany. As tensions increased, Sir Frederick Banting began lobbying the British government to establish a research program into the research and development of biological weapons to effectively deter the Germans from launching a biological attack. Banting proposed a number of innovative schemes for the dissemination of pathogens, including aerial-spray attacks and germs distributed through the mail system.

With the onset of hostilities, the Ministry of Supply finally established a biological weapons programme at Porton Down, headed by the microbiologist Paul Fildes. The research was championed by Winston Churchill and soon tularemia, anthrax, brucellosis, and botulismtoxins had been effectively weaponized. In particular, Gruinard Island in Scotland, during a series of extensive tests was contaminated with anthrax for the next 48 years. Although the UK never offensively used the biological weapons it developed, its program was the first to successfully weaponize a variety of deadly pathogens and bring them into industrial production.

When the USA entered the war, mounting British pressure for the creation of a similar research program for an Allied pooling of resources, led to the creation of a large industrial complex at Fort Detrick, Maryland in 1942 under the direction of George W. Merck.The biological and chemical weapons developed during that period were tested at the Dugway Proving Grounds in Utah. Soon there were facilities for the mass production of anthrax spores, brucellosis, and botulism toxins, although the war was over before these weapons could be of much operational use.

However, the most notorious program of the period was run by the secret Imperial Japanese Army Unit 731 during the war, based at Pingfan in Manchuria and commanded by Lieutenant General Shirô Ishii. This unit did research on BW, conducted often fatal human experiments on prisoners, and produced biological weapons for combat use. Although the Japanese effort lacked the technological sophistication of the American or British programs, it far outstripped them in its widespread application and indiscriminate brutality. Biological weapons were used against both Chinese soldiers and civilians in several military campaigns. Three veterans of Unit 731 testified in a 1989 interview to the Asahi Shimbun, that they contaminated the Horustein river with typhoid near the Soviet troops during the Battle of Khalkhin Gol. In 1940, the Imperial Japanese Army Air Force bombed Ningbo with ceramic bombs full of fleas carrying the bubonic plague. A film showing this operation was seen by the imperial princes Tsuneyoshi Takeda and Takahito Mikasa during a screening made by mastermind Shiro Ishii. During the Khabarovsk War Crime Trials the accused, such as Major General Kiyashi Kawashima, testified that as early as 1941 some 40 members of Unit 731 air-dropped plague-contaminated fleas on Changde. These operations caused epidemic plague outbreaks.

Many of these operations were ineffective due to inefficient delivery systems, using disease-bearing insects rather than dispersing the agent as an bioaerosol cloud. Nevertheless, some modern Chinese historians estimate that 400,000 Chinese died as a direct result of Japanese field testing and operational use of biological weapons.

Ban Shigeo, a technician at the Japanese Army's 9th Technical Research Institute, left an account of the activities at the Institute which was published in "The Truth About the Army Nororito Institute". Ban included an account of his trip to Nanking in 1941 to participate in the testing of poisons on Chinese prisoners. His testimony tied the Noborito Institute to the infamous Unit 731, which participated in biomedical research.

When the war ended, the US Army quietly enlisted certain members of Noborito in its efforts against the communist camp in the early years of the Cold War. The head of Unit 731, Shiro Ishii, was granted immunity from war crimes prosecution in exchange for providing information to the United States on the Unit's activities. Allegations were made that a "chemical section" of a US clandestine unit hidden within Yokosuka naval base was operational during the Korean War, and then worked on unspecified projects inside the United States from 1955 to 1959, before returning to Japan to enter the private sector.

Some of the Unit 731 personnel were imprisoned by the Soviets, and may have been a potential source of information on Japanese weaponization.

Postwar Period

Considerable research into BW was undertaken throughout the Cold War era by the US, UK and USSR, and probably other major nations as well, although it is generally believed that such weapons were never used. In Britain, the 1950s saw the weaponization of plague, brucellosis, tularemia and later equine encephalomyelitis and vaccinia viruses. Trial tests at sea were carried out including Operation Cauldron off Stornoway in 1952. The programme was cancelled in 1956, when the British government unilaterally renounced the use of biological and chemical weapons.

The United States initiated its weaponization efforts with disease vectors in 1953, focused on Plague-fleas, EEE-mosquitoes, and yellow fever - mosquitoes (OJ-AP). However, US medical scientists in occupied Japan undertook extensive research on insect vectors, with the assistance of former Unit 731 staff, as early as 1946.

The United States Army Chemical Corps then initiated a crash program to weaponize anthrax (N) in the E61 1/2-lb hour-glass bomblet. Though the program was successful in meeting its development goals, the lack of validation on the infectivity of anthrax stalled standardization. The United States Air Force was also unsatisfied with the operational qualities of the M114/US bursting bomblet and labeled it an interim item until the Chemical Corps could deliver a superior weapon.

Around 1950 the Chemical Corps also initiated a program to weaponize tularemia (UL). Shortly after the E61/N failed to make standardization, tularemia was standardized in the 3.4" M143 bursting spherical bomblet. This was intended for delivery by the MGM-29 Sergeant missile warhead and could produce 50% infection over a 7-square-mile (18 km^2) area. Although tularemia is treatable by antibiotics, treatment does not shorten the course of the disease. US conscientious objectors were used as consenting test subjects for tularemia in a program known as Operation Whitecoat. There were also many unpublicized tests carried out in public places with bio-agent simulants during the Cold War.

In addition to the use of bursting bomblets for creating biological aerosols, the Chemical Corps started investigating aerosol-generating bomblets in the 1950s. The E99 was the first workable design, but was too complex to be manufactured. By the late 1950s the 4.5" E120 spraying spherical bomblet was developed; a B-47 bomber with a SUU-24/A dispenser could infect 50% or more of the population of a 16-square-mile (41 km^2) area with tularemia with the E120. The E120 was later superseded by dry-type agents.

Dry-type biologicals resemble talcum powder, and can be disseminated as aerosols using gas expulsion devices instead of a burster or complex sprayer. The Chemical Corps developed Flettner rotor bomblets and later triangular bomblets for wider coverage due to improved glide angles over Magnus-lift spherical bomblets. Weapons of this type were in advanced development by the time the program ended. From January 1962, Rocky Mountain Arsenal "grew, purified and biodemilitarized" plant pathogen Wheat Stem Rust (Agent TX), Puccinia graminis, var. tritici, for the Air Force biological anti-crop program. TX-treated grain was grown at the Arsenal from 1962-1968 in Sections 23-26. Unprocessed TX was also transported from Beale AFB for purification, storage, and disposal. Trichothecenes Mycotoxin is a toxin that can be extracted from Wheat Stem Rust and Rice Blast and can kill or incapacitate depending on the concentration used. The "red mold disease" of wheat and barley in Japan is prevalent in the region that faces the Pacific Ocean. Toxic trichothecenes, including nivalenol, deoxynivalenol, and monoace tylnivalenol (fusarenon- X) from Fusarium nivale, can be isolated from moldy grains. In the suburbs of Tokyo, an illness similar to "red mold disease" was described in an outbreak of a food borne disease, as a result of the consumption of Fusarium- infected rice. Ingestion of moldy grains that are contaminated with trichothecenes has been associated with mycotoxicosis.

Although there is no evidence that biological weapons were used by the United States, China and North Korea accused the US of large-scale field testing of BW against them during the Korean War (1950–1953). At the time of the Korean War the United States had only weaponized one agent, brucellosis ("Agent US"), which is caused by *Brucella suis*. The original weaponized form used the M114 bursting bomblet in M33 cluster bombs. While the specific form of the biological bomb was classified until some years after the Korean War, in the various exhibits of biological weapons that Korea alleged were dropped on their country nothing resembled an M114 bomblet. There were ceramic containers that had some similarity to Japanese weapons used against the Chinese in World War II, developed by Unit 731.

Cuba also accused the United States of spreading human and animal disease on their island nation.

During the 1948 Israel War of Independence, International Red Cross reports raised suspicion that the Israeli Haganah militia had released Salmonella typhi bacteria into the water supply for the city of Acre, causing an outbreak of typhoid among the inhabitants. Egyptian troops later claimed to have captured disguised Haganah soldiers near wells in Gaza, whom they executed for allegedly attempting another attack. Israel denies these allegations.

Biological and Toxin Weapons Convention

In mid-1969, the UK and the Warsaw Pact, separately, introduced proposals to the UN to ban biological weapons, which would lead to the signing of the Biological and Toxin Weapons Convention in 1972. United States President Richard Nixon signed an executive orderon November 1969, which stopped production of biological weapons in the United States and allowed only scientific research of lethal biological agents and defensive measures such as immunization and biosafety. The biological munition stockpiles were destroyed, and approximately 2,200 researchers became redundant.

Special munitions for the United States Special Forces and the CIA and the Big Five Weapons for the military were destroyed in accordance with Nixon's executive order to end the offensive program. The CIA maintained its collection of biologicals well into 1975 when it became the subject of the senate Church Committee.

The Biological and Toxin Weapons Convention was signed by the US, UK, USSR and other nations, as a ban on "development, production and stockpiling of microbes or their poisonous products except in amounts necessary for protective and peaceful research" in 1972. The convention bound its signatories to a far more stringent set of regulations than had been envisioned by the 1925 Geneva Protocols. By 1996, 137 countries had signed the treaty; however it is believed that since the signing of the Convention the number of countries capable of producing such weapons has increased.

The Soviet Union continued research and production of offensive biological weapons in a program called Biopreparat, despite having signed the convention. The United States had no solid proof of this program until Dr. Vladimir Pasechnik defected in 1989, and Dr. Kanatjan Alibekov, the first deputy director of Biopreparat defected in 1992. Pathogens developed by the organization would be used in open-air trials. It is known that Vozrozhdeniye Island, located in the Aral Sea, was used as a testing site. In 1971, such testing led to the accidental aerosol release of smallpox over the Aral Sea and a subsequent smallpox epidemic.

During the closing stages of the Rhodesian Bush War, the Rhodesian government resorted to biological warfare. Watercourses at several sites close to the Mozambique border were deliberately contaminated with cholera and the toxin Sodium Coumadin, an anti-coagulant commonly used as the active ingredient in rat poison. Food stocks in the area were contaminated with anthrax spores. These biological attacks had little impact on the fighting capability of ZANLA, but caused considerable distress to the local population. Over 10,000 people contracted anthrax in the period 1978 to 1980, of whom

200 died. The facts about this episode became known during the hearings of the South African Truth and Reconciliation Commission during the late 1990s.

After the 1991 Persian Gulf War, Iraq admitted to the United Nations inspection team to having produced 19,000 liters of concentrated botulinum toxin, of which approximately 10,000 L were loaded into military weapons; the 19,000 liters have never been fully accounted for. This is approximately three times the amount needed to kill the entire current human population by inhalation, although in practice it would be impossible to distribute it so efficiently, and, unless it is protected from oxygen, it deteriorates in storage.

According to the U.S. Congress Office of Technology Assessment 8 countries were generally reported as having undeclared offensive biological warfare programs in 1995: China, Iran, Iraq, Israel, Libya, North Korea, Syria and Taiwan. Five countries had admitted to having had offensive weapon or development programs in the past: United States, Russia, France, the United Kingdom, and Canada.Offensive BW programs in Iraq were dismantled by Coalition Forces and the UN after the first Gulf War (1990–91), although an Iraqi military BW program was covertly maintained in defiance of international agreements until it was apparently abandoned during 1995 and 1996.

21ST CENTURY

On September 18, 2001 and for a few days thereafter, several letters were received by members of the U.S. Congress and American media outlets which contained intentionally prepared anthrax spores; the attack sickened at least 22 people, of whom five died. The identity of the bioterrorist remained unknown until 2008, when an official suspect, who had committed suicide, was named.

Suspicions of an ongoing Iraqi BW program were not substantiated in the wake of the March 2003 invasion of that country. Later that year, however, Muammar Gaddafi was persuaded to terminate Libya's BW program. In 2008, according to a U.S. Congressional Research Service report, China, Cuba, Egypt, Iran, Israel, North Korea, Russia, Syria and Taiwan are considered, with varying degrees of certainty, to have some BW capability. By 2011, 165 countries had officially joined the BWC and pledged to disavow biological weapons.

ENTOMOLOGICAL WARFARE

Entomological warfare (EW) is a type of biological warfare that uses insects to attack the enemy. The concept has existed for centuries and research and development have continued into the modern era. EW has been used in battle by Japan and several other nations have developed and been accused of using an entomological warfare program.

DESCRIPTION

Entomological warfare (EW) is a specific type of biological warfare (BW) that uses insects in a direct attack or as vectors to deliver abiological agent, such as plague or cholera. Essentially, EW exists in three varieties. One type of EW involves infecting insects with apathogen and then dispersing the insects over target areas. The insects then act as a vector, infecting any person or animal they might bite. Another type of EW is a direct insect attack against crops; the insect may not be infected with any pathogen but instead represents a threat to agriculture. The final method of entomological warfare is to use uninfected insects, such as bees, to directly attack the enemy.

Early History

Entomological warfare is not a new concept; historians and writers have studied EW in connection to multiple historic events. A 14th century plague epidemic in Asia Minor that eventually became known as the Black Death is one such event that has drawn attention from historians as a possible early incident of entomological warfare. That plague's spread over Europe may have been the result of a biological attack on the Crimean city of Kaffa.

According to Jeffrey Lockwood, author of *Six-Legged Soldiers* (a book about EW), the earliest incident of entomological warfare was probably the use of bees by early humans. The bees or their nests were thrown into caves to force the enemy out and into the open.Lockwood theorizes that the Ark of the Covenant may have been deadly when opened because it contained deadly fleas.

During the American Civil War the Confederacy accused the Union of purposely introducing the harlequin bug in the South. These accusations were never proven, and modern research has shown it more likely that the insect arrived by other means. The world did not experience large-scale entomological warfare until World War II; Japanese attacks in China were the only verified instance of BW or EW during the war. During, and following, the war other nations began their own EW programs.

WORLD WAR II

Canada

Among the Allied Powers, Canada led the pioneering effort in vector-borne warfare. After Japan became intent on developing the plague flea as a weapon, Canada and the United States followed suit.

Cooperating closely with the United States, Dr. G.B. Reed, chief ofKingston's Queen's University's Defence Research Laboratory, focused his research efforts on mosquito vectors, biting flies, and plague infected fleas during World War II. Much of this research was shared with or conducted in concert with the United States.

Canada's entire bio-weapons program was ahead of the British and the Americans during the war. The Canadians tended to work in areas their allies ignored; entomological warfare was one of these areas. As the U.S. and British programs evolved, the Canadians worked closely with both nations. The Canadian BW work would continue well after the war,including entomological research.

France

France is known to have pursued entomological warfare programs during World War II. Like Germany, the nation suggested that theColorado potato beetle, aimed at the enemy's food sources, would be an asset during the war. As early as 1939 biological warfare experts in France suggested that the beetle be used against German crops.

Germany

Germany is known to have pursued entomological warfare programs during World War II. The nation pursued the mass-production, and dispersion, of the Colorado potato beetle (*Lepinotarsa decemlineata*), aimed at the enemy's food sources.

The beetle was first found in Germany in 1914, as an invasive species from North America. There are no records that indicate the beetle was ever employed as a weapon by Germany, or any other nation during the war. Regardless, the Germans had developed plans to drop the beetles on English crops.

Germany carried out testing of its Colorado potato beetle weaponization program south of Frankfurt, where they released 54,000 of the beetles. In 1944, an infestation of Colorado potato beetles was reported in Germany. The source of the infestation is unknown, speculation has offered three alternative theories as to the origin of the infestation.

One option is Allied action, an entomological attack, another is that it was the result of the German testing, and still another more likely explanation is that it was merely a natural occurrence.

Japan

Japan used entomological warfare on a large scale during World War II in China. Unit 731, Japan's infamous biological warfare unit led by Lt. General Shirô Ishii, used plague-infected fleas and flies covered with cholera to infect the population in China. The Japanese military dispersed the insects by spraying them from low-flying airplanes and dropping bombs filled with a mixture of insects and disease. Localized and deadly epidemics resulted and nearly 500,000 Chinese died of disease. An "international symposium" of historians declared in 2002 that Japanese entomological warfare in China was responsible for the deaths of 440,000.

The late Ban Shigeo, a technician at the Japanese Army's 9th Technical Research Institute, left a rare and valuable account of the activities of Noborito Research Institute which was published in Rikugun Noborito Kenkyujo no shinjitsu - The Truth About the Army Nororito Institute available only in the Japanese language. Of the Japanese Army's ten numbered institutes, only the 9th Army Technical Research Institute came under the covert operations section of the Army General Staff's Second Bureau (Intelligence). On the sensitive issue of Japanese biological warfare, Ban did not shrink from including an account of his trip to Nanking in 1941 to participate in the testing of poisons on Chinese prisoners.

One of his book's contributions is to further tie Noborito to the Japanese Army's infamous Unit 731, which participated in biomedical research. When the war ended, the US Army quietly enlisted certain members of Noborito in its efforts against the communist camp in the early years of the Cold War.

The author notes near the end of the book that Ban led the "chemical section" of a US clandestine unit hidden within Yokosuka naval base during the Korean War, and then worked on unspecified projects inside the United States from 1955 to 1959, before returning to Japan to enter the private sector. Shirô Ishii of Unit 731, having not been charged as a war criminal, also continued his work to consult with American authorities, especially during the height of the Cold War, and died in 1959 of throat cancer.

In 1989, a British study of Unit 731 strongly supported the theory of United States-Japanese BW culpability in Korea. Chinese experts doggedly insist today that BW weapons created in an American-Japanese collaboration were used in the Korean war.

Further evidence that Japanese continued to assist the United States Chemical, Biological warfare, as well as Radiological effects and Entomological warfare program efforts continued after the Korean war into Vietnam includes a visit to Rocky Mountain Arsenal in September of 1962 by Japanese delegation I-63.

Among many other activities, from January 1962-October 1969, Rocky Mountain Arsenal "grew, purified and biodemilitarized" plant pathogen wheat stem rust [Puccinia graminis, var. tritici] (Agent TX) for the Air Force biological anti-crop program.

TX-treated grain was grown at the Arsenal from 1962-1968 in Sections 23-26. Unprocessed TX was also transported from Beale AFB for purification, storage, and disposal.

Trichothecenes Mycotoxin is a toxin that can be extracted from Wheat Stem Rust and Rice Blast and can kill or incapacitate depending on the concentration used.

The "red mold disease" of wheat and barley in Japan is prevalent in the region that faces the Pacific Ocean. Toxic trichothecenes, including nivalenol, deoxynivalenol, and monoace tylnivalenol (fusarenon- X) from Fusarium nivale, can be isolated from moldy grains. In the suburbs of Tokyo, an illness similar to "red mold disease" was described in an outbreak of a food borne disease, as a result of the consumption of Fusarium- infected rice.

Ingestion of moldy grains that are contaminated with trichothecenes has been associated with mycotoxicosis.

United Kingdom

A British scientist, J.B.S. Haldane, suggested that Britain and Germany were both vulnerable to entomological attack via the Colorado potato beetle. In 1942 the United States shipped 15,000 Colorado potato beetles to Britain for study as a weapon.

COLD WAR

Soviet Union

The Soviet Union researched, developed and tested an entomological warfare program as a major part of an anti-crop and anti-animal BW program. The Soviets developed techniques for using insects to transmit animal pathogens, such as foot and mouth disease — which they used ticks to transmit. The nation also used avian ticks to transmit *Chlamydophila psittaci* to chickens. In addition, the Soviet Union claimed to have developed an automated mass insect breeding facility, capable of outputting millions of parasitic insects per day.

United States

The United States seriously researched the potential of entomological warfare during theCold War. The United States military developed plans for an entomological warfare facility, designed to produce 100 million yellow fever-infected mosquitoes per month. A U.S. Armyreport titled "Entomological Warfare Target Analysis" listed vulnerable sites within the Soviet Union that the U.S. could attack using entomological vectors. The military also tested the mosquito biting capacity by dropping uninfected mosquitoes over U.S. cities.

North Korean and Chinese officials leveled accusations that during the Korean War the United States engaged in biological warfare, including EW, in North Korea.

The claim is dated to the period of the war, and has been thoroughly denied by the U.S. In 1998, Stephen Endicott and Edward Hagermann claimed that the accusations were true in their book, *The United States and Biological Warfare: Secrets from the Early Cold War and Korea* The book received mixed reviews, some called it "bad history" and "appalling",while other praised the case the authors made. Other historians have revived the claim in recent decades as well. The same year Endicotts' book was published Kathryn Weathersby and Milton Leitenberg of the Cold War International History Project at the Woodrow

Wilson Center in Washington released a cache of Soviet and Chinese documents which revealed the North Korean claim was an elaborate disinformation campaign. During the 1950s the United States conducted a series of field tests using entomological weapons. Operation Big Itch, in 1954, was designed to test munitions loaded with uninfected fleas (*Xenopsylla cheopis*). Big Itch went awry when some of the fleas escaped into the plane and bit all three members of the air crew. In May 1955 over 300,000 yellow fevermosquitoes (*Aedes aegypti*) were dropped over parts of the U.S. state of Georgia to determine if the air-dropped mosquitoes could survive to take meals from humans.

The mosquito tests were known as Operation Big Buzz. Operation Magic Sword was a 1965 U.S. military operation designed to test the effectiveness of the sea-borne release of insect vectors for biological agents. The U.S. engaged in at least two other EW testing programs,Operation Drop Kick and Operation May Day.

A 1981 Army report outlined these tests as well as multiple cost-associated issues that occurred with EW. The report is partially declassified — some information is blacked out, including everything concerning "Drop Kick" — and included "cost per death" calculations. The cost per death, according to the report, for a vector-borne biological agent achieving a 50% mortality rate in an attack on a city was $0.29 in 1976 dollars. Such an attack was estimated to result in 625,000 deaths.

The United States has also applied entomological warfare research and tactics in non-combat situations. In 1990 the U.S. funded a $6.5 million program designed to research, breed and drop caterpillars. The caterpillars were to be dropped in Peru on coca fields as part of the American War on Drugs. As recently as 2002 U.S. entomological anti-drug efforts at Fort Detrick were focused on finding an insect vector for a virus that affects the opium poppy.

BIOTERRORISM

Clemson University's Regulatory and Public Service Program listed "diseases vectored by insects" among bioterrorism scenarios considered "most likely". Because invasive species are already a problem worldwide one University of Nebraska entomologist considered it likely that the source of any sudden appearance of a new agricultural pest would be difficult, if not impossible, to determine. Lockwood considers insects a more effective means of transmitting biological agents for acts of bioterrorism than the actual agents. Insect vectors are easily gathered and their eggs easily transportable without detection. Isolating and delivering biological agents, on the other hand, is extremely challenging and hazardous.

In one of the few suspected acts of entomological bioterrorism an eco-terror group known as The Breeders claimed to have releasedMediterranean fruit flies (medflies) amidst an ongoing California infestation. Lockwood asserts that there is some evidence the group played a role in the event. The pest attacks a variety of crops and the state of California responded with a large-scale pesticides praying program.

At least one source asserted that there is no doubt that an outside hand played a role in the dense 1989 infestation. The group stated in a letter to then Los Angeles Mayor Tom Bradley that their goals were twofold. They sought to cause the medfly infestation to grow out of control which, in turn, would render the ongoing Malathion spraying program financially infeasible.

5

Chemical Weapons Convention

A chemical weapon (CW) is a device that uses chemicals formulated to inflict death or harm on human beings.

They are classified as weapons of mass destruction though they are separate from biological weapons (diseases), nuclear weapons, and radiological weapons (which use radioactive decay of elements).

Chemical weapons can be widely dispersed in gas, liquid and solid forms and may easily afflict others than the intended targets. Nerve gas, tear gas and pepper spray are three modern examples.

Lethal, unitary, chemical agents and munitions are extremely volatile and they constitute a class of hazardous chemical weapons that are now being stockpiled by many nations. (Unitary agents are effective on their own and require no mixing with other agents.)

The most dangerous of these are nerve agents GA, GB, and VX, and vesicant (blister) agents which are formulations of sulfur mustard such as H, HT, and HD. All are liquids at normal room temperature, but become gaseous when released. Widely used during theFirst World War, the effects of so-called mustard gas, phosgene gas and others caused lung searing, blindness, death and maiming.

Pepper spray is of common use today. It is potentially lethal. There are no recent records of pepper spray being used in war, despite the fact that it inflicts less injuries and has less side-effects if compared with impact and explosive weapons. Under the Chemical Weapons Convention (1993), there is a legally-binding, world-wide ban on the production, stockpiling, and use of chemical weapons and their precursors. Notwithstanding, large stockpiles thereof continue to exist, usually justified as only a precaution against putative use by an aggressor.

INTERNATIONAL LAW ON CHEMICAL WEAPONS

Before the Second World War

International law has prohibited the use of chemical weapons since 1899, under theHague Convention: Article 23 of the Regulations Respecting the Laws and Customs of War on Land adopted by the First Hague Conference "especially" prohibited employing "poison and poisoned arms"; also, a separate Declaration stated that in any war between signatory powers, the parties would abstain from using projectiles "the object of which is the diffusion of asphyxiating or deleterious gases."

The Washington Naval Treaty, signed February 6, 1922, also known as the Five-Power Treaty, aimed at banning CW—but did not succeed because the French rejected it. The subsequent failure to include CW has contributed to the resultant increase in stockpiles.

The Geneva Protocol, officially known as the *Protocol for the Prohibition of the Use in War of Asphyxiating, Poisonous or other Gases, and of Bacteriological Methods of Warfare*, is an International treaty prohibiting the use of chemical and biological weapons. It was signed at Geneva June 17, 1925 and entered into force on February 8, 1928. 133 nations are listed as state parties to the treaty—Ukraine acceded August 7, 2003 and is the most recent member nation. This treaty states that chemical and biological weapons are "justly condemned by the general opinion of the civilised world." While the treaty prohibits the use of chemical and biological weapons, it does not address the production, storage, or transfer of these weapons. Later treaties did address those omissions and have been enacted.

Modern agreements

The Chemical Weapons Convention (CWC) is the most recent arms control agreement with the force of International law. Its full name is the *Convention on the Prohibition of the Development, Production, Stockpiling and Use of Chemical*

Weapons and on their Destruction. That agreement outlaws the production, stockpiling and use of chemical weapons. It is administered by the Organisation for the Prohibition of Chemical Weapons (OPCW), which is an independent organization based in The Hague.

The OPCW administers the terms of the CWC to 188 signatories which represents 98% of the global population. Of the stockpiles, 44,131 of the 71,194 tonnes declared (61.99%) have been destroyed. The OPCW has conducted 4,167 inspections at 195 chemical weapon-related and 1,103 industrial sites. These inspections have affected the sovereign territory of 81 States Parties since April 1997. Worldwide, 4,913 industrial facilities are subject to inspection provisions.

Use

Chemical warfare (*CW*) involves using the toxic properties of chemical substances as weapons. This type of warfare is distinct from Nuclear warfare and Biological warfare, which together make up NBC, the military initialism for Nuclear, Biological, and Chemical (warfare or weapons). None of these falls under the term conventional weapons which are primarily effective owing to their destructive potential.

Chemical warfare does not depend uponexplosive force to achieve an objective. Rather it depends upon the unique properties of the chemical agent weaponized. A lethal agent is designed to injure or incapacitate the enemy, or deny unhindered use of a particular area of terrain. Defoliants are used to quickly kill vegetation and deny its use for cover and concealment. An agent can also be used against agriculture and livestock to promote hunger and starvation. Chemical payloads can be delivered by remote controlled container release, aircraft, or rocket. Protection against chemical weapons includes proper equipment, training, and decontamination measures.

COUNTRIES WITH STOCKPILES

CWC States with Declared Stockpiles

Of 190 signatory nations to the CWC, state parties listed below have also declared stockpiles, agreed to monitored disposal, and verification, and in some cases, used CW in conflict. Both military targets and civilian populations have been affected—the affected populations were not always damaged collaterally, but rather at times, the target of the attack. As of 2012, only four nations are confirmed as having chemical weapons: the United States, Russia, North Korea and Syria.

India

India declared its stock of chemical weapons in June 1997. India's declaration came after the entry into force of the CWC that created the OPCW. India declared a stockpile of 1044 tonnes of sulphur mustard in its possession. On January 14, 1993 India became an original signatory to the CWC. By 2005, from among the six nations that had declared possession of chemical weapons, India was the only one to meet its deadline for chemical weapons destruction and for inspection of its facilities by the OPCW. By the end of 2006, India had destroyed more than 75 percent of its chemical weapons/material stockpile and was granted extension for destroying (the remaining stocks by April 2009) and was expected to achieve 100 percent destruction within that time frame. On May 14, 2009, India informed the United Nations that it has destroyed its stockpile of chemical weapons.

Iraq

The Organisation for the Prohibition of Chemical Weapons which oversees destruction measures has announced "The government of Iraq has deposited its instrument of accession to the Chemical Weapons Convention with the Secretary General of the United Nations and within 30 days, on 12 February 2009, will become the 186th State Party to the Convention". Iraq has also declared stockpiles of CW, and because of their recent accession is the only State Party exempted from the destruction time-line. On September 7, 2011 Mr. Hoshyar Zebari entered the OPCW headquarters, becoming the first Iraqi Foreign Minister to officially visit since the country joined the CWC.

On June 28, 1987, Iraqi aircraft delivered what was believed to be mustard gas in an attack against the Iranian city of Sardasht. On two separate attacks against four residential areas, victims were estimated as 10 civilians dead and 650 civilians injured.

Japan

Japan stored chemical weapons on the territory of mainland China between 1937 and 1945. The weapons mostly contained a mustard gas-lewisite mixture. The weapons are classified as abandoned chemical weapons under the CWC and Japan has started their destruction in September 2010 in Nanjing using mobile destruction facilities.

Libya

Libya used chemical weapons under Muammar Gaddafi's regime in a war with Chad. In 2003 Gaddafi agreed to accede to the convention in exchange for "rapprochement" with western nations. At the time of the Libyan uprising against Gaddafi, Libya still controlled approximately 11.25 tons of poisonous mustard gas. Because of destabilization, concerns have increased regarding possibilities and likelihood that control of these agents could be lost. With terrorism as a core concern, international bodies are seeking to ensure Libya is held to its obligations under the treaty. Libya's post-Gaddafi National Transitional Councilis cooperating with the Organization for the Prohibition of Chemical Weapons regarding the destruction of all legacy chemical weapons in the country. After assessing the chemical stockpiles the Libyan government will receive a deadline from the OPCW to destroy the weapons.

Russia

Russia entered the CWC with the largest declared stockpile of chemical weapons. By 2010 the country had destroyed 18,241 tonnes at destruction facilities located in Gorny(Saratov Oblast) and Kambarka (Udmurt Republic)—where operations have finished—andShchuchye (Kurgan Oblast), Maradykovsky (Kirov Oblast), Leonidovka (Penza Oblast) while installations are under construction in Pochep (Bryansk Oblast) and Kizner (Udmurt Republic).

United States

The U.S. stored its chemical weapons at eight U.S. Army installations within the Continental United States (CONUS). The stockpiles were maintained in exclusion zones at the following Department of Army installations (the percentages shown are reflections of amount by weight):

- Tooele Army Depot (TEAD), Utah (42.3% of total stockpile)
- Pine Bluff Arsenal (PBA), Arkansas (12%)
- Umatilla Depot Activity (UMDA), Oregon (11.6%)
- Pueblo Depot Activity (PUDA), Colorado (9.9%)
- Anniston Army Depot (ANAD), Alabama (7.1%)

- Aberdeen Proving Ground (APG), Maryland (5%)
- Newport Army Ammunition Plant (NAAP), Indiana (3.9%)
- Blue Grass Army Depot (BGAD), Kentucky (1.6%).

The remaining 6.6% was located on Johnston Atoll in the Pacific Ocean.

Currently stockpiles have been eliminated at Johnston Atoll, APG, NAAP, UMDA,PBA TEAD., and ANAD. PUDA will begin elimination during FY 2015, and complete in FY 2017. BGAD will be last to complete this elimination which tentative dates have not been set.

The U.S. policy on the use of chemical weapons is to reserve the right to retaliate. First use, or preemptive use, is a violation of stated policy. Only the president of the United States can authorize the first retaliatory use. Official policy now reflects the likelihood of chemical weapons being used as a terrorist weapon.

Syria

Prior to September 2013, Syria was one of only 7 states which are not party to the Chemical Weapons Convention. However, it is party to the 1925 Geneva Protocol prohibiting the use of chemical weapons in war but has nothing to say about production, storage or transfer.

Syrian officials have stated that they feel it appropriate to have some deterrent against Israel's similarly non-admitted nuclear weapons program when questioned about the topic, but only on July 23, 2012, the Syrian government acknowledged for the first time that it had chemical weapons

Independent assessments indicate that Syrian production could be up to a combined total of a few hundred tons of chemical agent per year. Syria reportedly manufactures Sarin, Tabun, VX, and mustard gas types of chemical weapons.

Syrian chemical weapons production facilities have been identified by Western nonproliferation experts at approximately 5 sites, plus one suspected weapons base:

- Al Safir (Scud missile base)
- Cerin
- Hama
- Homs
- Latakia
- Palmyra

In July 2007, a Syrian arms depot exploded, killing at least 15 Syrians. Jane's Defence Weekly, a U.K. magazine reporting on military and corporate affairs, believed that the explosion happened when Iranian and Syrian military personnel attempted to fit a Scudmissile with a mustard gas warhead. Syria stated that the blast was accidental and not chemical related.

On July 13, 2012, the Syrian government moved its stockpile to an undisclosed location.

In September 2012, information emerged that the Syrian military had begun chemical weapons tests and was reinforcing and resupplying a base housing these weapons located east of Aleppo in August.

On March 19, 2013, news emerged from Syria indicating the first use of chemical weapons since the beginning of the Syrian uprising.

On August 21, 2013, testimony and photographic evidence emerged from Syria indicating a large-scale chemical weapons attack on Ghouta, a populated urban center.

On October 14, 2013, Syria officially acceded to the Chemical Weapons Convention.

NON-CWC STATES WITH STOCKPILES

Israel

Although Israel has signed the CWC, it has not ratified the treaty and therefore is not officially bound by its tenets. The country is believed to have a significant stockpile of chemical weapons, likely the most abundant in the Middle-East, according to the Russian Foreign Intelligence Service. In a 1983 CIA Report, it was stated that Israel, after "finding itself surrounded by front-line Arab states with budding CW capabilities, became increasingly conscious of its vulnerability to chemical attack... undertook a program of chemical warfare preparations in both offensive and protective areas... In late 1982 a probable CW nerve agent production facility and a storage facility were identified at the Dimona Sensitive Storage Area in the Negev Desert. Other CW agent production is believe to exist within a well-developed Israeli chemical industry." In 1992, El Al Flight 1862 crashed on its way to Tel Aviv and was found to be carrying CWC schedule 2 chemical, which is a precursor to the production of sarin nerve gas, a prohibited chemical weapon of mass destruction prohibited by the CWC. Israel insisted at the time that the materials were non-toxic. This shipment was coming from a US chemical plant to the IIBR under a US Department of Commerce license.

In 1993, the U.S. Congress Office of Technology Assessment WMD proliferation assessment recorded Israel as a country generally reported as having undeclared offensive chemical warfare capabilities.

North Korea

North Korea is not a signatory of CWC and has never officially acknowledged the existence of its offensive CW program. Nevertheless, the country is believed to possess a substantial arsenal of chemical weapons. It reportedly acquired the technology necessary to produce tabun and mustard gas as early as the 1950s. In 2009 the International Crisis Group reported that the consensus expert view was that North Korea had a stockpile of about 2,500 to 5,000 tonnes of chemical weapons, including mustard gas, sarin (GB) and other nerve agents.

Framework for Elimination of Syrian Chemical Weapons

An agreement was reached September 14, 2013 called the Framework For Elimination of Syrian Chemical Weapons; leading to the elimination of Syria's chemical weapon stockpiles by mid-2014.

MANNER AND FORM

There are three basic configurations in which these agents are stored. The first are self-contained munitions like projectiles, cartridges, mines, and rockets; these can contain propellant and/or explosive components. The next form are aircraft-delivered munitions. This form never has an explosive component. Together they comprise the two forms which have been weaponized and are ready for their intended use. The U.S. stockpile consisted of 39% of these weapon ready munitions. The final of the three forms are raw agent housed in one-ton containers. The remaining 61% of the stockpile was in this form. Whereas these chemicals exist in liquid form at normal room temperature, the sulfur mustards H, and HD freeze in temperatures below 55 °F (12.8 °C). Mixing lewisite with distilled mustard lowers the freezing point to "13 °F ("25.0 °C).

Higher temperatures are a bigger concern because the possibility of an explosion increases as the temperatures rise. A fire at one of these facilities would endanger the surrounding community as well as the personnel at the installations. Perhaps more so for the community having much less access to protective equipment and specialized training.The Oak Ridge National Laboratory conducted a study to assess capabilities and costs for protecting civilian populations during related emergencies, and the effectiveness of expedient, in-place shelters.

Disposal

The stockpiles, which have been maintained for more than 50 years, are now considered obsolete. Public Law 99-145, contains section 1412 which directs the Department of Defence (DOD) to dispose of the stockpiles. This directive fell upon the DOD with joint cooperation from the Federal Emergency Management Agency (FEMA). The Congressional directive has resulted in the present Chemical Stockpile Disposal Program.

Some places where chemical weapons were tested, such as the San Jose Project in Panama, were not included in the disposal program. Thousands of mines on the island are still full of chemical gas and can be set off by passersby.

Historically, chemical munitions have been disposed of by land burial, open burning, and ocean dumping (referred to as Operation CHASE). However in 1969, the National Research Council (NRC) recommended that ocean dumping be discontinued. The Army then began a study of disposal technologies, including the assessment of incineration as well as chemical neutralization methods. In 1982, that study culminated in the selection of incineration technology, which is now incorporated into what is known as the *baseline*system. Construction of the Johnston Atoll Chemical Agent Disposal System (JACADS) began in 1985.

This was to be a full-scale prototype facility using the baseline system. The prototype was a success but there were still many concerns about CONUS operations.

To address growing public concern over incineration, Congress, in 1992, directed the Army to evaluate alternative disposal approaches that might be "significantly safer", more cost effective, and which could be completed within the established time frame.

The Army was directed to report to Congress on potential alternative technologies by the end of 1993, and to include in that report—"any recommendations that the National Academy of Sciences makes...". In June 2007 the disposal program achieved a milestone reaching 45% destruction of the chemical weapon stockpile. The Chemical Materials Agency (CMA) releases regular updates to the public regarding the status of the disposal program. By October 2010, the program had reached 80% destruction status.

Lethality

Chemical weapons are said to "make deliberate use of the toxic properties of chemical substances to inflict death". At the start of World War II it was reported in newspapers that "entire regions of Europe" would be turned into "lifeless wastelands". However, chemical weapons were not used to the extent feared.

An unintended chemical weapon release occurred at the port of Bari. A German attack on the evening of December 2, 1943, damaged U.S. vessels in the harbour and the resultant release of mustard gas inflicted a total of 628 casualties.

The U.S. Government was highly criticized for exposing American service members to chemical agents while testing the effects of exposure. These tests were often performed without the consent or prior knowledge of the soldiers affected. Many Australian service personnel were also exposed as a result of the "Brook Island trials" carried out by the British Government to determine the likely consequences of chemical attack in tropical conditions, about which little was then known. Some chemical agents are designed to produce mind altering changes rendering the victim unable to perform their assigned mission. These are classified as incapacitating agents and lethality is not a factor of their effectiveness.

UNITARY VERSUS BINARY WEAPONS

Binary munitions contain two, unmixed and isolated chemicals which do not react to produce lethal effects until mixed. This usually happens just prior to battlefield use. In contrast, unitary weapons are lethal chemical munitions which produce a toxic result in their existing state. The majority of the chemical weapon stockpile is unitary and most of it is stored in one-ton bulk containers.

THE CHEMICAL WEAPONS CONVENTION (CWC) AT A GLANCE

The Chemical Weapons Convention (CWC) is a multilateral treaty that bans chemical weapons and requires their destruction within a specified period of time. The treaty is of unlimited duration and is far more comprehensive than the 1925 Geneva Protocol, which outlaws the use but not the possession of chemical weapons.

CWC negotiations started in 1980 in the UN Conference on Disarmament. The convention opened for signature on January 13, 1993, and entered into force on April 29, 1997.

The CWC is implemented by the Organization for the Prohibition of Chemical Weapons (OPCW), which is headquartered in The Hague with about 500 employees. The OPCW receives states-parties' declarations detailing chemical weapons-related activities or materials and relevant industrial activities. After receiving declarations, the OPCW inspects and monitors states-parties' facilities and activities that are relevant to the convention, to ensure compliance.

The CWC is open to all nations and currently has 189 states-parties. Two signatories—Israel and Myanmar—have yet to ratify the convention. Key non-signatories included North Korea and Syria. Syria acknowledged it had CW in 2012, and according to the United States, United KIngdom and France, Syria has used its CW stockpiles. On September 12, 2013, Syria sent a letter to the United Nations Secretary General which said that Assad signed a legislative decree providing the accession of Syria to the Chemical Weapons Convention. In the letter, Assad said Syria woud observe its CWC obligations immediately, as opposed to 30 days from the date of accession, as stipulated in the treaty. But it remains to be seen if Syria will follow through on its treaty obligations.

Prohibitions

The Chemical Weapons Convention prohibits:

Developing, producing, acquiring, stockpiling, or retaining chemical weapons.

The direct or indirect transfer of chemical weapons.

Chemical weapons use or military preparation for use.

Assisting, encouraging, or inducing other states to engage in CWC-prohibited activity.

The use of riot control agents "as a method of warfare."

Declaration Requirements

The CWC requires states-parties to declare in writing to the OPCW their chemical weapons stockpiles, chemical weapons production facilities (CWPFs), relevant chemical industry facilities, and other weapons-related information. This must be done within 30 days of the convention's entry into force for each member state.

Chemical Weapons Stockpiles—States-parties must declare all chemical weapons stockpiles, which are broken down into three categories:

Category 1: chemical weapons based on Schedule 1 chemicals, including VX and sarin.

Category 2: chemical weapons based on non-Schedule 1 chemicals, such as phosgene.

Category 3: chemical weapons including unfilled munitions, devices and equipment designed specifically to employ chemical weapons.

Other weapons-related declarations states-parties must make include:

Chemical weapons production facilities on their territories since January 1, 1946.

Facilities (such as laboratories and test sites) designed, constructed, or used primarily for chemical weapons development since January 1, 1946.

"Old" chemical weapons on their territories (chemical weapons manufactured before 1925 or those produced between 1925 and 1946 that have deteriorated to such an extent that they are no longer useable).

"Abandoned" chemical weapons (abandoned by another state without consent on or after January 1, 1925).

Plans for destroying weapons and facilities.

All transfers or receipts of chemical weapons or chemical weapons-production equipment since January 1, 1946.

All riot control agents in their possession.

Chemical Industry—The CWC requires states-parties to declare chemical industry facilities that produce or use chemicals of concern to the convention. These chemicals are grouped into "schedules," based on the risk they pose to the convention. A facility producing a Schedule 1 chemical is considered a Schedule 1 facility.

Schedule 1 chemicals and precursors pose a "high risk" to the convention and are rarely used for peaceful purposes. States-parties may not retain these chemicals except in small quantities for research, medical, pharmaceutical, or defensive use. Many Schedule 1 chemicals have been stockpiled as chemical weapons.

Schedule 2 chemicals are toxic chemicals that pose a "significant risk" to the convention and are precursors to the production of Schedule 1 or Schedule 2 chemicals. These chemicals are not produced in large quantities for commercial or other peaceful purposes.

Schedule 3 chemicals are usually produced in large quantities for purposes not prohibited by the CWC but still pose a risk to the convention. Some of these chemicals have been stockpiled as chemical weapons.

The CWC also requires the declaration of facilities that produce certain nonscheduled chemicals.

Destruction Requirements

The convention requires states-parties to destroy:

All chemical weapons under their jurisdiction or control.

Category 1 chemical weapons destruction must start within two years after the CWC enters into force for a state-party. States-parties must destroy 1 percent within three years of the CWC's entry into force, 20 percent within five years, 45 percent within seven years, and 100 percent within 10 years (by April 29, 2007). The OPCW may extend these deadlines due to "exceptional circumstances," but states-parties are supposed to destroy their entire stockpiles by April 29, 2012. In December 2006, the OPCW Executive Council granted nearly all possessors extensions of differing lengths. The only exception was Albania, which was the sole state-party nearing the complete destruction of its stockpile at that time,

The latest possessor state to join the convention, Iraq, has not been given a date by which to complete destruction. Its requirement is guided by paragraph 8, article 4, which states that destruction will take place as soon as possible. (A chart at the end of this fact sheet shows the status of each possessor state's destruction activities.)

Category 2 and 3 chemical weapons destruction must start within one year after the CWC enters into force for a state-party. All chemical weapons production facilities under their jurisdiction or control.

Destruction of CWPFs capable of producing Schedule 1 chemicals must start within one year after the CWC enters into force for a state-party. States-parties must complete destruction by April 29, 2007.

Destruction of other CWPFs must start within one year after the CWC enters into force for a state-party. States-parties must complete destruction by April 29, 2002.

States-parties may request to convert CWPFs to facilities that they can use for nonprohibited purposes. Once their requests are approved, states-parties must complete conversion by April 29, 2003.

As of July 2010, 64 of the 70 CWPFs declared to the OPCW have either been destroyed (43) or converted for peaceful purposes (21).

Chemical weapons abandoned on other states' territories.

Old chemical weapons.

On-Site Activity

The convention establishes three types of on-site activities that aim to generate confidence in states-parties' CWC compliance. These include:

"Routine inspections" of chemical weapons-related facilities and chemical industry facilities to verify the content of declarations and to confirm that activities are consistent with CWC obligations.

"Challenge inspections" which can be conducted at any facility or location in states-parties to clarify questions of possible noncompliance. (To prevent abuse of this measure, the OPCW's executive body can vote by a three-quarters majority to stop a challenge inspection from going forward.) Investigations of alleged use of chemical weapons.

Trade

The convention encourages trade among states-parties, calling upon them not to maintain restrictions on one another that would hamper the trade of chemical-related items to be used for peaceful purposes.

The convention does restrict trade with non-states-parties, outlawing the transfer of Schedule 1 and 2 chemicals. To ensure that Schedule 3 transfers to non-states-parties are not used for purposes prohibited by the convention, the CWC requires exporting states-parties to obtain an end-use certificate from importing states.

PENALTIES FOR NONCOMPLIANCE

If states-parties are found to have engaged in prohibited actions that could result in "serious damage" to the convention, the OPCW could recommend collective punitive measures to other states-parties.

In cases of "particular gravity," the OPCW could bring the issue before the UN Security Council and General Assembly.

States-parties must take measures to address questions raised about their compliance with the CWC.

If they do not, the OPCW may, inter alia, restrict or suspend their CWC-related rights and privileges (such as voting and trade rights).

AN ARMS CONTROL TREATY AND CHEMICAL WEAPONS CONVENTION

The Chemical Weapons Convention (CWC) is an arms control treaty which outlaws the production, stockpiling, and use of chemical weapons and their precursors. The full name of the treaty is the Convention on the Prohibition of the Development, Production, Stockpiling and Use of Chemical Weapons and on their Destruction and it is administered by the Organisation for the Prohibition of Chemical Weapons (OPCW), an intergovernmental organization based in The Hague, Netherlands. The treaty entered into force in 1997.

The parties' main obligation under the convention is to prohibit the use and production of chemical weapons, as well as the destruction of all chemical weapons. The destruction activities are verified by the OPCW.

As of September 2013, around 82% of the declared stockpile of chemical weapons has been destroyed. The convention also has provisions for systematic evaluation of chemical and military plants, as well as for investigations of allegations of use and production of chemical weapons based on intelligence of other state parties.

As of October 2013, 190 states have given their consent to be bound by the CWC. Two of the remaining six states, Israel and Myanmar, have signed but not ratified the agreement. Most recently, Syria deposited its instrument of accession to the CWC on 14 September 2013 and agreed to its provisional application pending entry into force on 14 October 2013.

HISTORY

Intergovernmental consideration of a chemical and biological weapons ban was initiated in 1968 within the 18-nation Disarmament Committee, which, after numerous changes of name and composition, became the Conference on Disarmament (CD) in 1984.

On 3 September 1992 the Conference on Disarmament submitted to the U.N. General Assembly its annual report, which contained the text of the Chemical Weapons Convention. The General Assembly approved the Convention on 30 November 1992, and The U.N. Secretary-General then opened the Convention for signature in Paris on 13 January 1993. The CWC remained open for signature until its entry into force on 29 April 1997, 180 days after the deposit of the 65th instrument of ratification (by Hungary).

The convention augments theGeneva Protocol of 1925 for chemical weapons and includes extensive verification measures such as on-site inspections. It does not, however, cover biological weapons.

Organisation for the Prohibition of Chemical Weapons (OPCW)

The convention is administered by the Organization for the Prohibition of Chemical Weapons(OPCW), which acts as the legal platform for specification of the CWC provisions (theConference of the States Parties is mandated to change the CWC, pass regulations on implementation of CWC requirements etc.). The Technical Secretariat of the organization furthermore conducts inspections plants to ensure compliance of member states. These inspections target destruction facilities (where permanent monitoring takes place during destruction), chemical weapons production facilities which have been dismantled or converted for civil use, as well as inspections of the chemical industry. The Secretariat may furthermore conduct "investigations of alledged use" of chemical weapons and give assistance after use of chemical weapons.

The 2013 Nobel Peace Prize was awarded to the organization because it had, with the Chemical Weapons Convention, "defined the use of chemical weapons as a taboo underinternational law" according to Thorbjørn Jagland, Chairman of the Norwegian Nobel Committee.

Key points of the Convention

- Prohibition of production and use of chemical weapons
- Destruction (or monitored conversion to other functions) of chemical weapons production facilities
- Destruction of all chemical weapons (including chemical weapons abandoned outside the state parties territory)
- Assistance between State Parties and the OPCW in the case of use of chemical weapons
- An OPCW inspection regime for the production of chemicals which might be converted to chemical weapons
- International cooperation in the peaceful use of chemistry in relevant areas

Controlled Substances

The convention distinguishes three classes of controlled substance, chemicals which can either be used as weapons themselves or used in the manufacture of weapons.

The classification is based on the quantities of the substance produced commercially for legitimate purposes. Each class is split into Part A, which are chemicals that can be used directly as weapons, and Part B which are chemicals useful in the manufacture of chemical weapons.

Separate from the precursors, the convention defines toxic chemicals as "[a]ny chemical which through its chemical action on life processes can cause death, temporary incapacitation or permanent harm to humans or animals. This includes all such chemicals, regardless of their origin or of their method of production, and regardless of whether they are produced in facilities, in munitions or elsewhere."

- Schedule 1 chemicals have few, or no uses outside of chemical weapons. These may be produced or used for research, medical, pharmaceutical or chemical weapon defence testing purposes but production above 100 grams per year must be declared to theOPCW. A country is limited to possessing a maximum of 1 tonne of these materials. Examples are sulfur mustard and nerve agents, and substances which are solely used as precursor chemicals in their manufacture. A few of these chemicals have very small scale non-military applications, for example minute quantities of nitrogen mustard are used to treat certain cancers.

- Schedule 2 chemicals have legitimate small-scale applications. Manufacture must be declared and there are restrictions on export to countries which are not CWC signatories. An example is thiodiglycol which can be used in the manufacture of mustard agents, but is also used as a solvent in inks.
- Schedule 3 chemicals have large-scale uses apart from chemical weapons. Plants which manufacture more than 30 tonnes per year must be declared and can be inspected, and there are restrictions on export to countries which are not CWC signatories. Examples of these substances are phosgene, which has been used as a chemical weapon but which is also a precursor in the manufacture of many legitimate organic compounds, and triethanolamine, used in the manufacture of nitrogen mustard but also commonly used in toiletries and detergents.

The treaty also deals with carbon compounds called in the treaty *discrete organic chemicals*. These are any carbon compounds apart from long chain polymers, oxides, sulfides and metal carbonates, such as organophosphates. The OPCW must be informed of, and can inspect, any plant producing (or expecting to produce) more than 200 tonnes per year, or 30 tonnes if the chemical contains phosphorus, sulfur or fluorine, unless the plant solely produces explosives or hydrocarbons.

MEMBER STATES

165 states signed the CWC prior to its entry into force in 1997, allowing them to ratify the agreement after obtaining domestic approval. Following the treaty's entry into force, it was closed for signature and the only method for non-signatory states to become a party was through accession. As of October 2013, 190 states, representing over 98 percent of the world's population, are party to the CWC.

Of the sixUnited Nations Member States that are not parties to the treaty, two have signed but not yet ratified the treaty (Burmaand Israel) and four states have not acceded to the treaty (Angola, North Korea, Egypt, and South Sudan). Angola and Burma have committed to ratifying the CWC.Taiwan, though not a Member State, has stated that it complies with the treaty.

Key Organizations of Member States

Member states are represented at the OPCW by their permanent representative. This function is generally combined with the function of Ambassador. For the preparation of OPCW inspections and preparation of declarations, member states have to constitute anational authority.

WORLD STOCKPILE OF CHEMICAL WEAPONS

The total world declared stockpile of chemical weapons by the parties to the convention was about 13,024 tons in September 2013. A total of 71,315 tonnes of agents, 8.67 million munitions and containers, and 70 production facilities were declared to OPCW before destruction activities began. In addition, several countries that are not members are suspected of having chemical weapons, especially Egypt, Israel, and North Korea. Some member states (including Iran) have been accused by others of failing to disclose their stockpiles.

Progress of Destruction

By May 2012, a total of 50,619 tonnes or 71.10% of declared chemical weapons (of Category 1, which is the main category) had been destroyed, as well as all Category 3 declared chemicals. Category 2 remained at 52% complete. More than 45% (3.95 million) of chemical munitions and containers have been destroyed. (Treaty confirmed destruction totals often lag behind state-declared totals.) Only about 50% of countries had passed the required legislation to outlaw participation in chemical weapons production.

Three state parties, Albania (included 16,678 kilograms of mustard agent, lewisite, adamsite, and chloroacetophenone), an unspecified state party (widely believed to be South Korea) and India have completed the destruction of their stockpiles. Russia and the United States, which declared the largest amounts of chemical weapons, are in the process of destruction and have processed 57% and 90% of their respective stockpiles. The deadline set for both countries of April 2012, however, was not met.The destruction of Libya's Category 1 chemical weapons was completed in 2014; destruction of its chemical weapon precursors is scheduled to finish in 2016. Iraq has yet to start destruction. Japan and China started in October 2010 the destruction of World War II era chemical weapons abandoned by Japan in China by means of mobile destruction units and reported destruction of 35,203 chemical weapons (75% of the Nanjing stockpile).

Iraqi Stockpile

When Iraq joined the CWC in 2009, it declared "two bunkers with filled and unfilled chemical weapons munitions, some precursors, as well as five former chemical weapons production facilities" according to OPCW Director General Rogelio Pfirter. No plans were announced at that time for the destruction of the material, although it was noted that the bunkers were damaged in the 2003 war and even inspection of the site must be carefully planned. Most of Iraq's chemical weapons were previously destroyed under a United Nations reduction program after the 1991 Gulf War. Approximately five hundred degraded chemical munitions have been found in Iraq since the 2003 invasion of Iraq, according to a report of the US National Ground Intelligence Center. These weapons contained sarin andmustard agents but were so badly corroded that they could not have been used as originally intended.

Financial Support for Destruction

Financial support for the Albanian and Libyan stockpile destruction programmes was provided by the United States. Russia received support from a number of nations, including the United States, the United Kingdom, Germany, the Netherlands, Italy and Canada; some $2 billion given by 2004. Costs for Albania's program were approximately 48 million U.S. dollars. The U.S. had spent $20 billion and expected to spend a further $40 billion.

As of the end of March 2012, all 70 declared facilities had been deactivated and 92% (64) have been certified as destroyed or converted to civilian use. In 2009, Iraq declared five production sites which were put out of commission by damage in the 1991 and 2003 wars; OPCW inspections were still required.

DISARMAMENT TREATY AND CHEMICAL WEAPONS CONVENTION

Chemcal Weapons Convention is a universal non-discriminatory, multilateral, Disarmament Treaty which bans the development, production, acquisition, transfer, use and stockpile of all chemical weapons. The Treaty puts all the States Parties on an equal footing. Countries having stockpiles of chemical weapons are required to declare and destroy them in a specified time frame and those who produce and use chemicals that can be conveniently converted into chemical weapons have to be open and transparent about the use they put these chemicals to. The Convention was opened for signature on 13th January, 1993 in Paris. India signed the Convention on 14th January, 1993.

The Convention entered into force 180 days after deposit of 65th instrument of ratification. India's instrument of ratification was deposited on 3rd Sept., 1996 making India the 62nd States Party to ratify the Treaty. The 65th instrument of ratification was deposited on 31st October, 1996 and the Convention entered into force on 29th April, 1997. As on 30.11.2004, 167 countries are state parties to the Chemical Weapons Convention. Some of the important countries who have ratified the Treaty include USA, China, Japan, United Kingdom, France, Germany, Australia, Canada, Russia, Pakistan and the Netherlands.

The Chemical Weapons Convention (CWC) requires the State Parties to undertake not to develop, produce, otherwise acquire, stockpile or retain chemical weapons or transfer directly or indirectly chemical weapons to anyone and not to use chemical weapons and engage in military preparations. It also enjoins upon the States Parties to undertake destruction of all chemical weapons including old chemical weapons and abandoned chemical weapons in a stipulated time frame. The State Parties to the Convention are prohibited from using riot control agents as a method of warfare. Each State Party, however, has the right under the provisions of the Convention to develop, produce, otherwise acquire, retain, transfer and use toxic chemicalsand their precursors for purposes not prohibited under the Convention such as Industrial, agricultural, research, medical, pharmaceutical, protective and other peaceful purposes. The Convention classifies toxic chemicals into three schedules. Schedule 1 lists chemicals that are produced and stockpiled as chemical weapons. Schedule 2 contains such precursors which pose significant risk to the objective and purpose of CWC, since these chemicals are capable of generating Schedule 1 chemicals. In Schedule 3 are listed dual purpose chemicals that have large number of legitimate civilian commercial applications and which could also be used for purposes of developing chemical weapons. The list of scheduled chemicals is annexed.

The Chemical Weapons Convention entails a number of obligations on the State Parties which include regular reporting of data relating to production, processing, consumption, use and transfer in respect of chemicals, their plants and plant sites, chemical weapons, chemical weapons production facilities, riot control agents etc. The data contained in the declarations made is subject to verification through a mechanism of inspections by the Organisation for the Prohibition of Chemical Weapons (OPCW). India has hosted 16 OPCW inspections as on 30.10.2004. Therefore, the declarations have to be correct and complete in all respects. The Convention also provides for enactment of penal legislation prohibiting the activities not permitted by the convention to a State Party.

National Implementation Measures are required to be undertaken by the State Parties to fulfil their obligations under the Treaty.

Article VII of the Convention regarding the National Implementation Measures is as follows:

- Each State Party shall, in accordance with its constitutional processes, adopt the necessary measures to implement its obligations under this Convention. In particular, it shall:
  a. Prohibit natural and legal persons anywhere on its territory or in any other place under its jurisdiction as recognised by international law from undertaking any activity prohibited to a State Party under this Convention, including enacting penal legislation with respect to such activity.
  b. Not permit in any place under its control any activity prohibited to a State Party under this Convention; and
  c. Extend its penal legislation enacted under subparagraph (a) to any activity prohibited to a State Party under this Convention undertaken anywhere by natural persons, possessing its nationality, in conformity with international law.
- Each State Party shall cooperate with other State Parties and afford the appropriate form of legal assistance to facilitate the implementation of the obligations under the conventions.
- Each State Party, during the implementation of its obligations under this Convention, shall assign the

highest priority to ensuring the safety of people and to protecting the environment, and shall cooperate as appropriate with other States Parties in this regard.

- The Indian CWC Act 2000 was passed in August 2000. Section 18(1) of the Act requires that all persons engaged in activities related to scheduled chemicals and discrete organic chemicals will be required to submit applications for registration who are engaged in the activities of their facilities to the registration authority.

Relations between the State Party and the OPCW:

- In order to fulfil its obligations under this Convention, each State Party shall designate or establish a National Authority to serve as the national focal point for effective liaison with the Organisation and other State Parties. Each State Party shall notify the Organisation of its National Authority at the time that this Convention enters into force for it.
- Each State Party shall inform the Organisation of the legislative and administrative measures taken to implement this Convention.
- Each State Party shall treat as confidential and afford special handling to information and data that It receives in confidence from the Organisation in connection with the implementation of this Convention.
- It shall treat such information and data exclusively in connection with its rights and obligations under this Convention and in accordance with the provisions set forth in the Confidentiality Annex.
- Each State Party undertakes to cooperate with the Organisation in the exercise of all its functions and in particular to provide assistance to the Technical Secretariat".

6

Israel and Weapons of Mass Destruction

Israel is widely believed to possess weapons of mass destruction, and to be one of four nuclear-armed countries not recognized as a Nuclear Weapons State by the Nuclear Non-Proliferation Treaty (NPT). The US Congress Office of Technology Assessment has recorded Israel as a country generally reported as having undeclared chemical warfarecapabilities, and an offensive biological warfare program. Officially Israel neither confirms nor denies possessing nuclear weapons.

NUCLEAR WEAPONS

It is believed that Israel had possessed an operational nuclear weapons capability by 1967, with the mass production of nuclear warheads occurring immediately after the Six-Day War. Although no official statistics exist, it has been estimated that Israel possesses from 75 to as many as 400 nuclear weapons, which are reported to includethermonuclear weapons in the megaton range. Israel is also reported to possess a wide range of different systems, including neutron bombs, tactical nuclear weapons, andsuitcase nukes. Israel is believed to manufacture its nuclear weapons at the Negev Nuclear Research Center.

Delivery mechanisms include Jericho intercontinental ballistic missiles, with a range of 11,500 km, and which are believed to provide a second-strike option. Israel's nuclear-capable ballistic missiles are believed to be buried so far underground that they would survive a nuclear attack. Additionally, Israel is believed to have an offshore nuclear second-strike capability, using submarine-launchednuclearcapable cruise missiles, which can be launched from the Israeli Navy's *Dolphin*-class submarines. The Israeli Air Force has F-15I and F-16I Sufa fighter aircraft are capable of delivering nuclear weapons at long distances using conformal fuel tanks and their Aerial refueling fleet of modified Boeing 707's.

The Israeli government maintains a policy of deliberate ambiguity on whether it has nuclear weapons, saying only that it would "not be the first to introduce nuclear weapons in the Middle East." Former International Atomic Energy Agency Director General Mohamed ElBaradei regarded Israel as a state possessing nuclear weapons. Much of what is known about Israel's nuclear program comes from revelations in 1986 by Mordechai Vanunu, a technician at the Negev Nuclear Research Center who served an 18-year prison sentence as a result. Israel has not signed the Nuclear Non-Proliferation Treaty, but supports establishment of a Middle East Zone free of weapons of mass destruction.

CHEMICAL WEAPONS

Israel has signed but not ratified the Chemical Weapons Convention (CWC). In 1983 a report by the CIA stated that Israel, after "finding itself surrounded by frontline Arab states with budding CW capabilities, became increasingly conscious of its vulnerability to chemical attack... undertook a program of chemical warfare preparations in both offensive and protective areas... In late 1982 a probable CW nerve agent production facility and a storage facility were identified at the Dimona Sensitive Storage Area in the Negev Desert. Other CW agent production is believed to exist within a well-developed Israeli chemical industry."

There are also speculations that a chemical weapons program might be located at the Israel Institute for Biological Research (IIBR) in Ness Ziona.

190 liters of dimethyl methylphosphonate, a CWC schedule 2 chemical used in the synthesis of sarin nerve gas, was discovered in the cargo of El Al Flight 1862 after it crashed in 1992 en route to Tel Aviv. Israel insisted the material was non-toxic, was to have been used to test filters that protect against chemical weapons, and that it had been clearly listed on the cargo manifest in accordance with international regulations. The shipment was from a U.S. chemical plant to the IIBR under a U.S. Department of Commerce license.

In 1993, the U.S. Congress Office of Technology Assessment WMD proliferation assessment recorded Israel as a country generally reported as having undeclared offensive chemical warfare capabilities. Former US deputy assistant secretary of defence responsible for chemical and biological defence, Bill Richardson, said in 1998 "I have no doubt that Israel has worked on both chemical and biological offensive things for a long time... There's no doubt they've had stuff for years."

BIOLOGICAL WEAPONS

Israel is believed to have developed an offensive biological warfare capability. The US Congress Office of Technology Assessment records Israel as a country possessing a long-term, undeclared biological warfare program. Israel is not a signatory to the Biological Weapons Convention (BWC). It is assumed that the Israel Institute for Biological Research in Ness Ziona develops vaccines andantidotes for chemical and biological warfare. It has not been possible to conclude whether Israel currently maintains an offensive biological weapons program; it is speculated that Israel retains an active ability to produce and disseminate biological weapons.

NUCLEAR WEAPONS AND ISRAEL

Israel is widely believed to possess nuclear weapons and to be the sixth country in the world to have developed them. It is one of four nuclear-armed countries not recognized as a Nuclear Weapons State by the Nuclear Non-Proliferation Treaty (NPT), the others being India, Pakistan and North Korea. Israel maintains a policy known as "nuclear ambiguity" (also known as "nuclear opacity"). Israel has never officially admitted to having nuclear weapons, instead repeating over the years that it would not be the first country to "introduce" nuclear weapons to the Middle East, leaving ambiguity as to whether it means it will not create, will not disclose, will not make first use of the weapons or possibly some other interpretation of the phrase. The "not be the first" formulation goes back to the Eshkol-Comer memorandum of understanding made between Israel and the United States on March 10, 1965, which contained Israel's written assurance for the first time that it would not be the first to introduce nuclear weapons in the Middle East. Israel has refused to sign the NPT despite international pressure to do so, and has stated that signing the NPT would be contrary to its national security interests.

Israel started investigating the nuclear field soon after its founding in 1948 and with French support secretly began building a nuclear reactor and reprocessing plant in the late 1950s. Israel is alleged to have developed a nuclear weapon in the late 1960s, but it is not publicly confirmed. Mordechai Vanunu, a former Israeli nuclear technician, provided explicit details and photographs to the London *Sunday Times* of a nuclear weapons program in which he had been employed for nine years, "including equipment for extracting radioactive material for arms production and laboratory models of thermonuclear devices."

Estimates as to the size of the Israeli nuclear arsenal vary between 75 and 400 nuclear warheads, with most estimates at less than 200 warheads. It is estimated that theIsrael nuclear deterrent force has the ability to deliver them by intermediate-range ballistic missile, intercontinental ballistic missile, aircraft, and submarine-launched cruise missile.

DEVELOPMENT HISTORY

Pre-Dimona 1949–1956

Israel's first Prime Minister David Ben-Gurion was "nearly obsessed" with obtaining nuclear weapons to prevent the Holocaust from recurring. He stated, "What Einstein, Oppenheimer, and Teller, the three of them are Jews, made for the United States, could also be done by scientists in Israel, for their own people". Ben-Gurion decided to recruit Jewish scientists from abroad even before the end of the 1948 Arab–Israeli War that established Israel's independence. He and others, such as head of the Weizmann Institute of Scienceand defence ministry scientist Ernst David Bergmann, believed and hoped that Jewish scientists such as Oppenheimer and Teller would help Israel.

In 1949 a unit of the Israel Defence Forces Science Corps, known by the Hebrew acronym HEMED GIMMEL, began a two-yeargeological survey of the Negev. While a preliminary study was initially prompted by rumors of petroleum fields, one objective of the longer two year survey was to find sources of uranium; some small recoverable amounts were found in phosphate deposits. That year Hemed Gimmel funded six Israeli physics graduate students to study overseas, including one to go to the University of Chicago and study under Enrico Fermi, who had overseen the world's first artificial and self-sustaining nuclear chain reaction. In early 1952 Hemed Gimmel was moved from the IDF to the Ministry of Defence and was reorganized as the Division of Research and Infrastructure (EMET). That June Bergmann was appointed by Ben-Gurion to be the first chairman of the Israel Atomic Energy Commission (IAEC).

Hemed Gimmel was renamed Machon 4 during the transfer, and was used by Bergmann as the "chief laboratory" of the IAEC; by 1953, Machon 4, working with the Department of Isotope Research at the Weizmann Institute, developed the capability to extract uranium from the phosphate in the Negev and a new technique to produce indigenous heavy water. The techniques were two years more advanced than American efforts. Bergmann, who was interested in increasing nuclear cooperation with the French, sold both patents to the Commissariat à l'énergie atomique (CEA) for 60 million francs. Although they were never commercialized, it was a consequential step for future French-Israeli cooperation. In addition, Israeli scientists probably helped construct the G-1 plutonium production reactor and UP-1 reprocessing plant at Marcoule. France and Israel had close relations in many areas. France was principal arms supplier for the young Jewish state, and as instability spread through French colonies in North Africa, Israel provided valuable intelligence obtained from contacts with Sephardi Jews in those countries.

At the same time Israeli scientists were also observingFrance's own nuclear program, and were the only foreign scientists allowed to roam "at will" at the nuclear facility at Marcoule. In addition to the relationships between Israeli and French Jewish and non-Jewish researchers, the French believed that cooperation with Israel could give them access to international Jewish nuclear scientists.

After U.S. President Dwight Eisenhower announced the Atoms for Peace initiative, Israel became the second country to sign on (following Turkey), and signed a peaceful nuclear cooperation agreement with the United States on July 12, 1955. This culminated in a public signing ceremony on March 20, 1957, to construct a "small swimming-pool research reactor in Nachal Soreq", which would be used to shroud the construction of a much larger facility with the French at Dimona.

In 1986 Francis Perrin, French high-commissioner for atomic energy from 1951 to 1970 stated publicly that in 1949 Israeli scientists were invited to the Saclay nuclear research facility, this cooperation leading to a joint effort including sharing of knowledge between French and Israeli scientists especially those with knowledge from the Manhattan Project. According to Lieutenant Colonel Warner D. Farr in a report to the USAF Counterproliferation Center while France was previously a leader in nuclear research "Israel and France were at a similar level of expertise after the war, and Israeli scientists could make significant contributions to the French effort. Progress in nuclear science and technology in France and Israel remained closely linked throughout the early fifties." Furthermore, according to Farr, "There were several Israeli observers at the French nuclear tests and the Israelis had 'unrestricted access to French nuclear test explosion data.'"

DIMONA 1956–1965

Negotiation

The French justified their decision to provide Israel a nuclear reactor by claiming it was not without precedent. In September 1955 Canada publicly announced that it would help the Indian government build a heavy-water research reactor, the CIRUS, for "peaceful purposes". When Egyptian President Gamal Abdel Nasser nationalized the Suez Canal, France proposed Israel attack Egypt and invade the Sinai as a pretext for France and Britain to invade Egypt posing as "peacekeepers" with the true intent of seizing the Suez Canal. In exchange, France would provide the nuclear reactor as the basis for the Israeli nuclear weapons program.Shimon Peres, sensing the opportunity on the nuclear reactor, accepted. On September 17, 1956, Peres and Bergmann reached a tentative agreement in Paris for the CEA to sell Israel a small research reactor. This was reaffirmed by Peres at the Protocol of Sèvresconference in late October for the sale of a reactor to be built near Dimona and for a supply of uranium fuel.

Israel benefited from an unusually pro-Israel French government during this time. After the Suez Crisis led to the threat of Sovietintervention and the British and French were being forced to withdraw under pressure from the U.S., Ben-Gurion sent Peres and Golda Meir to France.

During their discussions the groundwork was laid for France to build a larger nuclear reactor and chemical reprocessing plant, and Prime Minister Guy Mollet, ashamed at having abandoned his commitment to fellow socialists in Israel, supposedly told an aide, "I owe the bomb to them," while General Paul Ely, Chief of the Defence Staff, said that "We must give them this to guarantee their security, it is vital." Mollet's successor Maurice Bourgès-Maunoury stated "I gave you [Israelis] the bomb in order to prevent another Holocaust from befalling the Jewish people and so that Israel could face its enemies in the Middle East."

The French–Israeli relationship was finalized on October 3, 1957, in two agreements whose contents remain secret: One political that declared the project to be for peaceful purposes and specified other legal obligations, and one technical that described a 24megawatt EL-102 reactor.

The one to actually be built was to be two to three times as large and be able to produce 22 kilograms ofplutonium a year. When the reactor arrived in Israel, Prime Minister Ben-Gurion declared that its purpose was to provide a pumping station to desalinate a billion cubic gallons of seawater annually and turn the desert into an "agricultural paradise". Six of seven members of the Israel Atomic Energy Commission promptly resigned, protesting that the reactor was the precursor to "political adventurism which will unite the world against us".

Excavation

Before construction began it was determined that the scope of the project would be too large for the EMET and IAEC team, so Shimon Peres recruited Colonel Manes Pratt, then Israeli military attaché in Burma, to be the project leader. Building began in late 1957 or early 1958, bringing hundreds of French engineers and technicians to the Beersheba and Dimona area. In addition, thousands of newly immigrated Sephardi Jews were recruited to do digging; to circumvent strict labor laws, they were hired in increments of 59 days, separated by one day off.

Creation of LAKAM

By the late 1950s Shimon Peres had established and appointed a new intelligence service assigned to search the globe and clandestinely secure technology, materials and equipment needed for the program, by any means necessary. The new service would eventually be named LEKEM (pronounced LAKAM, the Hebrew acronym for 'Science liaison Bureau'). Peres appointed IDF Internal Security Chief, Benjamin Blumberg, to the task. As head of the LEKEM, Blumberg would rise to become a key figure in Israel's intelligence community, coordinating agents' world wide and securing the crucial components for the program.

Rupture with France

When Charles de Gaulle became French President in late 1958 he wanted to end French–Israeli nuclear cooperation, and said that he would not supply Israel with uranium unless the plant was opened to international inspectors, declared peaceful, and no plutonium was reprocessed. Through an extended series of negotiations, Shimon Peres finally reached a compromise with Foreign Minister Maurice Couve de Murville over two years later, in which French companies would be able to continue to fulfill their contract obligations and Israel would declare the project peaceful. Due to this, French assistance did not end until 1966. However the supply of uranium fuel was stopped earlier, in 1963. Despite this, a French uranium company based in Gabon may have sold Israel uranium in 1965. The US government launched an investigation but was unable to determine if such a sale had taken place.

British Aid

Top secret British documents obtained by BBC *Newsnight* show that Britain made hundreds of secret shipments of restricted materials to Israel in the 1950s and 1960s. These included specialist chemicals for reprocessing and samples of fissile material—uranium-235 in 1959, and plutonium in 1966, as well as highly enriched lithium-6, which is used to boost fission bombs and fuel hydrogen bombs. The investigation also showed that Britain shipped 20 tons of heavy water directly to Israel in 1959 and 1960 to start up the Dimona reactor. The transaction was made through a Norwegian front company called Noratom, which took a 2% commission on the transaction. Britain was challenged about the heavy water deal at the International Atomic Energy Agency after it was exposed on Newsnight in 2005. British Foreign Minister Kim Howells claimed this was a sale to Norway. But a former British intelligence officer who investigated the deal at the time confirmed that this was really a sale to Israel and the Noratom contract was just a charade. The Foreign Office finally admitted in March 2006 that Britain knew the destination was Israel all along. Israel admits running the Dimona reactor with Norway's heavy water since 1963. French engineers who helped build Dimona say the Israelis were expert operators, so only a relatively small portion of the water was lost during the years since the reactor was first put into operation.

Criticality

In 1961, the Israeli Prime Minister David Ben-Gurion informed the Canadian Prime Minister John Diefenbaker that a pilot plutonium-separation plant would be built at Dimona. British intelligence concluded from this and other information that this "can only mean that Israel intends to produce nuclear weapons". The nuclear reactor at Dimona went critical in 1962. After Israel's rupture with France, the Israeli government reportedly reached out to Argentina. The Argentine government agreed to sell Israel yellowcake (uranium oxide). Between 1963 and 1966, about 90 tons of yellowcake were allegedly shipped to Israel from Argentina in secret. By 1965 the Israeli reprocessing plant was completed and ready to convert the reactor's fuel rods into weapons grade plutonium.

Costs

The exact costs for the construction of the Israeli nuclear program are unknown, though Peres later said that the reactor cost $80 million in 1960, half of which was raised by foreign Jewish donors, including many American Jews. Some of these donors were given a tour of the Dimona complex in 1968.

Weapons Production 1967–present

Israel is believed to have begun full scale production of nuclear weapons following the 1967Six-Day War, although it may have had bomb parts earlier. A CIA report from early 1967 stated that Israel had the materials to construct a bomb in six to eight weeks and some authors suggest that Israel had two crude bombs ready for use during the war. According to US journalist Seymour Hersh, everything was ready for production at this time save an official order to do so. Another CIA report from 1968 states that "...Israel might undertake a nuclear weapons program in the next several years." Moshe Dayan, then Defence Minister, believed that nuclear weapons were cheaper and more practical than indefinitely growing Israel's conventional forces. He convinced the Labor Party's economic bossPinchas Sapir of the value of commencing the program by giving him a tour of the Dimona site in early 1968, and soon after Dayan decided that he had the authority to order the start of full production of four to five nuclear warheads a year. Hersh stated that it is widely believed that the words "Never Again" were welded, in English and Hebrew, onto the first warhead.

In order to produce plutonium the Israelis needed a large supply of uranium ore. In 1968, the Mossad purchased 200 tons from Union Minière du Haut Katanga, a Belgian mining company, on the pretense of buying it for an Italian chemical company in Milan. Once the uranium was shipped from Antwerp it was transferred to an Israeli freighter at sea and brought to Israel. The orchestrated disappearance of the uranium, named Operation Plumbat, became the subject of the 1978 book *The Plumbat Affair.*

Estimates as to how many warheads Israel has built since the late 1960s have varied, mainly based on the amount of fissile material that could have been produced and on the revelations of Israeli nuclear technician Mordechai Vanunu.

By 1969, U.S. Defence Secretary Melvin Laird believed that Israel might have a nuclear weapon that year. Later that year, U.S. President Richard Nixon in a meeting with Israeli Prime Minister Golda Meir pressed Israel to "make no visible introduction of nuclear weapons or undertake a nuclear test program", so maintaining a policy of nuclear ambiguity. Before the Yom Kippur War Peres nonetheless wanted Israel to publicly demonstrate its nuclear capability to discourage an Arab attack, and fear of Israeli nuclear weapons may have discouraged Arab military strategy during the war from being as aggressive as it could have been.

The CIA believed that Israel's first bombs may have been made with highly enriched uraniumstolen in the mid-1960s from the U.S. Navy nuclear fuel plant operated by the Nuclear Materials and Equipment Corporation, where sloppy material accounting would have masked the theft.

By 1974 U.S. Intelligence believed Israel had stockpiled a small number of fission weapons, and by 1979 were perhaps in a position to test a more advanced small tactical nuclear weapon or thermonuclear weapontrigger design.

The CIA believed that the number of Israeli nuclear weapons stayed from 10 to 20 from 1974 until the early 1980s. Vanunu's information in October 1986 said that based on a reactor operating at 150 megawatts and a production of 40 kg of plutonium per year, Israel had 100 to 200 nuclear devices. Vanunu revealed that between 1980 and 1986 Israel attained the ability to build thermonuclear weapons. By the mid 2000s (decade) estimates of Israel's arsenal ranged from 75 to 400 nuclear warheads.

Several reports have surfaced claiming that Israel has some uranium enrichment capability at Dimona. Vanunu asserted that gas centrifuges were operating in Machon 8, and that a laser enrichment plant was being operated in Machon 9 (Israel holds a 1973 patent on laser isotope separation). According to Vanunu, the production-scale plant has been operating since 1979–80. The scale of a centrifuge operation would necessarily be limited due to space constraints. Laser isotope separation, however, if developed to operational status, could be quite compact. If highly enriched uranium is being produced in substantial quantities, then Israel's nuclear arsenal could be much larger than estimated solely from plutonium production. Uranium enrichment could also be used to re-enrichreprocessed uranium into reactor fuel to more efficiently use Israel's uranium supply.

In 1991 alone, as the Soviet Union dissolved, nearly 20 top Jewish Soviet scientists reportedly emigrated to Israel, some of whom had been involved in operating nuclear power plants and planning for the next generation of Soviet reactors. In September 1992, German intelligence was quoted in the press as estimating that 40 top Jewish Soviet nuclear scientists had emigrated to Israel since 1989.

In a 2010 interview, Uzi Eilam, former head of the Israeli Atomic Energy Commission, told the Israeli daily *Maariv* that the nuclear reactor in Dimona had been through extensive improvements and renovations and is now functioning as new, with no safety problems or hazard to the surrounding environment or the region.

NUCLEAR TESTING

According to Lieutenant Colonel Warner D. Farr in a report to the USAF Counterproliferation Center much lateral proliferation happened between pre-nuclear Israel and France stating "the French nuclear test in 1960 made two nuclear powers not one—such was the depth of collaboration" and "the Israelis had unrestricted access to French nuclear test explosion data." minimizing the need for early Israeli testing though this cooperation cooled following the success of the French tests.

In June 1976, a West Germany army magazine, *Wehrtechnik* ("military technology"), claimed that Western intelligence reports documented Israel had conducted an underground test in the Negev in 1963. The book *Nuclear Weapons in the Middle East: Dimensions and Responsibilities* by Taysir Nashif cites other reports that on November 2, 1966, the country may have carried out a non-nuclear test, speculated to be zero yield or implosion in nature at Al-Naqab, in the Israeli Negev desert region.

On September 22, 1979 Israel may have been involved in a possible South African nuclear bomb test also known as the Vela Incident in the southern Indian Ocean. A secret committee was set up under then U.S. president Jimmy Carter headed by Prof. Jack Ruina of MIT. Most of the committee's members assumed that South African navy vessels had sailed out of Simonstown port, near Cape Town, to a secret location in the Indian Ocean, where they conducted the nuclear test. The committee defined the nuclear device tested as compact and especially clean, emitting little radioactive fallout, making it very nearly impossible to pinpoint. Another committee assessment concluded a cannon had fired a nuclear artillery shell and the detected test was focused on a small tactical nuclear weapon. After renouncing their nuclear weapons South Africa was revealed to only have six large and of the most primitive aircraft deliverable atomic bombs with a seventh being built but no sophisticated miniaturized devices in the artillery shell size.

REVELATIONS

Dimona

The Israeli nuclear program was first revealed publicly on December 13, 1960, in a small *Time* article, which said that a non-Communist non-NATO country had made an "atomic development". On December 16, the *Daily Express* revealed this country to be Israel, and on December 18, US Atomic Energy Commission chairman John McCone appeared on *Meet the Press* to officially confirm the Israeli construction of a nuclear reactor and announce his resignation. The following day *The New York Times*, with the help of McCone, revealed that France was assisting Israel.

The news led Ben-Gurion to make the only statement by an Israeli Prime Minister about Dimona. On December 21 he announced to theKnesset that the government was building a 24 megawatt reactor "which will serve the needs of industry, agriculture, health, and science", and that it "is designed exclusively for peaceful purposes". Bergmann, who was chairman of the Israel Atomic Energy Commission from 1954 to 1966, however said that "There is no distinction between nuclear energy for peaceful purposes or warlike ones" and that "We shall never again be led as lambs to the slaughter".

Weapons Production

The first public revelation of Israel's nuclear capability (as opposed to development program) came from NBC News, which reported in January 1969 that Israel decided "to embark on a crash course program to produce a nuclear weapon" two years previously, and that they possessed or would soon be in possession of such a device. This was initially dismissed by Israeli and U.S. officials, as well as in an article in *The New York Times*. Just one year later on July 18, *The New York Times* made public for the first time that the U.S. government believed Israel to possess nuclear weapons or to have the "capacity to assemble atomic bombs on short notice". Israel reportedly assembled 13 bombs during the Yom Kippur War as a last defence against total defeat, and kept them usable after the war.

The first extensive details of the weapons program came in the London-based *Sunday Times* on October 5, 1986, which printed information provided by Mordechai Vanunu, a technician formerly employed at the Negev Nuclear Research Center near Dimona. For publication of state secrets Vanunu was kidnapped by the Mossad in Rome, brought back to Israel, and sentenced to 18 years in prison for treason and espionage. Although there had been much speculation prior to Vanunu's revelations that the Dimona site was creating nuclear weapons, Vanunu's information indicated that Israel had also built thermonuclear weapons.

Theodore Taylor, a highly respected former U.S. weapon designer leading the field in small, efficient nuclear weapons, reviewed the 1986 leaks and photographs of the Israeli nuclear program by Mordechai Vanunu in detail. Taylor concluded that Israel's thermonuclear weapon designs appeared to be "less complex than those of other nations," and as of 1986 "not capable of producing yields in the megaton or higher range." Nevertheless, "they may produce at least several times the yield of fission weapons with the same quantity of plutonium or highly enriched uranium." In other words, Israel could "boost" the yield of its nuclear fission weapons. According to Taylor, the uncertainties involved in the process of boosting required more than theoretical analysis for full confidence in the weapons' performance. Taylor therefore concluded that Israel had "unequivocally" tested a miniaturized nuclear device. The Institute for Defence Analyses (IDA) concluded after reviewing the evidence given by Vanunu that as of 1987, "the Israelis are roughly where the U.S. was in the fission weapon field in about 1955 to 1960." and would require supercomputers or parallel computing clusters to refine their hydrogen bomb designs for improved yields without testing, though noting they were already then developing the computer code base required.

In May 2008, former U.S. President Jimmy Carter stated that "Israel has 150 or more [nuclear weapons]."

According to a 2013 report by the Bulletin of the Atomic Scientists, which cited US Defence Intelligence Agency figures, Israel began the production of nuclear weapons in 1967, when it produced its first two nuclear bombs. According to the report's calculations, Israel produced nuclear weapons at an average rate of two per year, and stopped production in 2004. The report stated that Israel has 80 nuclear warheads and has enough fissile material to produce 190 more.

South African Documents

In 2010, *The Guardian* released South African government documents that it alleged confirmed the existence of Israel's nuclear arsenal. According to the newspaper, the documents are minutes taken by the South African side of alleged meetings between senior officials from the two countries in 1975. *The Guardian* alleged that these documents reveal that Israel had offered to sell South Africa nuclear weapons that year. The documents appeared to confirm information disclosed by a former South African naval commander Dieter Gerhardt – jailed in 1983 for spying for the Soviet Union, who said there was an agreement between Israel and South Africa involving an offer by Israel to arm eight Jericho missiles with atomic bombs. Waldo Stumpf—who led a project to dismantle South Africa's nuclear weapons program—doubted Israel or South Africa would have contemplated a deal seriously, saying that Israel could not have offered to sell nuclear warheads to his country due to the serious international complications that such a deal could have. Shimon Peres, now Israeli President and then Defence Minister, has rejected the newspaper's claim that the negotiations took place. He also asserted that *The Guardian*'s conclusions were "based on the selective interpretation of South African documents and not on concrete facts".

Avner Cohen, author of *Israel and the Bomb* and *The Worst-Kept Secret: Israel's Bargain with the Bomb*, said "Nothing in the documents suggests there was an actual offer by Israel to sell nuclear weapons to the regime in Pretoria."

US Pressure

The United States was concerned over possible Israeli nuclear proliferation. US intelligence began to notice the Dimona reactor shortly after construction began, when American U-2 spy planes overflew the reactor, which lead to a diplomatic clash. In 1960, the outgoing Eisenhower administration asked the Israeli government for an explanation for the mysterious construction near Dimona. Israel's response was that the site was a future textile factory, but that no inspection would be allowed. When Ben-Gurion visited Washington in 1960, he held a series of meetings with State Department officials, and was bluntly told that for Israel to possess nuclear weapons would affect the balance of power in the region. John F. Kennedy took office as US President in 1961, he put continuous pressure on Israel to open the plant to American inspection. Reportedly, every high-level meeting and communication between the US and Israeli governments contained a demand for an inspection of Dimona. To increase pressure, Kennedy denied Ben-Gurion a meeting at the White House - when they met in May 1961, it was at the Waldorf Astoria Hotel in New York. The meeting itself was dominated by this issue. Ben-Gurion was evasive on the issue for two years, in the face of persistent US demands for an inspection. Finally, in a personal letter dated May 18, 1963, Kennedy threatened Israel with total isolation unless inspectors were allowed into Dimona. However, Ben-Gurion resigned as Prime Minister shortly afterward. His successor, Levi Eshkol, received a similar letter from Kennedy.

Israel eventually accepted an inspection, and Kennedy made two concessions - the US would sell Israel Hawk anti-aircraft missiles after having refused to sell Israel any major weapon systems for years.

In addition, the US government agreed to the Israeli demand that the inspections would be carried out by an all-American team which would schedule its visits weeks in advance, rather than the IAEA.

In 1964, the US government tried to prevent Argentina's sale of yellowcake to Israel, with no success.

Allegedly, because Israel knew the schedule of the inspectors' visits, it was able to disguise the true purpose of the reactor. The inspectors eventually reported that their inspections were useless, due to Israeli restrictions on what parts of the facility they could investigate. According to British writer and intelligence expert Gordon Thomas, former Mossad agent Rafi Eitan told him how the inspectors were fooled:

A bogus control center was built over the real one at Dimona, complete with fake control panels and computer-lined gauges that gave a credible impression of measuring the output of a reactor engaged in an irrigation scheme to turn the Negev into a lush pastureland. The area containing the "heavy" water smuggled from France and Norway was placed off-limits to the inspectors "for safety reasons". The sheer volume of heavy water would have been proof the reactor was being readied for a very different purpose.

In 1968, the CIA stated in a top-secret National Intelligence Estimate that Israel had nuclear weapons. This assessment was given to President Lyndon B. Johnson. The basis for this claim was the CIA's belief, although never proven, that the uranium that went missing in the Apollo Affair had been diverted to Israel, as well as evidence gathered from NSA electronic eavesdropping on Israeli communications, which proved that the Israeli Air Force had engaged in practice bombing runs that only made sense for the delivery of nuclear weapons.

In 1969, the US government terminated the inspections. That same year, Richard Nixon became President. According to US government documents declassified in 2007, the Nixon administration was concerned with Israel's nuclear program, worrying that it could set off a regional nuclear arms race, with the Soviet Union possibly granting the Arab states a nuclear guarantee. In a memorandum dated July 19, 1969, National Security Adviser Henry Kissinger warned that "The Israelis, who are one of the few peoples whose survival is genuinely threatened, are probably more likely than almost any other country to actually use their nuclear weapons." However, Kissinger warned that attempting to force Israel to disarm could have consequences, writing that "Israel will not take us seriously on the nuclear issue unless they believe we are prepared to withhold something they very much need" (Kissinger was referring to a pending sale of F-4 Phantom fighter jets to Israel). Kissinger wrote that "if we withhold the Phantoms and they make this fact public in the United States, enormous political pressure will be mounted on us.

We will be in an indefensible position if we cannot state why we are withholding the planes. Yet if we explain our position publicly, we will be the ones to make Israel's possession of nuclear weapons public with all the international consequences this entails." Among the suggestions Kissinger presented to Nixon was the idea of the United States adopting a policy of "nuclear ambiguity", or pretending not to know about Israel's nuclear program.

According to Israeli historian Avner Cohen, author of *Israel and the Bomb*, historical evidence indicates that when Nixon met with Israeli Prime Minister Golda Meir at the White House in September 1969, they reached a secret understanding, where Israel would keep its nuclear program secret and refrain from carrying out nuclear tests, and the United States would tolerate Israel's possession of nuclear weapons and not press it to sign the Nuclear Non-Proliferation Treaty.

Stockpile

The State of Israel has never made public any details of its nuclear capability or arsenal. The following is a history of estimates by many different sources on the size and strength of Israel's nuclear arsenal. Estimates may vary due to the amount of material Israel has on store versus assembled weapons, and estimates as to how much material the weapons actually use, as well as the overall time in which the reactor was operated.

- 1967 (Six Day War)– 2 bombs; 13 bombs
- 1969– 5–6 bombs of 19 kilotons yield each
- 1973 (Yom Kippur War)– 13 bombs; 20 nuclear missiles plus developed a suitcase bomb
- 1974– 3 capable artillery battalions each with 12 175 mm tubes and a total of 108 warheads; 10 bombs
- 1976– 10–20 nuclear weapons
- 1980– 100–200 bombs
- 1984– 12–31 atomic bombs; 31 plutonium bombs and 10 uranium bombs
- 1985– at least 100 nuclear bombs
- 1986– 100 to 200 fission bombs and a number of fusion bombs
- 1991– 50–60 to 200–300
- 1992– more than 200 bombs
- 1994– 64–112 bombs (5 kg/warhead); 50 nuclear tipped Jericho missiles, 200 total
- 1995– 66–116 bombs (at 5 kg/warhead); 70–80 bombs; "A complete Repertoire" (neutron bombs, nuclear mines, suitcase bombs, submarine-borne)
- 1996– 60–80 plutonium weapons, maybe more than 100 assembled, ER variants, variable yields
- 1997– More than 400 deliverable thermonuclear and nuclear weapons
- 2002– Between 75 and 200 weapons
- 2004– 82
- 2006– Federation of American Scientists believes that Israel "could have produced enough plutonium for at least 100 nuclear weapons, but probably not significantly more than 200 weapons".
- 2008– 150 or more nuclear weapons.
- 2008– 80 intact warheads, of which 50 are re-entry vehicles for delivery by ballistic missiles and the rest bombs for delivery by aircraft. Total military plutonium stockpile 340–560 kg.
- 2009– Estimates of weapon numbers differ sharply with plausible estimates varying from 60 to 400.
- 2010– According to *Jane's Defence Weekly* Israel has

between 100 and 300 nuclear warheads, most of them are probably being kept in unassembled mode but can become fully functional "in a matter of days".

- 2010– "More than 100 weapons, mainly two-stage thermonuclear devices, capable of being delivered by missile, fighter-bomber, or submarine"

DELIVERY SYSTEMS

Israeli military forces possess land, air, and sea based methods for deploying their nuclear weapons, thus forming a nuclear triad that is mainly medium to long ranged, the backbone of which is submarine-launched cruise missiles and medium and intercontinental ballistic missiles, with Israeli Air Force long range strike aircraft fulfilling the role played by intercontinental strategic bombers in the Russian and American nuclear forces due to mostly regional threats. During 2008 the Jericho III ICBM became operational, giving Israel extremely long range nuclear strike abilities.

Missiles

Israel is believed to have nuclear second-strike abilities in the form of its submarine fleet and its nuclear-capable ballistic missiles that are understood to be buried deeply enough that they would survive a Pre-emptive nuclear strike. Ernst David Bergmann was the first to seriously begin thinking about ballistic missile capability and Israel test-fired its first Shavit II sounding rocket in July 1961. In 1963 Israel put a large-scale project into motion, to jointly develop and build 25 short-range missiles with the French aerospace company Dassault.

The Israeli project, codenamed Project 700, also included the construction of a missile field at Hirbat Zacharia, a site west of Jerusalem. The missiles that were first developed with France became the Jericho I system, first operational in 1971. It is possible that the Jericho I was removed from operational service during the 1990s. In the mid-1980s the Jericho II medium-range missile, which is believed to have a range of 2800–5000 km, entered service. It is believed that Jericho II is capable of delivering nuclear weapons with a superior degree of accuracy. The Shavit three stages solid fuel space launch vehicle produced by Israel to launch many of its satellites into low earth orbit since 1988 is a civilian version of the Jericho II. The Jericho III ICBM, became operational in January 2008 and some reports speculate that the missile may be able to carry MIRVed warheads.The maximum range estimation of the Jericho III is 11,500 km with a payload of 1000–1300 kg (up to six small nuclear warheads of 100 kt each or one 1 megaton nuclear warhead), and its accuracy is considered high. In January 2008 Israel carried out the successful test launch of a long-range, ballistic missile capable of carrying a nuclear warhead from the reported launch site at the Palmachim Airbase south of Tel Aviv. Israeli radio identified the missile as a Jericho III and the Hebrew YNet news Web site quoted unnamed defence officials as saying the test had been "dramatic" and that the new missile can reach "extremely long distances", without elaborating. Soon after the successful test launch, Isaac Ben-Israel, a retired army general and Tel Aviv University professor who is now an MP, told Israeli Channel 2 TV:

Everybody can do the math and understand that the significance is that we can reach with a rocket engine to every point in the world.

The test came two days after Ehud Olmert, then Israel's Prime Minister, warned that "all options were on the table to prevent Tehranfrom acquiring nuclear weapons" and a few months later Israel bombed a suspected Syrian nuclear facility built with extensive help from North Korea. At the same time, regional defence experts said that by the beginning of 2008, Israel had already launched a programme to extend the range of its existing Jericho II ground attack missiles. The Jericho-II B missile is capable of sending a one ton nuclear payload 5,000 kilometers. The range of Israels' Jericho II B missiles is reportedly capable of being modified to carry nuclear warheads no heavier than 500 kg over 7,800 km, making it an ICBM. It is estimated that Israel has between 50 and 100Jericho II B missiles based at facilities built in the 1980s. The number of Jericho III missiles that Israel possesses is unknown.

Aircraft

Israel is believed to use fighter bombers as a means to deliver nuclear weapons. The Israeli Aerial refueling fleet of modified Boeing 707sand the use of external and conformal fuel tanks gives Israeli F-15s and F-16s strategic reach as demonstrated in Operation Wooden Leg. F-16 fighter aircraft have been cited as possible nuclear delivery systems. While such aircraft are generally not favored as a delivery platform by other nuclear states due to their limited range and payload, the situation in Israel makes their potential use plausible. Most realistic targets for a possible Israeli nuclear strike are significantly closer than other nations envisaged making strikes and would likely only require a small number of warheads to ensure success, compared to hundreds or thousands needed by a first strike attack against the USSR or NATO. The U.S. Air Force has retained a tactical nuclear strike ability on it's F-15,F-15E, and F-16, so the capability is not unprecedented.

Present

The Israeli Air Force possesses the following types of strike fighters:

- Lockheed Martin F-16I Sufa ("Storm")
- McDonnell Douglas/Boeing F-15I Ra'am ("Thunder")

Marine

The Israeli Navy operates modern German-built *Dolphin*-class submarines. The first three Dolphins were delivered to Israel in 1999 and replaced the aging Gal class submarines, which had served in the Israeli navy since the late 1970s. Various reportsindicate that these submarines are equipped with Popeye Turbo cruise missiles that can deliver nuclear and conventional warheads with extremely high accuracy. The proven effectiveness of cruise missiles of its own production may have been behind Israel's recent acquisition of these submarines which are equipped with torpedo tubes suitable for launching long-range (1500–2400 km) nuclear-capable cruise missiles that would offer Israel a second strike capability. Israel is reported to possess a 200 kg nuclear warhead, containing 6 kg of plutonium, that could be mounted on cruise missiles. The missiles were reportedly test launched in theIndian Ocean near Sri Lanka in June 2000, and are reported to have hit their target at a range of 1500 km. In June 2002, former State Department and Pentagon officials confirmed that the US Navy observed Israeli missile tests in the Indian Ocean in 2000, and that the Dolphin-class vessels have been fitted with nuclear-capable cruise missiles of a new design. It is believed by some to be a version ofRafael Armament Development Authority's Popeye turbo cruise missile while some believe that the missile may be a version of the Gabriel 4LR that is produced by Israel Aircraft Industries. However, others claim that such a range implies an entirely new type of missile. During the second half of the 1990s, Israel asked the United States to sell it 50 Tomahawk land-attack cruise missiles to enhance its deep-strike capabilities. Washington rejected Israel's request in March 1998, since such a sale would have violated the Missile Technology Control Regime guidelines, which prohibit the transfer of missiles with a range exceeding 300 km.

Shortly after the rejection, an Israeli official told Defence News, "History has taught us that we cannot wait indefinitely for Washington to satisfy our military requirements. If this weapon system is denied to us, we will have little choice but to activate our own defence industry in pursuit of this needed capability." In July 1998, the Air Intelligence Center warned the US Congress that Israel was developing a new type of cruise missile.

According to Israeli defence sources, in June 2009 Israeli Dolphin-class submarine sailed from the Mediterranean to the Red Sea via theSuez Canal during a drill that showed that Israel can access the Indian Ocean, and the Persian Gulf, far more easily than before.IDF sources said the decision to allow navy vessels to sail through the canal was made recently and was a definite "change of policy" within the service. Israeli officials said the sub passed through the canal above water. In the event of a conflict with Iran, and if Israel decided to involve its Dolphin-class submarines, the quickest route would be to send them through the Suez Canal.

The Israeli fleet was expanded after Israel signed a 1.3 billion euro contract to purchase two additional submarines from Thyssen Krupp's subsidiary HDW in 2006. These two U212s are to be delivered to the Israeli navy in 2011 and are "Dolphin II" class submarines. The submarines are believed to be capable of launching cruise missiles carrying nuclear warheads, despite statements by the German government in 2006, in confirming the sale of the two vessels, that they were not equipped to carry nuclear weapons. The two new boats are an upgraded version of the old Dolphins, and equipped with an air-independent propulsion system, that allow them to remain submerged for longer periods of time than the three nuclear arms-capable submarines that have been in Israel's fleet since 1999. In October 2009 it was reported that the Israeli navy sought to buy a sixth Dolphin class submarine.

On June 4, 2012, *Der Spiegel* published an investigative article stating that Israel has armed its newest submarines with nuclear missiles. Numerous Israeli and German officials were quoted testifying to the nuclear capabilities of the submarines and the placement of nuclear missiles aboard the ships. In response to the article, officials from both Germany and Israel refused to comment. Several papers have stated the implications of Israel attaining these nuclear weapon carrying submarines are increased due to the threat of attacks upon Iran by Israel.

Other

It has been reported that Israel has several other nuclear weapons capabilities:

- Suitcase bomb: Seymour Hersh reports that Israel developed the ability to miniaturize warheads small enough to fit in a suitcase by the year 1973.
- Tactical nuclear weapon: Israel may also have 175 mm and 203 mm self-propelled artillery pieces, capable of firing nuclear shells. There are three battalions of the 175mm artillery (36 tubes), reportedly with 108 nuclear shells and more for the 203mm tubes. If true, these low yield, tactical nuclear artillery rounds could reach at least 25 miles (40 km), while by some sources it is possible that the range was extended to 45 miles (72 km) during the 1990s.
- EMP strike capabilities: Israel allegedly possesses several 1 megaton bombs, which give it a very large EMP attack abilities. For example, if a megaton class weapon were to be detonated 400 kilometers above Omaha, NE, USA, nearly the entire continental United States would be affected with potentially damaging EMP experience from Boston to Los Angeles and fromChicago to New Orleans. A similar high altitude airburst above Iran could cause serious damage to all of the electrical systems in the Middle East, and much of Europe.
- Enhanced Radiation Weapon (ERW): Israel also is reported to have an unknown number of neutron bombs.
- Nuclear land mine: Israel supposedly has deployed multiple defensive nuclear land mines in the Golan Heights.

POLICY

Israel's refusal to admit it has nuclear weapons or to state its policy on use of them make it necessary to gather details from other sources, including 'unauthorized' statements by its political and military leaders.

Possession

Although Israel has officially acknowledged the existence of Dimona since Ben-Gurion's speech to the Knesset in December 1960, Israel has never officially acknowledged its construction or possession of nuclear weapons. In addition to this policy, on May 18, 1966, Prime Minister Levi Eshkol told the Knesset that "Israel has no atomic weapons and will not be the first to introduce them into our region," a policy first articulated by Shimon Peres to U.S. President John F. Kennedy in April 1963. In the late 1960s, Israeli Ambassador to the US Yitzhak Rabin informed the United States State Department that its understanding of "introducing" such weapons meant that they would be tested and publicly declared, while merely possessing the weapons did not constitute "introducing" them. Avner Cohen defines this initial posture as "nuclear ambiguity", but he defines the stage after it became clear by 1970 that Israel possessed nuclear weapons as a policy of *amimut*, or "nuclear opacity".

In 1998, former Prime Minister Shimon Peres said that Israel "built a nuclear option, not in order to have a Hiroshima but an Oslo".The "nuclear option" may refer to a nuclear weapon or to the nuclear reactor near Dimona, which Israel claims is used for scientific research. Peres, in his capacity as the Director General of the Ministry of Defence in the early 1950s, was responsible for building Israel's nuclear capability.

In a December 2006 interview, Israeli Prime Minister Ehud Olmert stated that Iran aspires "to have a nuclear weapon as America, France, Israel and Russia". Olmert's office later said that the quote was taken out of context; in other parts of the interview, Olmert refused to confirm or deny Israel's nuclear weapon status.

Doctrine

Israel's nuclear doctrine is shaped by its lack of strategic depth: a subsonic fighter jet could cross the 72 kilometres (39 nmi) from theJordan River to the Mediterranean Sea in just 4 minutes. It additionally relies on a reservist-based military which magnifies civilian and military losses in its small population. Israel tries to compensate for these weaknesses by emphasising intelligence, maneuverability and firepower.

As a result, its strategy is based on the premise that it cannot afford to lose a single war, and thus must prevent them by maintaining deterrence, including the option of preemption. If these steps are insufficient, it seeks to prevent escalation and determine a quick and decisive war outside of its borders.

Strategically, Israel's long-range missiles, nuclear-capable aircraft, and possibly its submarines present an effective second strikedeterrence against unconventional and conventional attack, and if Israel's defences fail and its population centres are threatened, the Samson Option, an all-out attack against an adversary; would be employed. Its nuclear arsenal can also be used tactically.

Although nuclear weapons are viewed as the ultimate guarantor of Israeli security, as early as the 1960s the country has avoided building its military around them, instead pursuing absolute conventional superiority so as to forestall a last-resort nuclear engagement.

According to historian Avner Cohen, Israel first articulated an official policy on the use of nuclear weapons in 1966, which revolved around four "red lines" that could lead to a nuclear response:

1. A successful military penetration into populated areas within Israel's post-1949 (pre-1967) borders.
2. The destruction of the Israeli Air Force.
3. The exposure of Israeli cities to massive and devastating air attacks or to possible chemical or biological attacks.
4. The use of nuclear weapons against Israeli territory.

Use

On October 8, 1973, just after the start of the Yom Kippur War, Golda Meir and her closest aides decided to put eight nuclear armed F-4s at Tel Nof Airbase on 24 hour alert and as many nuclear missile launchers at Sedot Mikha Airbase operational as possible. Seymour Hersh adds that the initial target list that night "included the Egyptian and Syrian military headquarters near Cairo and Damascus".This nuclear alert was meant not only as a means of precaution, but to push the Soviets to restrain the Arab offensive and to convince the US to begin sending supplies. One later report said that a Soviet intelligence officer did warn the Egyptian chief of staff, and colleagues of US National Security Advisor Henry Kissinger said that the threat of a nuclear exchange caused him to urge for a massive Israeli resupply. Hersh points out that before Israel obtained its own satellite capability, it engaged in espionage against the United States to obtain nuclear targeting information on Soviet targets.

Israeli military and nuclear doctrine increasingly focused on preemptive war against any possible attack with conventional, chemical, biological or nuclear weapons, or even a potential conventional attack on Israel's weapons of mass destruction.

Louis René Beres, who contributed to Project Daniel, urges that Israel continue and improve these policies, in concert with the increasingly preemptive nuclear policies of the United States, as revealed in the Doctrine for Joint Nuclear Operations.

After Iraq attacked Israel with Scud missiles during the 1991 Gulf War, Israel went on full-scale nuclear alert and mobile nuclear missile launchers were deployed. In the build up to the United States 2003 invasion of Iraq, there were concerns that Iraq would launch an unconventional weapons attack on Israel. President George W. Bush, the then Israeli Prime Minister Ariel Sharonwarned "If our citizens are attacked seriously — by a weapon of mass destruction, chemical, biological or by some mega-terror attack act — and suffer casualties, then Israel will respond." Israeli officials interpreted President Bush's stance as allowing a nuclear Israeli retaliation on Iraq, but only if Iraq struck before the U.S. military invasion.

Maintaining Nuclear Superiority

Alone or with other nations, Israel has used diplomatic and military efforts as well as covert action to prevent other Middle Eastern countries from acquiring nuclear weapons.

For example, it is believed that Israel filed a false laser patent in the late 1970s to mislead Arab nuclear research. Mossad agents triggered explosions in April 1979 at a French production plant near Toulouse, damaging the two reactor cores destined for the Iraqi reactors. Mossad agents may also have been behind the assassinations of an Egyptian nuclear engineer in Paris as well as two Iraqi engineers, all working for the Iraqi nuclear program.

On June 7, 1981, Israel launched a preemptive air strike against Saddam Hussein's breeder reactor in Osirak, Iraq, in Operation Opera. The Mossad – as well as any number of other intelligence agencies – are also frequently said to have assassinated professor Gerald Bull, an artillery expert, who was allegedly building a massive cannon or "super gun" for Saddam Hussein in the 1980s, which was capable of delivering a tactical nuclear payload.

On September 6, 2007, Israel launched an air strike dubbed Operation Orchard against a target in the Deir ez-Zor region of Syria. While Israel refused to comment, unnamed US officials said Israel had shared intelligence with them that North Korea was cooperating with Syria on some sort of nuclear facility. Both Syria and North Korea denied the allegation and Syria filed a formal complaint with the United Nations. The International Atomic Energy Agency concluded in May 2011 that the destroyed facility was "very likely" an undeclared nuclear reactor.

Journalist Seymour Hersh speculated that this air strike might have been intended as a trial run for striking alleged Iranian nuclear weapons facilities. On January 7, 2007, *The Sunday Times* reported that Israel had drawn up plans to destroy three Iranian nuclear facilities with low-yield nuclear bunker-busters that would be launched by aircraft through "tunnels" created by conventional laser-guided bombs. These tactical nuclear weapons would then explode underground to reduce radioactive fallout. Israel swiftly denied the specific allegation and analysts expressed doubts about its reliability. However, in 2004 its then Defence minister said that it rules out no option. The death of the Iranian physicist Ardeshir Hassanpour, who may have been involved in the nuclear program, has been reported by the intelligence group Stratfor to have been a Mossad assassination. Iran is currently conducting atomic researchthat Israel fears is aimed at building a nuclear weapon. Israel has pressed for United Nations economic sanctions against Iran, and has repeatedly threatened to launch a military strike on Iran if the United States does not do so first.

The 2010 Stuxnet malware targeting Iran's nuclear program is widely believed to have been sponsored by Israel. In 2009, a year before Stuxnet was discovered, researcher Scott Borg suggested that Israel might prefer to mount a cyber-attack rather than a military strike on Iran's nuclear facilities. Iran uses IR-1 centrifuges at Natanz, which are based on the P-1 centrifuge, the design A. Q. Khanstole in 1976 and took to Pakistan. His black market nuclear-proliferation network sold P-1s to, among other customers, Iran and Libya. Experts believe that Israel also somehow acquired P-1s and tested Stuxnet on the centrifuges, installed at the Dimona facility that is part of its own nuclear program. The equipment may be from the United States, which received P-1s from Libya's former nuclear program.

Nuclear Non-Proliferation Treaty and United Nations' Resolutions

Israel was originally expected to sign the 1968 Nuclear Non-Proliferation Treaty (NPT) and on June 12, 1968, Israel voted in favour of the treaty in the UN General Assembly. But when the invasion of Czechoslovakia in August by the Soviet Union delayed ratification around the world, Israel's internal division and hesitation over the treaty became public. The Johnson administration attempted to use the sale of 50 F-4 Phantoms to pressure Israel to sign the treaty that fall, culminating in a personal letter from Lyndon Johnson to Israeli PMLevi Eshkol. But by November Johnson had backed away from tying the F-4 sale with the NPT after a stalemate in negotiations, and Israel would neither sign nor ratify the treaty. After the series of negotiations, U.S. assistant secretary of defence for international security Paul Warnke was convinced that Israel already possessed nuclear weapons. In 2007 Israel sought an exemption to non-proliferation rules in order to import atomic material legally.

In 1996, the United Nations General Assembly passed a resolution calling for the establishment of a nuclear-weapon-free zone in the region of the Middle East. Arab nations and annual conferences of the International Atomic Energy Agency (IAEA) repeatedly have called for application of IAEA safeguards and the creation of a nuclear-free Middle East. Arab nations have accused the United States of practicing a double standard in criticizing Iran's nuclear program while ignoring Israel's possession of nuclear weapons. According to a statement by the Arab League, Arab states will withdraw from the NPT if Israel acknowledges having nuclear weapons but refuses to open its facilities to international inspection and destroy its arsenal. In a statement to the May 2009 preparatory meeting for the 2010 NPT Review Conference, the US delegation reiterated the longstanding US support for "universal adherence to the NPT", but uncharacteristically named Israel among the four countries that have not done so. An unnamed Israeli official dismissed the suggestion that it would join the NPT and questioned the effectiveness of the treaty. *The Washington Times* reported that this statement threatened to derail the 40-year-old secret agreement between the U.S. and Israel to shield Israel's nuclear weapons program from international scrutiny, while Avner Cohen, author of *Israel and the Bomb*, argued that acknowledging its nuclear program would allow Israel to take part constructively in efforts to control nuclear weapons.

The Final Document of the 2010 NPT Review Conference calls for a conference in 2012 to implement a resolution of the 1995 NPT Review Conference that calls for the establishment of a Middle East Zone free of weapons of mass destruction. The United States joined the international consensus for Final Document, but criticized the section on the Middle East resolution for singling out Israel as the only state in the region that is not party to the NPT, while at the same time ignoring Iran's "longstanding violation of the NPT and UN Security Council Resolutions."

7

Chemical and Biological Warfare Threat

Future adversaries seeking asymmetric advantage will necessarily identify and attempt to exploit vulnerable U.S. Air Force (USAF) centres of gravity (COG). Drinking water is one such COG. Given that most if not all airmen (both operational and support personnel) drink water every day, an adversary could functionally destroy or disrupt USAF operations by injecting deadly chemicals or insidious infective agents into an air base water supply. This study addresses how an adversary might target water systems and with what chemical and biological weapons (CW/BW). The USAF needs to "check-six" before an adversary cuts its Achilles' Heel, grounding global engagement before "wheels are in the well."

Humans can live only minutes without air, perhaps several days without water and weeks without food. Yet, who deliberately forgoes water for even a day? It's axiomatic that in the course of everyday life all humans drink water. Americans in general take clean, potable water for granted because U.S. water systems produce some of the safest water in the world. Cholera, dysentery and other deadly waterborne epidemics are nightmares of the distant past, now relegated to the nightly news and the Third World. Or are they? Though the DESERT SHIELD RIVET JOINT and ABCCC aircrews and missions eventually recovered, had a saboteur laced the water with anthrax spore or sodium cyanide the results could have been catastrophic.

The study assumes the existence of adversaries (transnational or domestic terrorists and/or rogue states) who have the will to attack water supplies with CW/BW and the ability to produce or acquire sufficient quantities of a particular CW/BW agent. Base personnel are assumed to drink 2 to 15 liters per day (L/d), with the average drink being 0.25 liters. Mature theater air base water systems are assumed to generally conform to standard design criteria as outlined in Military Handbook 1164, *Operation and Maintenance of Water Supply Systems*. Bare base water systems in immature theatres are assumed to conform with Air Force Manual (AFM) 10-222, Volume 1, *Guide to Bare Base Development*. Water monitoring is assumed to be routine compliance sampling as required by Air Force Instruction (AFI) 48-119, *Medical Service Environmental Quality Programs*. This study references sources that identify biological and chemical agents and materials that are known to or presumably can cause acute illness or death from drinking water.

The analyses and findings are organized into three parts, followed by conclusions and a series of force protection recommendations. First, current USAF policy and conventional wisdom regarding water system vulnerability assessments and CW/BW attack are assessed. Though common in history, such attacks are largely ignored in official USAF policies and instructions, leaving operations potentially vulnerable. Next, to determine water system vulnerabilities, notional water systems are analyzed to identify common critical points (targets). Finally, the potential adversary's chemical and biological arsenals are examined. Various chemical weapon agents, industrial chemicals, pathogens and biological toxins are shown to be effective (cause incapacitating illness or death) from drinking water. Finally, this study concludes that if adversaries have access to certain chemical or biological weapons, and to the critical components of a base's water system, they may be able to cripple USAF operations. A series of recommendations are offered to focus attention on this significant force protection issue.

TAKING WATER FOR GRANTED

As the sole superpower, the United States is unlikely to be significantly challenged or defeated by conventional military means in the near future. Ironically, this superiority increases the likelihood of asymmetric attack against the U.S. and its fielded forces, as adversaries logically seek to exploit U.S. weaknesses. One such weakness is water. President Clinton targeted the risk in *A National Security Strategy for a New Century*:

Our military power and national economy are increasingly reliant upon interdependent critical infrastructures—the physical and information systems essential to the operations of the economy and government. They include telecommunications, energy, banking and finance, transportation, water systems and emergency services.... If we do not implement adequate protective measures, attacks on our critical infrastructures... might be capable of significantly harming our military power and economy.

Depending on objectives, an adversary could attack water in two ways. Physical or cyber attack on the system or its controls could deny water, degrading emergency services and organic community activity. Examples include destruction of dams, pumping stations, and distribution lines. To kill or disable humans, however, the adversary could deliberately contaminate the water with chemicals, biological pathogens or other toxins.

The President's Critical Infrastructure Assurance Office (CIAO) bluntly assessed the risk in *Preliminary Research and Development Roadmap for Protecting and Assuring Critical National Infrastructures*:

In general, vulnerability or risk evaluations that involve biological or chemical attacks by terrorists have not been performed for U.S. water-supply systems. However, a limited number of systems have been evaluated on behalf of the Commission. The results of these analyses indicated that most water supply systems are vulnerable to terrorist attack through the distribution network.

In the author's opinion and experience, the USAF would fare no better. Air Force vulnerability assessment guidance and practice isn't consistent among the various responsible agencies (Security Forces (SF), Bioenvironmental Engineering (BEE), and Civil Engineering (CE)). A disconnect exists between vulnerability assessments done by anti-terrorism experts (typically the SF and the USAF Office of Special Investigations (AFOSI)) and those done by water system experts in Bioenvironmental Engineering and Civil Engineering. The USAF Force Protection Battlelab agrees, summing up the situation like this:

[There is] No well institutionalized USAF process which addresses *intentional contamination* of food or water, especially from asymmetric attack. This vulnerability points out the need for assessing our food and water handling processes,...

The SF and AFOSI naturally focus on protection from physical attack. In the author's experience, vulnerability assessments conducted per this AFI are broad based installation assessments, and do not focus on the particular CW/BW threats and risk to water systems critical points. Additionally, the assessment teams rarely include a water system expert or a person versed in the water threats posed by CW/BW, such as one assigned to U.S. Air Force Bioenvironmental Engineering (BEE).

Per USAF policy the BEE is responsible for assessing water system vulnerability. Assessments are governed by AFI 48-119, *Medical Service Environmental Quality Programs*, and AFI 41-106, *Medical Readiness Planning and Training*. At fixed installations the BEE assesses as required by the various federal or state drinking water regulations, focusing on natural/unintentional contamination. These vulnerability assessments generally don't address deliberate contamination nor are they coordinated with AFI 31-210 assessments. There are no deployed location standards, though the 1991 Armstrong Laboratory report, *Water Vulnerability Assessments*, is a starting point and is used by some in the field.

The civil engineers operate and maintain USAF water systems and are the commander's principal advisors on CW/BW issues. Arguably, one would expect to find water system vulnerability assessment guidance in CE policy and instruction. The only significant discussion of deliberate waterborne risk is found in the field guide Air Force Handbook 10-222, *Guide to Civil Engineer Force Protection*. This handbook recognizes the possibility that CW/BW attacks in a deployed environment can be waterborne and provides a checklist of preventive measures. The primary CE contingency planning tool is the "Contingency Response Plan (CRP)." Annex P, "Main Water Supply and Distribution System," and Annex Q, "Alternate or Emergency Water Supply," to the Contingency Response Plan should address the threats, impacts and risks of deliberate CW/BW attack. In the author's experience as a MAJCOM evaluator, these annexes rarely address this contingency.

Perhaps the vulnerability assessment disconnect is the result of institutional myopia about the CW/BW risk to water systems. Air Force conventional wisdom focuses on aerial CW/BW attacks, omitting chemical threats to water and downplaying biological attacks as highly unlikely. Indeed, the Air Intelligence Agency report, *Worldwide Chemical-Biological Threat to USAF Air Bases: 1995-2005 (U)*, and USAF nuclear, biological and chemical (NBC) defence guidance (Air Force Manual (AFM) 32-4017, *Civil Engineer Readiness Technician's Manual for Nuclear, Biological and Chemical Defence)*, presume that CW/BW will be delivered by air (artillery, missiles, aircraft sprayers, etc.) against airmen, airfields and airplanes. Conventional wisdom also holds that any CW/BW risk to military water is from collateral (secondary) contamination of surface supplies. In this view, dilution and degradation in the air and water reduce weapon effectiveness. Additionally, since aerial attacks raise alarms, water contamination will be suspect and the water will be tested subsequently and treated prior to any consumption.

There is no dispute that aerial CW/BW attack could ground USAF operations, and it must not be discounted. However, downplaying the possibility and probability of water system attacks compromises USAF operational preparedness. In 20 pages of NBC hazard checklists, Air Force Manual (AFM) 32-4017 mentions water only twice, and not in terms of CW/BW threats ("Are there adequate supplies for drinking?" and "Do adequate supplies exist for contamination control and fire fighting activities?"). AFM 32-4017 leaves little doubt about the perceived risk of waterborne attack:

This method of delivery [water contamination] is probably of little threat to modern military and civilian populations because of advanced water treatment facilities. However, it may be a significant threat to less developed nations.

Information provided to senior leadership also downplays the waterborne risk. For example, even though Air Force Pamphlet 32-4019, *Chemical- Biological Warfare Commander's Guide*, recognizes covert operations have increased the potential for biological contamination of food and water supplies; nonetheless, when addressing protection, it makes no mention of securing water systems. Additionally, Air Force Handbook 32-4014,*USAF Operations in a Chemical and Biological (CB) Warfare Environment, Planning and Analysis*, fails to identify water as a significant threat vector, only recommending use of "approved food/water sources" in "low-risk" environments. However, this recommendation applies to all USAF operations regardless of CW/BW risk. The handbook offers no real mitigation for water system attacks. The airborne attack dogma has blinded force protection from historical realities.

Deliberate chemical and biological contamination of water supplies is common in history. Attacks have ranged from the crude dumping of human and animal cadavers into water supplies to well orchestrated contamination with anthrax and cholera. Cyanide has been used as a deadly waterborne poison for thousands of years. In ancient Rome, Nero eliminated his enemies with cherry laurel water (cyanide is the chief toxic ingredient). In the U.S. Civil War, Confederate soldiers shot and left farm animals to rot in ponds during General Sherman's march, compromising the Union water supply. During World War II, the Japanese attacked at least 11 Chinese cities, intending to contaminate food and water supplies with anthrax, cholera, and various other bacteria. Hitler's forces also released sewage into a Bohemia reservoir, deliberately sickening the rival population. Terrorists are using CW/BW. The Aum Shinrikyo Cult attacked a Tokyo subway with sarin gas in 1995 and they are known to have produced and unsuccessfully attempted to use anthrax and botulism toxin nine times as well. In 1985 the Rajneesh religious cult sickened 750 people in The Dalles, Oregon, by spreading salmonella bacteria on local salad bars. In an unprecedented violation of the Geneva Conventions, Yugoslav federal forces, or those allied with them, appear to have poisoned wells throughout Kosovo in October/November 1998. Those responsible dumped animal carcasses and hazardous materials (chemicals like paints, oil, and gasoline) into seventy percent of area wells, deliberately sickening the populace and denying them the use of the wells.

Despite a history of armies poisoning rival water supplies, USAF institutional dogma downplays the risk of asymmetric CW/BW attack on water. Nationally recognized as critical infrastructures, water systems, including the USAF's, are vulnerable to disabling attacks. At present, the USAF lacks an institutionalized assessment process of this threat. Instead, various agencies conduct discordant assessments, failing to scrutinize the primary risk of deliberate sabotage using CW/BW in water supplies.

WATER SYSTEM ANALYSIS

In order to successfully affect operations by water system attack, an adversary would have to dissect the water distribution system to target components vulnerable to attack. Air Force doctrine calls these components "critical points." This section is devoted to coarse analysis of notional water systems to identify potential critical points. Fixed-base water distribution systems, generally found in mature theatres of operation, are essentially community (city) water systems. Bare base systems are generally found in immature theatres of operations. Analyzing a notional community water system and a bare base (austere) system illuminates potential target sets for CW/BW attack.

Notional Community Water System

A community water system, whether it serves New York City, a summer camp in the Rocky Mountains, or a notional Air Force Base has four basic components. Arrows indicate water transport and flow direction in this system. Sources include treated water from other local systems, and raw water from deep wells and/or surface sources such as lakes, rivers or the ocean. Raw water is transported to a treatment plant to remove natural or manmade contaminants, ultimately producing drinking water. Drinking water is stored in clear wells or reservoirs and then pumped into the community's system under pressure. Within the system, pressure is maintained by booster pumps and usually one or more water towers. These towers store water and provide pressure in the system (known as "head") by force of gravity. The elevated water in the towers is typically not under pressure.

Raw water sources usually supply the system's water. Wells and surface sources might be geographically separated by miles from their treatment plants. In many cases they may be off the property boundary of the notional city or airbase. In properly constructed wells, submerged pumps collect water from relatively safe underground aquifers. Outside of the U.S., wells may be simple lined pits. All wells contain a confined volume of raw water that may be suitable for mixing or dissolving introduced CW/BW agents. Water is pumped to the surface, and then, as the arrows indicate, to the treatment system. Accessible wells are vulnerable. If a saboteur can circumvent the well casing, cap or other protection, he can contaminate the well. Because wells provide a potentially vulnerable confined volume from which water is transported directly into the distribution system, they are potential critical points for CW/BW attack.

While less vulnerable than wells, surface sources are also vulnerable critical points. Rivers, lakes and other surface bodies may also supply raw water. Collection systems vary, but essentially they all consist of an intake structure, pumps and pipes. Dilution makes effective contamination of these sources more difficult. The adversary must directly inject into the intake, or otherwise contaminate the source water to the poison's effective concentration in order to disrupt the community water system.

Local system water is the final water supply source. By policy, the USAF is required to use local municipal or regional systems whenever feasible. In this case two systems connect their distribution mains, allowing water transfer from one to the other. Valves usually control these connections, isolating the systems when necessary. Local water might be plumbed directly into the community system, or might be routed through the treatment plant first. In practice, the receiving system usually exercises little control over the operation and maintenance of the producing system. Therefore, since a saboteur could contaminate the receiving system via the local system, the local systems must be considered critical points.

Raw water is treated at the treatment plant to meet federal, state standards, or Department of Defence (for overseas fixed installations) guidelines and to improve its taste and corrosion characteristics. To meet standards, contaminants must be removed or neutralized. Treatment requirements vary greatly depending on raw water quality and community population (these factors affect which standards apply). A small system supplied by a secure well might only require simple chlorination. Larger systems with surface sources have multiple filtration, physical/chemical modification and disinfection units. Common in the U.S., but typically not used in Europe, chlorine disinfectant is added to kill microbial contamination and residual chlorine is maintained to control microbial life within the system. Examples of other chemical addition are precipitation of iron or other metals, reduction of the water's corrositivity and adding fluoride for children. Upon treatment, the water is considered potable or safe to drink.

By its very nature a treatment plant both provides security from and facilitates CW/BW attack. Treatment processes may very well remove/ neutralize an agent introduced into the raw water or local system. On the other hand, it is the controlling point for system quality where chemicals are deliberately and systematically added to the water. The plant lends itself as an ideal attack point for water downstream in the system. Therefore, treatment plants are potential critical points of a water distribution system.

After treatment, potable water is either pumped directly into the distribution system or stored in unpressurized clear wells (not a well, but a large, covered storage facility) or other reservoirs. From these the water is then pumped into the system. Clear wells and reservoirs provide disinfectant (typically chlorine) contact time and store system water. Unpressurized and typically only passively defended (usually covered, but not always locked), they are a relatively easy target for contamination. By design they provide contact time and mixing, and directly feed potable water into the distribution system, and therefore are critical points.

Water towers also store system water. Distribution system water is typically pumped up into the tower, which forms a reservoir and provides constant pressure in the system by force of gravity, reducing electric utility costs.

Like in the clear wells, these tanks are usually not under pressure. Similarly, they provide a high mixing volume and direct access to the potable water. They are passively defended with fences and gates on the ladders, and by the fact one must climb to the top to gain access. Like clear wells, they are critical points.

Post treatment and/or clear well, the water is pumped into the distribution system. The system is an underground network of iron, concrete or PVC (plastic) pipes that transport the treated water under pressure to the consumers. Ultimately, water is plumbed into each building from these underground mains. High pressure makes it difficult, though not impossible, to inject material into the typically buried lines. A distribution system typically has a variety of valve pits and other control points where maintenance personnel, or an adversary, may gain access to the water. Though relatively secure, the system pipes and valves are critical points.

Notional Austere Water System

The same four basic components make up a notional austere water system. They are source(s), treatment, storage and distribution. Transportation and storage differentiate the two system types. Trucks and above ground lines usually transport the water, and portable bladders are often used for storage.

Raw water sources face the same vulnerabilities as community systems. Wells may or may not exist, and those that do must be suspect until sanitary evaluations demonstrate their suitability. Third World wells often will not meet U.S. or European construction standards. Passively defended, they are vulnerable to sabotage and therefore are critical points. Surface sources are vulnerable to contamination, but this path is rendered inefficient by resultant dilution of the contaminant. To be effective, a saboteur must either con- taminate the entire source to the effective concentration, or inject directly into the intake. Though lower risk than wells, surface sources are critical points.

Transport to treatment will vary, from tanker truck or portable, above ground lines to, in some cases, buried semi-permanent lines. Anytime the water is above ground and/or not under pressure, access is relatively easy, facilitating sabotage. Treatment is typically reverse osmosis (RO) followed by chlorination. Portable RO units will remove nearly all suspended particulate (including biological matter) and many chemical contaminants. Again, treatment is a dual-edged sword. On the one hand it can provide protection from contaminants introduced at the source. But, in the wrong hands, it is a direct vector into the system's "potable" water. Therefore, bare base treatment is also a critical point.

Post treatment, water is typically pumped into unpressurized storage bladders. These bladders function as storage reservoirs. They suffer the same vulnerabilities (unpressurized, passive defence if any, long contact time, and feed the distribution systems) and therefore make inviting sabotage targets. Distribution of the water varies with the local conditions. Notionally, from the storage bladders it is trucked or piped to other bladders, and eventually distributed to the ultimate consumer. This might be from sinks and taps or from portable water buffaloes. In most cases the water isn't under high pressure and is only passively defended. Distribution at bare bases must be considered a critical point. In conclusion, water is an airbase center of gravity. The proceeding analyses of notional community and austere water systems reveals "critical points." These points provide potential targets for asymmetric CW/BW attacks. Wells, surface sources and local systems can be contaminated. Treatment operations are dual-edged, removing contaminants but also providing direct system access. Storage structures are ideal contamination points. Distribution networks may provide system access for potential adversaries.

CHEMICAL AND BIOLOGICAL THREATS IN DRINKING WATER

Any adversary with access to basic chemical, petrochemical, pharmaceutical, biotechnological or related industry can produce chemical or biological weapons. Compared to aerial attack (inhalation or skin contact), effective doses are easier to obtain in water (less dilution than air and directly ingested by the target airmen), and in many cases the materials are more stable (protected from ultraviolet and temperature extremes, although exposed to chlorine). To effectively kill or disable from drinking water chemical and biological agents must be:

1. Weaponized, meaning it can be produced and disseminated in large enough quantities to cause desired effect.
2. Water threat, meaning it is infectious or toxic from drinking water.
3. Stable, meaning the agent maintains it structural and virulent effects in water.
4. Chlorine resistance, meaning the agent isn't significantly oxidized by free available chlorine (FAC) present in most American water systems. USAF standard is typically 0.2 parts per million FAC. Chlorine susceptibility can be negated by inactivation of system chlorination devices.

Chemical weapons in this study are defined as the classic CW agents (nerve, blister, blood, etc.) and various industrial chemicals that could be used as water system poisons. Despite USAF institutional myopia in identifying threats to water attack, technical research by the USAF and Army public health communities has demonstrated the efficacy and effects of chemical or biological attacks on drinking water.

Summary of Applicable Studies

There are four major studies of the vulnerability of water supplies to CBW attacks. First, the seminal USAF study of CW/BW threats to water supplies is Major John Garland's Armstrong Laboratory Technical Report, *Water Vulnerability Assessments*, which focuses on water system emergency planning and identifies toxic concentrations of certain materials. Second, in another study by experts from the U.S. Army's Center for Health Promotion and Disease Prevention, titled *Natural And Terrorist Threats To Drinking Water Supplies*, identifies 11 CW/BW materials that are effective in drinking water. Third and fourth, the greatest volume of work, however, was by the National Research Council (NRC) and the Lawrence Livermore National Laboratory (LANL).

The NRC and LANL investigated the effects of CW agents and other chemicals in military (Army) field drinking water. The primary report is LANL's*Evaluation of Military Field-Water Quality*. In it a variety of CW agents and industrial chemicals are evaluated for the potential impact on military field operations. The NRC's Committee on Toxicology updated LANL's study with a more current assessment of the effects of specific CW agents in*Guidelines for Chemical Warfare Agents in Military Field Drinking Water*.

The LANL and NRC agree with conventional military CW/BW wisdom. The two reports assume natural or secondary contamination of the water source(s) versus contamination by direct attack or sabotage. The assumed at risk population is the average 70-kilogram soldier who, in field conditions will be drinking from 5 to 15 liters per day. The studies propose guideline contaminant concentrations below which military mission degradation isn't expected, but don't identify lethal or incapacitating doses.

The chemicals for which LANL and NRC propose acceptable guidelines are known or are expected to have certain human oral lethal/incapacitating dose levels. Those doses are necessarily greater than the reported acceptable consumption guidelines. Nonetheless, an adversary could conceivably inject sufficient material to generate concentrations well above the guideline acceptable doses, resulting in the death or disablement of all personnel who drank the water, causing major operational disruptions.

Chemical Agents

There are five types of CW agents: 1) nerve agents, 2) blister agents, 3) choking agents, 4) blood agents, and 5) hallucinogens. Many countries (Russia, China, North Korea, Iraq, and Iran for example) are known to possess, and in some cases have used, chemical weapons. The Aum Shinrikyo cult in Japan crossed a terrorist psychological barrier in 1995 when it attacked a Tokyo subway with sarin, a nerve agent. By design, these agents are most effective as vapor inhalation hazards, either through liquid or vapor contact. Even though their primary designed effects are through inhalation and by dermal exposure a few CW agents are lethal or incapacitating when placed in drinking water and ingested.

The LANL and NRC reports identify hydrogen cyanide (blood agent), the nerve agents Tabun, Sarin, Soman and VX, the blistering agents Lewisite and sulfur mustard, and the hallucinogen BZ as potential drinking water poisons. Garland focuses on LSD (a hallucinogen), nerve agents (VX is listed as most toxic), arsenic (Lewisite) and cyanide (hydrogen cyanide). Burrows, et al, list BZ, LSD and VX. These agents, however, are not the only chemicals a saboteur might use in drinking water.

Industrial Chemical Poisons

The world is replete with dangerous industrial chemicals, hazardous materials, pesticides, fungicides, and the like. Many of these are acutely toxic to humans in doses obtainable by deliberate water system contamination. While it's beyond the current scope of this study to exhaustively survey all known chemicals and hazardous materials to determine potential drinking water threats, a summary review by major classes (pesticides and inorganic chemicals) can indicate areas of concern. The LANL report considers general classes of chemicals, while Garland identifies several toxic compounds, and Burrows, et al, list a few specific threat agents.

Pesticides and Related Chemicals. These materials for the most part are designed to kill insects, rodents, fungi, plants, etc., and are produced, distributed and used throughout the world. Organophosphate pesticides, chlorinated pesticides, and rodenticides are particularly toxic and their effects on humans are nearly identical to that of CW nerve agents. Commercial products contain low concentrations of active ingredient, but a determined adversary could easily acquire pure active ingredients in the open or black markets. Malathion, methyl parathion, and chlorpyrifos are chemically very similar to the organophosphate nerve agents, paralyzing an insect's nervous system. Organochlorine pesticides, like lindane, dieldrin, methoxychlor and endosulfan, also affect the nervous system. The rodenticides sodium fluoroacetate, strychnine, crimidine, yellow phosphorus, and thallium sulfate can cause incapacitation or death in humans at very small doses. Burrows, et al, list sodium fluoroacetate and parathion, and Garland lists dieldrin as potential threat agents.

Inorganic Chemicals. These metal salts, acids, and other substances offer a wide variety of options to the potential saboteur. Arsenic and cyanide are strong potential threats according to the LANL report. Garland focuses on cyanide, arsenic, fluoride, cadmium and mercury. Burrows, et al, single out sodium cyanide. Arsenic, the active agent of Lewisite, is readily available on the open market, is soluble, and lethal in high doses. Cyanide, particularly sodium cyanide, is available on the worldwide open and black markets, is soluble, and certainly is lethal in relatively low doses. Magnesium, a soluble metal, and sulfate (an inorganic anion) can cause diarrhea in high oral doses.

Biological Agents

Similar to CW agents, most biological warfare (BW) agents are developed for aerial dissemination of an aerosolized organism or toxin. However, many lung-targeting BW agents might be effective via the digestive track, and some, *Shigella* spp. and *Vibrio cholerae* for example, are probably solely water-borne threats. In his seminal report, *Biological Warfare Agents as Potable Water Threats*, Jerry A. Valcik, P.E., states:

Most biotoxins [biological agents] would probably be effective threats to drinking water under suitable conditions. For others, however, either there is no known infectious path through ingestion, or the agent cannot survive in water.

There are two types of biological threats, pathogens and toxins. Pathogens are live organisms, such as bacteria, viruses or protozoa, which infect and cause illness and/or death. The other are biological toxins, chemicals derived from organisms, primarily bacteria and fungi, which cause chemical toxicity resulting in illness and/or death. For less than $10,000, anyone with gear no more sophisticated than a home brewing kit, protein cultures and personal protection can cultivate trillions of bacteria with relatively little personal risk.

Pathogens

Mankind wages a constant battle against pathogens. Bacteria, viruses, protozoa, nematodes fungi, and others are the causes of most infectious diseases. Living organisms, they require a host population and certain environmental conditions (temperature, humidity/water, and protection from sunlight) for survival. Upon infection, the pathogen must "grow" in the host. This latency period requires time, depending on the organism, from hours to weeks. Therefore, pathogens are:b best suited for covert, terrorist or non-conventional attack, the types central to this study. "Threat Potential of Pathogens," lists the drinking water threat potential of pathogens. As indicated, many BW pathogens have the essential characteristics of effective weapons. The bacterial agents in particular show great utility as weapons. Infectious doses range from the miniscule, 25 organisms (Tularemia), to around 500,000 for C. Perfringens. Many are stable in water and exhibit chlorine resistance.

Biological Toxins

Biological toxins are chemicals derived from the natural metabolic processes of organisms. From a practical perspective, they more closely resemble chemical threats than biological pathogens. Large scale fermentation of the parent organism and toxin recovery are feasible; particularly for bacteria derived toxins. Some may be synthesized in a laboratory. Many are environmentally stable and water soluble. Effective doses are extremely small, facilitating sabotage.

CHEMICAL AND BIOLOGICAL MONITORING AND DETECTION

Rapid detection and quantification of a CW/BW attack on a water supply is difficult at best. Unlike aerial delivery, a CW/BW attack via water won't be heralded by incoming missiles or bombs and concomitant weapons detonation. Dumping a thermos of concentrated anthrax spores into a clear well won't garner much attention. The first evidence of attack is likely to be a flood of sick or dying at the emergency room. By the time water is recognized as the source, identification and quantification of the agent could take days if not weeks. To further complicate force protection, the adversary could tailor the effect based on his objective, using chemicals or fast acting pathogens for a quick kill, or slower incubating pathogens for delayed effects.

Two operational constraints cause this situation. First, there is currently no real-time detection capability for BW pathogens in water, and only a limited capability for chemicals. The Bioenvironmental Engineering Flight (BEF), a component of each base's Aerospace Medicine Squadron, normally conducts both fixed-base and bare-base water sampling. The BEF typically operates a coliform bacteria analytical laboratory while centralized military or contract laboratories perform the vast majority of chemical analyses (the BEF uses field kits to analyze chlorine residual and hydrogen ion concentration (pH)). Unfortunately, a coliform analysis does not detect any of the pathogens. Microbiological analyses for BW pathogens, from collection to reporting results, can vary from a day to weeks, depending on transportation logistics and analytical complexity. If the pathogen is in a spore or cyst form, it may be extremely difficult to identify and enumerate. Turn-around times for chemical samples can take just as long.

Certain deployable BEF units might maintain the M272 Chemical Agent Monitor Water (CAMW) kits and/or chemical test strips for cyanide and arsenic. However, these kits are not maintained by all units or at all bases. In addition to war reserve materiel, some BEF may own and operate a direct-reading chemical spectrophotometer, which may be able to detect a limited number of inorganic chemicals. The BEF has no in-house capability to detect or monitor organic chemicals and pesticides. The USAF and Army are developing the Joint Chemical/Biological Agent Water Monitor (JCBAWM) with a prototype due in the field in 2001.

The second operational constraint is sampling frequency. Fixed-base routine water sampling is conducted to meet certain national public health standards in accordance with AFI 48-119, *AF Medical Service Environmental Quality Programs*, the various state drinking water regulations, and the various Environmental Final Governing Standards (for overseas bases.) These are public health standards, designed for the detection of some acute contaminants (coliform bacteria and nitrate for protection of infants) and a variety of chronic contaminants (pesticides, heavy metals, etc.). Monitoring schedules range from weekly checks for coliform bacteria to every three years for many other chemicals. The USAF has no deployed or bare-base standards, and sampling is based on risk assessment and logistical constraints.

The Civil Engineers, as operators of the water distribution system, typically sample chlorine residual and pH at the treatment plant. Frequency of tests varies greatly depending on manpower and system operational requirements. Even if the USAF had the detection capability, under current policy and manning the odds are good that an attack would not occur on a sampling day.

NOTIONAL EXAMPLES OF DISABLING ATTACK

Botulism Toxin

Assuming adversaries could produce or acquire Botulinium Toxin, how much material is needed to effectively poison a person with 0.25 liter of water? Botulinium Toxin's effective dose is 0.07 mg, it is stable in water, and it is resistant to chlorine at the normal level of 1.0 ppm. Assuming the notional community water system has a clear well with a 200,000-gallon volume (750,000 liters, typical of a medium-sized system), and perfect mixing and solubility, just 0.21 kilograms (kg, equal to 0.46 pounds, less than a cup of water) could generate a disabling dose. As the water entered the distribution system, unsuspecting and unprotected personnel would consume the water, thereby functionally killing such USAF global engagement operations in that region.

Sodium Cyanide

Sodium cyanide (NaCN) presents a special challenge to USAF force protection because it is in plentiful supply in the mining and metals technology industries. An Internet search for "sodium cyanide" reveals a plethora of suppliers throughout the world. It is an odorless white salt, which is stable and highly soluble in water (around 80 percent at 35°C). Death or incapacitation can result from a 25 mg oral dose. Cyanide exerts its lethal effect by stopping cell aerobic metabolism, thereby suffocating the body's cells. To generate 25 milligrams in the first quarter liter (about a cup) a person drank would require that 188 kg (415 pounds) of NaCN be dumped into a 200,000 gallon clear well or water similar reservoir.

Thus, a saboteur with four and a quarter 100-pound "cement" bags of NaCN, with access to the clear wells, or storage bladders in the austere case, could generate a poisonous slug of water that could kill or incapacitate every consumer downstream. Properly timed, a "construction worker" could cripple operations through a relatively cheap and simple asymmetric attack.

Cholera

Cholera is an acute intestinal disease in man, caused by the bacterium *Vibrio cholerae*. Symptoms include profuse watery diarrhea, rapid dehydration, and a state of collapse. Treatment consists of replacement of fluid and electrolytes; untreated, the victim may die within hours after onset. This disease is responsible for mass epidemics when basic sanitation and water supply break down. It is inactivated by chlorine.

How might the saboteur proceed this time? What if the notional treatment plant wasn't manned 24-hours per day and didn't remotely and continuously control chlorine levels? At the end of a work shift, a saboteur might shut off the chlorinator, and several hours later start dumping cultured *V. cholerae*into the clear well, or maybe into a water tower.

Within hours of consumption, profuse diarrhea would disable all consumers. An attack at a austere location could severely strain health care resources. Left untreated, many could die. Properly timed, the resultant epidemic could paralyze on-scene operations.

In summary, potential adversaries have a veritable supermarket menu of weapon choices. Chemical warfare agents, such as hydrogen cyanide, Lewisite, or VX could be used to poison water.

Many industrial chemicals and pesticides are close chemical cousins to the usual CW agents. These materials are readily available in the world market, and, when concentrated and employed in water, can produce lethal or incapacitating doses. Many pathogens and biological toxins are water-borne threats. An adversary could turn these age-old enemies on a friendly water system for devastating, system-wide effects. The USAF isn't currently equipped to sample and analyze most CW/BW water threats, and monitoring programs are managed for peacetime compliance instead of the detection of deliberate attack. A thermos full of Botulinium Toxin or concentrated *Vibrio cholerae* is nearly impossible to detect and intercept as it crosses base boundaries.

The problem is even harder to prevent if the base supply shares an offbase water supply with the local regional community. Once dumped into the water supply, the first evidence of such an attack will likely be casualties at the clinic. For less than $10,000 an adversary could wage an unsophisticated asymmetric attack, perhaps delivering a knockout blow to unprepared and unsuspecting USAF units dependent on those water supplies.

PROTECTING THE FORCE

Clearly, USAF operations could be severely degraded by CW/BW attacks on an air base water system or by attacks on a community water supply that the air base is dependent upon. A center of gravity, drinking water is essential to the airmen who operate and support USAF weapon systems. It is collected, treated, stored, and delivered in systems with common critical points.

These points, if vulnerable, are potential CW/BW targets. A terrorist bent on killing Americans, or a rogue nation seeking asymmetric advantage in a pre-emptive strike, has available a plethora of CW/BW agents and materials that are effective in drinking water. Rhetorically, why use ballistic missiles when a thermos laced with cholera or botulism toxin, or a couple of bags of "cement" (sodium cyanide), could functionally destroy operations?

As these examples demonstrated, chemicals, pathogens and toxins are cheap, ubiquitous, and deadly in water. Very little material is needed to inflict lethal or incapacitating doses in an unsuspecting and unprepared population. Adversaries seeking asymmetric advantage could focus on the water attack scenario, severing the USAF's proverbial "Achilles' Heel," grounding operations before "wheels are in the well."

Though plainly delineated as a security threat at the national level, the USAF institutionally fails to recognize water system risk resulting in a disjointed vulnerability assessment process. Civil Engineering contingency planning inadequately addresses the threats, risks and impacts of deliberate CW/BW attack. Bioenvironmental Engineering vulnerability assessments have traditionally focused on ambient pollution and operational condition risks, not deliberate contamination. Civil Engineering contingency plans and BEE water system vulnerability assessments are rarely rolled into SF and AFOSI installation vulnerability assessments.

Official CW/BW policy and threat assessments focus on airborne CW/BW attack. Any water impact is assumed to be secondary contamination of surface sources. In this scenario, dilution, degradation and targeted treatment render the weapon less effective, resulting in the conclusion that operations are at little risk from waterborne CW/BW attack.

The institutional focus on the threat of adversary missiles and bombs blinds force protection personnel to the CBW water threat. Yet, direct attacks on water systems overcome dilution and some forms of degradation (ultraviolet and temperature extremes), and can circumvent treatment.

This study has clearly demonstrated that a variety of traditional CW agents, industrial chemicals, pathogens and biological toxins are potentially deadly weapons when targeted through drinking water. Assuming an adversary could produce or acquire the CW/BW material, delivery could be deceptively easy. It may only be a matter of time before CW/BW attack with a thermos and bolt cutter evolves from the theoretical to reality.

Recommendations

Force protection is a commander's highest priority concern. To protect the force, commanders must give higher priority to drinking water vulnerability. Though defence against chemicals and bacteria may not seem immediately relevant to those conducting air operations, the service must "check six" and secure its critical infrastructure. This chapter proposes four risk reduction thrusts:

- comprehensive threat and risk assessment;
- focused water system vulnerability assessments;
- re-evaluation of the CW/BW conventional wisdom;
- and a critical review of Civil Engineering water system outsourcing and management practices.

Comprehensive threat and risk assessment starts at the high-threat bases. It is essential that installation commanders in those areas assess their water system critical point security. A combined team of CE, BEE and SF/AFOSI experts is best suited for this task. Are the passive defenses adequate? Are active defenses dictated? Does the base control who has access to the system's critical points? If the system can't be secured, verifiably safe bottled water should be provided for drinking and cooking. Concurrent with the high threat area assessments, the USAF must embark on a detailed evaluation of the CW/BW threat to its critical water infrastructures, starting with the intelligence community.

This analysis should raise some eyebrows. It posits that an adversary could disable USAF operations with a thermos of bacteria for less than $10,000. Therefore, it is first recommended that the USAF should bring the assets of the intelligence community to bear on this critical force protection problem, the potential in various regions of an adversary poisoning USAF unit water supplies. Focusing outside the "aerial delivery against massed troops or airfields" and concomitant secondary source water contamination paradigms, the agents, materials and delivery systems that pose operational threats to water supplies need to be identified and assessed. Building on the cited preventive medicine community's CW/BW threat, this should also include the threats of physical attack, cyber-attack, and radioactive materials attack. Concurrently, by expanding this study's critical points analysis, the CE, BEE and civilian water authorities (the Critical Infrastructure Assurance Office and civilian water industry) can focus protection efforts on the highest risk vulnerabilities. Together these data will focus force protection training and vulnerability assessments in the various commands.

The second recommendation is for more focused water vulnerability assessments. This requires BEE and CE integration into the SF/AFOSI vulnerability assessment process. Integrated MAJCOM and/or installation teams, backed by the intelligence assessment of actual water CW/BW vulnerabilities and critical points analysis, can re-evaluate all USAF water systems, including off-base community water systems on which the USAF is dependent, on a prioritized basis. Concurrently, including the detailed CW/BW threat and critical point analysis in Level II and III anti-terrorism training will help raise the general awareness level throughout the USAF. Threat and risk based assessment of the passive defenses protecting the sources, treatment, storage and distribution system components is critical. In the end, defending priority components from sabotage is likely the most practical counter to CW/CW attack. Offered in Appendix A is a water system CW/BW vulnerability assessment checklist as a starting point for these teams.

Concurrently, real-time detection systems for the most likely and damaging CW/BW attack scenarios might prove to be mission savers. Based on the threat and risk, Civil Engineering as water system managers and Bioenvironmental Engineers as primary samplers should identify detection requirements. The Critical Infrastructure Assurance Office addresses many of these needs in *Preliminary Research and Development Roadmap for Protecting and Assuring Critical National Infrastructures*. They include rapid and continuous detection of contaminants of concern and enhanced chlorine detection systems. Chlorine could be used as a detection surrogate for contaminants, under the theory that residual chlorine will react with injected CW/BW, necessarily reducing the ambient chlorine concentration. Unexplained chlorine concentration variations could indicate CW/BW attack.

Third, the USAF can no longer afford to ignore the vulnerability to CW/BW attacks on its water system's critical points. Reducing this vulnerability must be given a top priority in USAF force protection efforts. The conventional USAF wisdom, reflected in policy and guidance, assumes aerial attack and dissemination of CW/BW. Little attention outside military medical communities has been placed on water system attack. And the majority of those reports assume only secondary contamination of surface water supplies. The Civil Engineering readiness community, as those with the primary responsibility (OPR) for NBC readiness and training, can rectify this by incorporating the intelligence community's threat and risk assessments into official policy and training guidance. Concurrently, the Bioenvironmental Engineering NBC reconnaissance teams must update their training regimens.

Fourth, a final recommendation is that there be a critical review of USAF water system management practices. Civil Engineering has outsourced or privatized many water system functions. This could seriously impact mission security and operational readiness. Has the USAF placed its people and mission at risk in the effort to save money? If USAF water systems in a region have critical vulnerable points, and a successful CW/BW attack could cripple such USAF operations, shouldn't the USAF be concerned about who's running the show? Should military, civil service or contract personnel undergo special security or reliability checks periodically when working with the water systems? What about overseas, where the host nation may control the sources and distribution of water? These force protection concerns demand a bottom-up review of the CE outsourcing program with respect to the risk and threats of CW/BW weapons in drinking water.

8

Chemical Warfare Agents and Weapons of Mass Destruction

Among the Weapons of Mass Destruction, chemical warfare (CW) is probably one of the most brutal created by mankind in comparison with biological and nuclear warfare. Chemical weapons are inexpensive and are relatively easy to produce, even by small terrorist groups, to create mass casualties with small quantities. The characteristics of various CW agents, general information relevant to current physical as well as medical protection methods, detection equipment available and decontamination techniques. A brief note on Chemical Weapons Convention is also provided.

Among the Weapons of Mass Destruction (WMD), chemical warfare (CW) is probably one of the most brutal created by mankind. CW agents are extremely toxic synthetic chemicals that can be dispersed as a gas, liquid or aerosol or as agents adsorbed to particles to become a powder. These CW agents have either lethal or incapacitating effects on humans. They differ from explosive chemicals in which the destructive effects are caused by shear force and are localized. Thousands of toxic substances are known, but only some of them are considered as CW agents based on their characteristics, viz. high toxicity, imperceptibility to senses and rapidity of action after dissemination and persistency, and are listed as scheduled chemicals in the Chemical Weapons Convention (CWC). According to the CWC, chemical weapons are defined as toxic chemicals and their precursors, munitions and devices, and any equipment specifically designed for use directly in connection with such weapons.

The use of poisonous chemicals from plant extracts to poison individuals is widely documented throughout the Middle Ages and Renaissance, but it was not until the expansion of industrial chemistry in the 19th century that mass production and deployment of CW agents in war became a possibility. Thus, the birth of modern CW was ushered in by the German gas attack with chlorine on 22nd April 1915 at Ypres, Belgium. The use of these toxic chemicals, including phosgene, sulfur mustard and lewisites caused 100,000 deaths and 1.2 million casualties in World War I (WWI). Millions of innocent civilians were killed by the Nazis with Zyklon B gas (hydrogen cyanide gas) during World War II. Agent Orange – a defoliant – was used by the USA during the Vietnam War. The only major use of CW since WWI occurred during the Iran–Iraq War in the 1980s. The largest single CW attack killing around 5,000 people followed an Iraqi nerve agent attack on the Kurdish civilian population of Halabja. This attack illustrates the one single characteristic of CW agents that allows them to be considered as WMD. This incident, together with the relative simplicity of their production, makes them an attractive terrorist weapon. This has been made particularly evident by the Sarin attacks by a Japanese cult in Matsumoto city (1994) and the Tokyo subway system (1995), causing 5,500 injuries and 12 deaths. The threat of using CW agents in domestic terrorist attack was demonstrated for the first time in these cases. However, mass casualties were prevented not as a consequence of the medical response but because of the inefficiency of the delivery method. Subsequent investigations revealed that the sect had also produced Tabun, Soman, Vx and Botulinum toxin. Thus, even small groups of individuals can use CW agents to create massive and extensive human suffering without any warning.

Terrorists have previously used more conventional means of violence, such as bombings, assassinations and hostage taking, to promote their causes. Terrorism and criminal activities achieved a whole new quality after incidents like the repeated assaults on the World Trade Center in New York culminating in its destruction on September 11, 2001 and the subsequent dissemination of anthrax-letters. On April 6, 2004, news agencies reported that the British police foiled a plot by members of the El-Qaeda to prepare and detonate a bomb containing OsO_4 in London. Following these, over the last decade, it has been feared that terrorists might be tempted to acquire and use such weapons against innocent civilians. The major reasons for the production and use of such weapons are manifold. First, chemical weapons are cost-effective, particularly when used against concentrated forces or populations. Second, they may be used at lower levels of concentration with an aim to cause panic and disorder among civilians. Among the CW agents, chlorine, phosgene and cyanides are widely used in the manufacturing processes of various chemical or pharmaceutical industries. Thus, the act of terrorism might also occur in the form of a toxic chemical release, e.g. when such industrial plants, stocks or transports become a target of terrorist attacks. In the Tokyo subway attack, a simple plastic bag containing the CW agent Sarin was kept on an underground train, allegedly piercing it with umbrella tips before the cult's escaped. Therefore, intentional release of such agents during National or International events can be easily achieved by transporting them in the form of water bottles, cold drink cans, ampoules or even pens, etc. to the site. The effect of intentional release of CW agent varies greatly, depending on several factors, including the toxicity of the compound, its volatility and concentration, the route of exposure, the duration of the exposure and the environmental conditions. The release of such agents in an enclosed place could deliver doses high enough to injure or kill a large number of people, whereas in an open area, chemical cloud would become less concentrated as it spreads, leading possibly to numerous mild casualties.

In the present time, all over the world, chemical terrorism is a serious threat to the security of mankind, whose scale essentially exceeds the impact of use of the most modem firearms. Probably about 70 different chemicals or mixtures of chemicals have been used or stockpiled as agents for the purpose of CW during the 20th century. Taking recent technological advances into consideration, easy access to raw materials, the ready availability of technical information on the internet, increasing crime and corruption and state-sponsored terrorism and globalization, it is not difficult for the terrorists to use CW agents to achieve their goals. This review provides a comprehensive account of the CW agents, which includes current status of protective equipment available, detection and decontamination methods. The role of the CWC is also briefly mentioned.

CLASSIFICATION OF CW AGENTS

The CW agents possess different characteristics and belong to various classes of compounds with pronounced physicochemical, physiological and chemical properties. Thus, they are classified in many ways. Based on their volatility, they are classified as persistent or non-persistent agents. The more volatile an agent, the quicker it evaporates and disperses. The more volatile agents like chlorine, phosgene and hydrogen cyanide are non-persistent agents whereas the less volatile agents like sulfur mustard and Vx are persistent agents. Based on their chemical structure, they can be classified as organophosphorus (OP), organosulfur and organofluorine compounds and arsenicals. In general, classification in terms of physiological effects produced on humans by the CW agents is used for many decades. Thus, the CW agents used in warfare are classified as follows:

- Nerve agents
- Vesicants (blistering agents)
- Bloods agents (cyanogenic agents)
- Choking agents (pulmonary agents)
- Riot-control agents (tear gases)
- Psychomimetic agents
- Toxins.

Nerve Agents

Nerve agents acquired their name because they affect the functioning of the nervous system. Nerve agents do not occur naturally and belong to a group of OP compounds. The first known nerve agent, Tabun (GA), was first developed by the German chemist, Gerhard Schrader, in the 1930s during his research in the development of new OP insecticides. Following this, a series of nerve agents known as the G-agents, which include Sarin (GB) and Soman (GD), were developed.

Germany had stockpiles of nerve agent munitions during World War II, but did not use them. A variety of nerve agents were developed till 1960 for military use. Much importance was given to increase their potency and environmental persistence. Thus, the V-agents, as more stable versions of the "G" agents, were developed. Thus VX, a sulfur-containing OP, is more potent than sarin, is more stable, less volatile and less water-soluble, acting through direct skin contact, and persisting in the environment up to several weeks after release. Nerve agents are more toxic than the other reported CW agents. They are highly toxic and can cause death within few minutes to few hours after exposure, depending on the concentration. Nerve agents were not used during World War II. The only known battlefield use of nerve agents was in the Iraq-Iran conflict during the 1980–8 war; Iraq reportedly used nerve agents against Iranian troops and later against members of its Kurdish population in northern Iraq. The chemical structures and some of the properties of the more powerful nerve agents.

In the pure state, all nerve agents are colorless liquids. The G-agents give off a fruity odor whereas the V-agents give off an amine odor. Sarin is infinitely soluble in water, Soman is sparingly soluble in water and Tabun and Vx are of intermediate character in this respect. The reactions of nerve agents take place through P-X bond cleavage. Thus, the reaction of G-agents with alkali gives non-toxic phosphonic acid. On the other hand, the hydrolysis product of Vx leads to another extremely toxic product.

The mode of action of nerve agents is well documented in the literature. Nerve agents exert their biological effects by irreversibly inhibiting the enzyme acetyl cholinesterase (AChE). This enzyme is responsible for hydrolyzing acetylcholine (ACh), a neurotransmitter liberated at the nerve synapse, nerve–muscle (neuromuscular) junction and nerve–gland junction. In a normal individual, a small quantity of ACh is continuously liberated and hydrolyzed by AChE. Inhibition of AChE causes accumulation of Ach, leading to overexcitation or paralysis. As soon as the nerve agents enter the system, symptoms of poisoning appear.

The effects of nerve agents are the result of the action on the muscurinic and nicotinic receptors on the receptors within the central nervous system. They include constriction of the pupil (meiosis), increased production of saliva, running nose, increased perspiration, urination, defecation, bronchosecretion, bronchoconstriction, decreased heart rate and blood pressure, muscular twitches and cramps, cardiac arrhythmias, tremors and convulsions. The most critical effects are paralysis of the respiratory muscles and inhibition of the respiratory center. Ultimately, death results due to respiratory paralysis. If the concentration of the nerve agent is high, death is immediate.

The treatment of nerve agent poisoning requires constant attention by the medical personnel. Three drugs, atropine, pralidoxime chloride and diazepam, are used to treat nerve agent exposure. Atropine competes with ACh for the muscuranic ACh receptors and thus helps to protect accumulation of excess ACh during nerve agent poisoning. Atropine is active against all nerve agents. Thus, atropine should be administered immediately and should be repeated, starting with an initial dose of 2 mg intramuscularly or intravenously. The administration of atropine should be continued till it is adequate, as indicated by dryness of mucosa of nose and mouth, and an increase in heart rate. The dosage of atropine should not hinder the performance of a non-intoxicated individual. Side-effects of 2 mg atropine in a normal individual are increased heart rate, drying of secretions, mydriasis (dilatation of pupil) and paralysis of accommodation. Most of the effects are reversible. 2-pyridine aldoxime chloride (2-PAM or pralidoxime) is used for the nicotinic effects of nerve agents, which include muscle fascilation followed by depolarization paralysis. Sometimes, 2-PAM helps to regenerate AChE, thereby restoring muscle repolariztion. Other than pralidoxime, obidoxime, also known as toxogonin, can also be used. But, these oximes are not effective for Soman poisoning. For this, H-series oximes are preferred (HI-6). The oximes should be administered in combination with atropine. The dose of pralidoxime chloride is 15–25 mg/kg by slow intravenous injection. The usual dose of toxogonin is 300 mg. Because these oximes are quickly excreted, further doses may be needed. The convulsions induced by nerve agent poisoning may cause brain damage. Diazepam is used as an adjunct to reduce the convulsions. The usual dose of diazepam is 5–10 mg, intramuscularly. It is important that the antidotes should be administered very quickly in the field itself in the form of first aid.

This is done by the use of autoinjectors, which does not require the help of medical personnel to inject the drug. Atropine and PAM chloride autoinjectors are available for immediate use. There are no accepted prophylactic antidotes for nerve agent poisoning, i.e. drugs administered before exposure to the agent. Pyridostigmine bromide has been introduced as a prophylactic drug. The dose is 30 mg, three-times a day. Although it may give some protection against nerve agent poisoning, it has side-effects.

Blistering Agents

Blistering agents or vesicants are toxic compounds that produce skin injuries resembling those caused by burns. These agents on inhalation affect the upper respiratory tract as well as the lungs, producing pulmonary edema. These agents can also cause severe eye injuries. There are two forms of vesicants: mustards and arsenicals. The most important substance in this class of CW agents is sulfur mustard and is called as king of CW agents. Other members include nitrogen mustards (HN1, HN2 and HN3) and lewisites (L1, L2 and L3).

Pure sulfur mustard is a colorless and odorless liquid; the impure product has a characteristic smell similar to mustard or garlic. It has low volatility. It is soluble in organic solvents readily but is barely soluble in water (0.8 g/L). Nitrogen mustards are also colorless liquids in the pure state. They are less volatile, less soluble and more resistant to oxidizing agents than sulfur mustard, but are less stable in storage. Pure lewisites are also colorless liquids with metallic odor and solubility in water is similar to sulfur mustard, these are but relatively unstable. Thus, nitrogen mustards and lewisites lack the basic requirement, i.e. storage stability of a CW agent.

Sulfur mustard is the vesicant with the highest military significance since its use in WWI. The nitrogen mustards were synthesized in the 1930s but were not produced in large amounts for warfare. Mechlorethamine (HN2, Mustargen) has found more peaceful applications as a cancer chemotherapeutic agent and has remained the standard compound for this purpose for many years. Lewisite (L) was synthesized in 1918 for military purpose due to its non-flammable property and toxicity similar to mustard, but has probably not been used on a battlefield.

The mustards are radiomimetic and are extremely toxic to dividing cells. Mustards are lipophilic and readily penetrate the skin, most textiles and rubber. After passing through the cellular membrane, sulfur mustard is converted to highly reactive sulphonium ion. It irreversibly alkylates DNA, RNA and protein, causing cell death; the most important target is DNA. Mustard alkylates the purine bases of DNA and damages them. Lewisite is absorbed by the skin ten-times faster, and it causes immediate pain and irritation in the affected organ and produces more systematic symptoms. It directly binds to the sulfhydryl groups and inactivates them.

The clinical hallmark of mustard exposure is the relative lack of symptoms following exposure. The length of this latent period and rapidity and intensity of symptom development depend on the mode of exposure, concentration of the agent and environmental conditions. In the form of gas or aerosol, mustard attacks the skin, eyes and the respiratory tract. Chemical damage begins in 1–2 min after contact, but onset of pain is delayed for 4–6 h. Eye damage ranges from conjunctivitis to corneal opacification, ulceration and rupture. Skin injury ranges from sun burn-like erythema to vesicles, which coalesce into blisters. Liquid exposure can cause coagulation necrosis of the dermis. The effect of mustard gas on the respiratory tract also depends on the degree of exposure. If the exposure is mild, swelling and erythema will be present in the nose, larynx and trachea. The laryngeal edema and necrosis may lead to respiratory obstruction. There is a danger of bacterial infection of the lungs, which may result in bronchopneumonia. The latter may be responsible for death following mustard exposure. Severe exposure to mustard may induce bone marrow damage, leading to leucopenia. Ingestion of food or water contaminated by liquid mustard produces nausea, vomiting, pain and diarrhea. Even exposure to the skin alone can cause malaise, vomiting and cardiac abnormalities.

There is no specific antidote for mustard toxicity and the treatment is similar to that of burn injuries. The eyes should be washed with uncontaminated water. If the eyelids are sticky, then sterile petroleum jelly can be applied. Blepharospasm can be relieved by instilling one drop of atropine solution (1%) three to four-times a day. Secondary infection, if any, can be treated by instilling ciprofloxacillin eye drops. The skin area should be immediately decontaminated using Fuller's Earth. Povidone–iodine ointment or framycetin ointment should be applied on the mustard blisters. Systemic analgesics and antihistamines can be used to relieve itching and pain. Pharyngitis due to inhalation exposure can be relieved by taking alkaline gargle. For persistent cough, codeine can be taken.

Unlike mustard, specific treatment for lewisite poisoning is available. 2,3-dithiocaptopropanol, commonly known as British Anti Lewisite (BAL), is a specific chelating agent for arsenicals. Lewisite is a potent inhibitor of anaerobic glycolysis, an effect reversible with BAL. If the eye or skin is contaminated,

BAL ointment should be applied immediately. The other treatment measures are similar to that of mustard. If the contamination is very severe, BAL should be administered systemically. BAL in oil (10% solution) should be given by deep intramuscular injection at a dose of 5 mg/kg and repeated after 4, 8 and 12 h. Due to the toxicity and side-effects of BAL, less-toxic and more-specific new arsenic antidotes such as meso-dimercaptosuccinic acid (DMSA), 2,3-dimercapto-1-propanesulphonic acid (DMPS) and 2,3-dithioerythritol (DTE) are being studied.

Blood Agents

Blood agents are cyanide group of chemicals that affect bodily functions by preventing the normal utilization of oxygen by body tissues. The term "blood agent" is a misnomer because these agents do not typically affect the blood, although they may interrupt the production of blood components. Rather, they exert their toxic effect at the cellular level by interrupting the electron transport chain in the inner membranes of the mitochondria. These agents are also known as systemic agents as they inhibit certain specific enzymes. Hydrogen cyanide (HCN) and cyanogen chloride (CNCl) are the main CW agents in this class.

Hydrogen cyanide, first discovered by a Swedish chemist in 1872, was used as an industrial chemical long before the realization of its potential as a CW agent during the first World War. The French were the first to consider it for this purpose and used shells made from this material in the battle of Somme in 1916. Cyanogen chloride was also available in plenty as a commercial product having applications as an industrial intermediate during the first World War. It was introduced to overcome the disadvantages encountered in the use of HCN, i.e. a heavier gas with cumulative effects in low concentrations. Cyanogen chloride has powerful lachrymatory and choking effects also. The agent penetrates the filter elements of a gas mask more readily than any other agent. The worldwide industrial development has become a major threat so far as cyanide is concerned. This was used by Iraq in her conflict with Iran during the 1983–88 war. The very high volatility of the blood agents makes them less useful as CW agents, but their use as a terrorist weapon rests on their efficacy if deployed in enclosed spaces.

Cyanide has a very high affinity for iron in the ferric (Fe^{+3}) state. On entering the biological system, it readily reacts with trivalent iron of cytochrome oxidase (an end-chain enzyme of cellular respiration) to form a complex, thereby impairing the utilization of oxygen in the tissues. Eventually, death follows as a result of respiratory failure. The onset and intensity of symptoms depend on the concentration of inhaled toxic vapor and duration of the exposure. Symptoms on exposure to low doses of HCN are weakness, giddiness, headache, confusion and, sometimes, nausea and vomiting. Clinical signs appear only at high levels of exposure, which include fast and painful respiration, lack of coordination of movement, cardiac irregularities, hypoxic convulsions, coma and respiratory failure culminating in death. Diagnosis may be aided by characteristic odor of cyanide (bitter almond) or a faint pale-red hue of the skin.

Artificial respiration and oxygen are given as first aid to victims of cyanide poisoning. The patient should be removed from the contaminated environment. The aim of the treatment is to dissociate the cyanide ion from the cytochrome oxidase–cyanide complex. This can be accomplished by binders like amyl nitrite, sodium nitrite and 4-dimethylaminophenol (DMAP), which oxidize hemoglobin to methemoglobin, which subsequently sequesters the cyanide ion to form cyanmethemoglobin. Amyl nitrite is usually administered by inhalation while sodium nitrite (10 ml of 3%) is given intravenously (i.v.). Sodium thiosufhate (50 ml of 25% solution, i.v.), a sulfur donor to enzyme rhodanese present in the liver, augments the elimination of cyanide as thiocyanate. Other chelating compounds like hydroxocobalamin (vitamin B12a, 20 mg, i.v.) and kelocyanor (cobalt-EDTA) are also effective antidotes. Recent studies have also shown that disodium 2-ketoglutarate, either alone or in combination with sodium thiosulfate, is very effective in antagonizing lethal cyanide poisoning in experimental animals. Hyperbaric oxygen also potentiates the efficacy of known antidotes. Other supportive therapy include diazepam (3 mg × 10 mg, i.v.), sodium bicarbonate and methylene blue (30 ml of 1%, i.v.). Treatment of cyanide poisoning must be rapid to be effective.

Choking Agents

Choking agents injure an individual mainly in the

respiratory tract, i.e. in the nose, throat, and particularly, the lungs. In extreme cases, membranes swell, the lungs become filled with liquid and death results from lack of oxygen; thus, these agents "choke" the unprotected individuals. Fatalities of this type are referred to as "dry-land drownings." Chlorine and phosgene are the best known among this class, although diphosgenes, nitric oxide and perfluoroisobutylene (PFIB) also belong to this group. Choking agents were among the first CW agents produced in large quantities and were used extensively during WWI. They are generally heavier than air. Both chlorine and phosgene are used in many chemical industrial processes, making the control of these compounds difficult, and these can be used as a devastating low-tech weapon in the hands of terrorists.

At room temperature, chlorine is a pungent, green-yellow gas. It can be liquefied under moderate pressure. Even at toxic levels, phosgene gas has little distinguishing odor and usually kills its victims only after a considerable delay (up to 24 h). Phosgene was alone responsible for about 80% death by chemicals in WWI. Being liquid at room temperature, diphosgene, another WWI agent, is generally easier to handle than phosgene, and it is more persistent than either chlorine or phosgene. Diphosgene is basically phosgene with chloroform grafted onto it, and it has the capability to penetrate through canisters. PFIB is an industrial gas generated as a byproduct from overheating and during the production of polytetrafluoroethylene (Teflon). Like phosgene, PFIB has a latency period between exposure and symptoms. Because of its high toxicity (about 10-times as toxic as phosgene), its protective filters breakthrough property and wide availability, PFIB is listed in the Scheduled 2 toxic substance in the CWC.

There is no uniform view regarding the mechanism of action of phosgene intoxication. Phosgene is highly reactive and combines with the –SH, $-NH_2$ and –OH groups of biological macromolecules, including enzymes, and this may account for its toxic effects. Poisoning is mainly attributed to acylation of certain tissue elements of the lungs and increased permeability of the alveolar mucous membrane resulting in pulmonary edema with consequent anoxia and death. Inhalation of low concentrations of phosgene produces rapid and shallow breathing, reduced respiratory volume, bradycardia and hypotension. Many cholinergic symptoms like increased salivation, nausea, micturition and defecation are also observed. Exposure to higher concentration may produce more specific effects on the vital functions of the lungs and, eventually, development of pulmonary edema culminating in death. The immediate cause of death is usually paralysis of the respiratory center due to anoxia.

Treatment of phosgene poisoning is essentially palliative. The main objective of the treatment is to prevent the development of pulmonary edema and other secondary effects arising out of anoxia. Treatment is extended in three steps. Under first aid, the victim should be allowed fresh air and should be kept warm. The treatment is phased in a manner to provide basic therapy within 30 min of exposure followed by selected additional therapy. Immediate medical aid involves artificial respiration along with the administration of cortisone (hexamethasone or beclamethasone) and sodium bicarbonate assisted by positive pressure breathing. Coughing worsens the prognosis and can be suppressed with codeine. Sedatives are not recommended. Antibiotic therapy is recommended when bronchitis or pneumonitis develops. The selected additional therapy includes supplementary oxygen and i.v. injection of sodium bicarbonate. Relief from airway obstruction may be achieved by theophylline and prostaglandin E1 (PGE1) followed by surfactant supplementation with dipamitoyl phosphatidylcholine or cholesterol palmitate aerosols. Intensive care and supervision is required for more than 24 h.

Riot Control Agents

Riot control agents are compounds that cause temporary incapacitation by irritation of the eyes (tearing and blepharospasm), causing them to close, and irritation of the upper respiratory tract. They are often called irritants, lachrymators and harassing agents. The general public usually calls them tear gases. Many tear-stimulating substances were tested as CW agents. On exposure, they cause pain in the eyes, flow of tears and skin irritation. Sensations like skin irritation and lachrymation caused by the tear gases are so strong that victims cannot behave rationally, which will hinder and incapacitate the performance of coordinated activities of the exposed people. Three types of riot control agents are recognized: lachrymators, which primarily cause lachrymation and eye irritation; sternutators, which mainly cause sneezing and irritation of the upper respiratory tract; and vomiting agents, which additionally cause vomiting. Among a long series of chemical substances used as riot control agents, only three chemical agents, viz. CN, CS and CR are of significant importance.

CN, CS and CR are solid at room temperature and are dispersed as aerosols. They are relatively insoluble in water but soluble in most of the organic solvents. They are characterized by rapid onset of effects, short duration of action and a high safety ratio. The eye is the most sensitive organ, with pain arising rapidly, accompanied by conjunctivitis, blepharospasm and lacrymation. The symptoms are felt within 10–30 s. For each of the acute symptoms of pain, the probable mode of action is a direct chemical action on sensory receptors in skin and mucosa that involves a nicotinamide adenine dinucleotide hydrogenase (NADH)-dependent enzymatic process. The peripheral nature of their site of action distinguishes these agents pharmacologically from other incapacitating agents that affect the central nervous system, such as psychochemicals.

The treatment for lachrymator exposure requires immediate decontamination of the clothing and eyes. The victim should be brought to fresh air and the eyes and the skin should be decontaminated with water. Inflammation of skin may be treated with calamine lotion.

Psychomimetic Agents

Chemical agents that consistently produce changes in thought, perception and mood, without causing any major disturbances in the autonomic nervous system or other serious disability, are classified as psychomimetic agents. Therefore, this group of agents usually includes substances which, when administered in low doses (<10 mg), cause conditions similar to psychotic disorders or other symptoms emanating from the central nervous system, such as loss of feeling, paralysis, hallucinations, etc.

The civil use of this type of agents dates back to antiquity and includes the use of plants such as thorn apple (*Datura stramonium*)that contain various anticholinergic alkaloids. Psychomimetic agents were used for the first time as an incapacitating agent during war time in 600 BC, when Solon's soldiers threw hellebore roots into streams supplying water to enemy troops, who then developed diarrhea. Hannibal's army in 184 BC used belladonna plants to induce disorientation in the enemy. During World War II, the US military investigated a wide range of possible non-lethal, psychobehavioral chemical incapacitating agents containing indole moiety such as lysergic acid diethylamide (LSD) and marijuana derivatives as well as several glycolate anticholinergics. One of the anticholinergic compounds, 3-quinuclidinyl benzilate, was developed and weaponized in the 1960s as a new chemical agent for battlefield use as a psychochemical and assigned the NATO code BZ.

The psychedelics group includes a large variety of compounds. Among them, LSDis the most well known member. LSD remained as a drug of great interest from the 1950s. Systematic testing of LSD as a possible incapacitating agent was carried out mostly from 1959 to 1965. LSD was proved to be a highly potent incapacitating agent that could produce complete incapacitation, i.e. producing unpredictable behavior by giving an oral dose of approximately 2.5 μg/kg. Affected individuals usually can neither follow a series of instructions given to them nor concentrate on any task. Studies conducted in simulated military exercises demonstrated conclusively that even well-trained units become totally disorganized by giving oral doses of <200 μg. Psilocybin, ibogaine and harmine are also examples of psychedelics, but none of these share the potency of LSD. The aerosolized dose of LSD that capacitates 50% of the exposed individuals (ID_{50}) is estimated to be 6 μg/kg.

BZ is a potent anticholinergic drug that is 25-times more potent than atropine. The ID_{50} for BZ is 6 μg/kg. Less than 1 mg of BZ can produce acute brain syndrome, characterized by delirium lasting for 2–3 days, which can be reversed by physostigmine and other anticholinesterases.

The common signs and symptoms produced by the psychomimetic agents are:

a) restlessness, dizziness or giddiness; failure to obey orders, confusion, erratic behavior; stumbling or staggering; vomiting
b) dryness of mouth, tachycardia at rest, elevated temperature, flushing of face; blurred vision, pupillary dilation; slurred or non-sensical speech; hallucinatory behavior; disrobing; mumbling and picking behavior; stupor and coma

c) inappropriate smiling or laughter, irrational fear, distractibility, difficulty expressing self, perceptual distortions and phobias

The mechanism by which LSD causes such profound effects on the human perception still has not been established. LSD stimulates centres of the sympathetic nervous system in the midbrain, which leads to pupillary dilation, increase in body temperature and rise in the blood sugar level. LSD also has a serotonin-blocking effect. Serotonin is a hormone-like substance occurring naturally in various organs of warm-blooded animals. Concentrated in the midbrain, it plays an important role in the propagation of impulses in certain nerves and, therefore, in the biochemistry of psychic functions. LSD also influences neurophysiologic functions that are connected with dopamine, which is another naturally occurring hormone-like substance. Most of the brain centres receptive to dopamine become activated by LSD, while the others are depressed. The structure of LSD is very similar to other hallucinogenic drugs such as mescaline and psilocybin, all of which contain a substituted indole ring (or a related structure).

Clinical effects from ingestion or inhalation of psychedelics appear after an asymptomatic or latent period that may be as little as 30 min or as long as 20 h; the usual range is 0.5–4 h. However, there is no effect even after 36 h on skin exposure to BZ and other psychedelics. General supportive management of the patient includes decontamination of skin, clothing, weapons and other related items from the patient. The greatest risks to the patient's life are injuries from his or her own erratic behavior and hyperthermia, especially in patients who are in hot or humid environments or are dehydrated from overexertion or insufficient water intake. Management of heat stress assumes a high priority in a severely exposed patient.

Toxins

Poisonous chemical compounds synthesized in nature by living organisms such as bacteria, fungi, terrestrial or marine animals are called toxins. They are classified on the basis of chemical nature, molecular weight, source, preferred targets in the body and mechanism of action. Thus, they are two groups: protein toxins consisting of long, folded chains of amino acids and non-protein toxins, which generally are small molecules with a complex chemical nature. Because of the hybrid nature of toxins, they have sometimes been considered CW agents and sometimes BW agents. Similarly, based on their mechanism of action, they are grouped as cardiotoxins, dermatotoxins, hepatotoxins, neurotoxins, etc. The most potent toxins are neurotoxins such as botulinum toxin and tetanus toxin, but there also are others such as staphylococcal enterotoxin. Different bacteria produce each of these biotoxins. Botulinum toxin is the most toxic agent known ever to man and is a very potent neurotoxin, which blocks the release of AChE from the cholinergic nerves of the human nervous system. The lethal dose for humans of such toxins is in the sub-microgram range, which is many times lower (more toxic) than the dosage for nerve agents. Some of the toxins, their origin and mode of action.

Botulinum toxin is also known as agent X. Arnon *et al.* estimated that if 1 g of this toxin is aerosolized, it would kill more than one million people. The lethal dose for a 70-kg human is estimated to be approximately 0.7 μg if inhaled or 70 μg if ingested. Ricin is a very potent toxin of plant origin, isolated from the seeds of caster oil, *Ricinus communis*. It inhibits ribosome proteins, and the toxic dose for humans is about 0.1–1.0 μg/kg, depending on the mode of administration. It was used in the famous "umbrella tip" assassination of the Bulgarian journalist. Iraq produced and weaponized several highly potent toxins such as botulinum toxin and aflatoxin.

Considerations such as production, weaponization, delivery, environmental stability and host factors place practical limits on their use; toxins as warfare agents are restricted to assassinations or strictly localized terrorist attacks. The two most important toxin threats are botulinum toxin due to its toxicity and Staphylococcus Enterotoxins B, an incapacitating toxin, which cannot be destroyed by boiling. Cases of food poisoning, especially during summer, are due to this bacterial toxin. Ricin and the trichothecene mycotoxins, including T-2 mycotoxin, are of lesser concern, but are still potential threats. The treatment for toxins is passive immunization with antitoxins, with a variety of antitoxins currently being investigated.

PROTECTION DURING CHEMICAL EMERGENCIES

In case of a suspected or proven release of unknown chemicals or CW agents, the important elements of emergency response are: (i) detection and identification of the agent, (ii) physical and medical protection against the agent and (iii) decontamination.

Detection

The rapid identification and qualitative and quantitative determination of the unknown agent is necessary for the selection of adequate protective measures (protective masks and clothing as well as medical treatment), the mapping of contamination area and decontamination procedures. For onsite verification, especially involving CW agents, several handheld detection devices are available, including Three Colour Detector (TCD) paper, Residual Vapor Detection (RVD) Kit, Water Poison Detection Kit (WPDK) and chemical agent monitors. These devices have several limitations, such as low specificity and inability to detect all CW agents. Definitive identification of an agent can be carried out onsite in a mobile analytical laboratory or in an off-site laboratory, and this will generally take many hours.

Clinical symptoms and signs in exposed individuals may be the most useful indicators of the likely agent. This is followed by an on-the-spot analysis with detection paper (TCD). The paper, impregnated with reagents, reacts with the liquid CW agents to produce three distinct colors. The paper sticks to any surface and the colour change occurs within 30 s, mustard agent turns it red, G-nerve agent turns it yellow and V-nerve agent turns it green. The disadvantage is that it may give false-positive results with many other substances. The RVD kit is a portable, disposable CW agent detector kit that can detect CW vapors in air with a high specificity. The detection tubes are made of glass with break-off tips and are filled with impregnated chemicals on silica. A definite volume of air is sucked by pump strokes. Colour change of the silica indicates the presence of a particular agent. Detection tubes are available for individual agents. Blister and nerve agents, phosgene, cyanogens chloride and hydrogen cyanide in the atmosphere can be detected by this kit. Similarly, poisonous substances present in water sources can be detected with the help of WPDK. This kit contains different reagents marked with numbers, test procedures for known CW agents and results based on simple colour change for detection.

Many instruments are available for point detection of CW agents. These are mainly based on three principles: ion mobility spectrometers (IMS), gas chromatograph (GCs) and surface acoustic wave sensors (SAWS). Hand-held chemical agent monitors, based on the principle of ion-mobility spectrometry (IMS), are the most common devices used for the detection of CW agents, particularly blister and nerve agents. The GID-3 (Smiths) is a British IMS for onsite detection of common CW agents. The GID-2A is another version for fixed locations designed for unattended operation and continuous monitoring. The hand-held improved chemical agent monitor (ICAM) is a portable IMS device. The M8A1 is another IMS-based automatic CW alarm detector used during the 1991 Gulf war and it is replaced with the Automatic Chemical Agent Alarm (ACADA), which is a high-resolution IMS. ACADA can detect agents in a few seconds and can clean itself for fresh detection within 1 min. The other variants of IMS are RAID (Bruker's) and M-90 (Environics).

Handheld CW agent detectors, viz. AP2C (France) or CHASE (Israel) based on the flame photometry principle, is also frequently used. It can detect chemiluminescent reactions of sulfur or phosphorus-containing organic compounds in a hydrogen/air flame.

Surface Acoustic Wave Sensors (SAWS) work in the same manner as do Quartz Crystal Microbalances (QCMs), but at higher frequencies and greater sensitivities. The Joint Chemical Agent Detector (JCAD) employs an SAW-based technology. The JCAD is a handheld, lightweight CW detector and it combines with an electrochemical cell.

Portable gas chromatograph is used for automatic real-time continuous agent monitoring. In this, air is used as carrier gas and air sample is drawn through a pre-concentrator loop filled with an adsorbent material. A photoionization detector (PID) is used to detect the agents. The entire cycle from sample collection to detection takes about 5–10 min.

Gas chromatograph coupled with mass detector (GCMS) fitted on a vehicle can be used for unambiguous detection of most of the organic compounds, including CW agents, at very low concentrations. However, this hyphenated technique is complex, requires a skilled operator, is difficult to maintain and does not provide much advantage in comparison with off-site analysis, especially when chemical incident occurs at remote site when the mobile lab cannot approach easily. The commercially available portable GCMS-based instruments include HAPSITE (Inficon's), EM series (Bruker's), MM1 or MM2. No suitable onsite detection equipment or methods for the detection of psychomimetic agents are available except GCMS.

In addition to the above electrochemical-based detectors for nerve agents (NAD), standoff detection instruments (M21, RAPID) are also available. The M21 remote sensing chemical agent alarm (RSCAAL) is based on a passive infrared detector and is capable of detecting nerve and blister agents in the vapor phase from a distance of up to 5,000 m. Instruments based on other techniques, such as molecularly imprinted polymer (MIP) sensors, biosensors, surface plasmon resonance (SPR), conductive polymer sensors, etc. are under development stage.

All the detection methods have susceptibility to interferences or false-positive results. The best way is to use two types of detectors working on different principles to obtain accurate data.

Protection

The main twin aspects of physical protection are the creation of an artificial barrier between the toxic agent and the individuals and the provision of "breathable air." The barrier has to provide protection against liquids, aerosols or gases. The breathable air is accomplished by two ways: directly connected to a source (oxygen or pure air cylinder) or detoxification of contaminated air by passing through a canister. However, the use of a respirator can cause physiological discomforts such as breathing resistance, heat stress and vision and communication problems, resulting in the loss of efficiency.

The canister contains a "high-efficiency particulate aerosol (HEPA) filter media" for the aerosol retention and the gaseous contaminants from air are removed by the impregnated carbon through adsorption, catalytic decomposition and chemisorption processes. Thus, full-face protective masks provide good protection for both the respiratory tract and the eyes. The face mask should have a good field of vision and speech transmission preferably with a microphone. These respiratory protective masks in different sizes are required to suit different face sizes.

In case of body protection, liquid-impermeable full protective gears should be used for highly contaminated areas whereas toxic vapor-impermeable/air-permeable protective suits can be used. The impermeable suit is made up of nylon fabric coated outside with neoprene and another side with butyl rubber. The permeable protective clothing consists of three layers: the upper layer is oil, water and fire retardant nylon fabric, the middle layer is a carbon-coated non-woven fabric and the third layer is a simple cotton fabric layer. The protection gloves consist of an outer butyl rubber glove for chemical protection and an inner cotton glove for the absorption of perspiration water. Similar to gloves, overboots made up of butyl rubber are worn over the already used shoes to protect the footwear against contamination. The term "Personal Protective Equipment" (PPE) is used to denote complete protective gears i.e. face mask, suits, gloves and boots.

Collective protection to a group of people in vehicles or shelters is provided by providing purified air by filtration of contaminated air through large filters. The advantage of this is that individuals inside the protected area are not required to wear masks separately.

There are four levels of personal protection for dealing with hazardous substances. These are described as levels A, B, C and D for chemical protective clothing in combination with different types of respiratory protection. Level A protection should be worn when the highest level of respiratory, skin, eye and mucous membrane protection is needed. This protection consists of a fully encapsulated, vapor-tight, chemical-resistant suit, boots and gloves together with a self-contained breathing apparatus (SCBA). Level B protection should be selected when the highest level of respiratory protection is needed, but a lesser degree of skin and eye protection is required. This equipment consists of a chemical-resistant suit, chemical-resistant boots and gloves and SCBA. Level C protection should be selected when the types of airborne substance are known, concentration is measured, criteria for using air-purifying respirators are met and skin or eye exposures are unlikely. This PPE consists of a chemical-resistant suit, full-face mask with air-purifying canister-equipped respirator and chemical-resistant boots and gloves. Level D protection provides no respiratory protection and minimal skin protection and should not be worn on any site when respiratory or skin hazards exist.

A recent review brings out NBC protective clothing, their types, various clothing materials used, their evaluation procedures, washing methodologies and decontamination methods as well as the futuristic trends, such as detection and decontamination-integrated NBC protective clothing based on electrospun nanofiber technology and molecularly imprinted polymer technology.

Decontamination

Decontamination is the conversion of toxic chemicals into harmless products either by destruction or by detoxification. Decontamination is a complex process involving processes involving highly toxic chemicals with diverse properties, adverse conditions and a wide variety of subjects to be treated, e.g. human skin and eyes, equipment with metal/wooden/plastic surface, field, etc. In terms of CW agents, decontamination can be defined as reduction or removal of chemical agents. This may be accomplished by physically removing the agents or by chemically neutralizing them. Decontamination is most effective when conducted within 1 min of exposure, but this is practically rarely possible.

Physical decontamination is easy and acts universally, but is not as effective as chemical decontamination. It involves mainly adsorption of the toxic chemical on adsorbents such as Fuller's earth, kaolin, talc, activated carbon, etc., or removal of agents by spraying simple water or soap water under pressure. In emergency situations, the adsorbent may even be flour, saw dust or soil. There are many dry formulations containing Fuller's earth, such as PDK-1, PDK-2, M-291 kit that are available for decontamination of skin and equipment. The main disadvantage of the physical method is that the adsorbent or water used for decontamination should be detoxified later and disposed off carefully. Water spray should not be used in case of head or skin contaminated with mustards as it will spread to other body surfaces.

Chemical decontamination converts the toxic CW agents into innocuous products that can be handled safely. The chemical reactions that are generally applied in chemical decontamination methods are either nucleophilic reactions or oxidations. A commonly used skin decontaminant is the 0.5% hypochlorite solution or household bleach. Alkali (sodium or potassium hydroxide) dissolved in methanol or ethanol detoxifies most of the CW agents, but should not be used in decontaminating skin other than in extreme emergencies. Chloramines are effective against mustards and V-agents but are ineffective against G-agents. Sodium carbonate solution renders G-type nerve agents harmless, but with V-agents, it produces a toxic product.

Many ready-to-use effective chemical formulations have been developed and are commercially available. For example, DS2 is a universal decontamination solution for equipment and field use. This is investigated in depth and is available under different names. It is a composition of sodium hydroxide (2%), ethylene glycol monomethylether (28%) and diethylenetriamine (70%). The active ingredient in this formulation is ethylene glycol monomethylether, which acts as a nucleophile and hydrolyses the CW agents into non-toxic products. It is a clear, amber-colored solution and is used in the portable decontamination apparatus. DS2 reacts with GB and HD to effectively reduce their hazards within 5 min. Within 30 min contact time, DS2 neutralizes all known toxic chemical agents. It can damage paints as well as plastics, rubber and leather materials.

The American decontamination kit called M258A1 and M280 contain the active ingredients ethanol (72%), phenol (10%), NaOH (5%), ammonia (0.2%) and water (12%). Similarly, the German emulsion C8 is composed of tetrachloroethylene (15%), water (76%), anionic surfactant (1%) and calcium hypochlorite (8%). It is non-corrosive and can penetrate into paint to dissolve and react with the imbedded agent without damaging the paint.

The microemulsion-based (multi-purpose chemical, biological decontaminant) MCBD system contains water (60%), tetrachloroethylene (7%), n-cetyl trimethyl ammonium chloride (28%) and traces of cosurfactant, $(n\text{-Bu})_4$ NOH. To this microemulsion, Fichlor (4%), sodium 2-nitro-4-iodoxybenzoate (0.1%) and sodium borate are added for reactions with the agents. The MCBD system was designed to be superior to the C8 system because it is a more stable emulsion at a lower pH of 10, contains less tetrachloroethylene and is partially catalytic.

The variables that determine the effectiveness of decontamination are contamination time, temperature, contamination density and decontamination medium, nature of agent and nature of decontaminants. The requirements of an ideal decontaminant or decontamination formulation are rapid in action, efficiency, harmless to humans, non-corrosive, stability in long-term storage and washable with water. There is a great deal of recent discussion and re-evaluation of decontamination agents and strategies and, therefore, careful consideration of the most current recommendation is important. Decontamination must be performed on all victims and responders before they cross into the clean area.

CWC

On April 29, 1997, the world's first multilateral disarmament Treaty "Chemical Weapons Convention" entered into force. The CWC text has a preamble, 24 articles and three annexes, namely an annex on chemicals, an annex on verification and a confidentiality annex. The main objective of the CWC is to prohibit development, production, acquisition, retention, stockpiling transfer and use of chemical weapons. It mandated the Organisation for the Prohibition of Chemical Weapons (OPCW), with its headquarters at The Hague, the Netherlands, to eliminate the scourge of chemical weapons forever. It requires every country signatory to this Convention to destroy existing CW stockpiles and chemical weapons production facilities under its jurisdiction. The most unique feature of the Treaty is its comprehensiveness and a strict inspection and verification regime. In addition, each State Party undertakes to provide protection and assistance through the Organisation if chemical weapons have been used against a State Party or if a State Party is threatened by such weapons. The CWC also provides for international cooperation among States Parties in the pursuit of chemistry for peaceful purposes. As on date, 188 countries are signatories to the convention. OPCW inspectors also verify the consistency of industrial chemical declarations and, together with State Parties, monitor the non-diversion of chemicals for activities prohibited under this convention. It has been estimated that more than 100,000 compounds are controlled under the CWC, although, in practical terms, the actual number of CW agents, precursors and degradation products that are contained in the OPCW database is in thousands. The OPCW Central Analytical Database is a compilation maintained by the OPCW laboratory, and it contains analytical data of the chemicals that fall under the CWC.

WEAPON OF MASS DESTRUCTION

A "weapon of mass destruction" (WMD or WoMD) is a nuclear, radiological, biological,chemical or other weapon that can kill and bring significant harm to a large number of humans or cause great damage to man-made structures (e.g. buildings), natural structures (e.g. mountains), or the biosphere. The scope and application of the term has evolved and been disputed, often signifying more politically than technically. Coined in reference to aerial bombing with chemical explosives, it has come to distinguish large-scale weaponry of other technologies, such as chemical, biological, radiological, ornuclear. This differentiates the term from more technical ones such as chemical, biological, radiological, and nuclear weapons (CBRN).

EARLY USES OF THE TERM

The first use of the term "weapon of mass destruction" on record is by Cosmo Gordon Lang, Archbishop of Canterbury, in 1937 in reference to the aerial bombardment of Guernica, Spain:

Who can think at this present time without a sickening of the heart of the appalling slaughter, the suffering, the manifold misery brought by war to Spain and to China? Who can think without horror of what another widespread war would mean, waged as it would be with all the new weapons of mass destruction?

At the time, the United States (with help from Western Allies) had yet to develop and use nuclear weapons. Japan conducted research on biological weapons, and chemical weapons had seen wide use, most notably in World War I.

Following the atomic bombings of Hiroshima and Nagasaki that ended World War II, and progressing through the Cold War, the term came to refer more to non-conventional weapons.

He credits James Goodby (of the Brookings Institution) with tracing what he considers the earliest known English-language use soon after the nuclear bombing of Hiroshima and Nagasaki (although it is not quite verbatim): a communique from a 15 November 1945, meeting of Harry Truman, Clement Attlee and Mackenzie King (probably drafted by Vannevar Bush– or so Bush claimed in 1970) referred to "weapons adaptable to mass destruction".

That exact phrase, says Safire, was also used by Bernard Baruch in 1946 (in a speech at the United Nations probably written by Herbert Bayard Swope). The same phrase found its way into the very first resolution adopted by the United Nations General assemblyin January 1946 in London, which used the wording "...the elimination from national armaments of atomic weapons and of all other weapons adaptable to mass destruction." This resolution also created the Atomic Energy Commission (predecessor of theInternational Atomic Energy Agency (IAEA)).

An exact use of this term was given in a lecture "Atomic Energy as an Atomic Problem" by J. Robert Oppenheimer. The lecture was delivered to the Foreign Service and the State Department, on 17 September 1947. The lecture is reprinted in *The Open Mind* (New York: Simon and Schuster, 1955).

"It is a very far reaching control which would eliminate the rivalry between nations in this field, which would prevent the surreptitious arming of one nation against another, which would provide some cushion of time before atomic attack, and presumably therefore before any attack with weapons of mass destruction, and which would go a long way toward removing atomic energy at least as a source of conflict between the powers".

The term was also used in the introduction to the hugely influential US Government Document known as NSC-68 written in April 1950.

During a televised presentation about the Cuban Missile Crisis on 22 October 1962, John F. Kennedy made reference to "offensive weapons of sudden mass destruction."

An early use of the exact phrase in an international treaty was in the Outer Space Treaty of 1967, however no definition was provided.

Evolution of its Use

During the Cold War, the term "weapons of mass destruction" was primarily a reference to nuclear weapons. At the time, in the Westthe euphemism "strategic weapons" was used to refer to the American nuclear arsenal, which was presented as a necessary deterrent against nuclear or conventional attack from the Soviet Union.

The term "weapons of mass destruction" continued to see periodic use throughout this time, usually in the context of nuclear arms control; Ronald Reagan used it during the 1986

Reykjavík Summit, when referring to the 1967 Outer Space Treaty. Reagan's successor, George H.W. Bush, used the term in an 1989 speech to the United Nations, using it primarily in reference to chemical arms.

The end of the Cold War reduced U.S. reliance on nuclear weapons as a deterrent, causing it to shift its focus to disarmament. This period coincided with an increasing threat to U.S. interests from Islamic nations and independent Islamic groups. With the 1990 invasion of Kuwait and 1991 Gulf War, Iraq's nuclear, biological, and chemical weapons programs became a particular concern of the first Bush Administration. Following the war, Bill Clinton and other western politicians and media continued to use the term, usually in reference to ongoing attempts to dismantle Iraq's weapons programs.

After the 11 September 2001 attacks and the 2001 anthrax attacks, an increased fear of non-conventional weapons and asymmetrical warfare took hold of the United States and other Western powers. This fear reached a crescendo with the 2002 Iraq disarmament crisisand the alleged existence of weapons of mass destruction in Iraq that became the primary justification for the 2003 invasion of Iraq. However, no WMD were found in Iraq. (Stockpiles of chemical munitions including sarin and mustard agents were found, but none were considered to be in a usable condition due to corrosion.)

Because of its prolific use during this period, the American Dialect Society voted "weapons of mass destruction" (and its abbreviation, "WMD") the word of the year in 2002, and in 2003 Lake Superior State University added WMD to its list of terms banished for "*Mis-use, Over-use and General Uselessness*".

In its Criminal Complaint against the main suspect of the Boston Marathon bombing of 15 April 2013, the FBI refers to a pressure-cooker improvised bomb as a "weapon of mass destruction".

DEFINITIONS OF THE TERM

United States

Strategic

The most widely used definition of "weapons of mass destruction" is that of nuclear, biological, or chemical weapons (NBC) although there is no treaty or customary international law that contains an authoritative definition. Instead, international law has been used with respect to the specific categories of weapons within WMD, and not to WMD as a whole. While nuclear, chemical and biological weapons are regarded as the three major types of WMDs, some analysts have argued that radiological materials as well as missile technology and delivery systems such as aircraft and ballistic missiles could be labeled as WMDs as well.

The abbreviations NBC (for nuclear, biological and chemical) or CBR (chemical, biological, radiological) are used with regards to battlefield protection systems for armored vehicles, because all three involve insidious toxins that can be carried through the air and can be protected against with vehicle air filtration systems.

However, there is an argument that nuclear and biological weapons do not belong in the same category as chemical and "dirty bomb" radiological weapons, which have limited destructive potential (and close to none, as far as property is concerned), whereas nuclear and biological weapons have the unique ability to kill large numbers of people with very small amounts of material, and thus could be said to belong in a class by themselves.

The NBC definition has also been used in official U.S. documents, by the U.S. President, the U.S. Central Intelligence Agency, the U.S. Department of Defence, and the U.S. Government Accountability Office.

Other documents expand the definition of WMD to also include radiological or conventional weapons. The U.S. military refers to WMD as:

Chemical, biological, radiological, or nuclear weapons capable of a high order of destruction or causing mass casualties and exclude the means of transporting or propelling the weapon where such means is a separable and divisible part from the weapon. Also called WMD.

This may also refer to nuclear ICBMs (intercontinental ballistic missiles).

The significance of the words *separable and divisible part of the weapon* is that missiles such as the Pershing II and the SCUD are considered weapons of mass destruction, while aircraft capable of carrying bombloads are not.

In 2004, the United Kingdom's Butler Review recognized the "considerable and long-standing academic debate about the proper interpretation of the phrase 'weapons of mass destruction'". The committee set out to avoid the general term but when using it, employed the definition of United Nations Security Council Resolution 687, which defined the systems which Iraq was required to abandon:

- "Nuclear weapons or nuclear-weapons-usable material or any sub-systems or components or any research, development, support or manufacturing facilities relating to [nuclear weapons].
- Chemical and biological weapons and all stocks of agents and all related subsystems and components and all research, development, support and manufacturing facilities.
- Ballistic missiles with a range greater than 150 kilometres and related major parts, and repair and production facilities."

Chemical weapons expert Gert G. Harigel considers only nuclear weapons true weapons of mass destruction, because "only nuclear weapons are completely indiscriminate by their explosive power, heat radiation and radioactivity, and only they should therefore be called a weapon of mass destruction". He prefers to call chemical and biological weapons "weapons of terror" when aimed against civilians and "weapons of intimidation" for soldiers.

Testimony of one such soldier expresses the same viewpoint. For a period of several months in the winter of 2002–2003, U.S. Deputy Secretary of Defence Paul Wolfowitz frequently used the term "weapons of mass terror," apparently also recognizing the distinction between the psychological and the physical effects of many things currently falling into the WMD category.

Gustavo Bell Lemus, the Vice President of Colombia, at 9 July 2001 United Nations Conference on the Illicit Trade in Small Arms and Light Weapons in All Its Aspects, quoted the Millennium Report of the UN Secretary-General to the General Assembly, in which Kofi Annan said that small arms could be described as WMD because the fatalities they cause "*dwarf that of all other weapons systems – and in most years greatly exceed the toll of the atomic bombs that devastated Hiroshima and Nagasaki*".

An additional condition often implicitly applied to WMD is that the use of the weapons must be strategic. In other words, they would be designed to "*have consequences far outweighing the size and effectiveness of the weapons themselves*". The strategic nature of WMD also defines their function in the military doctrine of total war as targeting the means a country would use to support and supply its war effort, specifically its population, industry, and natural resources.

Within U.S. civil defence organizations, the category is now Chemical, Biological, Radiological, Nuclear, and Explosive (CBRNE), which defines WMD as:

(1) Any explosive, incendiary, poison gas, bomb, grenade, or rocket having a propellant charge of more than four ounces,missile having an explosive or incendiary charge of more than one-quarter ounce, or mine or device similar to the above. (2) Poison gas. (3) Any weapon involving a disease organism. (4) Any weapon that is designed to release radiation at a level dangerous to human life.

Military

For the general purposes of national defence, the U.S. Code defines a weapon of mass destruction as:

- any weapon or device that is intended, or has the capability, to cause death or serious bodily injury to a significant number of people through the release, dissemination, or impact of:
- toxic or poisonous chemicals or their precursors
- a disease organism
- radiation or radioactivity

For the purposes of the prevention of weapons proliferation, the U.S. Code defines weapons of mass destruction as "chemical, biological, and nuclear weapons, and chemical, biological, and nuclear materials used in the manufacture of such weapons."

Criminal (civilian)

For the purposes of US criminal law concerning terrorism, weapons of mass destruction are defined as:

- any "destructive device" defined as any explosive, incendiary, or poison gas - bomb, grenade, rocket having a propellant charge of more than four ounces, missile having an explosive or incendiary charge of more than one-quarter ounce, mine, or device similar to any of the devices described in the preceding clauses
- any weapon that is designed or intended to cause death or serious bodily injury through the release,

dissemination, or impact of toxic or poisonous chemicals, or their precursors

- any weapon involving a biological agent, toxin, or vector
- any weapon that is designed to release radiation or radioactivity at a level dangerous to human life

The Federal Bureau of Investigation's definition is similar to that presented above from the terrorism statute:

- any "destructive device" as defined in Title 18 USC Section 921: any explosive, incendiary, or poison gas - bomb, grenade, rocket having a propellant charge of more than four ounces, missile having an explosive or incendiary charge of more than one-quarter ounce, mine, or device similar to any of the devices described in the preceding clauses
- any weapon designed or intended to cause death or serious bodily injury through the release, dissemination, or impact of toxic or poisonous chemicals or their precursors
- any weapon involving a disease organism
- any weapon designed to release radiation or radioactivity at a level dangerous to human life
- any device or weapon designed or intended to cause death or serious bodily injury by causing a malfunction of or destruction of an aircraft or other vehicle that carries humans or of an aircraft or other vehicle whose malfunction or destruction may cause said aircraft or other vehicle to cause death or serious bodily injury to humans who may be within range of the vector in its course of travel or the travel of its debris.

Indictments and convictions for possession and use of WMD such as truck bombs, pipe bombs, shoe bombs, and cactus needles coated with a biological toxin have been obtained under 18 USC 2332a.

As defined by 18 USC §2332 (a), a Weapon of Mass Destruction is:

- (a) any destructive device as defined in section 921 of the title;
- (B) any weapon that is designed or intended to cause death or serious bodily injury through the release, dissemination, or impact of toxic or poisonous chemicals, or their precursors;

- (C) any weapon involving a biological agent, toxin, or vector (as those terms are defined in section 178 of this title); or
- (D) any weapon that is designed to release radiation or radioactivity at a level dangerous to human life;

Under the same statute, conspiring, attempting, threatening, or using a Weapon of Mass Destruction may be imprisoned for any term of years or for life, and if by death, be punishable by death or by imprisonment for any terms of years or for life. They can also be asked to pay a maximum fine of $250,000.

The Washington Post reported on 30 March 2006: "Jurors asked the judge in the death penalty trial of Zacarias Moussaoui today to define the term 'weapons of mass destruction' and were told it includes airplanes used as missiles". Moussaoui was indicted and tried for the use of airplanes as WMD.

The surviving Boston Marathon bombing suspect, Dzhokhar Tsarnaev, was charged in April 2013 with the federal offense of "use of a weapon of mass destruction" after he and his brother allegedly placed crude shrapnel bombs, made from pressure cookers packed with ball bearings and nails, near the finish line of Boston's most famous race. His alleged terrorist act resulted in three deaths and at least 282 injuries.

TREATIES

The development and use of WMD is governed by several international conventions and treaties, although not all countries have signed and ratified them:

- Partial Test Ban Treaty
- Outer Space Treaty
- Nuclear Non-Proliferation Treaty (NPT)
- Seabed Arms Control Treaty
- Comprehensive Test Ban Treaty (CTBT, has not entered into force as of 2012)
- Biological and Toxin Weapons Convention (BWC)
- Chemical Weapons Convention (CWC)

USE, POSSESSION AND ACCESS

Nuclear Weapons

The only country to have used a nuclear weapon in war is the United States, which dropped two atomic bombs on the

Japanese cities of Hiroshima and Nagasaki during World War II. There are eight countries that have declared they possess nuclear weapons and are known to have tested a nuclear weapon, only five of which are members of the NPT. The eight areChina, France, India, North Korea, Pakistan, Russia, the United Kingdom, and the United States.

Israel is considered by most analysts to have nuclear weapons numbering in the low hundreds as well, but maintains an official policy of nuclear ambiguity, neither denying nor confirming its nuclear status.

South Africa developed a small nuclear arsenal in the 1980s but disassembled them in the early 1990s, making it the only country to have fully given up an independently developed nuclear weapons arsenal. Belarus, Kazakhstan, and Ukraine inherited stockpiles of nuclear arms following the break-up of the Soviet Union, but relinquished them to the Russian Federation.

Countries with access to nuclear weapons through nuclear sharing agreements include Belgium, Germany, Italy, the Netherlands, andTurkey. North Korea has claimed to have developed and tested nuclear devices. Although outside sources have been unable to unequivocally support the state's claims, North Korea has officially been identified to have nuclear weapons.

UNITED STATES POLITICS

Due to the indiscriminate impact of WMD, the fear of a WMD attack has shaped political policies and campaigns, fostered social movements, and has been the central theme of many films. Support for different levels of WMD development and control varies nationally and internationally. Yet understanding of the nature of the threats is not high, in part because of imprecise usage of the term by politicians and the media..

Fear of WMD, or of threats diminished by the possession of WMD, has long been used to catalyze public support for various WMD policies. They include mobilization of pro- and anti-WMD campaigners alike, and generation of popular political support. The term WMD may be used as a powerful buzzword or to generate a culture of fear. It is also used ambiguously, particularly by not distinguishing among the different types of WMD.

A television commercial called *Daisy*, promoting Democrat Lyndon Johnson's 1964 presidential candidacy, invoked the fear of a nuclear war and was an element in Johnson's subsequent election.

More recently, the threat of potential WMD in Iraq was used by President George W. Bush as justification for the 2003 invasion of Iraq. Broad reference to Iraqi WMD in general was seen as an element of President Bush's arguments. The claim that Iraq possessed Weapons of Mass Destruction (WMD) led to the invasion of Iraq in 2003 by Coalition forces. However, WMDs were not found.

In 2004, Polish troops found nineteen 1980s-era rocket warheads, thwarting an attempt by militants to buy them at $5000 each. Some of the rockets contained extremely deteriorated nerve agent.

Media Coverage

In 2004, the Center for International and Security Studies at Maryland (CISSM) released a report examining the media's coverage of WMD issues during three separate periods: nuclear weapons tests by India and Pakistan in May 1998; the US announcement of evidence of a North Korean nuclear weapons program in October 2002; and revelations about Iran's nuclear program in May 2003. The CISSM report notes that poor coverage resulted less from political bias among the media than from tired journalistic conventions. The report's major findings were that:

1. *Most media outlets represented WMD as a monolithic menace, failing to adequately distinguish between weapons programs and actual weapons or to address the real differences among chemical, biological, nuclear, and radiological weapons.*
2. *Most journalists accepted the Bush administration's formulation of the "War on Terror" as a campaign against WMD, in contrast to coverage during the Clinton era, when many journalists made careful distinctions between acts of terrorism and the acquisition and use of WMD.*
3. *Many stories stenographically reported the incumbent administration's perspective on WMD, giving too little critical examination of the way officials framed the events, issues, threats, and policy options.*

4. *Too few stories proffered alternative perspectives to official line, a problem exacerbated by the journalistic prioritizing of breaking-news stories and the "inverted pyramid" style of storytelling.*

In a separate study published in 2005, a group of researchers assessed the effects reports and retractions in the media had on people's memory regarding the search for WMD in Iraq during the 2003 Iraq War. The study focused on populations in two coalitioncountries (Australia and USA) and one opposed to the war (Germany). Results showed that US citizens generally did not correct initial misconceptions regarding WMD, even following disconfirmation; Australian and German citizens were more responsive to retractions. Dependence on the initial source of information led to a substantial minority of Americans exhibiting false memory that WMD were indeed discovered, while they were not. This led to three conclusions:

1. *The repetition of tentative news stories, even if they are subsequently disconfirmed, can assist in the creation of false memories in a substantial proportion of people.*
2. *Once information is published, its subsequent correction does not alter people's beliefs unless they are suspicious about the motives underlying the events the news stories are about.*
3. *When people ignore corrections, they do so irrespective of how certain they are that the corrections occurred.*

A poll conducted between June and September 2003 asked people whether they thought evidence of WMD had been discovered in Iraq since the war ended. They were also asked which media sources they relied upon. Those who obtained their news primarily from Fox News were three times as likely to believe that evidence of WMD had been discovered in Iraq than those who relied on PBS and NPR for their news, and one third more likely than those who primarily watched CBS.

In 2006 Fox News reported the claims of two Republican lawmakers that WMDs had been found in Iraq, based upon unclassified portions of a report by the National Ground Intelligence Center. Quoting from the report, Senator Rick Santorum said "Since 2003, coalition forces have recovered approximately 500 weapons munitions which contain degraded mustard or sarin nerve agent". According to David Kay, who appeared before the US House Armed Services Committee to discuss these badly corroded munitions, they were leftovers, many years old, improperly stored or destroyed by the Iraqis. Charles Duelfer agreed, stating on NPR's *Talk of the Nation*: "When I was running the ISG – the Iraq Survey Group – we had a couple of them that had been turned in to these IEDs, the improvised explosive devices. But they are local hazards. They are not a major, you know, weapon of mass destruction."

PUBLIC PERCEPTIONS

Awareness and opinions of WMD have varied during the course of their history. Their threat is a source of unease, security, and pride to different people. The anti-WMD movement is embodied most in nuclear disarmament, and led to the formation of the British Campaign for Nuclear Disarmament in 1957. In order to increase awareness of all kinds of WMD, in 2004 the nuclear physicist and Nobel Peace Prize winner Joseph Rotblatinspired the creation of The WMD Awareness Programme to provide trustworthy and up to date information on WMD world wide.

In 1998 University of New Mexico's Institute for Public Policy released their third report on US perceptions – including the general public, politicians and scientists – of nuclear weapons since the breakup of the Soviet Union. Risks of nuclear conflict, proliferation, and terrorism were seen as substantial.

While maintenance of a nuclear US arsenal was considered above average in importance, there was widespread support for a reduction in the stockpile, and very little support for developing and testing new nuclear weapons.

Also in 1998, but after the UNM survey was conducted, nuclear weapons became an issue in India's election of March, in relation to political tensions with neighboring Pakistan. Prior to the election the Bharatiya Janata Party (BJP) announced it would "declare India a nuclear weapon state" after coming to power.

BJP won the elections, and on 14 May, three days after India tested nuclear weapons for the second time, a public opinion poll reported that a majority of Indians favored the country's nuclear build-up.

On 15 April 2004, the Program on International Policy Attitudes (PIPA) reported that US citizens showed high levels of concern regarding WMD, and that preventing the spread of nuclear weapons should be "a very important US foreign policy goal", accomplished through multilateral arms control rather than the use of military threats.

A majority also believed the US should be more forthcoming with its biological research and its Nuclear Non-Proliferation Treatycommitment of nuclear arms reduction, and incorrectly thought the US was a party to various non-proliferation treaties.

A Russian opinion poll conducted on 5 August 2005 indicated half the population believes new nuclear powers have the right to possess nuclear weapons. 39% believes the Russian stockpile should be reduced, though not fully eliminated.

In Popular Culture

Weapons of mass destruction and their related impacts have been a mainstay of popular culture since the beginning of the Cold War, as both political commentary and humorous outlet.

COMMON HAZARD SYMBOLS

Radioactive Weaponry/hazard Symbol

The international radioactivity symbol (also known as trefoil) first appeared in 1946, at the University of California, Berkeley Radiation Laboratory. At the time, it was rendered as magenta, and was set on a blue background. It is drawn with a central circle of radius R, the blades having an internal radius of $1.5R$ and an external radius of $5R$, and separated from each other by 60°. It is meant to represent a radiating atom.

The International Atomic Energy Agency found, however, that the symbol is unintuitive and can be variously interpreted by those uneducated in its meaning, and that its role as a hazard warning was compromised as it did not clearly indicate "danger" to many non-Westerners and children who encountered it. As a result of research, a new radiation hazard symbol was developed to be placed near the most dangerous parts of radiation sources featuring a skull, someone running away, and using the colour red rather than yellow as the background.

9

The Global Health Effects of Nuclear War

Ever since the first nuclear bomb was exploded at Alamogordo, New Mexico, on 16 July 1945, the threat of nuclear war has existed. So far the only nuclear bombs used in war were the two dropped by the United States on Hiroshima and Nagasaki on the sixth and ninth of August 1945. Today the United States possesses some 30,000 nuclear weapons, the Soviet Union some 20,000, and China, France and Britain several hundred to a few thousand each. A few other countries such as Israel have or may soon have small nuclear arsenals.

The Hiroshima and Nagasaki bombs killed a total of perhaps 300,000 people - different estimates have been offered. What would be the result of all-out nuclear war using today's weapon arsenals? This question has become more important in many people's minds in the 1980s as world attention has again focused on the threat of nuclear war.

In the immediate vicinity of a nuclear explosion, most casualties result from blast, heat and fallout during the first few days. The blast or heat from a one megatonne bomb - about 75 times the power of the Hiroshima bomb, and a size often found in nuclear arsenals - would kill almost all people, even those in shelters, out to a distance of two kilometres. Beyond ten kilometres the chance of death even for people without special protection would be very small. If the bomb is exploded at an altitude higher than the radius of the fireball from the explosion, as happened at Hiroshima and Nagasaki, local fallout is minimal. If exploded at or near the earth's surface, fallout lethal to unprotected people will be deposited downwind - most often to the east toward which prevailing upper atmospheric winds blow - for a distance of up to hundreds of kilometres. After a fortnight the radiation levels will have dropped to about one thousandth of what they were one hour after the blast. A major global nuclear war could kill up to 400-500 million people from these effects, mainly in the United States, Soviet Union and Europe, and to a lesser extent China and Japan. The death toll would depend on a range of factors, such as the areas actually hit by weapons and the extent of evacuation and fallout protection. This death toll would be made up mainly of the people in the immediate vicinity or downwind of nuclear explosions, and would total about ten percent of the world's population. The largest population centres in countries all around the world were bombed, but there are no known plans for systematically bombing the largest population centres in areas such as India, Southeast Asia and China. On the other hand, if a nuclear war were limited in any sense - for example, restricted to Europe or to military targets - the immediate death toll would be less.

If agricultural or economic breakdown or epidemics occurred in the aftermath of nuclear war, many more people could die, perhaps as many as a few hundred million in the worst case. These would be primarily in the most heavily bombed areas, namely the United States, Soviet Union and Europe.

Nuclear war would also result in various long range effects, beyond the range of blast, heat and local fallout. These effects - effects hundreds or thousands of kilometres from nuclear explosions - are known as 'global' effects. The most well known is global radioactive fallout. Many people believe that this fallout, or some other effect, would cause the death of most or all the people on earth in the event of major nuclear war. This is the idea portrayed in the popular novel On the Beach. However, the available scientific evidence provides no support for such a doomsday scenario. My aim here is to describe in general terms the main global effects of nuclear war with direct consequences for human health. Four main categories will be treated: global fallout, ozone, climate and fires.

Global Fallout

When a nuclear bomb is exploded, energy is released by the fissioning (splitting) of either uranium-235 or plutonium. There are a range of products of this fissioning, many of which are radioactive - that is, they are unstable and decay sooner or later by emission of energetic radiation or particles. The most well-known fission product is strontium-90, which decays by emission of a beta particle. About half the strontium-90 nuclei decay in this way in a period of about 28 years, called the half-life. Different radioactive atoms have different half-lives, ranging from a fraction of a second to many millions of years. Other biologically important radioactive species produced by nuclear explosions are caesium-137 (half-life: 27 years), iodine-131 (half-life: eight days) and carbon-14 (half-life: 5600 years).

A nuclear bomb like that exploded over Hiroshima produces a total of about 800 grammes of fission products, measured one hour after the blast. The enormous heat generated by the explosion creates a huge upwards surge of air, resulting in the familiar mushroom cloud. The height of the cloud depends on the size of the explosion. Most of the fission products are carried into the atmosphere by this initial updraft. They become dangerous to humans when they return to earth.

If the bomb is exploded at or near the surface of the earth, a large amount of dust, dirt and other surface materials will also be lifted with the updraft. Some of the fission products will adhere to these particles, or onto the material used to construct the bomb. The very largest particles - stones and pebbles - will fall back to earth in a matter of minutes or hours. Lighter material - ash or dust - will fall to earth within a few days, or perhaps be incorporated in raindrops. The radioactive material which returns to earth within 24 hours is called early or local fallout. It is the most dangerous.

The fission products contain a mixture of different types of radioactive atoms, some of which decay quickly and others much more slowly. A rough rule of thumb is that as time increases by a factor of seven, the average decay rate drops by a factor of ten. Thus, compared to the decay rate one hour after the explosion, the rate will be about ten per cent at 7 hours, about one per cent at two days (about 7 x 7 hours), and about 0.1 per cent at two weeks (7 x 2 days). (After about six months the fall in the decay rate becomes faster than this.) For this reason, exposure to early fallout is the greatest danger due to radioactivity generated by nuclear explosions.

Radioactive material which takes longer than 24 hours to return to earth is called delayed or global fallout. Some of the delayed fallout remains in the troposphere for days, weeks or months. This tropospheric fallout usually returns to earth within ten or 15 deg of latitude of the original explosion, mostly by being incorporated in raindrops as they are formed. The clouds of nuclear explosions larger than about one megatonne penetrate partially or wholly into the stratosphere, and deposit fission products there, which become stratospheric fallout. Since the stratosphere has no rain formation and is less turbulent than the troposphere, radioactive particles in the stratosphere can take months or years to return to earth. During this time the particles can move to any part of the globe.

By the time stratospheric fallout reaches the earth, its radioactivity is greatly reduced. For example, after one year, the time typically required for any sizable amount of fission products to move from the northern to the southern stratosphere, the rate of decay will be less than a hundred thousandth of what it was one hour after the blast.

It is for this reason that stratospheric fallout does not have the potential to cause widespread and immediate sickness or death. A dose of ionising radiation of four to five sieverts to the body of a person at a single time is enough to cause death in about half the people exposed to it.

Doses of one to two sieverts cause sickness, while a dose of one half sievert often causes no overt symptoms, though it may have long term effects. For comparison, the average annual ionising radiation dose to individuals from 'natural' causes - from cosmic rays, radioactivity in rocks and other sources - is about one thousandth of a sievert (one millisievert). An average of another millisievert is contributed, for those with Western lifestyles, by sources of human origin, mainly medical x-rays. What ionising radiation exposure would result from a major nuclear war?

In the 1950s and early 1960s a large number of nuclear weapons were exploded in the atmosphere - a total of 430 megatonnes (Mt). This has led and is leading to an average ionising radiation exposure, both external and internal, of about two millisieverts over 30 years for people in the northern hemisphere, and about one-third this level in the southern hemisphere. A major nuclear war resulting in the explosion of 4000Mt would, according to simple scaling, lead to an average exposure ten times as great as occurred from previous tests.

Many of the 1950s-1960s explosions were very high yield, up to 60Mt, but most nuclear weapons are now 2Mt or smaller. Therefore, stratospheric fallout from a 4000Mt war would probably be less than ten times as great as from previous atmospheric tests. Furthermore, because material injected into the lower stratosphere is less likely to move great distances before returning to the troposphere, relative fallout levels in the southern hemisphere due to northern hemisphere explosions are likely to be smaller than the previous one-third ratio.

The lower injection of radioactive material into the stratosphere means correspondingly higher levels of tropospheric fallout, especially near the latitudes of the explosions. Since tropospheric fallout returns to earth more quickly than stratospheric fallout, it is more radioactive and dangerous. Thus the shift to lower yield nuclear weapons has reduced the health risk of nuclear war from radioactivity to people who are far from the main regions of nuclear conflict, but increased it for those near the latitudes of numerous nuclear explosions. These conclusions are tentative, since it is possible that the rapid explosion of 4000Mt of nuclear weapons could greatly alter the atmospheric circulation, with unknown consequences for the distribution of fallout.

There are two main hazards from exposure to low levels of ionising radiation: cancers and genetic defects. In essence, the energetic radiation and particles from radioactive decay can disrupt the structure of cells in the body or in genetic material, causing or contributing to cancer or genetic defects. For several decades, a scientific controversy has raged over the effect of exposure to low levels of ionising radiation. Since the cancers and genetic defects caused by this radiation are usually impossible to distinguish from cancer and genetic defects due to other causes, available evidence is not adequate to measure the effect at low doses. The controversy concerns which theory is most appropriate to use to extrapolate from evidence at higher exposures (above one-half to one sievert).

An authoritative report on the effect of ionising radiation, called Beir III, concludes that exposure of the whole body to 100 millisieverts will result in an increase in the naturally occurring cancer death rate of 0.5 per cent to 1.4 per cent, and 50 to 750 additional serious genetic disorders per million live births. An average exposure of 20 millisieverts from delayed fallout from a nuclear war could, according to these figures, cause 600,000 to 1,700,000 additional cancer deaths and 40,000 to 600,000 additional genetic defects, manifested over a period of 50 years or more. Figures on risks of cancer and genetic defects from exposure to ionising radiation used by the International Commission on Radiological Protection for radiation protection purposes lie within the range of uncertainty specified by the Beir report. If the effects of carbon-14 over many thousands of years are included, these figures should be doubled.

There were two dissenting statements in Beir III, one suggesting the estimates are too high and the other that they are too low. Recent evidence on ionising radiation and cancer appears to support the latter view. Recent evidence also suggests that the Beir III figures for genetic defects may be too large. In any case, the figures are very uncertain, and could easily be ten times too small or ten times too large.

NUCLEAR REACTORS

Nuclear power reactors contain an enormous amount of radioactive material. Much attention has been focused on the possibility that reactor containment systems might fail, leading to escape of radioactivity and the possible death of up to tens of thousands of people. The meltdown and dispersal of a portion of the core of a nuclear power reactor could readily result from attack on a nuclear power plant by conventional or nuclear weapons which disabled cooling and other control systems. Even more devastating, though, would be the result of direct hit by a nuclear weapon on a nuclear power reactor, with the nuclear reactor's radioactive inventory being directly incorporated into the fireball of the nuclear explosion. This inventory would then be incorporated into the fallout cloud from the explosion.

The short-lived decay products in the reactor mostly decay away during its operation, leaving the longer-lived products such as strontium-90 and caesium-137. Therefore, while the radioactivity from a one megatonne nuclear explosion remains higher than that from a large (1000MW) nuclear power reactor for a few days, afterwards the reactor's radioactivity poses a greater danger. If many reactor cores were vapourised in this way, large areas of countryside could be made highly radioactive for long periods of time.

It is possible that nuclear power reactors would be nuclear targets, because of their high economic value, because of their capability of producing plutonium for making nuclear weapons, or because of the devastating radioactivity that would be spread about.

The latter effect could also be achieved by attacking radioactive waste repositories or reprocessing plants. The main concentrations of large nuclear reactors are found in the United States, Europe, the Soviet Union and Japan, that is, those areas most likely to be involved in nuclear war in any case. If nuclear power facilities were attacked, therefore, most of the extra deaths and injuries would result in those regions. Because reactor cores are very well protected, dispersal of the core materials is unlikely to occur unless they are the specific target of highly accurate weapons.

Plutonium

One special product of nuclear explosions is plutonium. Plutonium-239 is a fissionable substance and is used to construct nuclear weapons. It is also a highly dangerous radioactive material. It decays by emitting an alpha particle, which cannot penetrate a piece of paper or the skin. But once inside the body, plutonium-239 is a potent cancer-inducing agent. Experiments have shown that less than one milligramme of insoluble plutonium oxide is definitely enough to cause lung cancer in beagle dogs. It is not known how much plutonium is required to induce lung cancer in humans, but estimates as low as a few millionths of a gramme have been made.

Previous nuclear explosions have injected an estimated 5 tonnes of plutonium into the atmosphere. No one knows what effect this is having on human health. One of the highest estimates of the consequences is by John Gofman, who thinks 950,000 people worldwide may die of lung cancer as a result of this plutonium, over a period of many decades. A 4000Mt nuclear war could cause the release of ten times as much plutonium, some 50 tonnes, with ten times the consequences. Large nuclear power reactors contain an average inventory of perhaps 300 kilogrammes of plutonium. If it is assumed that all the plutonium from 20 large reactors - more than one tenth of the world total - were dispersed in a 4000Mt nuclear war, this would add another six tonnes of plutonium to the total released into the atmosphere. This would be about one tenth the amount directly released by the nuclear explosions themselves.

The cancers and genetic defects caused by global fallout from a nuclear war would only appear over a period of many decades, and would cause only a small increase in the current rates of cancer and genetic defects. The scientific evidence clearly shows that global fallout from even the largest nuclear war poses no threat to the survival of the human species. Nevertheless, the fact that hundreds of thousands or millions of people who would suffer and die from global fallout cannot be ignored. Furthermore, many more people than this would die from exposure to fallout in the immediate vicinity of nuclear explosions.

IMPORTANCE OF THE OZONE LAYER

The sun emits light or radiation at a large range of energies or frequencies. Much of this radiation is absorbed by the earth's atmosphere and does not reach the surface. Human eyes have evolved to be highly receptive to radiation in the so-called visual spectrum which is not absorbed very much at all by the atmosphere. At the violet, high-energy end of this band of transmitted light lies what is called ultraviolet light or uv.

Ultraviolet light with high energies is strongly absorbed by molecular oxygen - the oxygen we breathe - in the upper atmosphere. This absorption can cause the molecular oxygen to break into two oxygen atoms each of which in turn can react with other molecular oxygen to form ozone, a compound made up of three oxygen atoms. In turn, ozone strongly absorbs ultraviolet light itself, including uv with energies lower than that absorbed by molecular oxygen. Small amounts of uv can be beneficial, especially in forming vitamin D in the skin. But large amounts can be harmful, especially of the more energetic uv, causing sunburn and skin cancer in humans and adversely affecting the growth of many plants. Many scientists believe that much of biological evolution took place under the protective uv shield of upper atmospheric ozone.

In the early 1970s scientists first became aware that oxides of nitrogen play a large role in reducing ozone levels through catalytic destruction: a single nitric oxide molecule can help destroy many molecules of ozone without being destroyed itself. This knowledge soon led to concern about the effects of oxides of nitrogen from supersonic transport aircraft (SSTs) on ozone and led to studies on this problem and later to studies of other threats to ozone such as from fluorocarbons from aerosol sprays and refrigerants.

Another major threat to ozone comes from nuclear explosions. Nitric oxide is produced essentially by the 'burning' of nitrogen in the atmosphere, and this occurs whenever air temperatures are sufficiently hot: in automobile engines, in aircraft engines and in nuclear explosions. Studies of the creation of oxides of nitrogen by nuclear explosions were first undertaken as part of the SST debate, to determine whether the nuclear weapons tests in the 1950s and 1960s had reduced observed ozone levels. It was only in 1974 that John Hampson made a point which had been overlooked, namely that large-scale nuclear war could cause a major and disastrous reduction in ozone levels.

Calculations made in the mid-1970s assuming large nuclear arsenals with many high-yield explosions concluded that reductions of ozone could reach 50 per cent or more in the northern hemisphere, with smaller reductions in the southern hemisphere. But since the number of high-yield weapons in present nuclear arsenals is now smaller, much less oxides of nitrogen would be deposited in the stratosphere by nuclear war than assumed in earlier calculations, and so significant ozone reductions are unlikely.

This conclusion remains tentative. The actual behaviour of stratospheric ozone is quite complicated, involving many chemical compounds and numerous chemical reactions, the changing effects of temperature, the angle and intensity of sunlight, and the effect of air motions. Computer models of the effects of nuclear war on ozone are able to take into account only a part of this complexity, and new information about chemical reaction rates in particular have led in the past to periodic revisions in the calculated effects of added oxides of nitrogen.

If significant ozone reduction did occur, the most important direct effect on humans would be an increase in skin cancer. However, this is seldom lethal, and could be avoided by reducing exposure to sunlight. Potentially more serious would be effects on crops. Some of the important grains, for example, are sensitive to uv. Whether the net effects on crop yields would be significant is hard to estimate. But whatever the reduction in ozone, ozone levels would return pretty much to normal after a few years. It seems unlikely that in the context of a major nuclear war the changes in uv alone would be of serious concern. In particular, the threat of human extinction raised by Jonathan Schell in The Fate of the Earth, based mostly on effects of increased uv from ozone reduction, seems very small indeed.

It is sometimes claimed that nuclear war could destroy ozone to such an extent that humans and animals would be blinded by excess uv. Even if large numbers of high-yield weapons were exploded, this possibility seems very unlikely except for a contribution to snow blindness in the far north. Stratospheric ozone can never be completely removed, but at most reduced greatly. Even if a 50 per cent or more reduction in ozone occurred - and as noted this seems improbable with present nuclear arsenals - protection from uv for humans could be obtained from sunglasses or just ordinary glasses, which absorb uv. For animals, the following considerations are relevant. Ozone levels vary considerably from place to place and from time to time, both seasonally and daily (sometimes by up to 50 per cent). Sunlight at the equator typically passes through only half as much ozone as at the mid-latitudes, yet animals at the equator are not known to go blind more often than elsewhere. Furthermore, most ozone reductions from a nuclear war would be in the mid and high latitudes, where ozone levels are higher to start with and where the 'path length' of sunlight through ozone is increased due to its oblique angle of incidence. But this does not mean complacency is warranted, as the concerns of John Hampson illustrate.

HAMPSON'S ALTERNATIVE VIEW ON THE OZONE LAYER

The brief treatment given so far about the likely effects of nuclear war on ozone has presented for the most part the conventional scientific wisdom on this topic. But there is room for disagreement. One of those who think that scientists may be underestimating the danger is John Hampson, who originally raised the alarm about the effects of nuclear war on ozone. Here some of Hampson's views will be outlined, both to present his provocative ideas and to illustrate the large imponderables associated with present understanding of the global effects of nuclear war.

Hampson's first major point is that the standard values given for the amount of oxides of nitrogen deposited by nuclear weapons in the upper atmosphere may be underestimated. He notes that one of the few observations of oxides of nitrogen in the wake of high-yield nuclear tests can be explained if four times as much oxides of nitrogen are produced in nuclear explosions as found in other studies, and that all this is deposited in the stratosphere.

Hampson's second major point is that a major ozone reduction might be caused by detonation of nuclear weapons at high altitudes. Because of the low atmospheric density at say 100 kilometres, much of the high level gamma radiation produced by a nuclear explosion will produce x-rays which penetrate to about 40 kilometres. Because of the low atmospheric density, a large fraction of the bomb's energy can go to produce oxides of nitrogen, perhaps up to 20 times as much as from a surface explosion.

If the oxides of nitrogen remained at 40 kilometres altitude, they would not cause a large reduction in total ozone, since much ozone resides at lower altitudes. But since the ozone in the 40 kilometre region would be greatly reduced, absorption of uv by ozone would be reduced and the upper stratosphere would be quickly cooled. This would result in upper stratospheric instability. Hampson thinks that the cloud of oxides of nitrogen would sink by maybe one kilometre per day, reaching the peak ozone altitude of 30 kilometres in 10 days. If enough explosive power were released, the result could be a drastic reduction in ozone levels.

Hampson considers several scenarios in which high altitude explosions might play a role. One scenario involves antiballistic missiles (ABMs). The Soviet Union has a set of ABMs around Moscow, designed to intercept incoming missiles by exploding their own nuclear weapons at high altitudes. Hampson suggests that if these ABMs were used accidentally, perhaps after a false alarm, a large amount of oxides of nitrogen could be produced in the upper stratosphere. In the ten or 15 days required for the oxides of nitrogen to settle down to 30 kilometres, the oxides of nitrogen cloud would have blown by prevailing upper atmospheric winds over North America, which might be exposed to intense uv for a week or so. This scenario raises the possibility of using an apparently 'inadvertent' use of ABMs or other nuclear explosions as a form of environmental warfare by creating localised depletions in the ozone layer.

Hampson agrees that high uv levels do not pose a serious direct threat to human health. But he is less optimistic about effects on the biosphere. He has his own ideas, contrary to the current scientific orthodoxy, about the evolution of the ozone layer in the history of the earth, and the evolution of life under it. Among many points he raises, he thinks that studies of the impact of changes in ozone should begin with organisms he calls procarytoids, which are capable of forming amino acids directly from natural elements. He thinks it should be determined whether increased uv from ozone reductions could eliminate procarytoids, and whether humans could survive without their existence.

Hampson's views are outlined here not as established fact - which they are not - but to show the sort of dangers which may exist unrecognised by prevailing scientific views. It is a telling commentary on scientific research priorities that the possibilities raised by Hampson - and many others - are receiving almost no study by scientists. There are several reasons for this. One is simply that there is much more money available for studying how to wage nuclear war - for example, how to make smaller nuclear weapons or more accurate missile guidance systems - than for studying the human consequences of nuclear war. Second, Hampson's ideas are somewhat outside the main stream of scientific thought about ozone and production of oxides of nitrogen. It is difficult enough to obtain jobs and research grants to study the effects of nuclear war even when staying firmly within prevailing scientific ideas.

Third; Hampson's concerns involve a close intermeshing of scientific and strategic factors. For example, the current hazard from high altitude ABM explosions is being reduced: of the original 64 Galosh ABMs around Moscow, 32 have been dismantled. But an investigation of Hampson's arguments would be unwelcome to military decision-makers, who would not want to be constrained in any use of high-yield weapons or deploying of future ABMs. Fourth, to study the issues raised by Hampson would require an interdisciplinary person or team, involving knowledge of non-equilibrium reaction kinetics, stratospheric chemistry and dynamics, ozone history and evolution, and nuclear strategies. Finally, Hampson himself lacks credibility and pull because, in spite of a long and productive scientific career, he has no current scientific or academic position. Although in principle scientific ideas are judged by their merit, independently of who presents them, scientific practice is different. Obtaining attention, credibility and funds depends substantially on one's formal position and political sway within the power structure of science.

A SUBURB OF HIROSHIMA AFTER THE BOMB HAD BEEN DROPPED IN 1945

The Effects of Nuclear War on Climate

A major nuclear war would deposit millions of tonnes of dust in the stratosphere. Some sunlight would be absorbed or reflected away from the earth by the dust, causing a decrease in the earth's temperature. This in turn could conceivably trigger a major climatic change. For example, lowered temperatures could cause an increase in snow and ice near the polar caps, thus an increased reflection of light, and further lowering of temperatures.

Stratospheric dust from a nuclear war seems unlikely to cause such climatic change. In 1883 the volcanic eruption at Krakatoa deposited some 10 to 100 thousand million tonnes of dust in the stratosphere, and the 1963 Mt Agung eruption about half as much. These injections seem to have caused a minor cooling of the surface temperature of the earth, at most about half a degree Celsius, lasting a few years, with no long term consequences. A nuclear war involving 4000Mt from present arsenals would probably deposit much less dust in the stratosphere than either the Krakatoa or Mt Agung eruptions.

Another possibility is that decreases in ozone or increases in oxides of nitrogen levels in the stratosphere, caused by nuclear war, could lead to climatic change. A reduction in ozone levels by a factor of two could cause a decrease in surface temperature of one half to one degree Centigrade, but including oxides of nitrogen in the calculation reduces this effect. Whether or not a change in temperature at the earth's surface by this amount for a few years could cause irreversible climatic change is hard to assess. The National Academy of Sciences study concluded that the effects of dust and oxides of nitrogen injection into the stratosphere 'would probably lie within normal global climatic variability, but the possibility of climatic changes of a more dramatic nature cannot be ruled out'. Since the Academy assumed a nuclear war with the explosion of many more high-yield weapons than are presently deployed, the danger of climatic change from dust or oxides of nitrogen is almost certainly less than assessed in their report.

Fires and Smoke

In mid 1982, Paul Crutzen and John Birks drew attention to a previously overlooked major effect of nuclear war. They note that nuclear attacks would ignite numerous fires in cities, industry and especially in forests, crop areas and oil and gas fields. These fires would produce immense amounts of particulate matter which would remain in the lower atmosphere for weeks even after the fires ceased. The smaller particles, called aerosols, would absorb sunlight. A large nuclear war with many fires and large aerosol production could lead to a reduction in sunlight in the mid-northern hemisphere by 90 per cent or more for a period of a few months. This reduction would pose no direct threat to human health, but indirect effects could be widespread. If the nuclear war occurred during the agricultural growing season of the northern hemisphere, food production could be virtually eliminated for that season. This could greatly increase the chance of mass starvation in the north, though it is possible that stored food and changes in dietary habits could prevent this. If the reduction in ground level sunlight were 99 per cent or more, this could lead to the death of most of the phytoplankton and herbivorous zooplankton in half the northern oceans. This could lead to extinction of species and unpredictable changes in the balance of life on earth. Another effect of the fires would be production of large amounts of oxides of nitrogen and reactive hydrocarbons in the lower atmosphere, changes in lower atmospheric dynamics, and creation of ozone and other potent air pollutants. (While ozone plays a useful role in the stratosphere it can be harmful to living things at ground level.) In effect, much of the northern hemisphere could be exposed to severe photochemical smog for a period of weeks. This could cause health problems in susceptible people, especially the aged. Potentially more disastrous would be the negative effect of the smog on agricultural productivity, further increasing the chance of crop failure and consequent starvation.

Effects on Australia

The available evidence suggests that the global health effects of a major nuclear war are likely to be much less devastating than the immediate effects of blast, heat and local fallout. Present knowledge indicates that a large nuclear war in the northern hemisphere would have the following effects on Australia:

- from fallout, death of perhaps 1000 people from cancers and genetic defects over 50 years;
- from changes in ozone, a negligible effect;
- from climatic changes, a tiny chance of any effect;
- from fires, a negligible effect.

But this conclusion does not mean that the global effects should be ignored by Australians.

First, many people will die worldwide from cancers and genetic defects caused by global fallout, and possibly from other global effects. Whether the total is 10,000 or 10,000,000, the suffering and death will be real for those who experience it, and should not be discounted by use of comparisons. Second, there does exist a chance that major climatic changes, alterations in agricultural productivity, or consequences for global ecology could result from nuclear war.

NOW-FAMILIAR MUSHROOM CLOUD FROM A NUCLEAR BOMB BLAST

Third, simply not enough is known to predict with confidence all the global effects of nuclear war. The implications for ozone were not publicised until 1974 and the consequences of fires were first publicised in 1982. This suggests that further significant effects may remain to be discovered. Furthermore, the exact consequences of known processes are a subject of scientific controversy. John Hampson's scenario for possible inadvertent destruction of ozone in a local region is an example of what may happen within the limits of scientific possibility. Until much more study is made of the effects of nuclear war, a high level of uncertainty will remain. Fourth, whatever the scale of global effects of nuclear war, the potential for immediate death and destruction in areas directly attacked is more than sufficient to justify the most strenuous efforts to eliminate the nuclear threat.

Nuclear war will hit hardest at the areas bombed, not only directly from blast, heat and local fallout but also from delayed tropospheric fallout, fires and possible agricultural or economic breakdown. Since physical effects far from the regions of nuclear explosions are much less, the most important threat to a country such as Australia is direct nuclear attack. The prime targets in Australia are the United States military bases at Pine Gap, Nurrungar and North West Cape. Attacks on these bases would kill perhaps a few thousand people. There is a smaller chance of attacks on Cockburn Sound and on Darwin RAAF base, which are hosts for United States strategic nuclear ships, submarines and aircraft. Nuclear bombing of these two facilities, which are close to the population centres of Perth and Darwin respectively, could kill up to one hundred thousand people, depending on the wind direction at the time. Perhaps least likely, but certainly most devastating, would be nuclear attacks on major population centres. For example, the ports of major Australian cities could well be bombed if United States warships carrying strategic nuclear weapons were in harbour. Major population centres might also be hit as a consequence of attacks on associated military or economic facilities. Such attacks could kill from a few hundred thousand to several million people.

In the absence of direct attacks, the major indirect effects of nuclear war on a country such as Australia would not be physical but economic, political and social. Economically, nuclear war would cause an enormous disruption of world production and trade. Politically, nuclear war seems likely to cause massive upheavals not only in countries directly involved but in many of those far from the direct destruction. The social effects of nuclear war would be many, and include the psychological effects of massive nuclear destruction and the more immediate stresses of large numbers of refugees from Europe and North America. Study of and planning for these non-physical effects of nuclear war has been meagre or nonexistent. But unless the almost total lack of progress towards nuclear disarmament since 1945 is somehow reversed, these possible effects seem certain to become reality sooner or later.

EXPLOSIVE POWER IN A GLOBAL NUCLEAR WAR

The nuclear bomb exploded over Hiroshima had an explosive power of about 13 kilotonnes, denoted 13kt. One kt is the equivalent of one thousand tonnes (of one thousand kilogrammes each) of chemical explosives. The Hiroshima bomb was an enriched uranium fission bomb and the Nagasaki bomb of 21kt was a plutonium fission bomb. Much greater explosive power can be obtained by using an enriched uranium fission explosion as a trigger to cause nuclear fusion in a mixture of lithium and deuterium (heavy hydrogen). This is the thermonuclear, fusion, hydrogen or H-bomb. Unenriched uranium is often put around the fusion bomb to absorb emitted neutrons and cause further fissions and thus increase explosive power. This is the standard fission-fusion-fission bomb, whose explosive power is usually measured in megatonnes (denoted Mt), with 1Mt equal to 1000kt. The largest atmospheric nuclear explosion was one by the Soviet Union in 1961, of about 60Mt yield.

A typical large-sized nuclear explosive in the 'strategic' arsenals of the United States or the Soviet Union used to be about 1Mt, and many weapons of this size are deployed today in the payloads of ballistic missiles. The trend in the United States for the past decade or so, and in the Soviet Union for a few years, has been to switch from a single large warhead to several smaller warheads in the payload of strategic ballistic missiles. For example, a single 1Mt bomb might be replaced by ten 50kt bombs, each independently targetable. In this case this change reduces total explosive power by one half, while the total surface area that potentially can be destroyed is increased by one third.

The overwhelming bulk of nuclear explosive power resides in the arsenals of the two nuclear superpowers, the United States and the Soviet Union. In 1960 this explosive power totalled perhaps 60,000Mt. But due to the trend noted above, present arsenals total about 11,000Mt: about 3,500Mt for the United States and 7,500Mt for the Soviet Union. While the trend to larger numbers of smaller warheads increases the potential area destroyed by nuclear weapons, the reduction in total megatonnage reduces the potential global effects. This is especially the case since the clouds from nuclear explosions of 1Mt or less are unlikely to rise high into the stratosphere, reducing stratospheric fallout and effects on ozone.

What fraction of the 11,000Mt would be exploded in a major nuclear war? This is hard to assess, but almost certainly much will not be exploded. Both the United States and the Soviet

Union place a high priority on targeting their opponent's military forces, nuclear forces in particular. A sizable fraction of nuclear arsenals is likely to be destroyed before use (attacks on nuclear submarines, airfields, missile silos), be unavailable for use (submarines in port, missiles cut off from communications) or fail to perform properly.

One estimate is that one sixth to one third of superpower arsenals will be used, depending on whether the war occurs suddenly or builds up gradually.

Overkill

'Overkill: the ability to exterminate a population more than once. "Both the US and the Soviet Union now possess nuclear stockpiles large enough to exterminate mankind three or four - some say ten - times over" (Philip Noel-Baker, Nobel Peace Prize winner, 1971).'

Many people believe that the capacity of nuclear weapons for 'overkill' means that all or most of the people on earth would die in a major nuclear war. In spite of the prevalence of this idea, there is little scientific evidence to support it.

Many calculations of 'overkill' appear to be made using the nuclear attacks on Hiroshima and Nagasaki as a baseline. Estimates of the number of people killed at Hiroshima from a 13kt bomb range from 63,000 to over 200,000. Adopting a figure of 130,000 for illustrative purposes gives ten people killed for each tonne of nuclear explosive. By linear extrapolation, explosion of a third of a million times as much explosive power, 4000Mt, would kill a third of a million times as many people, namely 40,000 million, or nearly ten times the present world population.

But this factor of ten is misleading, since linear extrapolation does not apply. Suppose the bomb dropped on Hiroshima had been 1000 times as powerful, 13Mt. It could not have killed 1000 times as many people, but at most the entire population of Hiroshima perhaps 250,000. Re-doing the 'overkill' calculation using these figures gives not a figure of ten but of only 0.02. This example shows that crude linear extrapolations of this sort are unlikely to provide any useful information about the effects of nuclear war. 'Overkill' can be meaningful if applied to specific targets which will be attacked by several nuclear weapons. But applied to the entire world population the concept of 'overkill' is misleading. By the same logic it might be said that there is enough water in the oceans to drown everyone ten times.

It has been argued that if the megatonnage in nuclear arsenals were increased by ten or 100 times and used in war, the fallout would be sufficient to threaten the life of most people on earth. Since total megatonnage has been decreasing in recent years, this particular possibility remains hypothetical, at least at the moment.

THE HUMANITARIAN CONSEQUENCES OF NUCLEAR WAR

In March, 130 nations gathered in Oslo for a two-day conference on the humanitarian consequences of nuclear war. The five countries that the nuclear Nonproliferation Treaty (NPT) recognizes as nuclear-weapon states staged a coordinated boycott, arguing that a meeting that discussed what will actually happen if nuclear weapons are used would somehow distract them from the important initiatives they are pursuing to lower the number of nuclear weapons that they possess.

Next February, there will be a follow-up conference in Mexico to further delineate the medical effects of nuclear war as they are now understood and to consider the circumstances under which nuclear war might occur.

Far from being a distraction, these meetings are helping to create the conditions necessary for the elimination of nuclear weapons. The United States and the four other NPT nuclear-weapon states should participate in the Mexico conference and actively promote the process launched in Oslo to educate policymakers and the general public about the catastrophic humanitarian consequences of nuclear war.

This task is particularly urgent in view of the new data that have emerged over the last few years. This information indicates that even a very limited nuclear war, confined to one region of the globe, would have devastating effects worldwide.

In 2006, climatologist Alan Robock; Brian Toon, a professor of atmospheric and oceanic sciences; and four colleagues examined the consequences of a potential limited nuclear war between India and Pakistan. They chose to examine the effects of this scenario because of the two countries' long history of conflict and the ongoing risk of a nuclear exchange. India and Pakistan have fought three wars since they gained independence in 1947 and have come close to war twice when armed with nuclear weapons. During one crisis in the 1990s, it was reported that Pakistani planes armed with nuclear bombs were kept on the runway with their engines running 24 hours a day so they would be ready for takeoff on a few minutes' notice. It is easy to imagine events, such as an increase in tension over the disputed territories in Kashmir or another terrorist attack like those at the Indian parliament in 2001 or in Mumbai in 2008, that could escalate into full-scale warfare and the use of nuclear weapons.

In their study, Robock and Toon assumed that each country used 50 nuclear bombs, each with an explosive power of 15 kilotons—the power of the bomb dropped on Hiroshima in 1945—against urban targets in the other country. The weapons involved represent less than one-half of the current Indian and Pakistani arsenals and less than 0.5 percent of the world's nuclear arsenals. The local effects were devastating: 20 million dead in the first week from blast effects, burns, and acute radiation exposure. Even more disturbing were their findings concerning the far-reaching disruption to global climate conditions that this conflict would cause.

The scientists found that the firestorms generated by these nuclear explosions would loft about 5 million tons of black soot high into the atmosphere. The soot would block out sunlight, dropping surface temperatures across the planet by an average of 1.3 degrees Celsius. The cooling would be much more severe in the internal regions of the major continents, shortening the growing season in areas where much of the world's grain is produced. In addition, the cooling would lower total precipitation worldwide as less water evaporated from the oceans to fall back as rain or snow, and there would be significant changes in precipitation patterns.

Further, by heating the upper atmosphere, the soot particles would cause a major decrease in stratospheric ozone. By allowing substantially more ultraviolet light to reach the earth's surface, this would further reduce crop yields. The soot particles would be injected so high in the atmosphere that they would not be washed out by rainfall. Their effects would persist for a full decade until they gradually settled back to earth.

The climate disruption predicted by the Robock-Toon study has been independently confirmed in separate studies done by climatologists Michael Mills2 and Andrea Stenke, each of whom considered the same limited war scenario but used a different climate model.

In the last two years, a number of studies have attempted to look at the effect this climate disruption would have on food production. Environmental scientist Mutlu Özdogan looked at soybean production and corn production in the U.S. Corn Belt and found an average decline of 7 percent in soybean production and 12 percent in corn production in the decade following a limited war in South Asia. Crop specialist Lili Xia and Robock examined the impact on middle-season rice production in China and found a 15 percent decline from the prewar level for the 10 years following this conflict.

The world is not prepared to deal with this kind of significant decline in food production. World grain reserves amount to less than 70 days of consumption and would not offer a significant buffer against a sharp and sustained reduction in grain harvests. In addition, 870 million people in the world today already are malnourished. They receive less than the 1,800 calories per day required for the average adult to maintain his or her body mass and do a small amount of physical work to gather or grow food. Even a 10 or 15 percent decline from these levels of food consumption, sustained over a full decade, would be catastrophic. The decline in food consumption, however, probably would be much larger than the decline in food production. Market forces would magnify the impact with large rises in food prices, making even the available food inaccessible to the poor, who are already malnourished precisely because they cannot afford enough food at current prices.

Furthermore, some 300 million people live in countries where, although most people enjoy adequate nutrition today, much of the food is imported. Most of the countries of North Africa and the Middle East and many of the wealthy industrial countries of East Asia, including Japan, South Korea, and Taiwan, fall into this category. In the face of significant declines in food production, it is probable that grain-exporting countries would suspend exports. This has happened repeatedly, for limited periods of time, over the last decade in response to local crop shortfalls. Thus, these 300 million people also would face severe food insecurity.

In April 2012, at the Nobel Peace Laureates Summit in Chicago, International Physicians for the Prevention of Nuclear

War (IPPNW) and its U.S. affiliate, Physicians for Social Responsibility, released a report, "Nuclear Famine," examining this potential catastrophe. The report concluded that more than one billion people might starve as a result of a limited, regional nuclear war.

Since then, Xia and Robock have generated new data examining the impact of a limited nuclear war in South Asia on grain crops other than rice in China. Their findings, which will be published later this year, show that these other grains are affected much more severely than rice. In particular, production of the second-largest grain crop, winter wheat, is projected to fall 31 percent.

These new findings suggest that the "Nuclear Famine" report may have seriously underestimated the extent of the catastrophe that would follow a regional nuclear conflict and that arms control advocates need to fundamentally rethink their assumptions about limited nuclear war. The report assumed that China, along with most of the rest of the industrial world, would be spared actual famine. The latest studies suggest that there might be widespread starvation in China, putting another 1.3 billion people at risk. At the very least, the predicted food shortfalls would create a decade of severe economic and social instability in China, which is the largest country in the world and has the world's second-largest and most dynamic economy. China also has a large nuclear arsenal of its own, estimated to be nearly 300 warheads, about 50 to 75 of which are deliverable by land-based intercontinental ballistic missiles.

There are no simulations examining whether there will be similar shortfalls in other temperate-zone grain producers such as Canada, Russia, the United States, and Europe except for Özdogan's study of corn and soybeans in the United States. In the absence of such studies, it seems prudent to assume that these countries might well suffer the same major food shortages that are now predicted for China.

REGIONAL WAR, GLOBAL IMPACT

In the 1980s, there was a general understanding that large-scale nuclear war between the United States and the Soviet Union would be a disaster, not just for those countries but for the whole planet. From the studies described above, it is clear that even a much more limited nuclear war would be a global catastrophe, with severe humanitarian consequences extending far beyond the countries directly involved in the conflict.

These findings have significant implications for nuclear weapons policy choices in South Asia and for the policies of other states toward India and Pakistan. Yet, the issue extends well beyond South Asia. The arsenals of China, France, Israel, and the United Kingdom are all capable of causing the same or greater degrees of climate disruption.

More worrisome are the arsenals of the nuclear superpowers. Each U.S. Trident submarine can carry 96 warheads, each of which is 10 to 30 times more powerful than the weapons that were considered in the South Asia study. That means that each of these submarines can cause this nuclear famine scenario many times over. The United States has 14 of them, as well as an arsenal of land-based missiles and a fleet of strategic bombers armed with cruise missiles and gravity bombs. The Russian arsenal has a similar degree of overkill capacity.

The danger of nuclear war is often dismissed as a low-probability event and therefore not a cause for concern. The vast majority of the population, including people who were intensely aware of the nuclear danger during the Cold War, behaves as if this were true. Yet, the danger of nuclear war did not go away when the Berlin Wall came down. The arsenals remain, and the chance of nuclear war is not at all remote. As the number of nuclear-armed states increases, especially as nuclear arsenals grow in areas of chronic and seemingly intractable conflict, such as South Asia and the Middle East, the danger becomes even greater.

The possibility of war between the nuclear superpowers also still exists. Even if the likelihood of a deliberate nuclear war between the United States and Russia has declined, there remains the very real possibility of an accidental nuclear war.

There have been at least five incidents since 1979 in which Moscow or Washington was prepared to start a nuclear war in the mistaken belief that it was already under attack by the other side. The most recent known incident occurred in January 1995, a full five years after the fall of the Berlin Wall. The conditions that existed then have not changed fundamentally.

Human error, a computer failure, or perhaps a cyberattack launched by a terrorist group all could lead to the unintended launch of nuclear weapons. The new understanding of the climatic consequences of nuclear war makes it clear that even a very limited use of these weapons would be disastrous.

In his June speech in Berlin, President Barack Obama called for further reductions in the U.S. and Russian arsenals, suggesting a new target of 1,000 warheads on each side. This is a useful and important step in the right direction, but only if it is indeed a step toward further reductions designed to eliminate nuclear weapons altogether. If these reductions serve to legitimize the indefinite retention of nuclear weapons at an "acceptable" level, they will not fundamentally reduce the nuclear threat, for arsenals of this size would still pose an existential threat to human civilization.

During the Cold War, there was a widespread understanding of the medical consequences of nuclear war. That understanding and the further understanding that nuclear war was a real and immediate possibility fostered the development of a large movement in civil society that played an important role in convincing the leadership of the nuclear superpowers to stop and then reverse the arms race.

Unfortunately, the problem of nuclear war did not end when the Berlin Wall came down. Many of the 70,000 nuclear weapons that existed at the height of the Cold War have been dismantled, but nearly 20,000 remain. Although the weapons did not go away, an understanding of their terrible destructive power faded from the world's consciousness. Today, the medical consequences of nuclear war are not widely known, and there is inadequate appreciation of how dangerous it is to formulate nuclear policy without this knowledge. A generation has come of age since the end of the Cold War, young people who have never been taught about the destruction that nuclear weapons can cause. People who lived through the Cold War, including many policymakers in nuclear-weapon states, have largely forgotten what will happen if these weapons are used and are completely unfamiliar with the new data on the catastrophic global effects of a "limited" nuclear war.

Attention Needed

An example of the dangerous inattention to the humanitarian consequences of nuclear war is the report released in January by the Defence Science Board, an advisory group to the U.S. Department of Defence. The report argued that "while the manifestation of a nuclear and cyber attack are very different, in the end, the existential impact to the United States is the same" and concluded that "the situation today is such that the ultimate U.S. deterrent, including response against a catastrophic full spectrum cyber attack, is the nuclear triad—intercontinental ballistic missiles (ICBMs), submarine-launched ballistic missiles (SLBMs), and nuclear-capable heavy bombers." Even the most worrisome estimate of the potential damage caused by a cyberattack does not envision anything like the death of a billion people. U.S. policy that equates these threats and considers nuclear war in retaliation for a cyberattack betrays a profound and dangerous failure to understand fully the threat that nuclear weapons pose.

This lack of information is not confined to the Defence Department. Senior officials at the Department of State have privately acknowledged that they have not been aware of the nuclear famine data and that this information has not factored into policy decisions.

Fortunately, there is a growing movement to promote understanding of the actual consequences of nuclear war and of the need to make these consequences the starting point from which future nuclear policy flows.

In November 2011, the International Committee of the Red Cross called for the complete elimination of nuclear weapons and called on all national Red Cross and Red Crescent societies to launch educational campaigns on "the catastrophic humanitarian consequences" of nuclear war and the inability of the Red Cross and Red Crescent to respond in a meaningful way if nuclear weapons are used.

In the nongovernmental community, the IPPNW has launched a new campaign, the International Campaign to Abolish Nuclear Weapons, which has grown far beyond the medical community to encompass a broad swath of civil society.

At an April 22-May 3 meeting in Geneva of the Preparatory Committee for the 2015 NPT Review Conference, South Africa presented a statement on behalf of 80 countries citing the impossibility of responding adequately to the catastrophic humanitarian consequences of nuclear war and calling for the abolition of nuclear weapons. By October 21, a similar statement at the United Nations had gained the signatures of 125 countries. On September 26, there was a high-level meeting of the UN General Assembly on nuclear disarmament. Statements delivered by a wide range of states reflected the same focus on humanitarian effects rather than security doctrines and power politics. These statements emphasized how such a focus leads to an understanding of the urgent need for nuclear abolition.

As Austrian President Heinz Fischer said,

"[T]he discourse on nuclear weapons has been dominated by traditional national security considerations.... [I]t is overdue to move beyond such a narrow perspective. ... Any nuclear weapons use would cause severe humanitarian emergencies and have global consequences for the environment, global health, the climate, the social order, human development and the economy. ... Nuclear weapons should be stigmatized, banned and eliminated before they abolish us."

All of these threads will come together at the upcoming meeting in Mexico. Perhaps this time, the United States and the other nuclear-armed states will choose to attend and use this important forum to build further international support for the complete elimination of these weapons.

Some of the countries that will attend the Mexico meeting are discussing a possible treaty to ban nuclear weapons, a treaty that will make the use or possession of nuclear weapons illegal. Such a treaty would not take the place of a nuclear weapons convention, an agreement among the nuclear-armed states that spells out the concrete steps and timeline for actual dismantlement of their nuclear arsenals and the verification and enforcement measures that will be needed to assure adherence to the convention.

A treaty banning nuclear weapons would help to further delegitimize nuclear weapons and put pressure on those nuclear-weapon states that are reluctant to meet their obligations under Article VI of the NPT. The Obama administration, which "seek[s] the peace and security of a world without nuclear weapons," should embrace this initiative.

A first principle of the medical community is that health care decisions must be based on informed consent: patients need to understand the consequences of proposed treatment and the consequences of declining that treatment. Yet, the world today continues to maintain arsenals of nuclear weapons that threaten its existence, and the public's continued consent to this profoundly dangerous situation cannot be considered informed. Indeed, even many decision-makers do not seem to be aware of the consequences that could arise from the policies they are pursuing.

THE SOCIAL AND ECONOMIC EFFECTS OF NUCLEAR WAR

Limited Nuclear War

In 1974, Secretary of Defence James Schlesinger formally acknowledged the adoption of limited nuclear war (counterforce) as a part of United States strategic doctrine. "Limited" nuclear war is conceived of as a nuclear attack on one or more elements of a nation's land-based strategic arsenal: Intercontinental ballistic missiles (ICBMs), strategic bombers, or nuclear-powered ballistic missile submarine support bases. Other variations on the concept include possible attacks on other critical military, industrial (war production), or command and control centres.

Individually, or in combination, these options could be used either as a means of paralyzing effective military response or to demonstrate the attacker's resolve and ability to employ the ultimate weapon. The adoption of this strategy rests on two assumptions.

The first is that it is possible to limit and structure a nuclear attack that will seriously damage ICBMs or other strategic targets without causing substantial direct or indirect damage to the civilian population. In other words, societal (and thus political) impacts would be so benign that the attacked nation would perceive it as "acceptable" and would not automatically trigger escalation toward a full-scale nuclear response.

The second, and inextricably related, assumption is that following a limited nuclear attack, effective political mechanisms would exist to constrain and terminate the nuclear exchange, preventing escalation to a full-scale nuclear conflict. Thus, it presupposes the physical survival of an effective chain of command as well as a central government that has sufficient credibility, legitimacy, and authority. Within the context of the goals of limited nuclear war, then, the central issue to be considered is not physical survival, but rather the domestic (and international) political acceptability of the damage inflicted by the attack. Essentially the question is whether after surveying the extent of the perceived damage, the national leadership of the country attacked would be able to pursue this so-called "rational" policy of restraint.

The effects discussed below are based on a representative hypothetical attack in which the targets would be the U.S. ICBM arsenal and Strategic Air Command bases. The United States has approximately 1000 ICBMs, which are based in the states of South Dakota, North Dakota, Missouri, Kansas, Arkansas, Montana, Wyoming, and Arizona. The 46 Strategic Air Command bases are spread throughout the nation.

For each ICBM target, it is assumed that two weapons, each one megaton, would be dropped at ground level. (For purposes of comparison, these weapons would then have approximately 80 times the force of the bombs dropped on Hiroshima and Nagasaki.) The resulting fallout from the ICBM attacks would cover substantial parts of the Farm Belt, the Midwest, and some of the South and Southeast. The bomber or submarine bases would be attacked by three and one, one-megaton weapons, respectively, exploded to maximize blast damage, rather than fallout.

Casualties

An initial Department of Defence projection in 1974 estimated less than one million fatalities in the original version of a "limited" attack scenario. The Office of Technology Assessment (OTA) reviewed attack scenarios and produced estimates of 7 to 15 million deaths. Other projections estimate 10 to 20 million injuries, most resulting from radiation exposure due to fallout. For comparison, during World War II the Soviet Union lost 20 million people, but over a period of four to five years; all U.S. combat fatalities in World War II were only 290,000.

Medical

What would this level of destruction mean? If in the most heavily contaminated and damaged regions, all the doctors survived and hospitals were usable, there would be one doctor for every 50 or 100 injured, and between 10 and 30 patients per available hospital bed. Even if the entire national health care system was used, the patient-doctor ratio would be between 25 and 50 to 1 and patients per hospital bed between 10 and 20 to 1. Care for patients suffering from other medical problems, such as heart attack and cancer, would be significantly degraded for an extended time because of the competing and continuing demands of those injured by fallout, the loss of physicians and hospitals (because of contamination) in specific regions, and potential reductions in the manufacture and distribution of medical supplies (about 30% of all drugs are manufactured in the regions most affected by fallout). For a more specific example, to treat a single patient exposed to substantial levels of radiation (200 Radiation Equivalent Man — REMS — or more) would require massive medical resources — intensive care, bone marrow transplants, blood transfusions and antibiotics. In this type of attack hundreds of thousands — perhaps millions — would require complex bone marrow transplants to assure survival. Because of reduced resistance to infectious diseases, all clinical cases (a radiation dose exceeding 50 REMS) would need continuous protection against infection, involving high doses of antibiotics, etc. Treating large numbers would rapidly drain existing supplies and professional energy. As antibiotics supplies dwindled and immunization proved ineffective in this radiation-weakened group, a huge reservoir of potential disease carriers would develop. Diseases such as polio might reappear. Other key elements of medical care support systems, such as medical insurance and records, would be disrupted and in chaos after evacuation.

Food Production

Fallout would also significantly damage the U.S. food-producing system. The states in the Midwest, Farm Belt, and South/Southwest would be most affected by fallout. They produce 40 to 80% of the U.S. grains, such as wheat, rye, corn, and soybeans, and contain 40% of the cattle and 60% of the nation's hogs. Overall, these states produce about half of the U.S. food energy (calories). With virtually no fallout protection, cattle, hogs, and other animals would be particularly vulnerable since relatively low radiation doses can cause injury or death, similar to levels injuring humans.

Besides direct destruction of crops or livestock, many farmers would be killed, injured, or permanently disabled, leaving the food production system without the skilled manpower needed to quickly renew its productivity. In addition, even if the skilled farmers are available, food producing areas would be contaminated; soil radiation levels would be higher than what is considered "acceptable" in peacetime for growing crops. There would also be residual levels of radiation representing unacceptable occupational (worker) and general population exposures. Thus, in vast areas of such states as Montana, North and South Dakota, Nebraska, Missouri, and Illinois, such land denial is certain to occur; crops would be lost and farms unusable for months, or even years, where there are radioactive "hot" spots. All these factors combined will result in severe disruption to the most significant and productive parts of the U.S. agricultural system for a period extending far beyond the attack.

Since it is not unusual to have food travel 1000 miles or more from farm to market, a breakdown of the distribution system is likely to cause imbalances of food supply among regions. (The Northeast, for example, produces only 15% of its needs.) Such a geographical imbalance could result in major conflict among regions. The reality is that with huge areas contaminated with radioactivity, tens — perhaps a hundred — million or more people evacuating their homes, regional hoarding likely, and social disorganization widespread, the distribution system would be ineffective for months. Prices also would rise dramatically, and major government intervention and controls would be likely results.

THE ECONOMIC SYSTEM

Casualties, evacuation, and land denial would create severe national and local economic dislocations. Approximately one-third of the U.S.'s manufacturing capacity lies within the geographic areas most affected by fallout. A major evacuation would leave the regional economy in a shambles. Because of economic interdependence, the problem of "bottlenecking" — serious disruption of the national economy — would be likely. Bottlenecking is the disruptive effect that losses in a key industry (e.g., steel) have on other dependent economic activities (automobiles and machine tool production). Even modest reductions in capacity of basic, pivotal industries can have severe, widespread effects on the economy. Despite the possibility of product substitution (e.g., plastics for steel) or high inventories of selected products, the short- and mid-term ramifications of a disruption of even 25 to 50% of the affected region's manufacturing activities (equivalent to 8 to 15% of national economic activities) would be a serious blow to the national economy. This disruption could easily last several months, and in a post-attack stalemate with the possibility of future attack requiring prolonged urban evacuation, it would become worse.

There are other likely consequences that are less obvious. The banking system would face a particularly severe burden, for example — potential bankruptcies; defaults on basic time payments, such as mortgages and major appliances; and major shifts of monies by individuals during evacuation. In contaminated areas individuals or businesses would be unable to gain access to money, especially in local banks, for long periods. In general, it would be virtually impossible for banks, either regionally or nationally, to pursue "normal" lending and borrowing policies. Payments such as rents and salaries to businesses or individuals would also have to be deferred.

Business insurance would certainly not cover this type of catastrophe. On a scale unknown in U.S. experience, there would probably be a massive outcry for the federal government to provide regional disaster loans to prevent bankruptcy and help resettle workers and their families from severely contaminated areas. The injured and evacuated population would create enormous social service demands (medical care, welfare, emergency housing, etc.) requiring huge sums of money to be spent rapidly. Unprecedented government intervention would probably be demanded to save industries from bankruptcies, allocate goods, and determine industrial priorities. Since individual, industrial, and even regional economic stability would depend on which industries and plants were decontaminated and/or received needed financial support first, implementing these governmental policies would be politically explosive.

Evacuation and Relocation

Fallout would be so intense that massive evacuation of the affected areas in the Midwest, South, and Farm Belt would be required; relocation would last for weeks, months, and in some cases, even years. At least 30 to 40 million people would be forced to leave. However, in a stalemated situation — as "limited" nuclear war is likely to be initially — well over 100 million people, mostly from major urban areas, would either leave spontaneously or be required to leave by government directive. The implications, particularly for the economy, are dramatic.

As Fred Ikle, current Undersecretary of Defence for Policy, concluded 25 years ago, "not only nonessential persons but most of the workers will remain evacuated as long after the first nuclear attack as further attacks appear likely." Certainly this would be the case in a limited nuclear war.

If evacuation were to result in a prolonged relocation, divisive social conflicts, as well as economic and social dislocation, would be likely. Under much more favourable conditions in Great Britain during World War II, relationships between evacuees and their hosts degenerated quickly under the influence of prolonged stress, uncertainty, substantial class and urban-rural differences, and inadequate social service resources.

This experience was not unique. Japan and Germany in World War II, and even the Netherlands in peacetime, experienced these type of conflicts. Under a limited war scenario in the United States, to absorb the evacuated population the number of people living in a single house or apartment in the host areas would have to increase six times (from three people to eighteen). It is not hard to imagine the conflict and stress that type for crowding would create. Thus these problems are likely to be much more intractable under the "limited" war scenarios because of insufficient social services and the massive numbers of people involved. In threatened but unaffected metropolitan areas, decisions about who will be evacuated and when could become politically explosive — fraught with fears of one group or another becoming the expendable victims. This is not to mention the problem of deciding when and how to evacuate special populations — prisoners, patients in acute and chronic care facilities, etc.

PSYCHOLOGICAL EFFECTS

From a psychological point of view, limited nuclear war probably is the worst of all worlds. The imagery of nuclear war, the pervasiveness of casualties, the possibility of massive media coverage and the intense fear of radioactivity that has been manifested in the United States, would spread widely the nuclear war survivor syndrome — the powerful sense of personal vulnerability, helplessness, guilt, isolation and fear — seen to varying degrees in the Hiroshima and Nagasaki survivors. If there is any doubt about the effects of the fear of radioactivity, the psychological effects and "loss of trust" described by the President's Commission, and subsequent studies of the accident at Three Mile Island, should provide ample evidence. This would be true of the fallout from an ICBM attack even without the additional impacts of a geographically dispersed SAC-based attack, since fallout would create throughout the nation the image of nuclear threat and vulnerability. The disorienting and debilitating nature of this type of psychological syndrome would threaten an individual's social and economic functioning.

International Consequences

Not only is the domestic economy highly integrated and interdependent, so is the international system. Consequences of a limited nuclear war would be felt beyond the U.S. Reductions in industrial and food production would trigger a severely imbalanced import/export trade. This would in turn under- cut the dollar's stability and the international monetary system.

The United States plays a key role as a world food producer, exporting food to many nations, such as Japan. The U.S. produces 50% of the wheat and 70% of the corn used for grain, and 80% of the soybeans traded in the world. As a result of a severely damaged food production and distribution system, exports would be severely limited, if they are permitted at all. Thus, a significant number of countries may find themselves inadvertent victims of this attack, with their own stability threatened.

Life After a Limited Nuclear Attack

Life would be severely disrupted. The medical care system would be overburdened providing intensive treatment to fallout victims, resulting in degraded regular, acute, chronic or preventive care. Support systems such as insurance and medical records would likely be in chaos, or at best in serious disarray, with some drugs in short supply. Food production and distribution systems, as well as the banking system, would be severely disrupted.

Judging from previous experience, survivors are likely to feel threatened and disoriented. Massive urban evacuation and prolonged relocation could provoke social tension, severely taxing limited social services. Choices to be made regarding evacuation and future aid to rebuild the post-attack economy could become politically explosive.

Effects would extend beyond the U.S. Industrial and food exports would decrease, or cease, tilting the balance of payments, destabilizing the dollar, and ultimately affecting other currencies. Countries dependent on the United States for food would probably experience shortages and face domestic political problems as a result. The international situation would likely be unstable.

LIMITED NUCLEAR WAR A VIABLE STRATEGY

Would these effects be acceptable? Would-events in the post-attack situation be controllable? Remember the critical criterion for acceptability, and thus control, is the perception that a benign military-oriented attack has taken place.

Since the point of comparison would be the pre-attack world, not a full-scale nuclear war, it is unlikely that a limited nuclear attack would be perceived as benign. Instead, the effects are likely to be perceived as catastrophic and threatening. As a result, the attacked nation may be even more resistant to negotiating a resolution of whatever crisis triggered the attack.

In reality, the subtle differentiation made by military strategists between counterforce (military) and countervalue (economic/human) attacks may be politically, as well as militarily, meaningless.

Attacks Against Economic Targets

The test of any effective strategic nuclear deterrent is its ability to answer any "surprise" attack with a counter- attack so powerful and destructive that an adversary would face such great damage to its society as to be "unacceptable." Hence, an apparently successful first strike would be pyrrhic victory at best. Comparing the consequences to society of different levels of nuclear attack, we now consider how much of an arsenal is needed to achieve this goal.

The nature of defining "How much is enough?" has changed with the dramatic increase in warheads attributed to the appearance of multiple independent reentry vehicles (MIRVs) and the parallel development of increased accuracy and reliability of land- and sea-based missiles.

It is now possible to target selectively for maximum damage key components of the U.S. or Soviet economic and urban infrastructure, using only a small proportion of the current nuclear arsenal — for either a first strike or counterattack. The combination of technological advances in weaponry plus the highly integrated nature of technical/industrial societies results in potentially devastating damage from a relatively small attack. To demonstrate this potential, the attacks hypothesized for this consideration use only a fraction of existing nuclear weapons. As already noted, this scenario takes place in the U.S., but there is ample evidence that the Soviet Union would be just as vulnerable — or even more so — to such a disciplined attack.

In our hypothetical scenario, 34 major categories of industry were assumed as targets. Standard Industrial Classification (SIC) codes were used to identify these major categories. The study established the geographical distribution, capacity and location, by plant, of these major industries. The 71 largest metropolitan areas for 1980 were assumed to be the major initial targets, since they contain the largest concentration of the 34 critical industries.

The attacks (designated A-1 the largest to A-4 the smallest) range in size from 800 weapons, with a total destructive power equivalent to about 500 weapons, to 400 weapons totaling 150 equivalent megatons. For comparison, the Soviet SS-18s (which represent 308 out of approximately 1600 of the USSR's ICBMs) are estimated to have over 2,400 warheads, each with the destructive power of at least one megaton.

These attacks had two elements: 100(A-4), 200(A-3), 300(A-2) and 500(A-1) one megaton weapons used against the 71 U.S. chief urban centres containing 60% of U.S. manufacturing capability; and a second part in which 200-300 smaller 100 kiloton weapons were employed specifically to destroy eight key elements of the economy such as petroleum refining, iron and steel works, nonferrous metals (aluminum, zinc, copper, lead), drugs, electrical distribution products, and engines and turbines, which would reduce these industries to only 2 to 3% of their pre-attack capacity. No fallout is produced in these attacks. Selective use of weapons producing fallout would increase the effects.

The largest or "reference" attack — A-1 — uses 500 one megaton warheads and 200-300 smaller 100 kiloton warheads. It is based on data developed in a 1970 study entitled Potential Vulnerabilities Affecting National Survival prepared for the Army s Office of Civil Defence. The PVANS study assumed a nuclear attack intended to cripple the national economy recovery capabilities of the United States. Its purpose was to determine the number and variety of weapons needed to accomplish this objective.

CASUALTIES AND ECONOMIC EFFECTS

Depending on the size of the attack, casualties would range from 20 to 45% of the U.S. population (40 to 90 million people) including 20 to 30 million injured. From 25 to 65% of the economy would be destroyed. The gross economic figures seriously understate the problem since even using the smallest attack A-4 (100 one megaton, 200-300 one hundred kiloton weapons), specifically targeted key industries are likely to be well over 50% destroyed — some as high as 80 to 90%. To put these numbers in perspective, a Stanford Research Institute (SRI) study for the Office of Civil Defence (the Federal Emergency Management Agency's predecessor) estimated that to recover from nuclear attacks in the range discussed here would take well over a decade.

We believe these estimates are based upon unrealistically optimistic assumptions — or as the authors themselves state, the "upper limits on potential recovery. Projected recovery rates should prove over optimistic when compared with rates actually realized in a real case."

If recovery is possible, and that is an open question, a more reasonable estimate would be several decades — perhaps 40 or 50 years. Of course the attacks described above are not full-scale exchanges; under those circumstances the number of warheads and megatons directed at urban/industrial targets could easily reach 2000, 3000, or more, as well as substantial fallout from ground bursts not included as part of attacks A-1 to A-4. In the case of a large-scale attack the damage would be even more severe and widespread than in the discussion to follow; combining the effects of Parts I and II might provide the minimum damage expected with a full-scale attack.

Despite the effects of so-called urban sprawl and industrial migration, industry and population remain concentrated in a relatively small number of urban areas which present particularly vulnerable targets to nuclear weapons. Nearly 60% of the U.S. population lives on only 1% of the total land area of the United States. This is a result of the fact that approximately 85% of the population of large metropolitan areas lives on only 10% of the total urban land area. The population within these metropolitan regions is concentrated in very high-density areas, rendering the U.S. even more vulnerable to an "economic" attack.

For example, the implications of urban concentration are illustrated by the smallest attack, A-4. It would cause the destruction of about 20 to 30% of total manufacturing capacity and 44 to 55% of the manufacturing capacity in the 71 largest metropolitan areas.

In cities as diverse as New York, Chicago, Los Angeles, and Akron, Ohio, A-4 would destroy approximately 50% or more of their manufacturing capacity. When the number of one megaton weapons in the attack on these cities is increased five-fold (500%), as in A-1, casualties and industrial damage increase only by approximately 200%.

Therefore, devastating economic destruction, disruption, and social disorganization would be caused even by the smaller attacks, since in terms of the destructive effects of nuclear weapons, population and industry are not really dispersed. In the Soviet Union, industry and population are concentrated even more densely than in the United States.

Impact on Regions

Not only would major metropolitan areas be heavily damaged, whole regions would be seriously incapacitated. This is true in part because major urban centres tend to be relatively close to one another, such as in the Northeast Corridor, along the southern rim of the Great Lakes, and in Southern California. The primary area of destruction would be the Northeast/East-Central tier of states from Massachusetts to Minnesota. The one-megaton weapon component of the larger attacks (A-3, A-4) would destroy 50% or more of the industrial capacity of every state in the area, except Wisconsin and Indiana, which would suffer between 40 to 50% Manufacturing Value Added (MVA) destruction. Thus, the nation's largest block of industrial states is unlikely to continue to exist as a significant functioning unit because of the loss of population, industrial plants, and economic systems.

Several other states or industrial regions are likely to suffer similar destruction and disruption, making their contribution to the survival or recovery of the surrounding territory highly problematic. Key parts of the Sunbelt, sections of Texas, Louisiana, Oklahoma, Missouri, and Florida; and the area covered by California, Arizona, Utah, and Colorado would be severely damaged.

These regional patterns of destruction suggest that there will not be large, undamaged areas able to provide adequate refuge and support for the surviving urban population or to foster a rapid economic recovery. Although extensive rural or semi-rural territory will remain undamaged, it is largely devoid of the industrial infrastructure needed for substantial economic recovery.

Selected Industries

Since industrial societies are so well integrated, the strategy of virtually obliterating selected critical industries (2 to 3% survival) appears to be a way of assuring devastating, long-term disruption. The section on limited nuclear war, "bottlenecks" are created that eliminate key industries on which a large number of other industries directly and indirectly depend. For example, attacking petroleum refining directly affects the petrochemical industry; indirectly it would affect the heating of workers' homes, fuel and electricity for factories, and fuel for farm machinery and for transportation of goods. The power of this type of economic bottlenecking is well established. For example, the SRI study of post-attack recovery made calculations that assumed that energy, specifically the petroleum refining industry, was the sole target of a nuclear attack.

It found that while potentially 85% of the Gross National Product (GNP) would survive, only one-quarter of the surviving GNP — that is, only one-fifth of the pre-attack economy — would be able to operate in the first two post-attack years. Thus an effective attack would lead to an economy in which even surviving capacity would be drastically under-utilized.

Only one critical sector was the target in that situation. The implications of a more systematic effort affecting several industries should be clear. Additional evidence supporting the effectiveness of this bottlenecking strategy is found in a study prepared for the U.S. Arms Control and Disarmament Agency. In this study, which was not designed to create the largest amount of economic damage and disruption, modest 10% reductions in the capacity of a single basic industrial sector caused an overall 30 to 40% reduction in over 100 defence-related sectors. As it turns out, defence-related sectors included industries with broader influence on the entire economy, such as manufacturing trucks, airplanes and machine tools. The study concluded, "Since the economic and institutional activities necessary to sustain a war-making capability are highly interactive, relatively low levels of MVA (manufacturing) destruction can lead to significant reduction in the ability to support a war effort."

A nuclear war would fragment the U.S. economic system; its integration as an effective system would be seriously in question. Economic attacks would not only damage the industrial base (factories, etc.), they would also thin the ranks of the technical and managerial personnel. Moreover, they would disrupt and destroy supporting financial structures, throwing into question the value and utility of money, as well as the value and ownership of goods and property; records of financial transactions would be destroyed, and the lending and borrowing system (banks and the Federal Reserve) would collapse with the disappearance of assets and the non-payment of debts.

Also associated with extensive industrial damage is injury to the basic physical support systems. In particular, the urban infrastructure in attacked areas — transportation, utilities, housing, fuel and food distribution systems, sanitation systems, and medical care services — would emerge either badly damaged or of very limited use in supporting industrial workers. To rebuild these systems or to duplicate them elsewhere would be a lengthy but necessary process, diverting resources from the economic expansion necessary to achieve rapid full recovery.

The casualties (dead and injured) resulting from this type of attack would be incomprehensible, even if some reduction due to strategies of civil defence (evacuation) were possible. While the monumental loss of skilled workers, managers and economic leadership has already been noted, the key to the reality of the postnuclear attack period is the staggering burden of 20 to 30 million injured, many of whom would never again be fully productive. Who would care for them? Who would provide the support? What would be the cost to society in delayed recovery and social stability? These are almost unanswerable questions, but one thing is clear: The physical resources left after a "limited" nuclear attack will not exist after an economic attack.

Food

The U.S. food system (production, processing, distribution) is both highly integrated and dispersed. Since food may travel 1000 miles or more from production to consumer, the system depends very heavily on effective transportation and organization. For example, almost one-third of the population lives in counties that produce less than a two-week supply of their grain needs, and half the population lives in counties with two months or less production capability. Approximately two-thirds of the nation's food (as measured by calories) is produced in the North Central tier of states from Indiana to Colorado, which themselves contain only about one-quarter of the population. Moreover, this system is highly dependent on petroleum (farm equipment), electricity (particularly dairy), and fertilizers and pesticides. If, for example, dairy farms lost electricity, many cows could not be milked adequately. Without proper milking a cow would simply dry up in less than a week until it calved nine months later. Finally, almost 90% of U.S. processing capacity (canning, baking and packaging) would be in regions destroyed or severely damaged by the attack.

The severe limitation of energy supplies, particularly the large-scale loss (97 to 98%) of petroleum refining capacity; the loss of key chemicals (such as pesticides and fertilizers); and the regional and national economic and social disorganization resulting from any size attack, would deeply affect the nation's food supplies. The results of attacks A-1 through A-4 on the nation's food distribution, processing, and production systems would be as follows: First, sufficient basic production capacity in most food categories in the mid-range would survive because the Farm Belt is not directly attacked and fallout is not generated. There are real limitations on the use of this capacity, however, due to inadequate fuel for running farm machinery and transportation; disruption of electricity production through loss of fuel supplies and key workers; shortages of fertilizer and pesticides to maintain productivity because of the severe losses in petroleum refining and heavy damage to the related chemical industry; uncontrolled population migration and social disorganization, and possibly radioactive fallout. Second, because of widespread urban destruction the transport and distribution system would be severely disrupted, raising the possibility of a sufficient food supply but no effective means to distribute it.

Regional maldistribution exacerbated by hoarding contains the seeds of profoundly disruptive political as well as survival problems. For example, in theory, over 200 days of grain supply could be available; for the surviving population, however, there is no certainty that food would be permitted to leave the producing areas by local residents. Third, food-processing industry losses of potentially 80 to 90% would lead to insufficient capacity, even if supplies of raw foodstuffs were adequate, and cause spoilage and shortages.

Therefore, while mechanization, automation, and widespread use of chemical fertilizers and pesticides have made American food production comparatively very efficient, they have also created a situation in which large urban populations distant from their suppliers are totally dependent for food supplies on a system that is highly vulnerable to nuclear attack.

Finally, as we noted in the discussion of limited nuclear war, many other nations that depend on U.S. food production will be affected. A disruption or partial destruction of U.S. agriculture will have implications throughout the world food market, dramatically cutting supplies and increasing prices. For surviving supplier nations, food could quickly become a major political weapon; for consumers, it could become a focal point of desperate conflict in international affairs. From a humanitarian and political perspective, this vulnerability is a serious concern.

Energy

The availability of energy is a critical element in national survival and economic power. The United States depends on fossil fuels for about 93% of its energy needs, with petroleum accounting for the largest share (49%). In the two largest attacks hypothesized in Life After Nuclear War (A-1 and A-2), 98% of the petroleum refining capacity in the country would be destroyed. Surviving capacity would be inadequate to meet even farm fuel needs. Less refinery capacity — but still well over 50% — would be destroyed in attacks A-3 and A-4, but damage and disruptions to pipelines, port facilities, rolling stock, and other associated facilities would reduce the effectiveness of the surviving capacity.

Adequate foreign petroleum supplies may not be available, depending on the post-attack international situation, the availability of tanker capacity, the willingness or ability of the

OPEC nations to maintain or increase production, and the willingness of oil-producing nations to provide petroleum to a country without the economic capacity to generate adequate funds for payment. In any case, most imported petroleum arrives in the United States as crude oil, and thus U.S. refinery capacity, plus its port and distribution system, is needed to render it usable.

Natural gas is produced primarily in Texas and Louisiana (74%) and also in Oklahoma, Kansas, and New Mexico. These states consume one-third of their own production; the remainder goes mainly to the Midwest, New England, Mid-Atlantic states and California. Most of this gas is shipped by pipelines, many of which could be damaged if targeted in the hypothetical attacks.

Although coal is the most abundant fossil fuel in the United States, substitution of coal for oil will be very limited in the near and mid-term because of existing constraints and those imposed by nuclear war on fuel conversion and coal mining capacity. Coal is mined by electrical and diesel equipment, and it is transported by trucks and trains which will be damaged and short of fuel themselves in the post-attack period.

Power generating stations that survive the attacks would also be affected by fuel shortages. As is the case with refining and transporting fossil fuels, efforts to maintain or expand electrical generating capacity will suffer from reduced maintenance capability and lack of equipment and replacement parts. In fact, the loss of skilled personnel is a potentially more significant threat to power plant operation than any physical losses.

Both household and industrial fuel consumption will decrease as a result of losses in manufacturing capacity, population, and housing. It is not possible to predict precisely whether surviving fuel and power resources will match demand, though under the assumed attacks, refining capacity losses exceed losses in industrial capacity. Nor can we know in advance precisely what sort of price system would exist — whether prices would be controlled by government — or even the extent to which barter would replace monetary transactions. It does seem clear that maldistribution of surviving fuel stocks and transportation system damage will create local shortages and hamper immediate relief efforts.

And what about recovery? Postwar experience in Europe and Japan indicates that to replace and rebuild the fuel processing and distribution systems, as well as electrical generating and transmission facilities, will be time-consuming. Even if domestic or imported fuel is available in adequate quantities — an uncertain assumption — the capacity to convert it efficiently to its end use is likely to be inadequate for several years, thereby retarding economic recovery from the post-attack base. The American economy depends on large quantities of electrical power and fossil-fueled transportation systems; combined with the vulnerability of petroleum refining facilities and significant dependence on foreign petroleum, this suggests that the magnitude of the difficulty of meeting energy needs may be one of the most critical determinants of the nation's long-term ability to recover economically from urban-oriented nuclear attacks.

Pursuing full economic recovery will place enormous demands on the damaged energy system, even if stringest rationing were imposed on individual consumption. It remains doubtful whether the badly damaged economy with its output greatly curtailed would be able to generate the enormous sums of capital and other resources required to refurbish the national energy system and to purchase foreign petroleum (assuming it is available). After a limited nuclear attack, people's time preferences would increase dramatically, and savings and investment would nearly grind to-a halt, even if the institutions to channel savings into rebuilding productive capacity should happen to survive. It is not a far-fetched prospect that the victim of an urban-oriented thermonuclear attack would find itself in the position analogous to many of today's least developed countries — in a vicious circle where essential consumption prevents accumulation of the surplus resources required to expand productivity and output.

MEDICAL EFFECTS

The potential losses in medical resources are dramatic, particularly because United States medical resources, especially specialists, are so heavily concentrated in urban areas: 68% of the physicians, including about 70% of the specialist, over 60% of the surgeons, and 64% of the dentists, are located in the 71 urban areas attacked. These urban areas contain only 55% of the total population. Likewise, the areas exposed to both the attack against 71 urban areas and the adjunct attack against selected industries contain 61% of the total U.S. population, but 71% of U.S. physicians and 68% of its dentists. Thus, physicians and dentists would be comparatively more vulnerable than the general populace in an urban/economic attack. Also concentrated in the urban areas are many of the most advanced hospitals and almost 80% of the hospital-based physicians.

The combination of physician losses and injuries on the order of 20-30 million would produce patient-physicians ratios of 100-600 to 1. In the early period, when the wounded and dying cannot be distinguished, ratios would be 1000 to 1, depending on the movement of physicians into and/or patients out of damaged areas. For perspective, an average physician sees perhaps 25 patients a day with only 20% having serious problems, usually not emergencies. Surviving hospitals would face ratios of 30 to 40 injured per bed. There would be hundreds of thousands of burn victims; most large burn units — found only in major hospitals — have about 10 beds, And few major urban hospitals would be left.

Under these attacks, medical care for the injured will be further complicated by the virtual elimination of the pharmaceutical industry, one of the eight critical industries targeted for maximum destruction. Even simple protection against infection will be difficult without antibiotics and other prophylactics. Urban stocks of these medicines will be largely destroyed and new supplies unavailable. Chronically ill individuals (heart disease, diabetes, etc.) who depend on drugs to sustain physical activity or life itself will also be affected.

Providing high quality medical care requires high capital investment and long training periods; thus post-attack medical care norms may continue to be dramatically below current standards for a considerable time, with negative implications for labor productivity and other aspects of economic recovery. Significant radioactive fallout or the breaching of immunological barriers in the aftermath of the attack would permit a high incidence of epidemic disease.. The loss of major medical research centres will be devastating to research on improved disease treatment. The heavy burden of chronically ill or permanently injured survivors will continuously tax the reduced medical capabilities and disoriented social service support system, leading to a general deterioration of all medical care.

Because malnutrition lowers resistance to disease, medical problems would be exacerbated if the food supply system proves ineffective. Serious mental health problems will arise from the impact of the attack — particularly a sense of impotence from watching people die who in a "normal" society would have lived — or from the stress of the post-attack recovery period.

The implications of all these problems would be a society burdened and preoccupied with human suffering, unable to cope successfully with its demands. The credibility of the remaining leadership and its ability to focus resources for recovery might very well hinge on how it was able to manage the medical effects of nuclear war.

Higher Education

America's economic and military power derives in large measure from its ability to maintain its technological leadership; higher education plays a central role in maintaining this lead. Universities and colleges provide trained personnel to assist in scientific and technological development. They also provide the institutional framework for basic research that becomes the basis of scientific discovery and technological innovation.

In the above attack on the 71 major urban areas, over 50% of the higher education system would be damaged or destroyed. Professional schools are even more vulnerable — over 70% of the students are concentrated in these urban areas, which contain only 55% of the general student population. Of equal significance, an attempt to measure not only quantity but also the quality of graduate (science and engineering) and professional (medical, law) schools found a disproportionate number — 70% — in attacked areas.

In other words, in the academic areas we evaluated, quality educational facilities tended to be highly concentrated in the major urban areas. In addition, these universities and professional schools attract or spin off important private research-and-development or consulting firms and high-technology manufacturing firms in close proximity.

Given the massive scale of population losses and casualties after nuclear attacks, it is likely that the concept of the function of the university would also change, assuming a more narrow role as a vocational and professional training ground.

The training could be at a very basic level, with many important intellectual pursuits and professions abandoned. The basic scientific and technological infrastructure could be the most seriously injured since even if the capacity remained, the justification for basic research during the post-attack recovery period would likely be questioned, and any diversion of energies in this direction challenged. Complex scientific experiments requiring extraordinary collaboration among scientific groups and expensive, sophisticated equipment would be eliminated or delayed for perhaps decades. The quality of research and the university's vital contribution to technology would diminish drastically in almost any nuclear attack. Thus, the damage to the higher education system would pose serious obstacles to a strong and rapid economic recovery.

Social Consequences

To understand the effects of a nuclear war it is important to distinguish it from common disasters, even World War II. Especially if hostilities continue or their resumption is threatened, all the elements that make a small disaster tractable will be lacking: limited damage, modest casualties, surviving leadership, a diminishing incidence of role conflict (desire to protect one's family rather than to perform emergency work) and large reservoirs of external, easily mobilized skilled workers, material resources, and organizational skills.

The massive and simultaneous destruction of economic and human resources would result in an inability to provide immediate and sufficient human and material aid to damaged areas.

There will be no time to adapt and to innovate as nations did in World War II (U.S.S.R. as previously cited is an example). More important, the lack of outside aid would create a sense of individual and communal isolation. Aid symbolizes a reconnection with a larger, normal world. This connection helps provide the impetus for rebuilding the damaged society, creating a sense of vitality and competence to dispel the continuing perception of isolation. It also has an important function for binding together society, restating a common thread of hope and shared aspirations that are the essence of national life. The post-attack situation could be like Japan near the end of World War II.

There could be "a drift toward accomplishing personal and private aims rather than those which are national... farmers...growing little more than is required for their own subsistence," or more likely, the complete demoralization seen in an earlier tragedy: "Survivors of the Black Death in growing helplessness fell into apathy, leaving ripe wheat uncut and livestock untended...no one had any inclination to concern themselves about the future." More pertinent, a panel of experts in a study of social consequence of nuclear war for the Office of Civil Defence concluded: "One month after the attack, less than half the potential labor force could be expected to work without immediately beneficial compensation, and that, of these, one in five would be able to function only at a level greatly degraded from his normal abilities."

The experience of nuclear war is likely to have devastating psychological effects, especially for Americans, whose homes and institutions have essentially escaped the ravages of recent wars. The very short period required to carry out highly destructive nuclear attacks would intensify the emotional impact, particularly those reactions associated with denial of the true extent of the damage or fostering flight from and resistance to reentering damaged areas.

Robert J. Lifton, in his study of Hiroshima survivors, described the psychological effect as "a sudden and absolute shift from normal existence to an overwhelming encounter with death." The reaction, as reported by a witness to the disaster, Father Siemes: "Among the passersby, there are many who are uninjured. In a purposeless, insensate manner, distraught by the magnitude of the disaster, most of them rush by and none conceives the thought of organizing help on his own initiative. They are concerned only with the welfare of their own families." In some cases even families were abandoned. The result of this experience was, as Fred Ikle described it 25 years ago, a deep aversion to returning to the cities to rebuild the economy. "And thus a very different situation will exist from that envisaged in most civil defence plans (in the 1950s)." The economic implications of this type of withdrawal would be serious.

A high incidence of abnormal behavior, ranging from the nonfunctional to the antisocial, could be anticipated. Specific psychological effects would include disorientation, fear, doubt, apathy, and antipathy toward authorities. The effects on Hiroshima/Nagasaki survivors provide ample evidence to support these concerns.

Families would be broken up by death, severe injury, disease, evacuation, or military and labour conscription. The young, elderly, and handicapped would suffer disproportionately since they depend most on society's material and institutional resources. For example, the young and elderly showed significant increases in accidental death attributed to neglect in Great Britain in World War II.

The loss of material and institutional resources in urban-industrial attacks would make survival in the post-attack period difficult for individuals and groups alike, compounding the psychological stresses of the attack itself. Satisfying even the simplest survival requirements — food, shelter, and clothing — would become major tasks.

Significant interpersonal, intergroup, and inter-regional conflicts would probably arise.

Ethnic, racial, regional, and economic conflicts present in the pre-attack society, while minimized in the period immediately after an attack, would be heightened after only a limited time by the extent of the deprivation and the resulting tensions. New antagonisms would develop between hosts and evacuees or refugees over the possession and use of surviving resources.

These phenomena were observed both in Britain and in Japan during World War II. The Allnutt study predicted these conflicts would be so serious that they "would necessitate the imposition of martial law or other authoritarian system in many localities, and the widespread use of troops to maintain order."

Continuing hostilities or prolonged threat of renewed war would engender even more profound changes in the social fabric. Major, possibly permanent, changes in social values and institutions could be expected as society sought to adjust to a radically altered environment dominated by the question of physical survival.

Economic destruction, loss of political leadership (especially at the local level), and the need to mobilize resources for relief and recovery would present extraordinary demands on weakened political institutions. In the interest of implementing survival programs, legal norms and practices would have to be suspended for prolonged periods in many areas. The character of political institutions and authority would almost certainly change, especially if hostilities or the threat of hostilities persisted. Both old and new political structures would be likely to suffer from greatly reduced credibility. Decentralization of political power and more authoritarian methods of political, social, and economic control would be probable responses to post-attack conditions.

The substance of these problems is acknowledged with an ironic optimism by the panel assembled for the Allnutt study:

Major institutions and organizations were seen as fragmenting in most cases and collapsing in others, but the seriousness of this result would be relieved somewhat by the irrelevancy of many of them to the early stages of recovery, and by the ability of social structures to spring back into action where physical conditions permit.

The Federal Government would make serious mistakes and suffer a loss of power and prestige, but not a loss of faith so serious as to favour the possibility of revolt. Financial institutions would be modified greatly, and barter would be a widespread reaction to inflation, but money was not seen as going out of style, nor was a barter economy foreseen.

Legal, judicial, and enforcement systems would similarly undergo great strains, being overwhelmed entirely in some areas, but again, due process, though delayed, would not be lost in principle.

Industries and commercial organizations were expected to fragment into autonomous, local entities until communications and transportation systems were repaired, but the goals of such corporations would not be greatly changed.

We are not similarly convinced that such massive dislocations would not create more significant changes in both the underlying goals and functions of economic, social and political institutions in the post-attack society.

To see the problem of nuclear war in its proper context, we must first return briefly to the concept of "unacceptable" damage. Although two levels of damage — biological survival of individuals and the functioning of regions — often appear in public discussion of nuclear war, neither makes much sense in terms of the normal expectations of organized technical/industrial society. Not only must individuals survive, but so must the institutions necessary to maintain a social order. Do the weapons surviving constitute a viable military force and by what process would they be employed? The surviving weapons cannot order the economy, rebuild productive industrial capacity or grow or distribute food. Thus, simple biological survival of some members of the population or survival at a regional level could not be an acceptable outcome for a nation as a whole, and still less for its government.

One test of acceptability would be to maintain the minimum economic, political, and social capacity required for full recovery of the nation within a reasonable period of time. A higher standard would be the continued ability to play an effective independent role, politically, economically, diplomatically, and militarily.

This ability would be measured in relation to the analogous surviving capability of the attacking nation(s) as well as to the capability of undamaged or less damaged nations which did not participate directly in the nuclear exchange.

Would it be acceptable in a post-nuclear war world to become a client state such as Japan and Germany were after World War II? The question then becomes, what constitutes an acceptable post-attack national status — what kind of entity remains to fend for itself in the post-attack world? This may not be easy to answer.

It is conceivable that on a superficial level, there may still be substantial military and strategic capability equal to or more potent than other nations. The social structure, however, would be in disarray or on the verge of collapse or political leadership unable to "control" the evolution of events. It is this perspective that underlies our conclusions.

The U.S. nuclear deterrent is adequate now and almost certainly through this century. This is true because weapons technology permits relatively small but sophisticated attacks that can deliver stunning damage to the industrial functioning of an adversary, or alternately to its key military infrastructure. The numbers of weapons needed to assure unacceptable damage to an adversary are indeed so small that it is difficult to conceive of any situation where U.S. forces would be inadequate. Even a surviving force of only 10% of U.S. ICBMs, or 100 missiles (assuming a functional command and control system) would possess devastating and potentially fatal power. Moreover, a surviving bomber and in vulnerable submarine nuclear force alone would be sufficient.

Therefore, the "window of vulnerability" projected for U.S. ICBMs in the 1980s is more a matter of perception and emphasis than of compelling reality. We make this assertion because the key underlying assumption of this short-term vulnerability issue is that "limited," controlled nuclear war is credible. That is, it is accepted that if ICBMs are successfully attacked, the U.S. will be paralyzed — unable or unwilling to retaliate for fear of further destruction of its urban areas. If, as we conclude, limited nuclear war is not a credible strategy, then the sophisticated scenarios for land-based missile vulnerabilities become significant only because they might be believed, encouraging action on a false, high-risk assumption.

To insure nuclear stability there must be a long-range commitment to maintaining the survivability of a mixed force, so that no single vulnerability can threaten the entire nuclear capability force and the command and control structure. In this longer term context, the vulnerability of land-based ICBMs is worrisome because other vulnerabilities could arise, particularly with regard to sea-based missiles. Yet given the huge nuclear capability available, improvements to assure continued survival are certainly not incompatible with a phased mutual reduction of total strategic nuclear weaponry.

What is more, the concept of "limited" nuclear war is illusory and thus dangerous. It propagates a notion that no Soviet and no U.S. planner should be encouraged to accept as a basis for policy-making — that is, that damage from a military attack would be benign or "acceptable."

As we have shown, damage to the fabric of civilian society from any effective attack against ICBMs and/or substantial numbers of military targets would create an imperative to retaliate and escalate. Thus the possibility of a controlled, rational "limited" nuclear war would be undermined. The perception of threat and vulnerability generated by this damage would eliminate the political option of control. Moreover, a number of commentators have raised the serious possibility that in a technical sense, the command and control structure would be so physically vulnerable that even purely mechanical communication requirements for controlling a nuclear response will not be available. The combination of these two elements makes the viability of a "limited" nuclear war strategy highly doubtful.

Finally, civil defence, particularly crisis relocation (evacuation), has been presented as a complementary element in nuclear strategy. It is ineffective at best. Its purpose is to minimize human destruction and thus purports to strengthen the basis for the possibility of successfully enduring a "limited" or even urban-oriented nuclear attack. This argument is tenuous. First, it is hard to believe that in a period of extreme tension, a full-scale urban evacuation by the U.S. or Soviet Union would be perceived as anything but a signal of intent to pursue a nuclear strike. Since an effective evacuation takes at a minimum four to five days to complete, certain actions are likely to be taken by the other side. Among the possibilities: a threat to attack if the evacuation is not stopped; an attack during the evacuation phase when the population is most exposed; and of course, the adoption of a strategy of "launch on warning," creating a hair trigger in a clearly dangerous situation. Ironically, a launch on warning would defeat the whole purpose of a first- strike strategy.

Even with a successful evacuation, destruction from a well-designed second strike against a major portion of urban economic and physical infrastructure (factories, housing, electricity generation, hospitals, etc.) would not necessarily leave a nation better off than no evacuation at all. A surviving population with no basic support systems is a prescription for human suffering, gross political instability, and eventually death on an incomprehensive scale. Even an evacuation without an attack would seriously damage the U.S. economy. And, as Fred Ikle succinctly put it, "The war will not end miraculously after the people have been moved into the nearest fields, and further problems of evacuation will then arise."

Taken together, the concepts of "limited" nuclear war and crisis relocation represent a kind of sophisticated exercise in self-deception; a Pollyanna-like vision of the world that crumbles when confronted with dispassionate, realistic analysis of the limits of resiliency or flexibility of an society damaged by nuclear war.

Therefore, it is time to rethink the purposes of our nuclear strategy and their implications. Particularly worrisome are the demands for more sophisticated strategic weapons and the direct and inadvertent growth of the technological capabilities to satisfy these demands. It is the potential for technological sophistication and the apparent control these technologies offer that permits military planners to construct scenarios that make nuclear war appear "benign" when analyzed superficially.

Unfortunately, there is no magical prescription to solve these problems. But it is clear that much of the debate about numbers of weapons and vulnerability has little to do with the real problem: We must establish a basis for the control of nuclear weapons, particularly sophisticated technology, and the appropriate strategic weapons mix to maintain a stable defence. This is the challenge confronting Congress, the executive branch, and the American people.

10

The Role of Nuclear Weapons in International Politics

THE DAWN OF THE NUCLEAR AGE

The Nuclear Age began with the World War II Manhattan Project (1942–46), which culminated in the Trinity test on July 16, 1945, of the "Gadget" and the August 1945 bombings of Hiroshima and Nagasaki. The Project was led by Gen. Leslie Groves; physicist J. Robert Oppenheimer directed the scientific research. The Trinity test took place on a test range north of Alamogordo, New Mexico. Gadget was a somewhat less than 20-kiloton implosion-type fission device. Its yield was the equivalent of the bomb load of 2000 fully loaded WWII B-29s. Reacting to the test, Oppenheimer quoted the Bhagavad-Gita: "I am become Death, the Shatterer of Worlds."

Less than a month later, "Little Boy" was dropped on Hiroshima, on August 6, 1945. A gun-type bomb, it had an explosive force of roughly 15 kilotons. It was relatively simple: one piece of uranium-235 was fired at another. When Little Boy was exploded in an airburst about 1900 feet over Hiroshima, some 80,000-140,000 people were killed instantly; another 100,000 were seriously injured. The burst's temperature was estimated to reach more than 1 million degrees Celsius. The surrounding air was ignited, resulting in an 840-foot fireball; in less than a second, it expanded to over 900 feet. The blast wave from the explosion shattered windows ten miles away and was felt 37 miles away. Over two-thirds of the buildings in Hiroshima were demolished. Virtually everything within about 4.4 miles of ground zero of the explosion was incinerated by the hundreds of fires ignited by the thermal pulse. About thirty minutes later, a heavy "black rain" infused with dirt, dust, soot, and radioactive particles began falling in areas of the city. All this was the result of a relatively small device by today's standards. A few days later, on August 9, "Fat Man," a roughly 21 kiloton bomb, was exploded over Nagasaki. According to Japanese estimates, almost 24,000 people were killed and another 23,000 wounded; the lower casualty rates despite the bomb's being larger had to do with the terrain—Nagasaki was much hillier than Hiroshima. More than 40 percent of the city was destroyed. Fat Man was an implosion-type fission weapon, a more complex plutonium bomb. Unlike Little Boy, this type of bomb had been tested—the Little Boy type had not been. This was not just continuing wartime activities using a new device, it was also a test.

On August 15, after these two uses of the bomb (and the Soviet entry into the war against Japan), Emperor Hirohito announced Japan's surrender.

THE NUCLEAR REVOLUTION IN MILITARY AFFAIRS

The Nuclear Revolution is both a revolution in military affairs (RMA) and more than an "ordinary" RMA. From the start, nuclear weapons were regarded as so qualitatively different that everything that came before was rendered "conventional." The most powerful bombs used in WWII until August 1945 contained 10 tons of TNT; the average yield of the Hiroshima and Nagasaki bombs was the equivalent of 18,000 tons of TNT. The first U.S. thermonuclear test, in November 1952, had a yield of over 10 megatons, almost 580 times the power of the nuclear devices exploded in August 1945. Today, one intercontinental ballistic missile (ICBM) warhead possesses the equivalent of the explosive power used in all of WWII.

A RMA has three components: technology, doctrine, and organization. The nuclear revolution was a technology-driven RMA. It was not the result of existing strategy. Certainly, the United States wanted to develop nuclear weapons before Germany did. But U.S. leaders didn't have a specific use in mind—that came later. The Manhattan Project was viewed as a technological race with the Germans. That prefigured what was to come with the subsequent U.S.-Soviet technological competition. New doctrine and strategy was developed. The

United States had to determine what role nuclear weapons were to play. Initially, the U.S. Army-Air Force (then the USAF after 1947) took the lead; relatively soon, the U.S. Army and the U.S. Navy went nuclear. New military organizations emerged—the Strategic Air Command, for instance. New service elites—strategic bomber pilots and intercontinental ballistic missiles (ICBM) operators in the USAF and nuclear submariners in the USN—appeared. New civilian structures were stood up, including the Atomic Energy Commission, which over time became the Department of Energy; subsequently, we saw the establishment of National Nuclear Security Administration.

There were further technological developments. Not only did we go from fission to fusion by 1952, but we also devised new delivery systems, truly intercontinental jet bombers developed relatively quickly during the 1950s, with the B-52 (which is still with us) making its appearance in the mid-1950s. In between going from bombers to ICBMs, the USAF worked on cruise missiles. The latter weren't particularly successful in the 1950s but reappeared in the 1970s and 1980s. The Navy developed submarine-launched ballistic missiles (SLBMs) that were put on new platforms, nuclear-powered submarines.

The nuclear revolution is an RMA with a difference that made a difference. There were other RMAs in the 20th century, such as the German blitzkrieg that emerged during the interwar period. Like earlier RMAs, the blitzkrieg was developed during peacetime and was tested and employed during wartime. The nuclear revolution emerged during a conflict, and nuclear weapons have not been used in war since August 1945. Their impact has greater off than on the battlefield. They have not been used against a nuclear foe. Fortunately, the world has not experienced "nuclear combat" on a "nuclear battlefield," much less a nuclear war. There have been many tests—and we think we know a lot about the effects of nuclear explosions as a result of all those tests—but there has never been anything that resembles nuclear combat, a nuclear battlefield, or a nuclear war.

The nuclear revolution had greater strategic than operational or tactical war-fighting implications. It has been about deterrence and how we think about deterrence rather than war-fighting. Deterrence became nuclear weapons' central role. Some, such as Bernard Brodie in 1946, recognized that very early on. Over time, a very high level of strategic interdependence developed among the states that possessed nuclear weapons, at least among those that possessed large quantities of them—the U.S. and USSR were very sensitive to each other's nuclear moves. Some argue that nuclear weapons are responsible for what historian John Lewis Gaddis called the "long peace" of the Cold War. We have not seen a major power war since August 1945. Gaddis and other analysts argue that this is a direct result of the nuclear revolution. So we have seen a revolution in *strategic*, not merely military, affairs.

Another difference is that this RMA was led by civilians rather than the military. From the Manhattan Project on, civilians—Americans, Canadians, British, former Germans—led this RMA. More important, those who were responsible for the systematic exploration and development of U.S. nuclear policy and strategy over the years have been primarily civilians, people like Bernard Brodie, a historian/political scientist at RAND and then UCLA; the mathematician Albert Wohlstetter, also at RAND; the Nobel Prize-winning economist Thomas Schelling, who was at Harvard and then the University of Maryland; and RAND's Herman Kahn, who wrote *Thinking About the Unthinkable* (1962). These and other civilians were the pioneers— Fred Kaplan called them the "Wizards of Armageddon"—in developing nuclear thought. In the past, new strategy and doctrine were developed by the military.

THE CENTRAL ROLE OF DETERRENCE

In 1946, Bernard Brodie, one of the Wizards of Armageddon, observed "Thus far the chief purpose of our military establishment has been to win wars. From now on its chief purpose must be to avert them. It can have almost no other purpose." Brodie here put deterrence front and center. Also in 1946, General H. A. P. Arnold provided a hint of how to think about deterrence: " ur first line of defence is the ability to retaliate even after receiving the hardest blow the military can deliver." This is about striking second, about being able to absorb a nuclear blow, having forces that would survive, and being able to retaliate and punish the enemy.

The objective of deterrence is to prevent aggression and war, not necessarily to be able to fight a war. In the past, we've often thought that the ability to deter depended on the ability to fight: to be able to defend yourself and to be able to go on the offense. Whether that logic applies to nuclear deterrence has been a matter of no little contention.

The United States has attempted to deter threats against itself and against its allies and friends. Deterrence of threats against the U.S. homeland has been referred to as core, central, or fundamental deterrence.

The deterrence of threats against allies and friends is known as extended deterrence. When we've talked about countries like South Korea or Japan being under the U.S. nuclear umbrella or about preventing Soviet aggression against our NATO allies, we were talking about extended deterrence.

Deterrence entails persuading potential aggressors that the costs and risks of aggression are sure to exceed its benefits. This requires the requisite capabilities and the willingness to use them. Extended deterrence is regarded as more difficult than core or central deterrence: would the United States really risk the destruction of New York or San Francisco to save Bonn or Paris? It is generally thought that the target of deterrence has to be a rational actor. A very limited definition of rationality is at play here. It doesn't mean than an adversary has to think like us; it simply has to recognize that the costs and risks of aggression will exceed the benefits. If you do A, we'll do B, which could well be the destruction of your society as you know it.

It's usually clear when deterrence has failed. If the Soviets had invaded Western Europe during the Cold War, deterrence would have failed. Some argue that the Iraqi invasion of Kuwait in 1990 was a deterrence failure. It's very difficult, however, to know for certain when deterrence is working. Does the fact that the USSR never invaded Western Europe mean that U.S. extended deterrence worked? That something we wanted to prevent, or deter, didn't happen doesn't necessarily mean that what we did worked. Conclusively demonstrating why something did not occur is always problematical.

During the Cold War, two ways were developed of persuading a potential adversary that the costs and risks of aggression would be greater than the benefits. The first approach emphasized the threat of punishment; aggression would be met with the infliction of unacceptable costs; an aggressor would pay an unacceptably high price. The second approach emphasized the denial of objectives: aggression would fail; an aggressor would be stopped and defeated. Although these two approaches were developed in the context of the dyadic, U.S.-Soviet Cold War relationship, they continue to frame the post-Cold War nuclear policy and strategy debate.

Punishment

What kind of nuclear capabilities are required to punish an aggressor, to impose unacceptable costs on an aggressor? Punishment is thought to require not only offensive strike capabilities, but also retaliatory, second- (rather than first-) strike capabilities.

The emphasis on second-strike capabilities requires survivable forces. Survivability is enhanced by dispersing forces, rather than concentrating them, by deploying them underground in concrete, steel-reinforced silos; or by putting them out at sea in submarines that cannot be easily tracked and targeted. Redundancy, in the form of the triad of bombers, ICBMs, and SLBMs, also enhances force survivability. Punishment embraces the defence of military systems, whether passive (dispersal, hardening) or active (point defence). It requires as well the ability to destroy urban/industrial or "countervalue" targets, a targeting capability that does not require an especially high degree of accuracy.

The threat of punishment does not require civil defence capabilities or national ballistic missile defence capabilities that would serve to erode an opponent's ability to punish you (population centres were to remain vulnerable—Reagan's SDI was seen as providing an offensive rather than a defensive capability). Punishment requires relatively low cost, finite, or absolute, capabilities. It provides an answer to "how much is enough?" Punishment came to be known as "Assured Destruction" or, when both sides subscribe to it, "Mutual Assured Destruction"—MAD. Advocates of this approach viewed the Anti-Ballistic Missile Treaty of 1972 as the enshrinement of punishment, assured destruction, and MAD. In their view, by embracing the ABM Treaty, both the U.S. and the USSR agree not to take their population centres out of hostage.

Denial

What kind of nuclear capabilities are required to deny an aggressor the accomplishment of objectives? Denial requires all the capabilities needed for punishment and more. It emphasizes the need for a full range of offensive and defensive capabilities. Denial requires offensive strike capabilities, not just to retaliate but to strike first. Some argue that extended deterrence necessitates a first-strike capability. Like punishment, denial requires survivability and redundancy. Needed too are robust, survivable C4ISR (command, control, communications, computers, intelligence, surveillance and reconnaissance) capabilities. Unlike punishment, denial places a premium on the ability to destroy not just countervalue but military, "counterforce," targets, especially the other side's nuclear capabilities, such as its ICBMs and command and control centres. Counterforce targeting is much more demanding than countervalue targeting; hardened, underground target and mobile targets must be put at risk. A much higher degree of accuracy, therefore, is required. Denial demands passive and active defensive capabilities to protect not only military capabilities but population centres. It requires civil defence (air raid shelters) and national anti-ballistic missile defence capabilities as well as point defence, hardening, concealment, dispersal, and mobility.

Denial, clearly, requires a full suite of nuclear war-fighting capabilities. It emphasizes relative rather than absolute capabilities—superiority matters. Since one can never have too much superiority, denial is essentially open ended. Thus a denial posture is a great deal more expensive than a punishment posture. Kennedy and McNamara came into office convinced that the Eisenhower approach, which emphasized massive retaliation, provided too few options—it appeared to be all or nothing. They initially embraced a move to a denial, or "Flexible Response," posture. Once McNamara realized how open ended this was, he moved to an assured destruction posture. With their emphasis on the need for not just a deterrent but a nuclear war-fighting capability, the proponents of Flexible Response became known as NUTs—nuclear utility theorists.

We see differences in objectives here. For Assured Destruction, it's all about the ability to deter and retaliate, to punish, to harm. Flexible Response is about the ability to deter, fight, and win a nuclear war. This is much more demanding. Flexible Response has a fallback; Assured Destruction does not. Does having a fallback make it more likely that deterrence will fail? Assured destruction answers "Yes"—and that this is an experiment we should not want to run. Does a nuclear war-fighting capability enhance or erode deterrence? According to Assured Destruction, it erodes deterrence; according to Flexible Response, it enhances deterrence.

Have we been MAD or NUTS? Both, actually. We've gone back and forth. At times we've been a combination of the two, even though the two are in tension with one another. In the 1950s, the declaratory policy of massive retaliation amounted, essentially, to an early version of Assured Destruction. Many argue that it was credible in the 1950s because the U.S. had nuclear superiority, and Assured Destruction wasn't mutual. As noted, Kennedy and McNamara initially shifted away from Assured Destruction to Flexible Response, saw how demanding and expensive it was, and moved back to Assured Destruction. It became MAD in the late 1960s-early 1970s. Nixon and Kissinger placed a declaratory emphasis on "essential equivalence," i.e., MAD. That's when the ABM Treaty was negotiated and signed. After James Schlesinger came in as secretary of defence, we moved away from Assured Destruction to Flexible Response and emphasized the development of limited nuclear options, especially counterforce options. Under Carter and Reagan we moved further away from Assured Destruction to Flexible Response.

Over the years, we've been MAD and NUTs. What should we be now? What specifically are we trying to deter with nuclear weapons?

- State use of nuclear and other weapons of mass destruction?
- State use of conventional weapons? Do we still need to use nuclear weapons to deter other states' use of conventional weapons?
- Non-state actor use of nuclear or other WMD? (Can terrorists be deterred the way states are deterred?)
- State support for non-state actor use of nuclear or other WMD?
- Non-state actor use of "conventional" weapons?
- State support for non-state actor use of "conventional" weapons?

Today most advocates of Assured Destruction, or a minimalist approach, argue that the only role for nuclear weapons is the deterrence of the use of nuclear weapons. The proponents of a Flexible Response, or a maximalist approach, continue to see a broader role for nuclear weapons.

NON-DETERRENT ROLES

Nuclear weapons have had a truncated war-fighting role. They were only used in August 1945; most of us think that's a good thing. A tradition of nonuse, which some think is sufficiently strong as to constitute a nuclear taboo, has developed over the years.

For some, nuclear weapons clearly are a status symbol, an indicator or attribute of major power status. The U.S. development of nuclear weapons was replicated by the USSR (1949), Britain (1952), France (1960), China (1964), Israel (1966/67), India (1974, 1998) and Pakistan (1998), and the DPRK (2006). Now we're concerned about Iran going nuclear. Is it a coincidence that the first five nuclear powers were the five permanent members of the UN Security Council? Of course they're also the only nuclear weapons states recognized by the Nonproliferation Treaty of 1968.

In addition to their role as status symbols, nuclear weapons have served as an equalizer. During the Cold War, nuclear weapons were relied upon by the United States and its NATO allies to counter, or offset, the conventional advantage of the Soviet Union and the Warsaw Pact. This was what, for instance, the Eisenhower administration's New Look was all about.

Today, the tables have been turned. It's the U.S. that possesses an enormous conventional advantage; Russia, which in conventional military terms is a mere rump state of the former Soviet Union, relies on its nuclear capabilities to the extent that it's concerned about the need to counter U.S. and NATO conventional capabilities. Others, state and non-state alike, seek a nuclear counter to U.S. conventional superiority. There are a number of reasons states seek to go nuclear. But to the extent that is U.S. military capabilities that spur them to do so, it is not U.S. nuclear capabilities but U.S. conventional capabilities, particularly the manner in which they have been used since 9/11, that is most prominently at play.

Nuclear weapons have thus served as a substitute for conventional forces. In the past, the U.S. and NATO quite explicitly substituted nuclear for conventional weapons. Today,

Russia is doing that; like the United States and NATO in the past, Russia more recently hasn't been able to afford, or hasn't wanted to pay for, the conventional capabilities required to match those of an erstwhile adversary. Again as in the past, nuclear weapons continue to play a role in dampening defence spending.

Finally, nuclear weapons arguably have played a role in discouraging both horizontal and vertical proliferation. Extended deterrence has provided an excuse for European states such as Germany and Asian states such as Japan, South Korea, and Taiwan for not going nuclear. It has been suggested as well that the sheer size of the U.S. (and Soviet or Russian) nuclear arsenals have dissuaded others from attempting to increase their nuclear capabilities or even joining the nuclear club since competing seriously with the likes of the United States is hopeless. For some (although not this author), this dissuasion effect is cause for not reducing the U.S. nuclear arsenal below the Moscow Treaty range of 1,700-2,200 warheads.

DELEGITIMISATION OF NUCLEAR WEAPONS

Though after the second World War some countries have revised their nuclear weapons programme, nuclear weapons still today are considered to be an established currency of politics and security. While the nuclear weapons states have agreed on a legally binding commitment to nuclear disarmament, they continue to rely heavily on such weapons in their security doctrines and continue to invest and modernise their arsenals. The way towards nuclear disarmament has many different paths and there are several approaches.

One such approach that is gaining more and more support is the delegitimisation of nuclear weapons. To delegitimise something means to "diminish or destroy the legitimacy, prestige or authority" of a given idea, concept or object.

In their advisory opinion in July 1996 the International Court of Justice stated that "the threat or use of nuclear weapons would generally be contrary to the rules of international law applicable in armed conflict, and in particular the principles and rules humanitarian law". Since the use of nuclear weapons is generally considered to be illegal, their overall utility is questionable. So in order to delegitimise nuclear weapons, there is a critical need to change the perception of their role and utility: from a position in which they occupied a central strategic place to one in which their role is seen as wholly unnecessary as well as undesirable. To be successful in this task other actors that are not bound to a specific state's security polices are of utmost importance, they can bring new ideas to the table and keep the discussion focused on the topic at hand. It all comes down to nuclear weapons not being very useful in today's world and the upholding of these weapons increasing the danger of them being used and thus causing devastation.

REVIEWING THE VALUE OF NUCLEAR WEAPONS

Different reasons are being put forward as to why Japan surrendered on August 10th, 1945. Some people believe that dropping two atomic bombs on Hiroshima and Nagasaki coerced Japan's leaders into ending World War II (WWII). This interpretation has certain plausibility, since only a short time after the USA bombed Hiroshima on August 6th, 1945, and Nagasaki on August 9th, 1945, Japan signalled a willingness to surrender.

But even a superficial review of the facts shows that there is almost no way that this interpretation can be true.

Both recent historical research in Japan and older research, conducted by researchers in the Soviet Union demonstrate that the destruction of the two Japanese cities by the U.S. did not significantly influence the willingness of Japan's General Staff and government to fight. It was rather the declaration of war by the Soviet Union on August 8th, 1945 that led Japan to surrender. It can be argued that for the Japanese government the bombings served as a face-saving justification for the surrender, when really their military could not have fought both the U.S. and the Soviet Union. From the perspective of the U.S. the bombings ended WWII and were therefore a legitimate means of warfare.

In 1968, a multilateral treaty limiting the spread of nuclear weapons was signed and entered into force in 1970. Member states of the Non-Proliferation Treaty (NPT), including France, China, Great Britain, the USA and the Soviet Union, committed themselves not to acquire nuclear weapons (those who did not posses them), to pursue good faith negotiations to disarm nuclear weapons and to recognise the right for peaceful use of nuclear energy.

The time of the Cold War is often used as a reference for the effectiveness of nuclear deterrence. However, it could be argued that the absence of any great catastrophe can be attributed rather to luck than anything else. More than once the decision for or against the use of a nuclear weapon was in the hands of one man and one misinterpretation of the situation could have started a nuclear war.

In 1969 after the Antarctica (1961) and Outer Space (1967) had already been declared Nuclear Weapon Free Zones (NWFZ), the Treaty of Tlataloco created the first continental-wide NWFZ. Other treaties followed and today there are nine NWFZs around the world.

INTERNATIONAL HUMANITARIAN LAW

The advisory opinion of the International Court of Justice (ICJ) in 1996 declares that "the threat or use of nuclear weapons would generally be contrary to the rules of international law applicable in armed conflict, and in particular the principles and rules of humanitarian law". This advisory opinion is based on the fact that nuclear weapons are in their nature indiscriminate, i.e. they do not distinguish between non-combatants and combatants. Therefore a nuclear attack would be incapable of sparing civilians (article 48 of Protocol I). International humanitarian law (IHL) states that it is unlawful to cause unnecessary suffering to combatants (The Hague Convention IV, Article 23 (e)) A nuclear bomb will, if used, have devastating consequences and the "[r]adiation released by a nuclear explosion would cause generic defects and illness in future generations". Furthermore, nuclear weapons cannot be confined in their effects in space and time. That means that other states close to the attack cannot be guaranteed not to be affected. IHL states that neutral states must be protected from damage caused by warfare (The Hague Convention V, Article 1). Drawn from the above the indiscriminate nature of a nuclear weapon would be a violation of IHL. The rules that are outlined both in the Geneva Conventions and the Hague Convention on respecting the laws and customs of war and conflict should be applied to nuclear weapons just as they are in any other aspect of armed conflict.

Additionally, nuclear weapons have the same destructive nature as biological and chemical weapons. The degree of destructive power was one of the main arguments when banning the use of biological and chemical weapons, so this argument must be a legitimate one also in the case of nuclear weapons.

In addition to IHL, human rights law and environmental law are also applicable during armed conflict. They both emphasise general principles such as proportionality and necessity and are just as relevant for nuclear weapons as for biological and chemical weapons. The non-use of nuclear weapons could be argued to be Customary Humanitarian International Law since nuclear weapons have not been used since WWII and many states, including nuclear weapons states, have stated that six decades of international norm of non-use of nuclear weapons should be strengthened and the non-use policy be extended forever. The five big nuclear weapons states, i.e. the U.S., Great Britain, France, China and Russia (the P5), have signed and ratified the NPT. The P5 have thereby committed themselves "to pursue negotiations in good faith on effective measures relating to cessation of the nuclear arms race at an early date and to nuclear disarmament, and on a treaty on general and complete disarmament under strict and effective international control". The ICJ also strongly emphasised this issue and summarised the twofold requirements of article VI to be both conducting negotiations and engaging in results leading to nuclear disarmament.

The 2010 NPT Action Plan also calls upon member states, in action 20, to recall the advisory opinion of the ICJ. In spite of the ICJ's opinion on the use of nuclear weapons the court did not find any international laws specifically prohibiting the threat of use or use of nuclear weapons during an armed conflict. The court also could not conclude definitively whether the threat of use or use of nuclear weapons would be lawful or unlawful in an extreme circumstance of self-defence.

Utility

It is now widely accepted that nuclear weapons have little or no utility as instruments of warfare. They are unfit to be used to acquire territory because of their long lasting environmental damage. Nor can they be used in today's second generation warfare, when war is no longer fought by individual states' armies on the front line. Today's armed conflicts are to a greater extent fought by and amongst civilians, which makes it difficult to aim weapons at a specific military target. The weapons are, furthermore, useless when it comes to fighting terrorism since most terrorist groups do not occupy a traditional site that could be targeted, neither can they be identified as combatants since they do not distinguish themselves from civilians. There is a strong taboo on the actual use, if not possession, of nuclear weapons: a profound normative constraint, as well as a practical one, against using weapons of such indiscriminate and disproportionate destruction. Because of the limited utility and the taboo of the use of nuclear weapons, the question is how big the actual threat for nuclear power states to use their weapons is. The main purpose of nuclear weapons today is their deterrent character, i.e. the possession of nuclear weapons prevents any other agent from attacking a nuclear weapon state.

In the 2010 Nuclear Posture Review Report The United States explains "[...] with the objective of making deterrence of nuclear attack on the United States or our allies and partners the sole purpose of U.S. nuclear weapons." The Review Report goes on saying; "[e]ffective missile defences are an essential element of the U.S. commitment to strengthen regional deterrence against states of concern." The French Ambassador Mr. Eric Danon stated in an interview during the 2010 NPT review Conference that nuclear deterrence is one of the systems in place today that is keeping the international stability and refraining states from attacking other states.

Countries that have reversed their Nuclear Options

After the end of the Cold War the former members of the Soviet Union, Belarus, Kazakhstan and Ukraine, decided to return the nuclear weapons based on their soil. At the same time under the umbrella of NATO nuclear sharing, U.S. nuclear weapons have been deployed in different non-nuclear NATO member states. In 2001 the U.S. removed its tactical nuclear weapons from Greece and the United Kingdom, though in case of a crisis they could probably be redeployed.

In 1989 South Africa dismantled its nuclear weapons programme and joined the NPT in 1991. In 1994 the International Atomic Energy Agency confirmed the transformation of South Africa's nuclear programme into peaceful applications. Up until today South Africa remains the only country that has abolished its nuclear weapons.

After several years of struggling to develop nuclear weapons Libya announced in December 2003 the elimination of its production of nuclear weapons and the admission of International Atomic Energy Agency (IAEA) personnel to supervise the process. To increase confidence Libya ratified the Comprehensive Test Ban Treaty in January 2004 and signed the additional protocol of the NPT giving IAEA inspectors greater authority in verifying the country's nuclear programme.

These examples show the possibility to disarm without jeopardising national security, regrettably these efforts are few in numbers. Despite of the lack of nuclear disarmament today most countries have clearly stated that nuclear disarmament is a priority and is in their national interest. Unfortunately these commitments are in many cases vague and are yet not seen translated into concrete actions that are in compliance with the principles of nuclear disarmament.

How to move Forward

In order to abolish nuclear weapons today, their role as a central strategic asset in states national security needs to be redefined and the security issues have to be more focused on human security concerns. This will not be easy since the Cold War-assumptions about the weapons' roles are deeply rooted in notions of deterrence and national security. Traditional nuclear arms control was established during the Cold War and was concerned with arms control and non-proliferation. This attitude has still strong advocates particularly in the nuclear weapons states. One example is the reluctance in negotiation a Fissile Material Treaty (FMT) instead of a Fissile Material Cut-off Treaty (FMCT) in the Conference on Disarmament, which include just halting the production of fissile material but not reducing the current stocks. There is a need to start talking about nuclear weapons in a different manner. When disarmament is treated as humanitarian action, it forces states to change their mind-sets. The humanitarian approach to weapons has shown to be successful in the past when landmines and cluster weapons were banned and delegitimised. Non-nuclear weapons states, in particular Norway and Switzerland, have taken with some success a leading role in the delegitimisation debates.

For the first time, in the 2010 NPT review outcome document, the humanitarian approach is mentioned: "[...]

catastrophic humanitarian consequences of any use of nuclear weapons and reaffirms the need for all States at all time to comply with applicable international law, including international humanitarian law." Together with Norway and Switzerland more non-nuclear states are placing themselves on the humanitarian side of nuclear weapons. During the 2011 session of the Conference on Disarmament several states have pointed out the clash of International Humanitarian Law with the use of nuclear weapons and the devastating humanitarian crises an attack would cause. The above mentioned states together with the non-alliance movement (NAM) countries are slowly starting to change the doctrine.

Civil society actors have for a long time worked to eliminate nuclear weapons. Non-governmental organisations (NGO) that have no obligations towards a state should help put more focus on the delegitimisation. International humanitarian action organisations such as the ICRC and IOM could help taking a leading role for NGO's working for the delegitimisation of nuclear weapons. More measures have to be taken to engage more and new people, groups of stats, civil societies, scientists and health practitioners need to work together to push for the issue on delegitimisation.

Action plan number 19 in the 2010 NPT Action Plan focuses on the importance and obligations of member states of the NPT to engage in cooperation with other national governments, the United Nations, as well as other international and regional organisations and civil society.

In May 2010 the James Martin Center for Non-proliferation Studies and the Monterey Institute of International Studies published a report on Delegitimising Nuclear Weapons.

In their report the authors bring light to a new and important actor: the military. "Not surprisingly, military leaders have continually questioned the usefulness and morality of nuclear weapons." Furthermore, the report reminds the reader of the important role military personnel have had in the disarmament negotiations banning landmines and cluster munitions. In conclusion, more diverse groups of actors need to be attacking and changing the doctrine and view on nuclear weapons.

Unfortunately, using the example of the Conference on Disarmament, expanding the forum to more member states and the inclusion of civil society, show some states reluctance to engage in a broader forum. Delegitimisation is a conceptual approach to nuclear disarmament, but should be complemented with specific and tangible steps by governments.

THE EFFECTS OF NUCLEAR WEAPONS

A nuclear weapon is not just a big bomb. It does not have the same make up as a terrorist bomb or heavy artillery fire seen on the news from any global conflict. It's very difficult to write, let alone read, what these weapons can do to people. But it's vital that we understand the differences.

With a conventional weapon, most of the damage is done by the sheer force of the explosion. In contrast, much of the power of nuclear weapons comes from thermal (heat) and ionising (nuclear) radiation, caused by the splitting or joining together of atoms. The effects of a nuclear weapon increase in relation to its explosive power. Also, a blast some distance above the earth would create different effects than one exploded at (or below) ground level.

To take one example, if a 20 kiloton nuclear bomb (about twice as powerful as the bomb dropped on Hiroshima) was exploded on a city, the heat and blast generated would vaporise all people and buildings in the immediate area, and make a crater that might be as much as 100 metres in diameter. The wind created by the blast could be several hundred km/hr. The destruction of buildings would increase death and injury due to flying glass and other debris. The release of ionising radiation is a phenomenon unique to nuclear explosions and causes additional casualties alongside those caused by blast and thermal effects. There would be a number of deaths from radiation sickness, for which there is really no effective medical treatment. Large amounts of earth, water and other debris in the area surrounding the explosion would be sucked up to form a "mushroom cloud" of radioactive debris. When this material returned to earth, as fallout, the effects could be spread even further, and might make the city (and an area of countryside stretching tens of kilometres downwind) uninhabitable for many weeks or even years.

HEALTH EFFECTS

"In the dim light of a hospital room, seven years old Jimmy was remembering the day on which he was told he had

leukaemia. He remembered his mother's tears, his father's bewildered anger, the alien feeling of the hospital's environment. His mind replayed the nausea and the diarrhoea caused byradiation therapy and chemotherapy, his hair falling out and kids laughing at him... Jimmy died gently, utterly exhausted having lost so much blood. His tissue had broken down completely, and he was bleeding from every body opening. His bed looked like a battlefield."

"On August 9, 1945, when the atomic bomb was dropped over the city of Nagasaki, Kasuko Yamashina was working at a distance of two kilometers from ground zero. He tried to get home after the dropping of the bomb, but the fire was too fierce for him to approach the district, so that night he had to sleep under a bridge alone. His house was located at a place situated about 350 metres from ground zero. As soon as the fire went down, he reached the house finding out that his parents were burned by the heat of 4,000 degrees and lay scorched black and carbonised. He couldn't find his brother and his sister, and all that he could see were burned bricks and dead bodies.

On the August 15, the war was over, but by that day Kasuko body had changed. He had black bleeding from the gums, and he wasn't able to walk becouse of fierce shivers caused by high fever.

Under that condition he left Nagasaki to enter a hospital in his home town.

On 19th September, the headquarters of General Mac Arthur set up a press code, ordering him and the other victims never to speak about the atomic bombs.

They announced that all the persons who should die of radiation effects, would die by December 1945. Those who would live at that time, would have been spared by radiation. The situation of radiation injuries was unknown at that time, even in Japan. Only in 1957, the Supporting Law of Atomic Victims was passed, and Kasuko was legally admitted as a Hibakusha, but he had to conceal his being in order to survive.

In 1963 he had a high fever, his body changed stiff and black. It took him three years to get back his original skin colour, and, during the nights, Kasuko was extremely scared, he heard the voices of the dead..."

Jimmy and Kasuko's stories are two of the hundreds of thousands similar stories related to the nuclear age.

Radiation released from each step in the nuclear weapons production cycle cause cancer, congenital defects, mental retardation, immune destruction, cancer, stillbirths and other health problems.

Similar syndromes have been observed among the workers exposed to radiation in nuclear power plants in Japan, or in down-winders living in the irradiated zones near Hanford, and in the Chernobyl children, as well as the areas close to the nuclear test sites.

In 1984 the United Nations Human Rights Committe noted that "it's evident that the designing, testing, manifacture, possession and deployment of nuclear weapons are among the greatest threats to the right to life which confront mankind today" and concluded that "the production, testing, possession, deployment and use of nuclear weapon should be prohibited and recognized as crimes against humanity."

In human terms the cost has been astronomical. Rosalie Bertel has estimated that "the global victims of the radiation pollution related to nuclear weapon production, testing, use and waste conservatively number 13 million."

ENVIRONMENTAL EFFECTS

The production of nuclear weapons has polluted vast amounts of soil and water at hundreds of nuclear weapons facilities all over the world. Many of the substances released, including plutonium, uranium, strontium, cesium, benzene, polychlorinated biphenyls (PCBs), mercury and cyanide, are carcinogenic and/or mutagenic and remain hazardous for thousands, some for hundreds of thousands, of years. Contaminants from nuclear weapons production and testing have often travelled far down wind and down stream. Production facilities for nuclear weapons are heavily polluted, for example in the United States there are over 4500 contaminated Department of Energy sites.

The manufacture and testing of weapons involves the leakage of nuclear material. Of all the activities concerning nuclear weapons, testing has been the most destructive of the environment. Even placing tests underground does not avoid atmospheric pollution. Radioactivity released from atmospheric nuclear testing - including plutonium, strontium, cesium, carbon-14, and radioactive iodine - has been widely dispersed throughout the world. Underground tests have contaminated soil and groundwater. Many square miles in Russia, Belarus and the US have been rendered unusable by contamination of the soil. Also the Irish sea and the Arctic Ocean have been poisoned.

In Russia nuclear submarines, some still armed with nuclear warheads, are rusting away in the fjords of Murmansk. Elsewhere, rivers have been polluted and open reservoirs and lakes have been used to hold large quantities of liquid radioactive materials. In 1957, a waste storage tank at the Chelyabinsk nuclear weapons site in Russia exploded and a radioactive cloud dispersed over more than 200 square kilometres of an agricultural region containing numerous rivers and lakes. Nearly all the trees within the most radioactive zone were damaged or killed. Radioactive waste has been routinely dumped into Lake Karachay, recognized as the world's most radioactive body of water, also at Chelyabinsk.

The environmental damage resulting from nuclear technology is not limited to the two largest nuclear weapons states, the United states and Russia. All nuclear weapons and nuclear energy producing nations have caused some level of environmental contamination, both in their own countries and abroad - such as, nuclear testing in the South Pacific, Nevada, Kazakhstan, China, India and Pakistan; water and airborne discharges from reprocessing plants in the UK and France; and uranium mining in Namibia, Canada, former East Germany and Australia.

Moreover, the ongoing production of both nuclear weapons and nuclear power continues to create nuclear waste. The mining of uranium causes radioactive pollution of the atmosphere and also otherwise damages the environment. Further pollution occurs during the transport and processing of the uranium. Production of nuclear weapons involves the generation of large quantities of waste material and contamination of surrounding areas. Clean-up of contaminated sites, disposition of excess fissile material and dismantling of nuclear weapons also contaminates the environment. New technologies will need to be developed in order to retrieve radioactive materials which have been released into the environment either through accident or by design. Nuclear warfare would result in the wholesale destruction of the environment. The burial of radioactive materials is presently being promoted as the solution to radioactive waste disposal. However, at present, there are no known disposal routes for long-lived radioactive materials. The burial of these materials must not be confused with their safe containment and isolation from the environment. Whether the storage containers, the store itself, or the surrounding rocks will offer enough protection to stop radioactivity from escaping in the long term is impossible to predict. One of the most likely mechanisms of pollution in connection with waste disposal in rock is the contamination of groundwater. Underground waters may come into contact with radioactive elements that have leached out from the waste and contaminate the drinking water of both local and distant communities.

SOCIAL EFFECTS

To understand the effects of a nuclear war it is important to distinguish it from conventional war or a natural disaster. In particular, all the factors that would make it possible to cope with a normal emergency situation would be lacking: limited damage, a relatively small number of casualties, surviving political or social leadership, a desire to perform common emergency work rather than look after ones own family, large reservoirs of external, easily mobilized skilled workers, material resources, and organizational skills.

The massive and simultaneous destruction of economic and human resources would result in an inability to provide immediate and sufficient human and material aid to damaged areas. There will be no time to adapt and to innovate as nations did in World War II. More importantly, the lack of outside aid would create a sense of individual and common isolation. Aid symbolizes a reconnection with a larger, normal world. This connection helps provide the impetus for rebuilding the damaged society, creating a sense of vitality and ability to dispel the continuing perception of isolation. It also has an important function for binding together society, restating a common thread of hope and shared aspirations.

Economic destruction, loss of political leadership (especially at the local level), and the need to mobilize resources for relief and recovery would present extraordinary demands on weakened political institutions. In the interest of implementing survival programs, legal norms and practices would have to be suspended for prolonged periods in many areas. The character of political institutions and authority would almost certainly change, especially if hostilities or the threat of hostilities persisted. Both old and new political structures would be likely to suffer from greatly reduced credibility. Decentralization of political power and more authoritarian methods of political, social, and economic control would be probable responses to post-attack conditions.

However, even before any outbreak of nuclear war, the presence of nuclear weapons has an enormous potential to distort social and economic priorities. Each of the nuclear weapons states has spent billions of dollars on constructing, maintaining and protecting its nuclear weapons. It is not necessary to point out that this money could have been better spent on providing health care, education or other public services.

The development of nuclear weapons also makes it necessary to create an unaccountable "nuclear elite", made up of scientists, military and civil servants, who work largely in secret to control the development, testing and deployment of nuclear weapons. This makes the presence of nuclear weapons incompatible with a democratic society.

It is possible to link an increased importance of the military, and a general increase in militarism, to a growth of xenophobia, racial and religious intolerance, as well as male chauvinism.

PSYCHOLOGICAL EFFECTS

The imagery of nuclear war, the widespread casualties, and the intense fear of radioactivity would lead to the "nuclear war survivor syndrome". This powerful sense of personal vulnerability, helplessness, guilt, isolation and fear, was seen to varying degrees in the Hiroshima and Nagasaki survivors. The powerful psychological effects of the fear of radioactivity, and the "loss of trust" were described in studies of the nuclear accident at Three Mile Island. The spread of radioactive fallout would create the image of nuclear threat and vulnerability across wide areas.

The very short period required to carry out highly destructive nuclear attacks would intensify the emotional impact, particularly those reactions associated with denial of the true extent of the damage or fostering flight from damaged areas.

Robert J. Lifton, in his study of Hiroshima survivors, described the psychological effect as "a sudden and absolute shift from normal existence to an overwhelming encounter with death." The reaction, as reported by a witness to the disaster, Father Siemes: "Among the passers-by, there are many who are uninjured. In a purposeless, insensate manner, distraught by the magnitude of the disaster, most of them rush by and none conceives the thought of organizing help on his own initiative. They are concerned only with the welfare of their own families." In some cases even families were abandoned. The result of this experience was a deep fear of returning to the cities to rebuild the any form of normal life that may be possible after a nuclear attack.

Families would be broken up by death, severe injury, disease, evacuation, or military and labour conscription. The young, elderly, and handicapped would suffer disproportionately since they depend most on society's material and institutional resources. For example, the young and elderly showed significant increases in accidental death attributed to neglect in Great Britain in World War II. The loss of material and institutional resources in urban-industrial attacks would make survival in the post-attack period difficult for individuals and groups alike, compounding the psychological stresses of the attack itself. Satisfying even the simplest survival requirements (food, shelter, and clothing) would become major tasks.

The entire post-war generation has lived under a cloud of fear - sometimes described as the 'shadow of the mushroom cloud', which pervades all thoughts about the human future. This fear, which has hung like a blanket of doom over the thoughts of children in particular, is an evil in itself and will last so long as nuclear weapons remain. The younger generation needs to grow up in a climate of hope, not one of despair that at some point in their life, there is a possibility of their life being snuffed out in an instant, or their health destroyed, along with all they cherish, in a war in which their country may not even take part.

A nuclear strategy requires a genocidal mentality. There are important parallels between nuclear strategies and the Nazi policies that led to the gas chambers. This 'genocidal mentality' consists of dissociative processes of the mind such as 'psychic numbing' and the 'language of non-feeling' and together with distancing, ideological ethics and a passion for problem-solving have the effects of allowing people to remain sane whilst carrying out insane policies.

Governments also have to psychologically prepare their populations for the idea that such insane and evil strategies are rational and necessary. This requires demonising the enemy. During the Cold War for example, the Russians were demonised in order to try to make it acceptable that in some circumstances it would be justifiable to kill millions of them within minutes, in retaliation for something their government may or may not have done.

THE NUCLEAR FREEZE AND ITS IMPACT

Thirty years ago, Randall Forsberg, a young defence and disarmament researcher, launched the Nuclear Weapons Freeze Campaign. Designed to stop the drift toward nuclear war through a U.S.-Soviet agreement to stop the testing, production, and deployment of nuclear weapons, the freeze campaign escalated into a mass movement that swept across the United States. It attracted the support of nearly all peace groups, as well as that of mainstream religious, professional, and labour organizations.

In addition, the freeze concept secured the backing of most of the general public and was made part of the Democratic Party's presidential campaign platform. By the early 1990s, despite fierce opposition from the administrations of Ronald Reagan and George H.W. Bush, the freeze campaign, bolstered by the activities of nuclear disarmament groups at home and abroad, had succeeded in securing its objectives and in building a grassroots, long-term disarmament organization in the United States.

Background

As a keen supporter of peace and nuclear disarmament, Forsberg had been giving talks to peace groups since 1975. Convinced that they needed greater unity of action and attainable goals, she suggested in mid-1979 that they coalesce behind two objectives: a nuclear freeze and a nonintervention regime. Both, she believed, would "fundamentally change the nature of government policies." In December, when addressing the annual meeting of Mobilization for Survival, a major anti-nuclear organization of that era, she scrapped the nonintervention idea and focused instead on the nuclear freeze. Actually, Mobilization for Survival and the major groups backing it—the American Friends Service Committee (AFSC), Clergy and Laity Concerned (CALC), and the Fellowship of Reconciliation (FOR)—were already promoting a U.S. moratorium on nuclear weapons production and deployment. Therefore, as Forsberg recalled, she told the assemblage that if peace activists turned this unilateral moratorium into a bilateral one, "the great majority of the American people would completely agree with you. And you could change the world!"

Forsberg's speech served as a catalyst for a new movement. Enthusiastic about her idea, peace group leaders urged her to draw up a formal proposal. In late December 1979, Forsberg began drafting the "Call to Halt the Nuclear Arms Race." Circulated widely among leading peace activists, the "Call" emphasized that the freeze would retain the existing nuclear parity between the United States and theSoviet Union, thereby halting the arms race and opening the way for deep reductions in or elimination of nuclear weapons in the future. In April 1980, having secured adequate feedback and individual endorsements, the AFSC, CALC, FOR, and Forsberg's own Institute for Defence and Disarmament Studies published the "Call" and began seeking endorsements from other peace groups. Meanwhile, Forsberg and peace activist George Sommaripa drew up a strategic plan designed to run from 1980 to 1984. The plan proposed that, after securing the support of peace organizations, the movement proceed to obtain the backing of major interest groups, mount a widespread public education campaign to convert Middle America, and, finally, inject the issue into electoral politics.

The Movement Advances

Thereafter, the freeze campaign surged forward. To the dismay of movement leaders, enthusiasts jumped the gun by placing a freeze resolution on the November 1980 election ballot in western Massachusetts. Determined not to lose this first test of strength, Randy Kehler, Frances Crowe, and other local activists swung into action, and the freeze emerged victorious in 59 of the 62 towns that voted on it. In March 1981, the first national conference of the freeze movement convened at the Center for Peace Studies at Georgetown University. Thanks to Forsberg's efforts to keep the movement respectable, this conclave, although led by pacifists and other longtime critics of military priorities, produced a strategy and movement designed to appeal to the political mainstream. Admittedly, Kehler, chosen as the first freeze coordinator, was hardly an average American, for he had been a conscientious objector during the Vietnam War and a longtime peace activist. Yet, he was also a clean-cut, articulate, consensus-building individual, anxious to keep the movement on a mainstream course. In addition, the organizers deliberately rejected the offers of East Coast peace groups to house the freeze and instead established its headquarters in St. Louis, deep in the country's heartland.

For the most part, early movement efforts focused on popularizing the idea of the freeze on the local level. Activists distributed vast quantities of literature about the nuclear arms race and brought freeze resolutions before organizations with which they were affiliated, as well as before town meetings, city councils, and state legislatures.

They gathered signatures on freeze petitions locally as part of a nationwide campaign and placed freeze referenda on the ballot in cities, counties, and states throughout the country. Although these activities were time consuming and labour intensive, they meshed nicely with the efforts of other groups, such as the Union of Concerned Scientists and Physicians for Social Responsibility, to alert the public to the dangers of nuclear war. In general, freeze activism was stronger in northern and western states than in the more conservative South. Nevertheless, by mid-1982 it had taken root in three-quarters of the nation's congressional districts.

These efforts helped produce a widespread display of resistance by Americans to the nuclear arms race. In March 1982, 159 out of 180 Vermont town meetings voted to back a nuclear weapons freeze by the U.S. and Soviet governments. On June 12, an anti-nuclear demonstration in New York City around the theme "Freeze the Arms Race—Fund Human Needs" produced the largest political rally up to that point in American life, with nearly a million participants. When the freeze campaign delivered its petitions to the U.S. and Soviet missions to the United Nations, they contained the signatures of more than 2,300,000 Americans. Moreover, that fall, when freeze referenda appeared on the ballot in 10 states, the District of Columbia, and 37 cities and counties around the nation, voters delivered a victory to the freeze campaign in nine of the states and in all but three localities. Covering about one-third of the U.S.electorate, this was the largest referendum on a single issue in U.S. history.

Opinion surveys confirmed the vast popularity of the freeze campaign. Five polls taken during 1983 found an average of 72 percent support for and 20 percent opposition to the freeze—results that were virtually unchanged from six polls taken in 1982. Writing in October 1983, Patrick Caddell, one of the nation's leading political pollsters, called the freeze campaign "the most significant citizens' movement of the last century.... In sheer numbers the freeze movement is awesome; there exists no comparable national cause or combination of causes, left or right, that can match...the legions that have been activated."

Organizational endorsements of the freeze provide yet another indication of the movement's strength. With the exception of fundamentalist denominations, all major U.S. religious bodies expressed their support for the freeze, including the National Council of Churches, the Roman Catholic Church, the United Presbyterian Church, the United Methodist Church, the Episcopalians, the Lutherans, and the Synagogue Council of America. Indeed, hundreds of national organizations—many of which had never before taken a stand on national defence issues—came out in favour of the freeze. They included the American Association of School Administrators, the American Association of University Women, the American Nurses Association, the American Pediatric Society, the American Public Health Association, Friends of the Earth, the National Council of La Raza, the National Education Association, the U.S. Conference of Mayors, and the Young Women's Christian Association. Although the labour movement had been rather hawkish during the Cold War, 25 national labour unions backed the freeze, as did the AFL-CIO. Furthermore, by November 1983, the freeze had been endorsed by more than 370 city councils, 71 county councils, and by one or both houses of 23 state legislatures. In 1984 it became part of the Democratic Party's presidential campaign platform.

Reagan Administration Reacts

From the standpoint of officials in the Reagan administration, who championed a vast nuclear buildup and talked glibly of fighting and winning a nuclear war, the rise of the nuclear freeze campaign was a disaster. As David Gergen, the White House communications director during those years, recalled, "There was a widespread view in the administration that the freeze was a dagger pointed at the heart of the administration's defence program." Queried years later about the freeze campaign, Robert McFarlane, Reagan's national security adviser, observed, "We took it as a serious movement that could undermine congressional support for the [nuclear] modernization program, and potentially...a serious partisan political threat that could affect the election in `84." In March 1982, after Senators Edward Kennedy (D-Mass.) and Mark Hatfield (R-Ore.) announced that they would introduce a freeze resolution in Congress, administration officials sharply assailed the idea and met to plan what McFarlane called "a huge effort" to counter the freeze campaign. According to McFarlane, they organized an interdepartmental group that he chaired and that included representatives from the CIA, the Department of Defence, the Department of State, the Joint Chiefs of Staff, and the U.S. Information Agency. McFarlane told the members of the group that they and their deputies should fan out across the United States and make public appearances assailing the freeze. Although the administration denied at the time that a government campaign existed to defeat the freeze referenda of 1982, the effort absorbed the energies of numerous officials, including Reagan. In July, he appeared in his home state of California, where he charged that the freeze "would make this country desperately vulnerable to nuclear blackmail."

That fall, as the freeze grew increasingly likely to emerge victorious at the polls and in Congress, Reagan grew increasingly strident. Addressing a gathering of veterans groups in early October, he insisted that the freeze was "inspired by not the sincere, honest people who want peace, but by some who want the weakening of America and so are manipulating honest people." On November 11, he told a press conference that "foreign agents" had helped "instigate" the freeze campaign. There was "plenty of evidence" for this, the president declared, although he did not produce any. Challenged on his allegations,

Reagan said that he had leaned heavily for his freeze information on two *Reader's Digest*articles and cited a report by the House Intelligence Committee. However, the committee chairman, Representative Edward Boland (D-Mass.), declared that according to FBI and CIA officials, there was "no evidence that the Soviets direct, manage, or manipulate the nuclear freeze movement"—a contention confirmed when a declassified version of the FBI report was released in March 1983. Reagan stubbornly continued to insist that "the originating organization" for the freeze was the Communist-dominated World Peace Council and that the first person to propose it was Soviet leader Leonid Brezhnev.

Results

Superficially, the Reagan administration managed to hold the line against the freeze campaign and other critics of its nuclear policies. Although the administration failed in its diligent efforts to prevent passage of almost all the state and local freeze referenda in the fall of 1982 and to prevent passage of a freeze resolution in the House of Representatives in the spring of 1983, it did manage to defeat a similar resolution in the Senate, where Republicans had a majority. Furthermore, despite adoption of the freeze proposal by the Democrats in 1984, Reagan won re-election that year and then saw to it that a bilateral freeze with the Soviet Union was never negotiated. In addition, with the freeze campaign's momentum blunted by these actions, as well as by a rapid falloff in coverage by the media after 1983, the movement dwindled and dropped out of sight in the late 1980s. Nevertheless, the nuclear freeze campaign was considerably more successful than it appeared.

Under enormous political pressure, the Reagan administration dramatically reversed its rhetoric. In April 1982, shortly after the freeze resolution was introduced in Congress, Reagan began declaring publicly and repeatedly that "a nuclear war cannot be won and must never be fought." He added, on the first occasion that, "[t]o those who protest against nuclear war, I can only say: 'I'm with you.'" Increasingly rattled, Reagan, who had opposed every nuclear arms control and disarmament agreement negotiated by his Democratic and Republican predecessors, also began reversing his nuclear policies. In the fall of 1983, as anti-nuclear protests swept across the United

States and Western Europe, he told his startled secretary of state, George Shultz, "If things get hotter and hotter and arms control remains an issue, maybe I should go see [Soviet leader Yuri] Andropov and propose eliminating all nuclear weapons." Although Shultz and other members of the administration were horrified by this turnabout, Reagan persisted with it and eagerly searched for a Soviet negotiating partner.

Starting in March 1985, he found one in Mikhail Gorbachev. With Gorbachev in power, the way was open for significant arms control and disarmament agreements. Gorbachev was not only a true believer in nuclear disarmament, but a movement convert. The Soviet leader's "New Thinking," as his advisers noted, was powerfully affected by the Western nuclear disarmament movement. Gorbachev himself declared, "The new thinking took into account and absorbed the conclusions and demands of...the public and the scientific community, of the movements of physicians, scientists, and ecologists, and of various antiwar organizations." Meeting frequently with leaders of the Western peace and disarmament movement, including leaders of the freeze campaign, Gorbachev followed their advice by agreeing to the removal of medium-range nuclear missiles from Europe, removing short-range nuclear missiles from Eastern Europe, negotiating major reductions in strategic weapons, and unilaterally halting Soviet nuclear testing.

The result was an important victory for freeze activists and other anti-nuclear campaigners. Boxed in by the movement and Gorbachev, Reagan and his successor, George H.W. Bush, were drawn into the most substantial burst of nuclear arms control and disarmament ventures in history. By the early 1990s, the United States and the Soviet Union had ceased the testing, development, and deployment of nuclear weapons and had reduced their nuclear arsenals. Bush even called on Forsberg to serve as a consultant to his administration on nuclear policy. Yet, the freeze campaign did not evaporate. In 1987 it merged with the National Committee for a Sane Nuclear Policy to become Peace Action, the largest grassroots peace and disarmament organization in the United States. Today, Peace Action remains the largest organization of this kind and continues to mobilize public support for nuclear disarmament.

The success of the freeze movement and its anti-nuclear counterparts of the era provides an important lesson for our own time. If substantial popular pressure can be stirred up by advocates of arms control and disarmament, government officials can be convinced to change their nuclear policies.

THE DEVELOPMENT AND PROLIFERATION OF NUCLEAR WEAPONS

The 20th century saw revolutionary breakthroughs in many fields of science and technology. Besides the many discoveries and inventions in the fields of electronics and telecommunications, few of the leaps forward had more direct impact on people's lives and society at large than the advances in nuclear science. Below you can learn more about one particular aspect of the nuclear revolution: the development and spread of nuclear weapons.

THE BIRTH OF THE ATOMIC AGE

In October 1939, just after the outbreak of World War II in Europe, the President of the United States Franklin D. Roosevelt received a letter from physicist Albert Einstein and his Hungarian colleague Leo Szilard, calling to his attention the prospect that a bomb of unprecedented power could be made by tapping the forces of nuclear fission. The two scientists, who had fled from Europe in order to escape Nazism, feared that Hitler-Germany was already working on the problem. Should the Germans be the first to develop the envisaged "atomic bomb," Hitler would have a weapon at his disposal that would make it possible for him to destroy his enemies and rule the world.

To avoid this nightmare, Einstein and Szilard urged the government of the United States to join the race for the atomic bomb. Roosevelt agreed, and for the next four and half years a vast, utterly secret effort was launched in cooperation with the United Kingdom. Code-named "The Manhattan Project," the effort eventually employed more than 200,000 workers and several thousands scientists and engineers, many of European background. Finally, on July 16, 1945, the first atomic bomb was tested in the midst of the Alamogordo desert in New Mexico. Its power astonished even the men and women who had constructed it. As he witnessed the spectacular explosion, Robert Oppenheimer, the physicist who had directed the scientific work on the bomb, remembered a line from the Vedic religious text Bhagavad-Gita: "I am become death, the shatterer of worlds."

By the time of the Alamogordo test, Germany had already surrendered. This meant that the potential threat of a Nazi atomic bomb no longer existed. But the war in the Pacific was still raging, and the President of the United States Harry S. Truman decided to use the atomic bomb in order to force the Japanese leadership to surrender as quickly as possible. Thus, on August 6 an atomic bomb with an explosive yield equivalent to 12.5 kilotons of the explosives TNT (trinitrotoluene) was dropped on the Japanese city of Hiroshima, instantly killing some 70,000 of its inhabitants, with another 70,000 deaths registered by the end of 1945. Meanwhile, on August 9, a second bomb was used against the city of Nagasaki. This explosion had a higher yield (equivalent to 22 kilotons of TNT) but caused fewer instant deaths. However, many of the survivors suffered from heavy burns, radiation sickness, etc., and the death toll continued to rise. By the end of the year more than 70,000 of Nagasaki's citizens had lost their lives. Five years later, as many as 340,000 people, or 54 percent of the original population, had died from the two explosions.

THE SPREAD OF NUCLEAR WEAPONS 1945-1968

After the Japanese surrender on August 15, 1945, many people called for a ban on nuclear weapons in order to avoid a nuclear arms race and the risk of future catastrophes like the ones in Hiroshima and Nagasaki. Both the United States and the Soviet Union declared that they were in favour of putting the atomic bomb under foolproof international control. In spite of these declarations, the big powers were, in fact, never ready to give up their own nuclear weapons programs. By the end of 1946 it was clear to everybody that the effort to prevent a nuclear arms race had failed. Indeed, the Soviet Union had already launched a full-speed secret nuclear weapons program in an attempt to catch up with the United States. Thanks in part to espionage, the Soviet scientists were able to build a blueprint of the American fission bomb that was used against Nagasaki and to conduct a successful testing of it on August 29, 1949.

In its turn, the fact that the Soviet Union had become a nuclear power figured heavily when President Truman in early

1950 decided to launch a crash program in order to develop a more advanced type of nuclear weapons, the so-called hydrogen bomb. In contrast to the first atomic bombs, which destructive power came from the process of nuclear fission, the "H-bomb" would use a small fission bomb to trigger a tremendously powerful process of nuclear fusion.

By 1954, both the United States and the Soviet Union had successfully tested their first generation of H-bombs. The tests proved that fusion bombs could easily be made to produce explosions more than 1,000 times as powerful as the fission bombs used in the Second World War. The most powerful explosion ever took place at Novaya Zemlya on October 30, 1961, when the Soviet Union tested a "monster bomb" with a yield equivalent to 50 megatons of TNT. It has been estimated that this explosion alone released more destructive power than all bombs and explosives used in the Second World War added together, including the three nuclear explosions of July and August 1945.

By 1961, two more countries had developed and successfully tested nuclear weapons. United Kingdom had started its program during the Second World War in close co-operation with the United States, and the first British bomb was tested on October 3, 1952. On February 13, 1960, France followed suit. The French program received very little technological and scientific support from other countries. Four and a half years later, on October 16, 1964, China became the fifth nuclear power after having received only reluctant assistance from the Soviet Union.

PREVENTING THE SPREAD OF NUCLEAR WEAPONS

In the early 1960s, many military experts and political leaders feared that the proliferation of nuclear weapons was bound to continue, and that within a decade or two a dozen additional countries were likely to cross the nuclear threshold. In an attempt to forestall such a development, the United States and the Soviet Union took the lead in negotiating an international agreement that would prohibit the further spread of nuclear weapons without banning the utilization of nuclear energy for peaceful purposes. The result was the Treaty on the Non-Proliferation of Nuclear Weapons, also referred to as the Non-Proliferation Treaty, or NPT, which opened for signature on July 1, 1968. By then, 21 countries in Latin America and the Caribbean had already established the world's first nuclear weapons-free zone by signing on to the Treaty of Tlatelolco.

When it came into force on March 5, 1970, the NPT separated between two categories of states: On the one hand, nuclear weapons states – that is, the five countries that were known to possess nuclear weapons at the time when the Treaty was signed (United States, Soviet Union, United Kingdom, France and China). On the other hand, non-nuclear weapons states – that is, all other signatories of the Treaty. According to its provisions, the nuclear weapons states on signing the NPT agree not to release nuclear weapons or in any other way help other states to acquire or build nuclear weapons. At the same time, the non-nuclear weapons states signatories agree not to acquire or develop "nuclear weapons or other nuclear explosive devices." In exchange for this self-denial, the nuclear weapons states promise to move toward a gradual reduction of their arsenals of nuclear weapons with the ultimate goal of complete nuclear disarmament.

The NPT was first signed by the United States, the United Kingdom, the Soviet Union together with 59 other countries. China and France acceded to the Treaty in 1992. In 1996, Ukraine, Belarus and Kazakhstan gave up their nuclear weapons, left over from the Soviet Union when it fell apart in 1991-92, and signed the NPT as non-nuclear weapons states parties. The NPT is now the most widely accepted arms control agreement. As of June 2003, all members of the United Nations except Israel, India, and Pakistan had signed the NPT. However, one signatory, North Korea, had recently threatened to withdraw from the Treaty.

OTHER NON-PROLIFERATION AGREEMENTS

The very first major nuclear arms control agreement was the Limited Test-Ban Treaty of 1963. The LTBT prohibited nuclear explosions in the atmosphere, in outer space, and under water. This treaty was motivated first of all by a desire to reduce and contain the health hazards caused by radioactive fall-out from nuclear explosions in the atmosphere. Due to the fact that many of the radioactive isotopes that were spread around the globe in the wake of such explosions have a lifetime of many tens or hundreds or even thousands of years, the continuation of atmospheric testing was likely to cause additional cancer deaths and other serious health problems on a large scale for many generations to come.

That being said, many countries supported the treaty for yet another reason: non-proliferation. Since it was considered very difficult to develop a reliable nuclear weapons capability without conducting at least one real-life test, a universal ban on testing would also serve as an effective measure against nuclear proliferation. It was probably for the very same reason that most of the threshold states – that is, countries under suspicion of pursuing secret nuclear ambitions – for a long time refused to sign the LTBT.

Also France and China withheld their signature, arguing that the LTBT was unfair since it allowed the technologically more advanced nuclear weapons states to continue testing underground.

Eventually, on October 24, 1996, a Comprehensive Test-Ban Treaty (CTBT) was signed that banned all nuclear explosions, including underground tests, for military as well as peaceful purposes. Both France and China were now ready to sign up. By June 2003, the CTBT had been signed by 167 and ratified by 100 out of altogether 197 countries. Among the countries that had still to sign and/or ratify the treaty were Afghanistan, Cuba, India, Iraq, Iran, Israel, North Korea, Pakistan, Saudi Arabia, Syria, and the United States (United States ratification has so far been stopped by the Senate).

THE ILLEGAL NUCLEAR WEAPONS STATES

As mentioned, the NPT distinguished between nuclear weapons states and non-nuclear weapons states as parties of the Treaty. However, from the very beginning there was in fact a third category of countries as well, namely, non-nuclear weapons states that for one reason or another had decided not to become parties of the NPT. Some countries, like Cuba, dismissed the NPT as an instrument that served to maintain the existing and, in their opinion, thoroughly unjust world order. Others simply wanted to reserve the option of developing their own nuclear arsenal: either to enhance their regional or international status, to deter military aggression or to underpin their political independence. Not surprisingly, most of the threshold states belonged to this group.

The first country outside the NPT to cross the nuclear threshold was India, which exploded a nuclear device in an atmospheric test in 1974. In 1998, both India and Pakistan conducted several nuclear underground tests, inviting a storm of international protests and some short-lived economic and political sanctions as well.

Meanwhile, the ending of white minority rule in South Africa in 1993 had led to the sensational disclosure that, in the mid-1980s, South Africa had developed and stockpiled a small number of nuclear weapons. The weapons had been dismantled and destroyed in the last years of apartheid because the white government feared that they might some day fall into the hands of militant black opposition groups and be used against the government. Subsequently, South Africa signed both the NPT (1991) and the CTBT (1996) as a non-nuclear weapons state.

Allegations about a secret Israeli nuclear weapons program were frequently heard in the 1960s and 70s. It was not until the mid-1980s, however, that the allegations were backed up with firm proof. In the fall of 1986, a former Israeli nuclear technician, Mordechai Vanunu, disclosed illegally possessed evidence proving that Israel, by all meaningful definitions of the term, was indeed a nuclear weapons state, and a powerful one as well. Drawing on Vanunu's photographs from the bomb factory underneath the small Dimona nuclear reactor, Western experts concluded that Israel at the time probably had acquired enough fissile material to produce more than 100 nuclear bombs and warheads. Today, Israel may possess as much as 150-200 nuclear weapons.

Thus, by June 2003 there were at least three countries – India, Israel, and Pakistan – that were both in possession of nuclear weapons and non-parties to the NPT. In addition, North Korea had announced its intention to withdraw from the NPT. The announcement came after repeated hints by North Korean representatives that their country already possessed a few nuclear weapons.

11

Science, Technology, and the Biological Weapons Convention

The 1972 Biological Weapons Convention (BWC), which currently has 165 states-parties, is the principal international legal instrument againstbiological warfare. Developments in science and technology pose a continuing challenge to the treaty and the broader biological weapons nonproliferation regime. If they are applied to state or nonstate biological weapons programs, these developments can undermine the treaty's prohibitions.

Therefore, the possible impact of science and technology on the development, production, stockpiling, transfer, or use of biological agents for "hostile purposes or in armed conflict," as the BWC puts it, needs to be assessed periodically. On the other hand, science and technology collaborations are critical to the full and effective implementation of the BWC's Article X provisions on economic cooperation and development. It is important for states to conduct periodic reviews of implementation at an operational level in order to achieve a proper balance between preventing biological warfare and fostering economic cooperation and development.

The need to prevent the spread of technology that would assist weapons programs while allowing and in fact promoting technology dissemination for peaceful purposes is not unique to the BWC. Debates on this issue are a regular feature of conferences to review the nuclear Nonproliferation Treaty. In the case of the BWC, however, the tension and the need for review may be particularly acute because of the rapid pace of advances in the life sciences.

At their review conference in December 2011, BWC states-parties agreed to continue the process of intersessional meetings—meetings that take place between the treaty's quinquennial review conferences—for 2012-2015 "to discuss, and promote common understanding and effective action" on agreed agenda items, including science and technology and cooperation and assistance. The first of these meetings of experts, chaired by Boujemâa Delmi of Algeria, took place July 16-20. The next meeting of parties will occur December 10-14.

As with the sets of intersessional meetings that preceded the 2006 and 2011 review conferences, states-parties will exchange views and best practices through the tabling of national papers. Notably, states-parties will consider science and technology systematically for the first time since the 1992-1993 Ad Hoc Group of Governmental Experts to Identify and Examine Potential Verification Measures from a Scientific and Technical Standpoint (VEREX).

The ways in which the new intersessional process may address Article X and science and technology, taking account of linkages between them. It poses broader questions of how the treaty can be upheld and strengthened in the light of scientific and technological advances. Governments, the public, and other interested parties should consider at least four overarching questions: Does the regime have the capacity to react to concerns that the treaty is not being fully implemented or that its implementation needs to be adapted to new developments? Is this view shared by all states-parties, as well as the broader international community including international organizations, industry, and civil society? What specific processes and decisions are required to maintain and strengthen the regime without hindering progress in science and technology and international cooperation in the life sciences? Finally, can the regime be used effectively to identify and explore new opportunities for peaceful cooperation among the parties?

Article X

The standing agenda items of the intersessional process are cooperation and assistance, with a particular focus on Article X; review of developments in the field of science and technology; and strengthening national implementation. The 2012 meetings also are considering ways to "enable fuller participation in the confidence-building measures," which are data declarations covering a variety of topics relevant to compliance with the convention, such as national biodefense programs and unusual outbreaks of infectious disease. In addition, as part of their consideration of science and technology, the meetings are focusing on so-called enabling technologies, that is, technologies that enable the practical application of discoveries in the life sciences or facilitate research and collaboration in this field.

The 2011 review conference mandated that the 2012-2015 intersessional process should cover the following broad subject areas: national reports by states-parties on how they are implementing Article X, practical measures to support full and complete implementation of Article X, improvement in the capacity of states-parties in selected areas such as biosafety and biosecurity and disease surveillance and response, and coordination of cooperation with other stakeholders.

In addition, the review conference participants decided to establish a database, administered by the BWC's Implementation Support Unit (ISU), to facilitate assistance and cooperation among member states. States-parties will submit data to the ISU on requirements for and offers of assistance, including transfers of equipment and material, as well as science and technology information regarding the peaceful use of biological materials and toxins. Requests are to be matched with offers of states-parties and relevant international organizations to provide or facilitate such assistance.

The underlying assumption behind the database project appears to be that the parties themselves and some international organizations are the principal drivers for collaboration in the life sciences. In the review conference's final document, however, the countries observed that the private sector plays a strong role in the transfer of technology and information.

There continues to be disagreement within the BWC regime over the legitimate extent of controls and restrictions on transfers of materials, equipment, and technology in the life sciences among states-parties in good standing. Countries from the Non-Aligned Movement in particular often have argued that transfer controls for arms control purposes are unjustified and discriminatory when the recipients are abiding by their obligations to the relevant multilateral treaty regime. In recent years, the legitimacy and utility of strategic trade controls have become more widely accepted, particularly in view of the measures states are obliged to take under the terms of UN Security Council Resolution 1540.

Nevertheless, there remains a tension between, on one hand, the obligation to promote technology transfers between states-parties for the purpose of fostering economic cooperation and development and, on the other hand, the requirements of strategic trade controls in cases where a state-party believes that another state poses a proliferation risk and therefore should not have access to dual-purpose materials, technology, equipment, or information. Furthermore, despite the generally agreed objective of reducing international trade restrictions, various other legal regimes require states to impose controls and oversight for such reasons as human and environmental health or for legal enforcement reasons such as investigating possible tax avoidance. The practical measures that states take to ensure that such control and oversight efforts are effective may coincide with transfer control measures adopted for BWC implementation purposes, thereby strengthening perceptions that the BWC requirement to promote collaborations and exchanges between states-parties is not being fully met.

Such divergence in perception is not unique to the BWC. The Organisation for the Prohibition of Chemical Weapons (OPCW) has long experienced challenges in its implementation of Article XI of the 1993 Chemical Weapons Convention (CWC). A 2011 report by a high-level advisory panel chaired by Ambassador Rolf Ekéus of Sweden addressed this point. The panel focused on the OPCW's priorities after the destruction of chemical weapons stockpiles, an activity that will gradually wind down, and proposed "an approach whereby any State Party feeling discriminated against over transfer denials could address a complaint to the Director-General, who might use his good offices to bring the parties together to discuss and if possible resolve the matter including by addressing the reasons that have led to the denial. Such a mechanism might increase transparency and help to dispel concerns." The CWC parties have not acted on that proposal, but could do so at next year's CWC review conference. Whether a similar approach could be discussed in the BWC context remains uncertain.

Science and Technology

Last year's BWC review conference mandated that the intersessional process consider new developments in science and technology that have potential hostile applications. At the same time, the discussions should identify possible measures to strengthen biological risk management, which could include voluntary codes of conduct or similar governance measures, as well as education and awareness raising in the life sciences community.

Developments in science and technology should also be reviewed so as to improve the efforts of international organizations that work in fields relevant to the BWC. A further special topic for 2012 is "advances in enabling technologies, including high-throughput systems for sequencing, synthesizing and analyzing DNA; bioinformatics and computational tools; and systems biology."

Many specific science and technology developments were assessed with regard to their possible impact on the BWC in the lead-up to the review conference. Rapid progress in the life sciences has created a "time compression effect" whereby the period from innovation to general application in society has shrunk from perhaps a century to a decade or less. Enabling technologies allow for the processing and quantitative analysis of vast amounts of data and their distribution and utilization by research groups internationally. New investigative techniques, instrumentation, and methods such as combinatorial synthesis and high-throughput screening facilitate the acquisition of large amounts of biological data.

Furthermore, biology is converging with disciplines including chemistry, engineering sciences, modeling, and simulation, thus creating new insights into the function of biological systems and new medical treatments as well as targeted drug delivery.

Although biology remains essentially an empirical science, there is a gradual shift from descriptive to predictive approaches. Once science overcomes certain obstacles, such as the generation of the vast amounts of required biological data and the development of more-sophisticated mathematical algorithms to deal with the complexities of biological systems, the transition of the life sciences to a new level of accelerated and fundamental advancement will be inevitable.

The OPCW advisory panel observed that the convergence between chemistry and biology, although not in itself a cause for treaty convergence, underlines the importance of "exchanges of experience and joint technical reviews" between the two regimes and recommends that the OPCW Technical Secretariat establish a "liaison" with the BWC implementation process. Notably, many of the same national delegates and technical experts attend both the BWC and CWC meetings. Both treaties are rooted in the 1925 Geneva Protocol, cover toxins, and have prohibitions that embody a "general purpose criterion," which prohibits all toxic chemicals and their precursors and biological materials except for permitted purposes. This criterion is the legal mechanism by which the treaties' prohibitions remain relevant in the face of scientific and technological developments. States-parties to both treaties have devoted insufficient attention to developing ideas for better operationalizing it.

Moving Forward

A key difficulty for the intersessional process is how to move beyond merely compiling and reviewing advances in science and technology to actually assessing their impact on the BWC and developing policies and practical measures to manage the associated risks and opportunities. There are numerous difficulties associated with the assessment of the possible and actual effects of science and technology on the BWC, especially when the assessment is carried out in a multilateral framework.

Some officials say they have difficulty envisaging whether or how the conduct of research or the application of new technology in the life sciences might constitute a treaty violation. This is particularly true in cases where such an application is not part of traditional state-level biological weapons programs. Another difficulty is how the implications of science and technology, in all of their variety and complexity, can be absorbed meaningfully by negotiators and acted on by policymakers.

Another important issue is the extent to which BWC representatives should focus science and technology discussions on achieving a better understanding of defence sector evaluation methodologies for assessing national security threats and military capacity requirements. Such methodologies reflect threat perceptions, domestic and international defence-related developments, and the drivers of weapons acquisitions programs.

Exchanges of views in such areas may raise red flags in national defence establishments and therefore should be approached with care and discretion.

Some of the interactions during the current BWC intersessional meetings will be process oriented, while others may focus on specific developments of concern, such as the 2012 publication describing the experimental increase in transmissibility of an avian influenza H5N1 strain in an animal model. The meetings, however, will not decide any collective actions by BWC states-parties. Practical steps will be left largely to national implementation measures. The intersessional process is not empowered with decision-making authority, and any multilateral decisions will have to wait until the next review conference in 2016. The gap between the pace of science and technology and the diplomatic processes to manage the risks associated with these advances is likely to expand further.

The intersessional process will discuss the various issues placed on its agenda by the 2011 review conference on an individual basis, but it may be worthwhile for the states-parties also to consider the operational interlinkages and relationships among them. Advances in science and technology create risks, but also present opportunities for the regime, for example by improving the conditions for Article X implementation. Science and technology advances often have been evaluated primarily in the context of Article I of the BWC, that is, with regard to how they affect the prohibitions against biological warfare. Yet, as the major documented and acknowledged biological weapons programs recede into history and the regime's focus is shifting to broader topics such as best practices in biosafety and biosecurity, this assessment has moved beyond a traditional threat assessment to an evaluation of strategies to mitigate the risks of science and technology advances, many of which are dual purpose.

To manage or contain such inherent, yet wide-ranging risks and simultaneously reap the benefits for humanity will require the right balance between maintaining controls and creating incentives and conditions that favour applications that benefit society, promote economic and technological development, and keep countries in compliance with the treaty. Such strategies will be essential given the nature of the science and technology process, but they come with a degree of uncertainty with regard to some states' intentions and a loss of some control over societal actors by states generally. This is a consequence of a shift toward a postproliferation context, which reflects the increasing international dissemination of science and technology and is not specific to the implementation of the BWC. Thus the dual-purpose nature of the science and technology must be managed, but is not amenable to a conventional solution such as technology transfer controls and denial.

In addition, some researchers and analysts have challenged the general appropriateness of applying export controls and censorship by states to certain research data. This became apparent in the debate about whether to publish the full research papers that show how a modified avian influenza virus strain became readily transmissible among ferrets. The weight of the scientific community, as expressed by a World Health Organization committee that was established to consider the appropriateness of withholding some of the research data from publication, was against any recommendation for the censoring of any of the research. As a result, both of the papers in question were published in full earlier this year.

One broad policy question raised by this episode is whether it is possible to describe scientific research on its merits for peaceful purposes alone when the research has the potential of causing security threats. A related question is how to determine the point in the research cycle at which potential dual-use issues should be addressed. This discussion affects research funding, publication policies, principles in research oversight, and safety and security standards. Some tension between the scientific community and national security establishments is likely and perhaps inevitable. A better-informed and more regular dialogue between these communities is needed to prevent them from drifting apart over how to manage the risks inherent in dual-use research.

In the context of the BWC, there is a need for an effective bridge between the security-driven discussions in the intersessional meetings and the mainstream of the science and industry communities. Past consideration of science and technology by VEREX was operationally focused on supporting states-parties in determining whether prohibited weapons activities were occurring. The dynamic of today's evaluation of science and technology by the intersessional process is more generic, more wide ranging, and tied to more of the other main provisions of the treaty. Advances in science and technology are assessed not merely with regard to their impact on the BWC's prohibitions, but also with regard to whether national implementation measures need to be adapted, how they affect international collaborations for peaceful purposes, whether they call for the adoption of additional governance measures in industry and research, and how they may enhance the ability of governments to investigate allegations that states or other actors have misused biological or toxin agents.

BIOLOGICAL WEAPONS CAUSE EPIDEMICS

Biological weapons are devices intended to deliberately disseminate disease-producing organisms or toxins in food, water, by insect vector, or as an aerosol. As would be the case following exposure to any infectious disease, those infected would experience an incubation period of variable duration, depending on the pathogen, the size, and route of the inoculum, and the immune response of the affected persons. The incubation period could be days to weeks. If sufficient numbers of people were infected by the dispersal of a biological weapon, or if the agent were contagious and person-to-person transmission outran disease control measures, the result could be large-scale, possibly catastrophic epidemics. It is this outcome—the prospect of a pestilence intentionally unleashed on large civilian populations—that most concerns physicians, public health experts, and political leaders.

Public health, medical, military, and law enforcement experts have met in a number of settings in efforts to identify the most threatening of the biological weapons, specifically those weapons that merit priority concern in the development of public health and medical preparedness measures. The criteria for this determination have included feasibility of aerosol dissemination (thought by many to be the most likely means of exposing large populations), high case-fatality rates, the potential for secondary spread, and the availability of protective vaccines or antimicrobial agents. A limited number of agents are consistently recognized as being of greatest concern: Variola major, Bacillus anthracis, Yersinia pestis, Botulinum toxin (produced by Clostridium botulinum),Francisella tularensis, and a number of the causative agents of the syndrome termed viral hemorrhagic fever. Recommendations for the medical and public health management of these weapons are being published elsewhere in a series of consensus papers.

The scope and impact of an epidemic caused by a biological weapon would depend on the characteristics of the pathogen or toxin, the design of the weapon or delivery system, the environment in which the weapon was used, and the speed and effectiveness of the medical and public health response. Fortunately, the few attempts to use biological weapons in this century have produced limited numbers of casualties. These efforts, however, were not supported by the technological resources of nation-states. There is little dispute that biological weapons have the capacity to initiate epidemics on a scale and with a degree of lethality unparalleled in modern history. Although it is impossible to predict the probability that a nation-state, a state-sponsored terrorist, or an autonomous group might use a highly destructive biological weapon, there is little disagreement among experts that such an event is both feasible and becoming more likely.

There are few modern analogs that provide insight into the potential ramifications of a major epidemic caused by one of the more serious biological weapons. In the United States, the single event that might most closely resemble the aftermath of a biological weapon would be the influenza pandemic of 1918–1919. That epidemic caused widespread societal disruption and placed enormous burdens on both the health care system and the civil infrastructure. Yet even in this comparison, crucial distinctions exist. Pandemic influenza resulted in estimated case-fatality rates ranging from 1.9% to 5% ; the case-fatality rate for smallpox would approximate 30%, and for untreated anthrax, it would exceed 80%.

The experience following the importation of 1 case of smallpox into Yugoslavia in 1972 suggests the events that might accompany a modern epidemic. A pilgrim returning from Iraq developed a mild illness with a nondescript rash and fever. Two weeks later, 11 persons who had been in close contact with him developed similar symptoms. None of the 11 knew one another, and no physician recognized smallpox in the initial case patient or in the subsequent 11 cases. (The last case of smallpox in Yugoslavia had occurred in 1927.) One of the 11 developed hemorrhagic smallpox, a uniformly fatal, highly contagious form of the disease. He alone infected 38 persons, including physicians and nurses. Ultimately, the outbreak was recognized 4 weeks after the initial case became ill. Although childhood population-wide smallpox vaccination was in place in Yugoslavia, the discovery of a growing epidemic of smallpox led to the mandatory vaccination of the entire nation's population of 20 million persons. In addition, some 10,000 contacts of patients were quarantined in hotels guarded by the military. All surrounding countries closed their borders to travel and commerce from Yugoslavia. The outbreak ended about 8 weeks after the first case patient became ill. There were a total of 175 smallpox cases and 35 deaths. Smallpox experts considered this a small outbreak.

BIOLOGICAL WEAPONS ARE AN INCREASING CONCERN

The technology associated with the manufacture of biological weapons is relatively inexpensive, and because it is similar to that used in vaccine production facilities, it is easy to obtain. The microbial agents needed for most biological weapons are widely available. It is difficult to gauge the extent of biological weapons development in other nations since production facilities require little space and are not easy to identify. The acquisition and dissemination of even the most highly restricted organism, Variola major, is not an implausible scenario.

In 1970, the United States abandoned its offensive bioweapons program by presidential executive order. There were several reasons for this decision, including the determination that biological weapons were not essential for national security. The 1972 Biological Weapons and Toxin Convention (BWTC) calls for banning the development, possession, or use of biological weapons. It has been signed by 162 states, including most of the 17 states suspected of having offensive biological weapons in a recent report. Seven of the 17 are named sponsors of international terrorism. States are not the only entities to pursue the development of biological weapons. Individuals and groups, both internationally and within the United States, have also done so.

Three events in particular have fueled recent concern about biological terrorism. First, investigations following the 1995 release of sarin nerve gas by the Aum Shinrikyo religious cult in the Tokyo subway system revealed that cult members made at least 9 failed attempts to use biological weapons in central Tokyo with the intent to kill tens of thousands.

Second, the vast extent and sophistication of the biological weapons program of the former Soviet Union has become increasingly evident over the past decade coincident with revelations provided by defectors from its program. There is growing concern that biological weapon designs or materials from this program might find their way to other nations or terrorist groups.

Finally, the series of revelations following the Gulf War regarding the true capacity and scope of Iraq's biological weapons program has been alarming. In addition to creating many tons of pathogens and toxins, including B. anthracis and C. botulinum toxin, Iraq also admitted that it had loaded bombs and missiles with biological agents.

DISEASES COMMUNITY CAN DO TO SUPPORT PREVENTION EFFORTS

The ID community has important contributions to make in crafting strategies to forestall the development or use of biological weapons. Prevention strategies of particular salience include raising awareness among researchers and practitioners about the risk, involving researchers from universities and industry in efforts to strengthen the BWTC, creating mechanisms to consider appropriate scientific response to research with potential bioweapons application, and supporting programs that seek to employ former bioweaponeers in peaceful pursuits.

Each state party to the BWTC undertakes "never in any circumstance to develop, produce, stockpile or otherwise acquire or retain microbial or other biological agents, or toxins ... of types and in quantities that have no justification for prophylactic, protective or other peaceful purposes". Although the 1972 BWTC may have served as a partial barrier to biological weapons proliferation, it has been unsuccessful in preventing a number of countries from undertaking substantial programs of research and development. Efforts to strengthen the treaty are now being debated. It is not yet evident whether these efforts will be supported with the necessary political will, whether these efforts will make the BWTC a more useful tool in combating biological weapons proliferation, or how treaty verification and enforcement procedures might impact biological research in industry or in universities. The ID community is vitally concerned about the likelihood and price of success of such treaty mechanisms and should participate in the development of modifications, revisions, or enhancements on the basis of a careful assessment of the threat and actions likely to prevent biological weapon proliferation.

The ID community is a logical home for new initiatives for international scientific collaboration. Efforts that seek to establish communication with and create structures that offer practical support for scientists who once researched and developed biological weapons but are now being asked to change course should be encouraged.

PREPARATION TO RESPOND TO BIOLOGICAL WEAPON USE

Existing prevention strategies are insufficient to guarantee that biological weapons will not be used. Furthermore, it is clear that biological weapons are proliferating. Supporting a broad awareness of the perils of biological weapons will itself advance understanding of useful response measures. The ID community could take a number of additional actions that would strengthen the nation's capacity to respond to the use of a biological weapons. ID expertise will be critical to early recognition of the diseases that would follow biological weapons use, to recommend the most rapid diagnostic procedures, to assist in the development of medical treatment strategies, to support the creation of hospital response policies, and to undertake research into new diagnostic and therapeutic interventions.

Awareness and education. ID professionals are called on every day to diagnose and treat patients with fever, pneumonia, rash, and flulike symptoms; therefore, it is the ID professional who would be among the clinicians most likely to recognize the diseases caused by biological weapons. Professional educational and training curricula should be enhanced so that ID professionals are better capable of recognizing the diseases that would follow use of a biological weapon such as anthrax, plague, or smallpox. The perils of delayed recognition of one of these diseases, both for the patient and for the involved community, would be grave. Fostering strong working relationships between clinically based ID professionals (especially hospital epidemiologists) and health department-based ID professionals is an important step toward improving the capacity to both detect and respond to bioterrorist attacks.

Laboratory diagnosis. Should the recognition of an unusual disease or pattern of illnesses prompt consideration of possible biological weapon use, members of the ID community will be called on to advise upon the most rapid procedures for diagnostic confirmation of disease. In anticipation of this, ID experts should become familiar with the processes by which either the hospital laboratory or the local or state health department, in consultation with the Centres for Disease Control and Prevention (CDC) as necessary, will perform diagnostic studies to implicate or exclude biological weapons use. A process that establishes criteria and training measures for laboratory diagnosis of these diseases is being undertaken jointly by the Association of Public Health Laboratories and the CDC.

Systems for distributing therapeutics. Should a biological weapon use be confirmed, treatment and intervention strategies for the ill and for the exposed but not yet ill will be critical. Depending on the disease, antibiotics, and/or vaccines or other therapies, as well as quarantine, could be lifesaving. Public health agencies have begun to explore systems for emergency distribution and treatment of antibiotics and vaccines, systems that would also be useful should emergency interventions be needed for naturally occurring epidemics, such as pandemic influenza. The ID community should play an important role in the shaping of such efforts.

Hospital response. Hospitals will bear the brunt of caring for the sick and dying should a biological weapon be used. Yet few hospitals are prepared to cope with even a handful of cases of a highly contagious, life-threatening disease, and few hospitals are prepared to manage even a modest surge in the numbers of seriously ill patients. Hospital leaders should examine current policies in relation to this threat and develop new policies as appropriate. Infection control practices are but one critical component of such planning efforts. Numerous other issues are of compelling importance, such as hospital roles and authorities, prevention of disease transmission amongst staff, personnel requirements, security needs, communication both within and outside the hospital, and media interactions. ID expertise is of clear relevance to many of these issues.

Scientific research. The ID community already does research that seeks new strategies for diagnosis, prevention, or treatment for infectious disease. Commensurate with this, the ID community might elect to encourage and reward basic science research efforts that seek to produce novel diagnostic technologies, preventive, or therapeutic interventions for the diseases caused by biological weapons. At the same time, ID professionals can be compelling advocates for directing increased funding or attention toward critical needs, such as substantially augmenting the smallpox vaccine reserve and the development of a second generation anthrax vaccine.

THE BIOLOGICAL WEAPONS CONVENTION

Since ancient times, the use in war of poison and pathogenic agents has been considered a treacherous practice. It was condemned by international declarations and treaties, notably by the 1907 Hague Convention (IV) respecting the laws and customs of war on land. Efforts to strengthen this prohibition resulted in the conclusion, in 1925, of the Geneva Protocol which banned the use of asphyxiating, poisonous or other gases, usually referred to as chemical weapons, as well as the use of bacteriological methods of warfare. The latter are now understood to include not only bacteria, but also other biological agents, such as viruses or rickettsiae which were unknown at the time the Geneva Protocol was signed. (On 1 January 1997, 1 32 States were party to this Protocol.) However, the Geneva Protocol did not prohibit the development, production and stockpiling of chemical and biological weapons. Attempts to achieve a complete ban were made in the 1930s in the framework of the League of Nations, but with no success.

Shortly after World War II, the United Nations called for the elimination of all weapons "adaptable to mass destruction". Biological and chemical weapons were included in this category of arms along with atomic and radiological weapons. Debates on their prohibition took place in the 1950s and 1960s in the context of proposals for general disarmament but, again, the debate remained inconclusive.

As a separate issue, the prohibition of chemical and biological weapons appeared on the agenda of the Eighteen-Nation

Committee on Disarmament in 1968. One year later, the United Nations published an influential report on the problems of chemical and biological warfare, and the question received special attention at the UN General Assembly.

The UN report concluded that certain chemical and biological weapons cannot be confined in their effects in space and time and might have grave and irreversible consequences for man and nature.

This would apply to both the attacking and the attacked nations. A report by the World Health Organization (WHO) on the health aspects of chemical and biological weapons, issued in 1970, stated that these weapons pose a special threat to civilians, and that the effects of their use are subject to a high degree of uncertainty and unpredictability.

Although simultaneous prohibition of chemical and biological weapons had been considered for many years as both desirable and necessary, towards the end of the 1960s it became clear that such a prohibition was not achievable. In the Eighteen-Nation Committee on Disarmament, where the issue was under discussion, the United Kingdom and a few other Western countries ado pted the view that biological weapons should be banned first.

The Socialist and many neutral and non-aligned States were opposed to a separate treatment of these weapons, but finally accepted the Western approach. A factor which facilitated this development was the unilateral renunciation of biological weapons by the United States, announced on 25 November 1969, and the decision by the US government to destroy its stockpile of these weapons, irrespective of a possible future international agreement.

On 14 February 1970, the United States also formally renounced the production, stockpiling and use of toxins for war purposes. It stated that military programmes for biological agents and toxins would be confined to research and development for defensive purposes. Subsequent negotiations on a global prohibition of biological weapons led to an international agreement. On 16 December 1971, the text of the convention worked out by the Conference of the Committee on Disarmament (CCD), the successor of the Eighteen-Nation Committee on Disarmament, was commended by the UN General Assembly.

A CRITICAL ANALYSIS OF THE BW CONVENTION

On 10 April 1972, the Convention on the Prohibition of the Development, Production and Stockpiling of Bacteriological (Biological) and Toxin Weapons and on their Destruction was opened for signature. It entered into force on 26 March 1975, after the deposit of the instruments of ratification by 22 signatory governments, including the governments of the Soviet Union, the United Kingdom and the United States, designated as depositaries. By 1 January 1997, the BW Convention had been joined by 140 States, including all the permanent members of the United Nations Security Council.

Scope of the Obligations

The BW Convention prohibits the development, production, stockpiling or acquisition by other means, or retention of microbial or other biological agents or toxins, as well as of weapons, equipment or means of delivery designed to use such agents or toxins for hostile purposes or in armed conflict (Article I).

The Convention has not defined the prohibited items nor the targets to which the prohibitions relate. There exists, however, an authoritative definition of biological agents formulated by the WHO. In its 1970 report, mentioned above, the WHO described biological agents as those that depend for their effects on multiplication within the target organism and are intended for use in war to cause disease or death in man, animals or plants; they may be transmissible or non-transmissible. Toxins are poisonous products of organisms; unlike biological agents, they are inanimate and not capable of reproducing themselves. The Convention applies to all natural or artificially created toxins, "whatever their origin or method of production" (Article I). It thus covers toxins produced biologically, as well as those produced by chemical synthesis. Since toxins are chemicals by nature, their inclusion in the BW Convention was a step towards the projected ban on chemical weapons.

Since the signing of the Convention, there have been no disputes among the parties regarding the definition of biological agents or toxins, but the lack of definition of "weapons, equipment or means of delivery" led to a controversy. In ratifying the BW Convention, Switzerland reserved the right to decide for itself which items fall within the definition of weapons, equipment or means of delivery designed to use biological agents or toxins. The United States entered an objection to this reservation, claiming that it would not be appropriate for States to reserve unilaterally the right to take s uch decisions. In its opinion, the prohibited items are those the design of which indicates that they could have no other use than that specified in the Convention, or that they were intended to be capable of the use specified. There are, however, few weapons, equipment or means of delivery which would meet such criteria.

Under the BW Convention, the prohibition to develop, produce, stockpile or otherwise acquire or retain biological agents and toxins is not absolute. It applies only to types and to quantities that have no justification for prophylactic, protective or other peaceful purposes. Retention, production or acquisition by other means of certain quantities of biological agents and toxins may thus continue, and there may be testing in laboratories and even in the field. According to the clarification given in the course of the negotiations, the term "prophylactic" encompasses medical activities, such as diagnosis, therapy and immunization, whereas the term "protective" covers the development of protective masks and clothing, air and water filtration systems, detection and warning devices, and decontamination equipment, and must not be interpreted as permitting possession of biological agents and toxins for defence, retaliation or deterrence. The term "other peaceful purposes" has remained unclear. One can assume that it includes scientific experimentation.

There are no provisions in the BW Convention restricting biological research activities. One reason for this omission may be that research aimed at developing agents for civilian purposes is difficult to distinguish from research serving military purposes, whether defensive or offensive. Moreover, in the biological field it is difficult to draw a dividing line between research and development; a country can develop warfare agents in research facilities. Once developed, these agents can be rapidly produced in significant quantities. This circumstance and the express authorization to e ngage in production (for peaceful purposes) of biological agents and toxins that may be used in warfare create a risk that the provisions of the Convention will be circumvented. The stipulation that any development, production, stockpiling or retention of biological agents or toxins must be justified does not carry sufficient weight. There are no agreed standards or criteria for the quantities of agents or toxins that may be needed by different States for the different purposes recognized by the Convention. The parties are not even obliged to declare the types and amounts of agents or toxins they possess and the use they make of them. The system of material accountancy that is useful in the verification of certain measures of arms control is not practicable in the case of biological or toxin agents. It is thus not evident how much of a given prohibited substance stocked by a given country would constitute a violation of the Convention. The secrecy surrounding biological research activities and, in particular, the maintenance of defensive preparations, which at certain stages may be indistinguishable from offensive preparations, could generate suspicions leading to allegations of breaches.

The Convention prohibits the transfer of agents, toxins, weapons, equipment or means of delivery, specified above, to "any recipient whatsoever", that is, to any State or group of States or international organizations, as well as sub-national groups or individuals. The provision of assistance, encouragement or inducement to acquire the banned weapons is likewise forbidden (Article III). These non-proliferation clauses appear hard to reconcile with the commitment of the parties to engage in the "fullest possible" exchange of biological agents and toxins, and of equipment for the processing, use or production of such agents and toxins for peaceful ends (Article X). For all such materials and technologies, as well as expertise, are dual-use and as such widespread. To reduce the risk of misuse, an informal forum of industrialized countries, known as the Australia Group (after the country which took the initiative to convene it), decided to apply certain restrictions on transfers of items relevant to the BW Convention. Many nations consider the control arrangements adopted by the Group as complementary to the BW Convention, because an export may be precluded if there is particular concern about its potential diversion for weapon purposes. Other nations consider these arrangements to be discriminatory, because they chiefly affect the developing world. The latter would like to see the Australia Group disbanded and have all export restrictions that might be agreed among all parties incorporated in a legally binding verification document.

Parties to the BW Convention have undertaken to cooperate in the further development and application of scientific discoveries in the field of biology for the prevention of diseases or for other peaceful purposes (Article X). However, since the Convention is essentially a disarmament treaty, it can hardly serve as an effective instrument for such cooperation. The participants in the latest BW Convention Review Conference acknowledged the existence of an increasing gap between the developed and developing countries in the field of biotechnology, genetic engineering, microbiology and other related areas.

The most remarkable feature of the BW Convention is the disarmament obligation of the parties: to destroy or divert to peaceful purposes all agents, toxins, weapons equipment and means of delivery (Article II). The BW Convention was the first treaty providing for the abolition of an entire category of arms. The envisaged destruction or diversion was to take place not later than nine months after entry into force of the Convention, it being understood that for States acceding to the Convention after its entry into force the destruction or diversion was to be completed upon accession. All the necessary safety precautions are to be observed during the destruction operations to protect "populations" (that is, not only the population of the country carrying out these operations) as well as the environment in general. The United States was the only State to announce that its stockpile of biological and toxin agents and all associated munitions had been destroyed, except for small quantities for laboratory defensive research purposes. It also made it known that former biological warfare facilities had been converted to medical research centres. No other State has made such an announcement. The United Kingdom said that it had no stocks of biological weapons. The Soviet Union stated that it did not possess any biological agents or toxins, weapons, equipment or means of delivery, as prohibited by the Convention, but this statement turned out to be untrue.

RELATIONSHIP WITH THE 1925 GENEVA PROTOCOL

The BW Convention does not expressly prohibit the use of biological or toxin weapons. It only states that the obligations assumed under the 1925 Geneva Protocol, which prohibits such use, r remain valid (Article VIII). However, adherents to the BW Convention are not necessarily parties to the Geneva Protocol. Moreover, the Convention stipulates that nothing in its provisions shall be interpreted as in any way limiting or detracting from the obligations assumed by States under the Geneva Protocol. This implies that the reservations to the Protocol, which form part of the obligations contracted by the parties, continue to exist. Insofar as the reservations concern the right to employ the banned weapons against non-parties or in retaliation against a party violating the Protocol, they are incompatible with the obligation of the parties to the Convention never "in any circumstances" to acquire biological weapons (Article I). They also contradict the parties' expressed determination to exclude "completely" the possibility of biological agents and toxins being used as weapons (ninth preambular paragraph). It is for this reason that, in acceding to the BW Convention in 1984, China declared that the absence of an explicit prohibition on the use of biological weapons was a defect which should be corrected "at an appropriate time". Indeed, over the years, a number of States have withdrawn their reservations to the Geneva Protocol, either with regard either to biological weapons alone, or to both biological and chemical weapons. They have thereby recognized that since the retention and production of biological weapons are banned, so must, by implication, be their use, because use presupposes possession.

Nonetheless, in 1996, Iran proposed that the Convention (its title and Article I) be amended so as to make the ban on use explicit rather than implicit. An amendment submitted by a party enters into force for each State accepting it upon its acceptance by a majority of the parties (Article XI). However, the Iranian proposal is opposed by many States which fear the risks of having other provisions of the Convention opened up for renegotiation as well. Some are apprehensive that States not accepting the Iranian-proposed amendment would appear to condone the use of biological weapons under certain circumstances, and since use would be possible only after breaking the BW Convention, the absolute character of the Convention prohibitions would be called into question. What seems less objectionable than an amendment is a solemn declaration of understanding by all parties that the use of microbial or other biological agents or toxins in any way that is not consistent with prophylactic, protective or other peaceful purposes, would be a violation of the Convention.

Verification of Compliance

No specific measures are set forth in the BW Convention to verify compliance with the obligation not to develop, produce, stockpile or otherwise acquire or retain biological agents or toxins for "hostile purposes". Indeed, hostile intentions, like any other intentions, cannot be verified. As mentioned above, the parties are not obliged to declare biological agents or toxins used in non-prohibited activities. Nor are they obliged to declare all laboratories engaged in research and development of substances that could be used as agents of warfare. This is a serious lacuna, because advances in biotechnology have made it possible to produce large quantities of potent toxic substances by a small number of people, in a short period of time, and in facilities which are difficult to identify.

Such substances may be stored in inconspicuous repositories and eventually "weaponized", that is, filled into missiles, bombs or spray systems.

Consequently, a violator could relatively easily break out from the Convention. What is even more incongruous, States joining the Convention are not required to declare the possession or non-possession of the banned weapons. Nor are States, which may have declared such possession, obligated to prove that they have destroyed the weapons or diverted them to peaceful purposes. The opening-up by the United States of some of its biological facilities for public inspection and international visitors, following the destruction of its stocks, was a voluntary act.

National technical means of verification cannot be relied upon to verify in other countries the non-development and non-production of biological agents and toxins for hostile purposes, and there are at present no international means to perform such tasks. Illegal possession of the banned weapons could be demonstrated indirectly through investigations which the UN Secretary-General is authorized to carry out in response to reports that may be brought to his attention on the possible use of chemical and biological or toxin weapons entailing a violation of the Geneva Protocol or of any other applicable rule of international treaty or customary law. However, such investigations, which may be initiated by UN member States (but not by individuals or non-governmental organizations), could also prove inconclusive, because the diseases allegedly caused by biological weapons might be similar to those occurring naturally, and because it might be difficult for the investigators to determine the identity of the aggressor.

Each party is obliged to take measures, in accordance with its constitutional processes, to prohibit and prevent the activities banned by the Convention from taking place within its territory and under its jurisdiction or control anywhere (Article IV). The term "measures" applies to legislative, administrative or regulatory measures, whereas the term "under its jurisdiction or control" (also used in Article II referred to above) extends the bans to non-self-governing territories administered by States parties, and to territories under military occupation.

"Anywhere" implies that even transnational corporations operating in the territories of non-parties to the Convention are covered by the prohibitions if they remain under the jurisdiction or control of the parties. Not all parties, however, have taken the steps required to ensure domestic compliance with the Convention.

This is all the more regrettable in that biological agents appear to be becoming attractive, for terrorist purposes, to players other than States According to reliable reports, the Aum Shinrikyo sect, which released nerve gas in a Tokyo subway train, had also been working on the development of biological weapons and in 1995, shortly before the arrest of its leader, was close to completing this programme.

On the international level, the parties have undertaken to consult one another and to cooperate in solving problems relating to the objective or the application of the provisions of the Convention. Such consultation and cooperation may also take place "through appropriate international procedures within the framework of the United Nations and in accordance with its Charter" (Article V). Since the Convention does not explain what "appropriate international procedures" amount to, the participants in the BW Review Conferences agreed that such procedures should include the right of any party to request that a "consultative meeting", open to all parties, be convened promptly at expert level.

The parties have the right to lodge with the UN Security Council complaints regarding breaches of the Convention. They have undertaken to coöperate in carrying out any investigation which the Security Council may initiate on the basis of the complaint received, and they are entitled to be informed of the results of such investigation. Each complaint must contain "all possible evidence" confirming its validity (Article VI). However, only a few States have the means to collect such evidence. Others may not be in a position to do so, and could not always count on obtaining relevant information from foreign sources, even from their allies. There is thus a possibility that, for political or other reasons (for example, unwillingness to disclose the nature or the source of the evidence), certain powers will deliberately overlook transgressions committed by some States to the detriment of others. A State which suspects a violation, but lacks reliable information and therefore does not possess sufficient evidence, may have its request for consideration rejected by the Security Council. Even if the Security Council agreed to discuss a charge which did not satisfy the above requirement, there would always be a danger that the case would not receive proper examination. For the Council is not entitled (or equipped) by the UN Charter to check compliance with arms control agreements; nor is it empowered to take action against violators of such agreements. Only when the Council finds that the situation created by the violation can lead to international friction may it recommend, under Chapter VI of the UN Charter, "appropriate procedures or methods of adjustment" to the State or States concerned. This may not always be the case.

In 1992, the President of the UN Security Council stated, on behalf of its members, that proliferation of weapons of mass destruction, which include biological weapons, would constitute a "threat to international peace and security", and that appropriate action would be taken to prevent it. That action could include the application of coercive measures under Chapter VII of the UN Charter. However, the statement of the President of the Security Council has no binding legal effect. Even if it were transformed into a formal decision of the Council to have such effect, it would not necessarily enable the Council to act in all pertinent instances. The power of veto possessed by the permanent members of the Council can always be used to protect violators of treaties, especially when the violator happens to be a great power. A suggestion, put forward during the BW negotiations, that the Security Council's permanent members should waive their right of veto at least with regard to resolutions concerning investigations of complaints, was not accepted This is why proposals have been repeatedly made that a representative body of States parties — rather than the United Nations — should deal with investigations of alleged breaches of the BW Convention. If, in 1982, the UN General Assembly requested the UN Secretary-General to investigate alleged violations of the ban on use of chemical and biological weapons, it did so primarily because the ban, as embodied in the 1925 Geneva Protocol, is widely considered to form part of international customary law to be observed by all States, parties and non-parties to relevant treaties alike.

The circumstance that the fact-finding stage of the complaints procedure is not clearly separated from the stage of legal/political consideration and judgment is a serious shortcoming of the BW Convention. It makes it difficult to ascertain a violation. Moreover, a State under suspicion of having violated its obligations has no international impartial mechanism to turn to in order to free itself from that suspicion. Ill-considered allegations can therefore be made with impunity.

In the case of an established violation, parties would have to provide or support assistance, in accordance with the UN Charter, to a party which so requested, if the Security Council decided that this party had been exposed to danger as a result of the violation (Article VII). It appears from the negotiating history that assistance was meant primarily as action of a medical or other humanitarian or relief nature. In the understanding of at least the United Kingdom and the United States, it would be for each party to decide whether it could or was prepared to supply the requested aid. In other words, assistance would be optional, not obligatory: it could be refused without incurring the charge of non-compliance.

The Convention provided for a review conference of the parties to be convened five years after its entry into force (Article XII). Later, the parties decided to meet at least every five years; these Conferences review the operation of the Convention, taking into account the relevant scientific and technological developments.

ALLEGATIONS OF NON-COMPLIANCE

Several allegations of non-compliance with the BW Convention have been made since the Convention entered into force. Those which received most attention were the "Sverdlovsk" and "Yellow Rain" cases.

The Sverdlovsk Case

In March 1980, the United States accused the Soviet Union of maintaining an offensive biological weapons programme which included production, weaponization and stockpiling of biological warfare agents. The accusation was based on the suspected airborne release of anthrax spores from a Soviet biological facility, which caused an outbreak of anthrax in the city of Sverdlovsk in April and May 1979. The Soviet Union confirmed that there had been an outbreak of anthrax in the Sverdlovsk region, but attributed this occurrence to the sale of anthrax-contaminated meat in violation of veterinary regulations. It provided little additional information. The issue was the subject of bilateral US/Soviet consultations, and various groups of scientists met to evaluate the Soviet account of the incident, but the US government maintained its accusation. In 1992, the Russian authorities admitted that a breach of the BW Convention had been committed. They undertook, under a decree issued by the President of the Russian Federation, to open secret military research centres to international inspection and convert them to civilian use.

The "Yellow Rain" Case

In 1981, the US government accused the Soviet Union of being involved in the production, transfer and use of trichothecene mycotoxins in Laos, Kampuchea and Afghanistan in violation of both the 1925 Geneva Protocol and the BW Convention. The allegation was categorically rejected by the Soviet Union. US charges were based on reports by alleged victims and eye-witnesses who stated that since the autumn of 1978 enemy aircraft had been spraying a toxic yellow material (hence the name of the case). Chemical analyses of samples of the yellow material and medical checks of the affected persons were conducted to substantiate the case. However, as the investigations proceeded, with the involvement of laboratories in different countries and a careful scrutiny of the eye-witnesses' reports, the reliability of the evidence was increasingly questioned. Some authoritative scientists found that the yellow substance consisted to a large extent of excrements of wild honeybees, and extensive analytical efforts in several laboratories failed to confirm the initial positive reports of trichothecenes.

Assessment

As compared to other arms control agreements, the negotiations for the BW Convention — conducted separately from those on chemical weapons with which they had been associated for decades — encountered few obstacles and were concluded relatively quickly, in a common taboo on use. The reasons were as follows.

Biological weapons are unpredictable in their effects and of limited value in combat. Since cheating under a BW Convention could not yield significant military advantages to the cheating party, a ban on biological weapons without verification of compliance was considered by the negotiators to be free of serious security risks. By contrast, chemical weapons are predictable, capable of producing immediate effects and, consequently, useful incombat. Banning their possession without elaborate and intrusive methods of verification was, therefore, deemed impossible. Most states which joined the BW Convention did so on condition that the complete prohibition of biological weapons would be recognized as a step towards a complete prohibition of chemical weapons (Preamble and Article XI).

The aim of the BW Convention was not so much to remove an immediate peril, as to eliminate the possibility that scientific and technological advances, modifying the conditions of production, storage or use of biological weapons, would make these weapons militarily attractive. Indeed, progress in biotechnology is making it increasingly possible to "improve" upon known biological agents. Normally harmless organisms which do not cause diseases can be modified so as to become highly toxic and produce diseases for which there is no known treatment. But the Convention is comprehensive enough to cover all relevant scientific and technological developments, including biological agents and toxins that could result from genetic engineering processes.

The disclosure by the UN Special Commission of an extensive biological weapons programme in Iraq, as well as reports that certain other nations, too, have or are seeking to acquire a biological weapon capability, indicate that the threat of biological warfare remains real. Since the BW Convention has no instruments to check compliance, there is a need for verification machinery to deter would-be violators. Negotiations for a verification protocol, or another legally binding document strengthening the Convention with measures of control, have been going on in an ad hoc group of States, open to all parties, since January 1995. So far, however, agreement has proved elusive. Until it is reached, parties to the Convention are expected to implement the confidence-building measures they have agreed at their Review Conferences. The most important among them are measures enhancing the transparency of activities involving biological agents and toxins. They include exchanges of information on facilities and research programmes relevant to the Convention, on vaccine production, and on significant and unusual outbreaks of diseases.

Eventually, to make possible a differentiation between treaty-prohibited and treaty-permitted activities, the objects of the prohibitions will have to be more clearly defined, and the criteria necessary to assess compliance will have to be unambiguously established. Moreover, apart from short-notice visits to declared sites, on-site inspections of undeclared sites will have to be accepted without reservation by all parties. It is, of course, understood that sensitive commercial proprietary information and national security information, not directly related to the BW Convention, must be reliably protected. A special organization will be needed to oversee the implementation of the parties' obligations.

12

Health Impact of Chemical Weapons

Chemical weapons are classified as arms that use toxic chemical substances to harm or kill people during war. According to the International Chemical Weapons Convention there are more than fifty different chemicals that have been produced with the expressed intent to use them as weapons of war also referred to as, 'chemical weapons agents,' or, 'CWA.' The majority of chemical weapons have been used either on the battlefields of WWI where greater than one-hundred thousand or 124,000 metric tons were used, have been dumped into the oceans during the 1950's and 1960's - around several hundred thousand metric tons, or were stored chemical nuclear warheads at a Russian stockpile until the 1990's - approximately 70,000 metric tons. By the summer of 2009, around half of these weapons had been destroyed. The remaining stockpiles are highly dangerous if they are not appropriately guarded and maintained.

How are people most often exposed to these chemicals? Chemical weapon agents or products of unregulated destruction such as sea-dumping, open-air incineration, or burial of chemicals such as dioxins, as well as furan reaction masses from open-pit burning or dumping are extremely toxic to human beings. Besides the risk of direct exposure, the main risk involves the migration of these chemicals into the ground and the water people drink where they rapidly, 'bio-accumulate,' in the food chain.

One Deadly Example

The dumping of diphosgene, phosgene, as well as picric acid into Lake Mokhovoe in Russia's Penza region released around 740 tons of hydrochloric acid into the lake. In the 1960's the water revealed an extremely low pH-level of 1.5-2.5, something that killed every plant and animal in the entire lake. While the lake has recovered somewhat in the time that has passed, it still remains at an unusually low pH-level of 4.2-4.8. Due to the acidity of the water there are still only a very few primitive life forms to be found in this lake today. The lake is one of the onlydrinking water sources for greater than 650,000 people of Penza.

The Health Impact of Chemical Weapons - Examples

Chemical agents fall into four general categories, according to the Organization for the Prohibition of Chemical Weapons. Upon looking at these categories, one has to wonder why they have been created at all. The certainty of suffering, pain, and death is associated with any chemical weapon that falls into these categories.

Blood Agents: Blood agents include cyanogen chloride, hydrogen cyanide, and arsine. The chemicals prevent a person's blood and tissue cells from accepting oxygen and cause rapid organ failure.

Choking Agents: Choking agents include phosgene, chlorine, chloropicrin, and diphosgene. These chemicals are absorbed through a person's lungs and cause the buildup of fluids, leading to choking and eventually – death.

Blister Agents: Blister agents include nitrogen mustard, sulfur mustard, and lewisite. These chemicals burn a person's mucous membranes, skin, and eyes and cause large blisters on any skin that is exposed. When a person inhales these chemicals as a vapor, the chemicals have the ability to burn a person's windpipe and lungs leading to their death.

Nerve Agents: Nerve agents include sarin, tabun, soman, and VX. The chemicals cause muscle paralysis – including paralysis of a person's diaphragm and heart. They also cause seizures and loss of body control. Nerve agents are the most deadly of chemical agents and amounts the size of a small drop comprises a lethal dose that can cause almost immediate death.

STOPPING THE CHEMICAL AGENT MADNESS

Understanding why humanity struggles with itself, choosing to pursue violence and spending vast amounts of effort and resources on the pursuit of military equipment and methods and means of destruction instead of unifying to work towards the betterment of humanity and the planet is exceptionally difficult. Not everyone on Planet Earth has succumbed to the military madness that seems to prevail.

The Chemical Weapons Convention (CWC) is an international treaty that specifically aims to eliminate military-deployable chemical weapons by prohibiting, 'the development, production, acquisition, stockpiling, transfer, and use of chemical weapons." As of August 2009 there were 188 member states out of 195 countries and four countries with declared Chemical Weapons stockpiles.

Green Cross Switzerland and partner organizations Green Cross Russia and Global Green USA have played key parts in facilitating the timely and safe destruction of chemical weapons in both Russia and America. These two nations together possess greater than 90% of the global chemical weapons stockpiles. In the year 2000, Green Cross Switzerland launched, 'Destroy Chemical Weapons Now,' an international information campaign with the goal of raising awareness of the approximately 70,000 tons of toxic chemical weapons that were still in existence around the world at that time.

The organization has also encouraged an international partnership toward global chemical disarmament and effective implementation of the Chemical Weapons Convention. Beginning in the year 1997, Green Cross and Global Green established a network of a dozen local and regional public information and outreach offices in Russia and initiated an annual National Dialogue meeting, something that brings together all the stakeholders.

Since the year 2007, Green Cross has been working with Blacksmith Institute to isolate three open pit burning sites in Russia's Penza region that threaten the drinking water supply of more than 600,000 people through the migration of furanes, dioxins, and arsenic released during the process of incineration into Penza's drinking water.

Any nation that creates, maintains, or dares to use chemical weapons must be considered to be a threat to not only its own population - but other populations around the world as well. There is no justification for the creation, possession, or use of any type of chemical weapon. All stockpiles of chemical weapons must be appropriately destroyed.

CHEMICAL WEAPONS AND THEIR DESTRUCTION

Chemical weapons are a weapon of mass destruction because of their ability to indiscriminately kill thousands. This has been the position of the international community for more than 100 years since the Geneva Protocol of 1925. The preamble of the Chemical Weapon Convention reaffirmed this by stating:

"Determined for the sake of all mankind, to exclude completely the possibility of the use of chemical weapons, through the implementation of the provisions of this Convention, thereby complementing the obligations assumed under the Geneva Protocol of 1925"

The most common form of chemical weapons used in international conflicts are nerve agents, such as sarin and VX, and blistering agents, such as mustard gas. Nerve agents affect the nervous system and produce death through depressing or preventing respiration. Blistering agents cause intense and painful blisters and can lead to death by blistering the respiratory system. The Organization for the Prohibition of Chemical Weapons recognizes nine types of chemical agents including psychotomimetic and riot control agents.

The first documented use of modern chemical weapons was in Ypres, Belgium during World War I. It is estimated that chemical weapons led to the death of 1.3 million during World War I and more than a million deaths since World War I.

The magnitude of death and destruction of World War I lead the international community to establish the Geneva Protocol of 1925 which prohibits the use in war of "poisonous, asphyxiating or other gases."

Since 1925, subsequent legal interpretations have concluded that "a general consensus in the international community on the principle that the use of chemical weapons is also prohibited in internal armed conflict."

Since the passage of the Geneva Protocol of 1925, chemical weapons have been used in the lead-up to World War II by Italy against Ethiopia (1935) and Japan against China (late 1930s). Chemical weapons were not used in combat during World War II. Iraq used chemical weapons in the 1980s against Iran and its domestic Kurdish population. In 1995, Aum Shinrikyo, a Japanese cult, used sarin gas in a terrorist attack on the Tokyo subway system killing 12 people and sickening 5,500.

THE CHEMICAL WEAPONS CONVENTION (CWC)

In the early 1990s, the Conference on Disarmament negotiated the Chemical Weapons Convention. The Convention was created in 1993 and President George H.W. Bush's administration signed the treaty that year. It entered into force in 1997. To date, 191 States have signed the treaty and 189 States have ratified it. Israel and Burma (Myanmar) have signed but not ratified the Convention. Five States have not signed the Convention: Syria, Egypt, North Korea, Angola and South Sudan.

The Convention prohibits members from developing, producing, storing, acquiring or transferring of toxic chemicals, munitions and devices to separate toxic chemicals and any equipment supporting the employment of munitions and devices. The Convention specifically states that a toxic chemical is "any chemical which through its chemical action on life processes can cause death, temporary incapacitation or permanent harm to humans or animals." The Convention also prohibits precursor chemicals, which are used to produce toxic chemicals.

Members of the Convention have declared 71,196 tons of chemical agents and more than 81 percent of the global stockpile has been destroyed. The United States and Russia possess the largest remaining chemical stockpiles among Convention members and both states have missed their destruction deadlines. Both countries asked to extend their original 10 year deadline for total destruction because of complications in the process and environmental concerns. The U.S. has destroyed nearly 90 percent of its declared 31,000 ton stockpile and Russia has destroyed 57 percent of its declared 41,000 metric ton stockpile.

The Organization for the Prohibition of Chemical Weapons is the Convention's verification body. It has conducted more than 2,600 inspections on chemical weapons sites and 1,800 inspections of industrial sites in 86 countries to ensure compliance with the Convention.

THE DESTRUCTION OF CHEMICAL WEAPONS

Once a State joins the Chemical Weapons Convention, it has ten years to destroy its chemical weapons stockpile. The Organization for the Prohibition of Chemical Weapons sets out the following timeline for Schedule 1 chemicals:1

Day 30 – Declaration of all stockpiles and facilities

Year 2 – The first destruction facility is tested

Year 3 – No less than one percent of Schedule 1 chemicals are destroyed

Year 5 – No less than 20 percent of Schedule 1 chemicals are destroyed

Year 7 – No less than 45 percent of Schedule 1 chemicals are destroyed

Year 10 – All Schedule 1 chemicals are destroyed

Schedule 22 and Schedule 33 weapons are to be destroyed within five years of joining the Convention in equal annual increments.

The Convention allows States to develop and use their own technologies to destroy chemical weapons. The two most popular technologies are incineration, used by the United States, and low-temperature neutralization, used by Russia and the United States. The application of low-temperature and more environmental friendly neutralization technology and practices as well as organizational turmoil has been cited as a cause of the U.S. failure to meet both the original and revised destruction deadline. The United States, Germany, Japan and others have also developed mobile destruction technologies, similar to mobile chemical waste treatment systems.

During the destruction process, countries must maintain the security of their stockpiles while ensuring destruction methodology has a limited environmental impact.

SUCCESS OF THE ORGANIZATION FOR THE PROHIBITION OF CHEMICAL WEAPONS

Under the Chemical Weapons Convention, seven countries have declared chemical weapons stockpiles and three countries have completely destroyed their chemical weapons. As of July 2013, the Organization for the Prohibition of Chemical Weapons had conducted 5,167 inspections in 86 States. The Organization has inventoried and verified all declared chemical weapons stockpiles and verified that all declared chemical weapons production facilities are inactive in the states that have ratified the convention. Of the 70 declared chemical weapons facilities, 43 have been destroyed, 14 are mothballed and 21 have been converted to peaceful uses.

COUNTRY SPECIFIC CASE STUDIES

Libya

In December 2003, Libyan leader Moammar Gadhafi announced that Libya would eliminate its weapons of mass destruction programs. From 2003 until the civil war of 2011, Libya was dismantling its chemical weapons stockpile. After nine years, Foreign Policy reported that Libya had only destroyed "barely half of its total mustard gas stockpile and just 40 percent of its stores of chemical weapons precursor elements." Following the ouster of Gadhafi and the installation of a new government, Libya reported an undeclared stockpile of mustard gas and munitions. On February 4th, 2014, the OPCW announced that Libya had completed the destruction of its "remaining mustard gas filled in artillery projectiles and aerial bombs."

United States

The U.S. signed the Chemical Weapons Convention in 1993 under the presidency of George H.W. Bush. The U.S. Senate approved the treaty in April of 1997 by a vote of 74-26, including 28 Republicans Senators, under President Clinton.

To date, the U.S. has destroyed 90 percent of its declared stockpile at an estimated cost of $28 billion dollars. Two facilities remain with chemical weapons at Pueblo, CO and Blue Grass, KY. The Pueblo facility uses biotreatment to destroy the weapons while the Blue Grass facility uses supercritical water oxidation to destroy the stockpile of 523 tons of agents and munitions including VX, GB and mustard gas at its location. The estimated cost is $10.6 billion dollars to complete the destruction.

The U.S. has revised its total chemical weapons disarmament deadline from 2010 and missed the new 2012 deadline as well, citing technological implementation and environmental concerns, including leak containment and community health. The U.S. is slated to complete stockpile destruction in 2023, after Russia is slated to complete its chemical disarmament.

Russia

The Russian Federation signed the Chemical Weapons Convention in 1993 and fully joined the treaty in December of 1997. Upon joining the Convention, Russia declared a 41,000 ton arsenal, the world's largest arsenal. The U.S. State Department has publicly questioned the totality of the Russian declaration. Since Russia joined the Convention, foreign aid has assisted the country in the destruction of its chemical weapons stockpile. In 2002, Russia applied for and was granted an extension to the Convention's destruction deadline, of 2007. However, like the United States, Russia has missed the revised destruction deadline slated for 2012. At present, Russia is slated for total stockpile destruction in 2018.

Syria's Chemical Arsenal

In 2012, Syria confirmed that it had a stockpile of chemical weapons for use in case of foreign aggression. It did not publicly reveal the size or composition of its arsenal.

Intelligence estimates are that Syria possesses approximately 1,000 metric tons of chemical weapons, mostly sarin and VX nerve agent as unmixed components. It also maintains stockpiles of mustard gas and other blistering agents. As of 2011, the Nuclear Threat Initiative believes Syria operated four research and production facilities near Damascus, Homs, Aleppo and Latakia and the Israel-based International Institute for Counter-Terrorism estimated that Syria uses 50 different sites to store chemical weapons. A 2012 Department of Defence estimate suggests that securing Syria's chemical weapons in a non-permissive environment would take more than 75,000 American troops.

On August 21, 2013, Syria used chemical weapons as part of its ongoing civil war. This triggered involved from the U.S., Russia, OPCW and United Nations. A full accounting can be found in the section entitled: "United Nations Security Council and Syria." Eventually, a framework agreement was announced on September 14th, 2013 to destroy Syria's chemical weapons by mid-2014.

The U.S.-Russia framework was highly ambitious given India and South Korea had destroyed similarly sized arsenals in 3-4 years following the lengthy creation of destruction facilities.

FURTHER READING ON SYRIA'S CHEMICAL ARSENAL

While no historic precedent exists for the internationalization and destruction of a country's chemical weapons stockpiles, some parallels can be drawn to the United Nationals Special Commission tasked with disarming Iraq's chemical weapons following the Gulf War.

In April 1991, the United Nations Security Council passed Resolution 687 establishing the United National Special Commission to oversee the destruction of Iraq's chemical and biological weapons as well as cooperate with the International Atomic Energy Agency to dismantle Iraq's nuclear program. The Special Commission supervised the destruction of 40,000 chemical munitions, 500,000 litres of chemical weapons and 1.8 million litres of precursor chemicals.

Following the international condemnation of Iraq's invasion of Kuwait, the Special Commission was given total access to Iraq and the ability to inspect any and all facilities without advance warning. This type of access will be nearly impossible to achieve because of the Syrian civil war.

The first, very difficult part of the Special Commission's task was getting accurate information from Saddam's government. To obtain this information, it took multiple threats of the use of force and one actual use of force, Operation Desert Fox, for Saddam to cooperate.

Hiding a chemical weapons program or stockpile is more difficult than hiding a nuclear or biological program. Despite the inspections, Saddam still managed to conceal some part of the program, but his overall capacity was significantly degraded, as the United States discovered in the wake of invading Iraq in 2003.

United Nations Security Council and Syria

On September 14th, 2013, the U.S. and Russia announced they had reached an agreement in which Syria would accede to the Chemical Weapons Convention and surrender its chemical weapons.

On September 14th, 2013, Syria submitted the necessary instruments of treaty accession to the Secretary-General of the United Nations joined the Convention on October 14, 2013. Under the plan, instead of the one month reporting period, Syria must declare its chemical weapons and associated military hardware and infrastructure within one week. The plan also seeks to destroy all of Syria's chemical weapons by early 2014, outside of Syria, if possible. The program is to be completed under the supervision of Organization for the Prohibition of

Chemical Weapons' inspectors with the assistance of the United Nations.

The U.S.-Russian framework was approved by the Executive Council of the Organization for the Prohibition of Chemical Weapons and thc U.S. and Russia sponsored a UN Security Council resolution that reinforces the decision and ensures Syrian compliance.

Following months of searching, no State was found to be willing to destroy Syria's chemical arsenal. The U.S. announced a plan that would export Syria's chemical arsenal, via Norwegian and Dutch vessels, to the Italian port of Gioia Turano, where they would be loaded aboard the Cape Ray for destruction.

As of January 31st, 2014 only two shipments have been removed from Syria prompting Ahmet Uzumcu, OPCW's Executive Director, to tell the OPCW's Executive Council: "While the two shipments (of chemicals) this month represent a start, the need for the process to pick up pace is obvious."

THE CHEMICAL WEAPONS CONVENTION: HAS IT ENHANCED U.S. SECURITY?

Long before the Chemical Weapons Convention (CWC) became international law, the United States decided that the possession and use of chemical arms was not in its national interest.

In November 1985, Congress mandated that the U.S. stockpile of unitary chemical weapons be unilaterally destroyed. Then, in May 1991, in the aftermath of the Persian Gulf War, President George Bush went one step further by declaring that the United States would formally forswear the use of chemical weapons for any reason, including retaliation, once the CWC entered into force.

By signing the convention in January 1993 and ratifying it in April 1997, the United States sought to ensure that other nations would also renounce the possession and use of chemical weapons, reducing the risk that U.S. civilians or soldiers would face poison gas at home or on the battlefield. The CWC requires member states to destroy all chemical weapons stockpiles and dedicated production facilities within a decade of entry into force and to renounce their reacquisition in the future. Functioning both as a disarmament and a non-proliferation measure, it is the first multilateral treaty to require the elimination of an entire category of weapons under strict international monitoring.

Although April 29 marks the fourth anniversary of the CWC's entry into force, the perceived threat of chemical weapons has not diminished significantly, raising the question of how effective the convention has been in enhancing U.S. security. That question is particularly germane now, with the arrival of a new administration in Washington. Despite the fact that the CWC was one of the major foreign policy legacies of the first Bush presidency, President George W. Bush and his advisers have generally taken a skeptical view of multilateral arms control.

The CWC may not be a panacea for the problem of chemical weapons proliferation—it must be augmented with other measures such as export controls and protective equipment—but it is a potentially powerful instrument in the U.S. policy toolkit. Compared with earlier treaties such as the Biological Weapons Convention and the nuclear Non-Proliferation Treaty, the CWC is unique in the depth and breadth of its verification mechanisms, which include national declarations, routine on-site inspections, consultation and clarification mechanisms, and state-party-initiated challenge inspections. The convention also breaks new ground in the extent to which it monitors dual-use facilities in the private sector, in this case, the commercial chemical industry.

Several key states of concern are not yet members of the CWC, but as the treaty approaches universality, it will cement a worldwide norm against the possession and use of chemical weapons. And although the convention is binding only on states, it has indirect effects on the problem of chemical-weapons terrorism because states-parties are required to pass domestic implementing legislation making the prohibitions in the treaty binding on their nationals living both at home and abroad and imposing punitive sanctions for violations.

Unfortunately, the United States has not used the CWC effectively over the past four years to benefit its own interests or to further international security. Instead, Washington has weakened the convention by not complying fully with its affirmative obligations and by failing to make use of mechanisms within the treaty, such as challenge inspections, to resolve compliance concerns.

ASSESSING CWC IMPLEMENTATION

The results of the first four years of CWC implementation have been mixed. On the positive side of the ledger, the number of states-parties has grown rapidly, reaching 143 by early 2001 and including major regional powers such as Russia, China, and Iran. Four countries—the United States, Russia, India, and South Korea—have declared chemical weapons stockpiles totaling 69,863 metric tons of chemical agents and nearly 8.4 million munitions and containers. Significantly, after many years of denials, India and South Korea decided to come clean about their chemical weapons stockpiles.

All of the declared possessors except Russia have begun destroying their chemical weapons and have met the first intermediate destruction deadline in the CWC to eliminate 1 percent of their most dangerous stocks by April of last year. To date, the agency overseeing CWC implementation, the Organization for the Prohibition of Chemical Weapons (OPCW), has helped to eliminate roughly 7 percent of the world's chemical agents and 15 percent of its chemical munitions and has conducted hundreds of inspections at chemical weapons sites and relevant industry facilities. In addition, 11 states-parties have declared current or past chemical weapons production facilities, which must either be dismantled or converted to peaceful purposes.

Despite these successes, Iraq, Libya, Syria, and North Korea—all states that are of particular concern to Washington and that are thought to possess chemical weapons—remain outside the regime, with no short-term prospect for their inclusion. The nonparticipation of these states and others, such as Egypt and Israel, poses a major obstacle to achieving the treaty's fundamental goal of eliminating chemical weapons from the planet.

Other dark clouds lurk on the horizon: a serious financial crisis at the OPCW threatens to force a major cutback in verification activities; Russia is experiencing serious delays in its chemical demilitarization program; growing constraints on the intrusiveness of on-site inspections are reducing the OPCW's ability to build confidence in compliance; and a lack of political will on the part of member states to confront suspected violators by launching challenge inspections lessens the likelihood that states will use this important tool to address compliance concerns. Unless these negative trends are reversed, they could fatally undermine the ability of the convention to achieve the security goals that the United States and other nations had in mind when ratifying the treaty. Ironically, although the United States played a key role in the CWC negotiations in Geneva and has the most to gain from a successful convention, a failure of U.S. leadership is at least partly to blame for many of the CWC's implementation problems.

Financial Crisis at the OPCW

Each CWC member state is obliged to contribute to the OPCW's $55 million annual budget. About two-thirds of states-parties have failed to pay their regular assessments, however, while others, including the United States, have not reimbursed the organization for the full costs of verification activities on their territory, as required by the convention. Compounding this problem is the unwillingness of many member states sitting on the OPCW's governing body, known as the Executive Council, to punish states for nonpayment of dues—apparently because they, too, are in arrears. As a result of these shortfalls, the organization is facing a serious financial crisis.

In February 2001, OPCW Director-General José Bustani warned that budgetary constraints threaten to cripple the operations of the organization. Unless this situation is remedied, the OPCW may have to reduce its verification activities at operating chemical weapon destruction facilities in the United States, India, and South Korea, and to cut the number of industry inspections from the 140 it conducted last year to 25. The longer the OPCW faces an acute shortage of funds, the more profound will be the consequences for the effective implementation of the organization's mandate.

Russian Chemical Demilitarization

Russia's vast stockpile of chemical weapons inherited from the Soviet Union, totaling 40,000 metric tons, is the largest in the world. The cost of destroying this stockpile has been estimated at roughly $6 billion, which Moscow cannot afford. Indeed, after Russia acceded to the CWC in November 1997, a lack of funds from domestic and international sources was a major reason it was unable to begin destroying its chemical weapons. Other impediments included political and bureaucratic infighting, disagreements between the Russian federal authorities and leaders of the six regions where the weapons are stored, and public concerns about the environmental impact of chemical weapons destruction. Given the current financial situation, it is extremely doubtful that Moscow will meet the CWC's deadline for the destruction of its entire stockpile even if it is granted a one-time, five-year extension that would give it until 2012 to finish the task.

A recent reorganization of the Russian bureaucracy in charge of the chemical demilitarization program has cast a ray of hope into this dark picture. The Putin administration transferred responsibility for the program from the Ministry of Defence to a new civilian body called the Russian Munitions Agency, led by a seasoned bureaucrat named Zinoviy Pak. In March 2001, Pak proposed overhauling the 1996 federal plan, which called for building separate destruction facilities at each of the seven depots where chemical weapons are stored. Instead, the number of future destruction facilities would be scaled down to three: one near the town of Shchuch'ye to destroy munitions filled with nerve agents and two near the towns of Gorny and Kambarka to destroy blister agents stored in bulk tanks that are in danger of leaking and cannot be moved. Chemical weapons from the other four storage sites would be transported to Shchuch'ye for destruction, significantly reducing costs. The main obstacle facing the proposed plan is that the transportation of chemical weapons among Russian regions is prohibited by a 1997 federal law and by local legislation. Whether these laws can be rescinded is an open question.

Fallout From U.S. Implementing Legislation

In drafting the domestic legislation to ratify and implement the CWC, Congress and the Clinton administration included three unilateral exemptions that have undermined the multilateral treaty by creating a separate set of rules for the United States. The most damaging provision allows a U.S. president to refuse an on-site inspection by the OPCW on the grounds that it could pose a threat to national security. A second exemption prohibits the removal of chemical samples from U.S. territory for detailed analysis at independent laboratories overseas. The third exemption sharply limits the number of U.S. chemical facilities subject to declaration and routine inspection.

These unilateral U.S. provisions have been serious impediments to effective implementation of the CWC, both because they violate the nondiscriminatory spirit of the treaty and because they set a bad example that other countries have begun to follow. Although Clinton administration officials sought to play down the impact of the exemptions, they have clearly had a corrosive effect. Several foreign governments have taken note of the provisions and some, such as India and Russia, have initiated steps to duplicate them. Even if a future U.S. president never invokes the national security waiver to block a challenge inspection, another country, such as Iran, might well decide to exploit this loophole. In that case, Washington would be in a weak position to criticize.

Beyond its flawed implementing legislation, the United States did not submit its declaration of relevant chemical industry facilities to the OPCW until early May 2000, three years after the deadline in the CWC. This delay, attributable to difficulties in passing the required implementing legislation and a squabble within the executive branch over which agency would have the lead for treaty implementation, seriously disrupted the industry inspection process. Because of Washington's extreme tardiness in preparing its industry declaration, U.S. chemical companies were unavailable for routine inspections for three years, forcing the European Union to bear the brunt of the industry inspection regime. The European states finally rebelled in 1999 and refused to accept additional CWC inspections until the United States came into compliance. Moreover, other countries that were late in filing their own declarations, including Iran, were only too happy to hide behind the U.S. example. Paralyzed by its own failure to comply with the letter of the treaty, Washington was in no position to point a finger at Tehran for technical—or even substantive—noncompliance.

Weakening of Verification Measures

The negotiators of the CWC sought to achieve a reasonable balance between two conflicting objectives: on the one hand, providing sufficiently intrusive verification to build confidence in compliance, and, on the other hand, protecting non-treaty-related trade secrets and national security information. Over the past four years, states-parties have increasingly shifted this delicate balance by giving precedence to protecting confidential information over transparency concerns, with the unfortunate result of eroding the intrusiveness of the CWC verification regime.

During inspections at industry sites, for example, states-parties have begun to adopt a number of practices that clearly diverge from the intent of the treaty negotiators. On the grounds of protecting proprietary or national security information, countries hosting inspections have sought to limit the access of OPCW inspectors to plant sites and facility records, preventing them from obtaining the data they need to accomplish the aims of their inspection mandate. Also, CWC members have approved procedures giving host governments the right to confiscate and retain any piece of recording equipment that host officials claim has not been satisfactorily cleared of data unrelated to treaty compliance.

Even more egregious, OPCW inspectors are currently required to allow host officials to copy all of the information in their notebooks, laptop computers, electronic cameras, and video recorders before they depart from an inspected industry site. This new policy clearly conflicts with provisions in the CWC guaranteeing the inviolability of inspection records so that the inspectors can perform their duties without undue interference from hostile government officials or plant managers. So far, the United States has been either unable or unwilling to block these negative developments.

Inspections at U.S. industrial plants that produce, process, or consume treaty-controlled chemicals provide another example of how CWC implementation has become less intrusive than the treaty negotiators intended. When hosting industry inspections, U.S. government officials have narrowly defined the perimeter of the plant site and restricted the access of OPCW inspectors to the point that they have been unable to verify the absence of prohibited chemicals. Although U.S. officials acknowledge the importance of this verification objective, they argue that inspectors cannot use it as justification to gain access to all parts of a facility or to visit undeclared chemical plants on the same plant site without specifying a particular "ambiguity," or compliance concern. If widely adopted by other countries, the restrictive practices endorsed by the United States would diminish confidence in the effectiveness of industry inspections.

The campaign to weaken the intrusiveness of the CWC verification regime also extends to "challenge inspections," which provide a safety net to detect, and thereby deter, the clandestine production of chemical weapons. Under the convention, a member state has the right to request the OPCW to conduct such an inspection of any site—declared or undeclared—on the territory of another state-party for which some evidence of noncompliance exists. The CWC stipulates that a state-party can request a challenge inspection at any time and that the inspection will proceed unless a three-quarters majority of the OPCW Executive Council votes within 12 hours to stop it on the grounds that it is frivolous, abusive, or beyond the scope of the convention.

Recently, however, China, Cuba, India, Iran, Pakistan, and Russia have argued that a state-party can request a challenge inspection only after all bilateral and multilateral consultative procedures for resolving compliance questions have been exhausted. Although it is true that the CWC provides for such consultative mechanisms, the treaty makes clear that these methods are alternatives to, and not prerequisites for, a challenge inspection. Reinterpreting the convention to curtail the right to launch a challenge inspection would seriously weaken a key element of the verification regime.

Despite the low probability that a challenge inspection would uncover "smoking gun" evidence of a treaty violation, such as undeclared chemical munitions, using this measure when appropriate would help to deter would-be cheaters. During the first four years of implementation, however, not a single state-party has invoked the challenge inspection provisions of the CWC, even though suspicions have been raised that some member states are in substantive noncompliance with the convention.

The United States, for example, has asserted publicly that Iran continues to produce chemical weapons in violation of its treaty obligations. U.S. intelligence officials have testified before Congress that Tehran still possesses "several thousand metric tons of weaponized and bulk agent" including nerve, blister, choking, and blood agents, and has sought assistance from Russia, China, and other countries to become more self-sufficient in chemical weapons production. For reasons that remain unclear, however, the United States has never followed up these allegations by requesting a challenge inspection in Iran. Perhaps Washington is reluctant to disclose the sensitive intelligence information on which its assessment of Iranian noncompliance is based or fears a retaliatory Iranian challenge inspection on U.S. territory.

Whatever the reason for its inaction, if the United States continues to raise questions about CWC compliance without requesting a challenge inspection, this powerful tool will lose all credibility. The longer the challenge inspection mechanism remains unused, the more politically charged the process will become and the greater the burden of proof the requesting state will have to bear. Thus, if no challenge inspections are launched in the near future, there is a real risk that the states-parties could lose this critical instrument for promoting the goals of the CWC.

Conclusions and Recommendations

Taken as a whole, these implementation shortcomings pose a serious threat to the viability of the CWC and, by extension, to the security benefits that the convention could provide to the United States. Although the fact that a few countries have begun destroying their chemical weapons stocks and production facilities means that the United States is marginally safer than it was four years ago, the treaty has yet to live up to its promise, in large part because of a lack of U.S. leadership.

The vast majority of the 143 states-parties lack any experience with arms control implementation, and most of them face no immediate threat of chemical attack. Because the United States is one of the countries at greatest risk from the spread of chemical arms, Washington's rhetorical support for chemical disarmament and non-proliferation must be turned into effective action. Although the OPCW possesses the necessary tools to monitor and enforce compliance, the real question is whether the states-parties, in particular the United States, have the political will to implement the CWC in a way that strengthens non-proliferation norms and reduces the security threat posed by chemical weapons.

To take the lead in strengthening CWC implementation, the United States should take the following actions:

Address the financial crisis at the OPCW. The United States should help put the organization's fiscal house in order by reimbursing in full the cost of verification activities conducted on its territory. (As of February 28, Washington owed nearly $1.7 million for these activities.) At the same time, Washington should urge the OPCW Executive Council to punish those member states that have failed to pay their assessments for the past two years by stripping them of their voting rights, as provided for by the convention.

Minimize the impact of unilateral exemptions in the U.S. implementing legislation. The United States should help to restore the integrity of the CWC's verification regime by repealing or otherwise mitigating the three unilateral exemptions in the U.S. implementing legislation, which have seriously weakened the treaty. Although the Clinton administration was reluctant to attempt to modify legislation that it had accepted as part of a deal with Senate leaders to secure CWC ratification, the Bush administration starts with a clean slate and thus has more room to maneuver. Given the probable resistance to changes from conservative members of Congress, it is unlikely that the administration could remove all three exemptions from the legislation. But it may be possible for President Bush to pledge that he will not invoke the "national security waiver" during his time in office. That step would enable Washington to launch a challenge inspection without risk that the challenged country would invoke the same "right" to refuse an inspection on national security grounds.

Restore funding for Russian chemical weapons destruction. To facilitate the construction and operation of the Shchuch'ye nerve agent destruction plant, Washington should strive to restore the financial support that the U.S. Congress eliminated for fiscal years 2000 and 2001. Congress' decision to eliminate all $125 million slated for the project was based largely on the premise that, in the words of Senator Pat Roberts (R-KS), "Chemical weapons pose more of an environmental threat to Russia than a security threat to the United States." In fact, Russian chemical munitions are in good condition, portable, and could easily be stolen by terrorists. Although security measures at the seven chemical weapons depots have been improved, only destroying the entire stockpile will remove the threat.

Resolve conflicts with the OPCW over industry inspections. Sharp differences of interpretation between the U.S. government (notably the Department of Commerce) and the OPCW over the extent to which the CWC authorizes inspectors access to chemical industry plant sites have led to an impasse. Although the inspected companies have generally been prepared to compromise with the inspectors, U.S. government officials have dug in their heels and refused to budge. The OPCW has retaliated by subjecting the inspected firms to multiple inspections at the same sites. Instead of forcing industry to bear the brunt of this dispute, the U.S. government should seek to clarify this issue within the policy-making forums of the OPCW.

Launch a challenge inspection within the next year. In order to strengthen the credibility of the CWC verification regime, the United States should plan to launch a challenge inspection of a country suspected of a substantive violation or assist a close ally with initiating such an inspection. To this end, the U.S. intelligence community should build a compelling case for noncompliance and be prepared to share the necessary supporting information with the OPCW. At the same time, the U.S. government should prepare to host a challenge inspection that might be requested as a form of retaliation by the challenged country.

During more than two decades of arduous negotiations at the UN Conference on Disarmament in Geneva, the CWC's framers successfully designed a treaty that could eliminate chemical weapons and give member states confidence that the threat of chemical warfare would gradually diminish and finally disappear. Non-proliferation treaties are only effective, however, when given adequate resources and political support by law-abiding states and when violators are punished. For this reason, the CWC requires strong leadership if it is to be a useful instrument of non-proliferation that significantly benefits U.S. security.

Over the past four years, Washington's general lack of interest and confidence in the treaty has unfortunately created a vicious circle in which ineffective implementation has weakened the regime further, making it even less capable of inspiring confidence. If this downward spiral is not reversed soon, the CWC may not recover, and the United States will have lost a potentially valuable tool for reducing the threat of chemical weapons.

RIDDING SYRIA OF CHEMICAL WEAPONS

Preventing further use of chemical weapons in Syria will be achieved by their elimination rather than punitive airstrikes. Selective airstrikes, as repeatedly threatened by France, the United Kingdom, and the United States, would not have altered the military situation in the civil war, as the Syrian opposition forces and their backers had hoped.

The airstrikes would most certainly not have degraded Syria's chemical weapons capacity to the point it would have become useless, and further chemical attacks would have remained a distinct possibility. Targeting chemical weapons storage sites risked releasing toxic clouds affecting combatants and noncombatants alike. Destroying other types of targets would have just added to the tally of conventional weapons casualties.

As the situation developed, within a mere seven weeks after the chemical weapons attacks in the Ghouta district just outside Damascus on August 21, Syria became the 190th party to the Chemical Weapons Convention (CWC). Following months of deteriorating bilateral relations, elimination of Syria's chemical warfare capacity offered Russia and the United States common cause to rekindle security cooperation. On September 14, after three days of intense negotiations in Geneva, the two countries jointly presented to the world a very ambitious framework agreement. Syria announced its accession to the CWC on the same day, the best indicator thus far that it was a behind-the-scenes partner to the deal. Two weeks later, the Executive Council of the Organisation for the Prohibition of Chemical Weapons (OPCW) adopted the foundation of the framework agreement, including the ultimate destruction deadline of mid-2014. Syria, which by then had already submitted two sets of documents relating to its initial declaration, declared itself bound by the CWC and the Executive Council decisions even before the CWC had entered into force for it. A few hours after the Executive Council decision, the UN Security Council endorsed it in Resolution 2118, which created the mandate for the UN secretary-general to support the disarmament project. To cap two months of extraordinary twists and turns, the OPCW won the 2013 Nobel Peace Prize.

Meanwhile, the Syrian civil war continues to rage. The insurgent forces have by and large rejected the September 14 framework agreement and subsequent decisions because of the international legitimacy they feel these documents bestow on Syrian President Bashar al-Assad and his government. Together with their continuing fragmentation and ideological realignments, this position may pose security and safety risks to the chemical weapons elimination project that exceed by far the technical and logistical challenges resulting from the very short time frames.

The tasks facing the OPCW and United Nations are unprecedented. Never before has the international community attempted to secure and destroy a chemical weapons stockpile in a war, let alone a civil war in which multiple factions are fighting each other for territorial and ideological control. Besides the challenges of collecting and eliminating the chemical weapons and the specialized equipment and facilities for producing them, the primary concern of both organizations will be the safety and security of their personnel.

The events that led to the decisions to eliminate Syria's chemical warfare capacity. It discusses the legal and practical consequences of the U.S.-Russian bilateral agreement and the OPCW and UN decisions, as well as the areas of uncertainty or ambiguity they have engendered. The final section outlines how this sequence of decisions may actually benefit longer-term peace and security in the Middle East and offer a starting point for inclusive discussions to end the Syrian civil war.

CHEMICAL WEAPONS USE

Early on August 21, several major chemical warfare incidents occurred in the Ghouta district. Hundreds of people died from the effects of poisonous gases. Many more will suffer from the long-term consequences of exposure to a neurotoxicant, now known to have been sarin.

The Ghouta attacks followed several other allegations of chemical weapons use since the end of 2012. In particular, a chemical incident near Aleppo on March 19 prompted the Syrian government to formally ask UN Secretary-General Ban Ki-moon to launch an investigation. France and the United Kingdom promptly called for an expansion of the investigative team's mandate to include earlier incidents, which they attributed to government troops rather than the insurgents. After months of diplomatic haggling, the UN team, headed by

Swedish scientist Åke Sellström and comprising experts from the OPCW and the World Health Organization (WHO), finally began its mission in Syria on August 19.

Although deaths and other casualties were reported before the Ghouta strikes, the total image of these incidents never fully added up to one of chemical warfare. The nature of the attack on the Ghouta district differed in many fundamental ways: the parallel mounting of several strikes into different areas, the number of victims, and the volume and immediacy of video footage, pictures, and corroborating witness accounts all immediately pointing to the seriousness of the event.

The investigative team presented its preliminary report to the UN General Assembly and Security Council on September 16. Although the authors do not identify the culprits—to preserve their impartiality, that was never part of the mandate—the document independently confirms chemical weapons use in the Syrian civil war. The report's undeniable conclusions rest on multiple types of samples, interviews with victims and medical doctors that had treated them, investigation of munition remnants and impact zones, and laboratory analyses. The investigators established and preserved the integrity of the chain of custody from the moment they obtained the samples to the time they handed over the evidence to the laboratories in accordance with formal operating procedures and protocols. Syrian government representatives were present until the handover and reportedly monitored work in the laboratories.

Nevertheless, the UN investigative report does not fully clarify certain elements relating to those attacks. Among the issues that have not been resolved beyond a reasonable doubt are those dealing with types of delivery systems and their ownership, the quality of the sarin and whether the agent was produced using an industrial or improvised process, and the high number of exposed people who seem to have made it to medical stations combined with the virtual absence of images of instantaneous death at the sites of impact. With Syria's detailed declarations of weapon holdings and the verification of their accuracy by OPCW inspectors, these uncertainties should be completely removed in the near future.

From Bombing to Disarmament

Now well into its third year, the Syrian civil war reportedly has cost more than 110,000 lives. Many times that number have been injured or maimed for life. Millions have fled into neighboring countries or are internally displaced. Despite pressure to act from humanitarian law or doctrines such as the responsibility to protect, no single incident in conventional warfare has been a sufficient trigger for action. After Ghouta, however, UK Prime Minister David Cameron, French President François Hollande, and U.S. President Barack Obama intensified their rhetoric to justify punitive military strikes against Syrian military assets with or without Security Council approval.

In an attempt to prepare public opinion for military strikes, the three leaders invoked many emotive images of women and children suffering from exposure to the toxicants. By overselling the limited evidence to implicate the Assad regime in the Ghouta strikes and asserting its responsibility for earlier alleged uses of chemical weapons, they accorded data fragments higher evidentiary value than these actually merited. This was the principal concern with the intelligence summaries published by the French, UK, and U.S. governments at the end of August. A document outlining the UK government's legal position for punitive attacks further illustrated the complex logic to link the Ghouta chemical weapons victims to overall humanitarian concerns.

Pressing for military action while the UN investigative team was still on the ground in Syria was another psychological error. These investigators were working in accordance with procedures negotiated and approved by the international community in order to ensure impartiality in the findings.

For many observers, these factors, taken together, carried too many echoes of the highly selective and misleading evidence provided to justify the invasion of Iraq in 2003. Cameron's failure to persuade the House of Commons to endorse military retaliation against Assad's forces took the wind out of the French and U.S. calls for military intervention. Obama, in particular, was caught between his political rhetoric of a year earlier—chemical weapons use marked a redline—and his reluctance to get the United States embroiled in yet another Middle Eastern war.

A change of direction was needed, and to be viable, Russia needed to be on board. Russia seized on a September 9 remark by U.S. Secretary of State John Kerry to place chemical weapons disarmament in Syria at center stage. The remark was seemingly offhand but might have been previously agreed between Washington and Moscow.

Disarmament involving two or more parties by definition requires international cooperation and is possible because of the almost exclusive focus on the weapons technology. Negotiators and experts are consequently focused more on the most threatening implements of war than on the motivations and objectives of their respective leaders. This was very clear from the way Russia and the United States were able to thrash out a joint framework agreement after intense negotiation and persuade Syria to join the CWC. Meanwhile, it is equally clear that the Syrian civil war requires a political solution that addresses its underlying causes. It appears that the disarmament route may renew peace negotiations, as well as inadvertently lead to opportunities to resolve wider regional political and security issues.

Complex Framework

The U.S.-Russian framework agreement, Syria's accession to the CWC on the same day, and subsequent decisions by the OPCW Executive Council and the UN Security Council have created a complex legal and operational framework. Several questions must be addressed to ensure the effective and complete elimination of Syria's chemical weapons program.

Security. Syria's civil war poses the most extraordinary of circumstances for a chemical weapons disarmament project. All verification and disarmament activities require special arrangements to protect the members of the UN-OPCW joint mission and any other personnel involved. At the same time, the chemical weapons and specialized equipment need to be protected from unauthorized access, diversion, and attack.

Article II of the relationship agreement between the United Nations and the OPCW forms the basis for their mutual cooperation. It allows for detailed bilateral arrangements similar to the one worked out for investigating alleged chemical weapons use. In addition, Security Council Resolution 2118 contains certain provisions that will affect security management during the joint mission:

A stipulation that Syria was already legally bound by the basic undertakings of the CWC even before becoming a party.

A request to the UN secretary-general and the OPCW director-general to cooperate closely, including on the ground.

A reference to the Convention on the Privileges and Immunities of the United Nations and the privileges and immunities of OPCW-designated personnel set out in Part II of the CWC Verification Annex, which create a Syrian legal obligation to ensure the safety of the UN and OPCW personnel. A request to all Syrian parties and interested UN member states with relevant capabilities to work closely with the OPCW and the UN to arrange for the security of the monitoring and destruction mission.

A recognition of the primary responsibility of the Syrian government to ensure the security of the mission.

A stipulation that the Security Council will promptly consider OPCW reports under Article VIII of the CWC concerning referrals of noncompliance.

Syria's submittals. Syria disclosed the size and nature of its chemical weapons program to the OPCW even before it had become a party to the CWC. It also submitted a request for technical assistance. This approach raises several interconnected issues.

The first is the legal status of Syria's disclosure. The Executive Council decision recalled that Syria had already submitted information on September 19, gave it seven more days to submit additional information, and reiterated the requirement under Article III of the CWC that Syria submit its initial declaration. The disclosure was a first step in a process of submitting a complete and accurate initial declaration, but not the declaration itself. It nevertheless constituted the basis for verification planning and informing CWC states-parties about the details of the Syrian chemical weapons program. Such informal processes have been utilized in the past, albeit on a voluntary basis. In the Syrian case, such cooperation was portrayed as an obligation. Although this is consistent with the general principle of cooperation set out in the CWC, it also owes to the extraordinary circumstances of the case.

Second, the Executive Council decision includes a requirement that Syria submit information on "chemical weapons production facilities, including mixing and filling facilities, and chemical weapons research and development facilities, providing specific geographical coordinates."

The reference to "mixing...facilities" perhaps reflects the configuration of the Syrian chemical weapons stockpile, most of which has been reported to be in precursor form. Mixing machines meet the criterion, under Article II.1(c) of the CWC, of equipment specifically designed for use in connection with the deployment of chemical weapons and thus fall under the CWC definition of chemical weapons. Therefore, their explicit inclusion in the Executive Council decision comes as no surprise.

The reference to "research facilities" is interesting because the CWC is silent on chemical weapons research. Also, the issue of what exactly constitutes a chemical weapons development facility remains to be determined by the OPCW. It is not clear whether this provision in the Executive Council decision attempted to create a new legal requirement for Syria, which would raise a number of questions, or was merely a clarification to avoid situations whereby facilities involved in the early stages of chemical weapons development could be left undeclared because ostensibly they were research facilities.

A third issue, concerning the completeness of Syria's disclosure, is addressed below.

Verification. Verification of the Syrian declarations and chemical weapons destruction operations will essentially be carried out according the procedures detailed in the CWC. Nevertheless, several issues in the area of verification deserve further analysis:

Ensuring that the tight timelines can be met under the given circumstances will require effective and timely decision-making. It remains to be seen whether the OPCW's consensus approach can deliver on this.

Circumstances may demand frequent inspections or even a permanent in-country presence. Past verification practice may not be an appropriate guide in the Syrian case, given the recent chemical weapons use and the unique security context.

It may not be possible to ensure that all destruction operations are conducted in the presence of inspectors. If not, what are acceptable alternatives?

The Executive Council decision stipulates that the OPCW Technical Secretariat must "inspect as soon as possible any other site identified by a State Party as having been involved in the Syrian chemical weapons programme, unless deemed unwarranted by the Director-General, or the matter resolved through the process of consultation and cooperation." In general, this follows the cooperation concept of Article IX. In procedure, it is a departure from the CWC's challenge inspection mechanisms. Whether these stipulations were within the powers and functions of the Executive Council may not matter in practice, given that the subsequent Security Council resolution sanctioned this mechanism.

Destruction. The tight timelines for the elimination of Syria's chemical weapons program and the conditions inside the country will likely lead to certain practical and legal issues:

The Security Council resolution foresees the possibility of removal of bulk agent and precursors from Syrian soil for destruction elsewhere. If this option were to be executed, it would need to be reconciled with the prohibition on chemical weapons transfer under Article I of the CWC. The Security Council resolution recognizes this and "authorizes Member States to acquire, control, transport, transfer and destroy chemical weapons identified by the Director-General of the OPCW, consistent with the objective of the Chemical Weapons Convention, to ensure the elimination of the Syrian Arab Republic's chemical weapons program in the soonest and safest manner." The legal authority for this decision does not emanate from the CWC itself, but from Articles 24 and 103 of the UN Charter. Some members of the Executive Council have expressed their reservations with regard to this part of the Security Council resolution. It may be prudent for the CWC states-parties conference to recognize the legality of any removal of Syrian chemical weapons for destruction abroad in order to avoid future time-consuming legal debates that could obstruct decision-making.

If chemical weapons destruction were undertaken abroad or foreign mobile destruction facilities were deployed within Syria or near its borders, it needs to be established who bears responsibility for the timeliness, completeness, and safety of destruction and for the costs of destruction and verification. Under the CWC, Syria is responsible, but Syria does not own or operate this type of facility and may not have the expertise to make informed decisions. Chemical weapons destruction in Albania with technical assistance from the United States and other states-parties may be a useful precedent in this regard. Albania received technical and financial support from several CWC parties (Germany, Greece, Italy, Switzerland, and the United States). U.S. program managers and a German contractor designed and equipped a small chemical weapons disposal facility in Germany, then transported it to Albania where it was operated by the contractor on behalf of the Albanian government.

Although some destruction operations in Syria could be improvised along lines similar to the ones followed before the 1997 entry into force of the CWC by the UN Special Commission that operated in Iraq after the 1991 Persian Gulf War, there are limits to such improvisation. In the Syrian case, CWC rules on destruction apply—no open-pit burning, sea dumping, or land burial. For example, partial chemical destruction at storage locations by manually mixing the agent with decontamination solution may be acceptable as a first step of putting the agent beyond use, but explosive destruction of chemical weapons in the open clearly would not. The question is whether CWC rules could be eased, for example, with regard to the destruction of certain precursor chemicals.

The OPCW-UN Relationship. The UN and the OPCW each have mandates and responsibilities for Syria's chemical weapons disarmament, a situation that raises the question of who ultimately is in charge of what. That issue may become more complex if other states assume responsibility for aspects of Syria's destruction program, as allowed by the Security Council resolution.

The resolution contains key building blocks for the design of the coordination and cooperation mechanisms needed. In addition, the Executive Council decision contains a stipulation that Syria is to designate an official as the main point of contact for the OPCW and provide him or her with the authority necessary to ensure that the decision is fully implemented. It will be important to develop effective arrangements for coordination between the UN and the OPCW in the joint mission to avoid operational friction and uncertainties in decision-making.

GLIMMERS OF HOPE FOR THE FUTURE

The Syrian civil war continues to bring the greatest devastation onto civilians by means of conventional weapons. Many commentators from the Middle East and representatives of human rights organizations fear that the individuals responsible for the carnage, most notably Assad, will escape justice for the gross violation of the laws of war as a consequence of the chemical weapons agreements. Yet, it is far from established that the limited, punitive military strikes advocated by France, the United Kingdom, and the United States could have bought more justice for the Ghouta victims and survivors.

Disarmament involves removing a discrete weapons category from the military doctrine of a political entity. Weapons destruction is one aspect, but losing the doctrinal capacity to deploy and employ those weapons is by far the most important factor in preventing future rearmament with those weapons. Once the weapons category has been removed from military doctrine, there is no longer any testing of munitions and delivery systems or any training of troops in the use of these weapons.

Disarmament is also about preventing the outbreak of war. Because particular weapons technologies are considered to be destabilizing to international relations, people view their elimination as a contribution to peace and security. Even if war breaks out, disarmament prevents their use in combat or escalation of hostilities.

Translated to the U.S.-Russian framework agreement and the OPCW and UN Security Council decisions, forcing Syria to give up its chemical weapons arsenal will prevent a future Ghouta from occurring during the civil war. By bringing about Syria's accession to the CWC and by identifying a central role for the OPCW, Russia and the United States have made chemical disarmament in Syria a longer-term responsibility of the global community rather than a temporary, ad hoc reaction to a pressing problem by a few.

If successful, those disarmament decisions may inject a fresh dynamic into the so-called Helsinki process on eliminating nonconventional weapons from the Middle East. The final document of the 2010 Nuclear Nonproliferation Treaty Review Conference still requires the convening of a meeting on that subject. Nevertheless, some of the core assumptions about regional security, in particular, with regard to the strategic relationships among Egypt, Israel, and Syria, will have to be revisited in terms of the doctrinal relationships between their respective weapons holdings. Thus, for example, Syria's chemical weapons served a doctrinal function similar to Israel's nuclear weapons as an instrument of last resort in case of an existential threat to the state. As the former will soon be eliminated, this could have an impact on current regional security postures or on the prospects of other countries joining the CWC or the Biological Weapons Convention. If Israel were to join the CWC after the completion of Syria's disarmament, Egypt would become wholly isolated, globally and within the Arab League, as a CWC nonparty. If Egypt were to join the CWC under international pressure, how would this affect its bargaining position within the NPT context?

The standoff over Iran's nuclear program may acquire a different dynamic. U.S. and Iranian statements on the margins of and to the UN General Assembly in late September suggest a newfound willingness to address concerns and desires in constructive ways. The first meeting in Geneva between the P5+1 (China, France, Germany, Russia, the United Kingdom, and the United States) and Iran ended with a positive joint declaration and commitment for speedy follow-on discussions. The Iranian presidential election in June may prove to have been a watershed event in reconnecting Tehran with the world in mutually beneficial ways. These outcomes will benefit the disarmament of Syria and possibly the Geneva negotiations attempting to end the civil war. Iran is set to play important roles in both processes.

Making progress on these multiple fronts will require a move toward an inclusive process of political transition in Syria. That transition could benefit from progress being made with Syria's chemical weapons disarmament if it built on some of the practical arrangements and dialogue that the disarmament process is establishing and the political transition process will require. At the same time, key steps in the disarmament process will depend on cooperation by the different parties of the Syrian conflict or at least their commitment not to derail it. If one accepts that there is no military solution to the Syrian conflict, then it would be shortsighted to portray chemical weapons disarmament as a tactical victory for the Assad regime. It should be seen as a step toward de-escalation enabling political dialogue aimed at a political transition.

CHEMICAL DISARMAMENT

Brief History of the Treaty

The Convention on the Prohibition of the Development, Production, Stockpiling and Use of Chemical Weapons and on their Destruction (otherwise known as the Chemical Weapons Convention or CWC) was opened for signature with a ceremony in Paris on 13 January 1993—130 States signed the Convention within the first two days. Four years later, in April 1997, the Convention entered into force with 87 States Parties—the ratification of the Convention by at least 65 States, achieved in November 1996, was a precondition to trigger the 180-day countdown until the Convention's entry into force. Currently, the CWC comprises 184 States Parties, as well as a fully functioning implementing Organisation, the Organisation for the Prohibition of Chemical Weapons (OPCW).

The Convention had been the subject of nearly 20 years of negotiations within the Conference on Disarmament in Geneva. The States involved in these negotiations were seeking to finalize an international treaty banning chemical weapons, and designed to ensure their worldwide elimination. This goal was indeed achieved.

The Convention is unique because it is the first multilateral treaty to ban an entire category of weapons of mass destruction (WMD) and to provide for the international verification of the destruction of these weapons. Furthermore, it is the first disarmament treaty negotiated within an entirely multilateral framework, leading to increased transparency and its application equally to all States Parties. The Convention was also negotiated with the active participation of the global chemical industry, thus ensuring industry's ongoing cooperation with the CWC's industrial verification regime. The Convention mandates the inspection of industrial facilities to ensure that toxic chemicals are used exclusively for purposes not prohibited by the Convention.

Altogether, the international community succeeded in producing a treaty that would verify the destruction of chemical weapons worldwide as well as ensure the non-proliferation of these weapons and the toxic chemicals used in their manufacture. The Convention also encourages international cooperation between States Parties in the peaceful uses of chemistry, and provides for assistance and protection to States Parties that are threatened or attacked by chemical weapons.

Before the Convention is considered in greater detail, it is useful to understand why such a treaty was necessary. Where does the threat from chemical weapons come from?

BRIEF HISTORY OF CHEMICAL WEAPONS USE

Although chemicals had been used as tools of war for thousands of years—e.g. poisoned arrows, boiling tar, arsenic smoke and noxious fumes, etc.—modern chemical warfare has its genesis on the battlefields of World War I.

During World War I, chlorine and phosgene gases were released from canisters on the battlefield and dispersed by the wind. These chemicals were manufactured in large quantities by the turn of the century and were deployed as weapons during the protracted period of trench warfare. The first large-scale attack with chlorine gas occurred 22 April 1915 at Ieper in Belgium. The use of several different types of chemical weapons, including mustard gas (yperite), resulted in 90,000 deaths and over one million casualties during the war. Those injured in chemical warfare suffered from the effects for the rest of their lives; thus the events at Ieper during World War I scarred a generation. By the end of World War I, 124,000 tonnes of chemical agent had been expended. The means of delivery for chemical agent evolved over the first half of the twentieth century, increasing these weapons' already frightening capacity to kill and maim through the development of chemical munitions in the form of artillery shells, mortar projectiles, aerial bombs, spray tanks and landmines.

After witnessing the effects of such weapons in World War I, it appeared that few countries wanted to be the first to introduce even deadlier chemical weapons onto the World War II battlefields. However, preparations were made by many countries to retaliate in kind should chemical weapons be used in warfare. Chemical weapons were deployed on a large scale in almost all theatres in the First and Second World Wars, leaving behind a legacy of old and abandoned chemical weapons, which still presents a problem for many countries.

During the Cold War, the United States and the Soviet Union both maintained enormous stockpiles of chemical weapons, amounting to tens of thousands of tonnes. The amount of chemical weapons held by these two countries was enough to destroy much of the human and animal life on Earth.

Iraq used chemical weapons in Iran during the war in the 1980s, and Iraq also used mustard gas and nerve agents against Kurdish residents of Halabja, in Northern Iraq, in 1988. The horrific pictures of Halabja victims shocked the world at the time of the negotiations in Geneva on the Chemical Weapons Convention. The two most recent examples of the use of chemical weapons were the sarin poisoning incident in Matsumoto, a Japanese residential community, in 1994, and the sarin attack on the Tokyo subway in 1995, both perpetrated by the Aum Shinrikyu doomsday cult. These two attacks re-focused international attention on the potential use of chemical weapons by terrorists, and on the dangers posed by chemical weapons.

The devastating impact chemical weapons have had in the past, and the potential for the use of modern—even more deadly—chemical agents not only by States at war but in other violent conflicts and by non-State actors, provide the imperative for the international effort to uphold the ban on such weapons and to work towards the complete, global elimination of chemical weapons.

BRIEF DESCRIPTION OF CHEMICAL WEAPONS

The general and traditional definition of a chemical weapon is a toxic chemical contained in a delivery system, such as a bomb or shell.

The Convention defines chemical weapons much more generally. The term chemical weapon is applied to any toxic chemical or its precursor that can cause death, injury, temporary incapacitation or sensory irritation through its chemical action. Munitions or other delivery devices designed to deliver chemical weapons, whether filled or unfilled, are also considered weapons themselves.

The toxic chemicals that have been used as chemical weapons, or have been developed for use as chemical weapons, can be categorised as choking, blister, blood, or nerve agents. The most well known agents are as follows: choking agents—chlorine and phosgene, blister agents (or vesicants)—mustard and lewisite, blood agents—hydrogen cyanide, nerve agents—sarin, soman, VX.

Of course some toxic chemicals, and/or their precursors, are utilised globally in industry. For example, toxic chemicals are employed as basic raw material, or as anti-neoplastic agents, which prevent the multiplication of cells, or as fumigants, herbicides or insecticides. Such chemicals are considered chemical weapons if they are produced and stockpiled in amounts that exceed requirements for those purposes that are not prohibited under the Convention.

The Convention is designed to ensure that toxic chemicals are only developed and produced for purposes unrelated to chemical weapons. Chemical technology must not be misused, and the OPCW has a mandate to monitor chemical industry to make certain that this is the case.

To aid the OPCW in this task, the Convention divides toxic chemicals and precursors that could be used as chemical weapons or that could be used in the manufacture of chemical weapons into three Schedules. Schedule 1 chemicals have been used as chemical weapons in the past and/or have very few or no peaceful uses, and thus pose the most direct threat to the Convention. Schedule 2 chemicals are primarily precursors to Schedule 1 chemicals and most have some industrial uses.

Schedule 3 chemicals are produced in large quantities commercially but in some cases were used as chemical warfare agents and can also serve as precursors to Schedule 1 or 2 chemicals. Production facilities of many organic chemicals termed discrete organic chemicals are also subject to declaration requirements and verification activities.

To help facilitate the destruction and verification process, chemical weapons are formally divided into three Categories. Into Category 1 fall Schedule 1 chemical agents and munitions filled with Schedule 1 agents. Category 2 covers munitions filled with other toxic chemicals and any other weaponised chemical agents—other than those in Schedule 1. Unfilled munitions and devices, and any other equipment specifically designed to aid in the deployment of chemical weapons, fall into Category 3. Destruction timelines are set by the Convention for the destruction of all three Categories of chemical weapons.

The international efforts made in the area of chemical disarmament since the seventeenth century, the structure and purview of the CWC, the structure and function of the OPCW, and the implementation of the CWC since 1997.

Nerve Agents

"Nerve agents", or "nerve gases", as they are sometimes called, are some of the most well known chemical weapons. They derive their name from their mode of action on the human body. They are organophosphorus compounds and are divided into two distinct chemical families, the "G-agents" (tabun, sarin, soman, etc.) and the "V-agents" (VA, VG, VX, etc.). Although chemically different, G- and V-agents have the same effect.

Electrical signals are transmitted to and from the brain to the various parts of the body via the nerve cells (neurons). At the junction (synapse) between two nerve cells there is a gap. To enable an electrical impulse to cross this gap, the nerve cells spontaneously generate a chemical transmitter. There are several such transmitters in different parts of the nervous system, one of which is acetylcholine. Once the electrical signal has crossed the gap, the acetylcholine is immediately hydrolyzed through catalysis by the enzyme acetylcholinesterase. Nerve agents function by inhibiting this enzyme and thus preventing it from breaking down the acetylcholine. The result is the rapid paralysis of the nerve cells throughout the body. If left untreated, such paralysis is quickly followed by death.

Nerve agents can be dispersed as liquids or in aerosol form, allowing them to be inhaled or absorbed through the skin. All nerve agents are extremely toxic. For example, just one drop of VX the size of a pinhead absorbed through the skin will be more than enough to cause death.

HISTORY OF CHEMICAL DISARMAMENT

For as long as chemicals have been used as a means of warfare, efforts to curtail such use have been undertaken internationally. The first international agreement limiting the use of chemical weapons dates back to 1675, when France and Germany came to an agreement, signed in Strasbourg, prohibiting the use of poison bullets. Almost exactly 200 years later, in 1874, the next treaty or agreement of this sort was concluded: the Brussels Convention on the Law and Customs of War. The Brussels Convention prohibited the employment of poison or poisoned weapons, and the use of arms, projectiles or material to cause unnecessary suffering. Before the turn of the century, a third agreement came into being; an international peace conference held in The Hague in 1899 led to the signing of an agreement that prohibited the use of projectiles filled with poison gas.

In the wake of World War I, during which the world witnessed the horrors of large-scale chemical warfare, international efforts to ban the use of chemical weapons and prevent such suffering from being inflicted again, on soldiers and civilians, intensified. The result of this renewed global commitment was the 1925 Geneva Protocol for the Prohibition of the Use of Asphyxiating, Poisonous or Other Gases, and Bacteriological Methods of Warfare. The Geneva Protocol does not, however, prohibit the development, production or possession of chemical weapons. It only bans the use of chemical and bacteriological (biological) weapons in war. Furthermore, many countries signed the Protocol with reservations permitting them to use chemical weapons against countries that had not joined the Protocol or to respond in kind if attacked with chemical weapons. Since the Geneva Protocol has been in force, some of these States Parties have dropped their reservations and accepted an absolute ban on the use of chemical and biological weapons. In 1971 the Eighteen Nations Disarmament Committee (ENDC) (later to become the Conference on Disarmament)completed negotiations on the text of the Convention on the Prohibition of the Development, Production and Stockpiling of Bacteriological (Biological) and Toxin Weapons, commonly referred to as the Biological Weapons Convention or BWC. In conjunction with the 1925 Geneva Protocol, it banned its States Parties from developing, producing, or possessing biological weapons, but contained no mechanism to verify the compliance of States Parties with these prohibitions. Included within the BWC was the stipulation that countries commit themselves to the negotiation of an international treaty banning chemical weapons.

Beginning in 1986, the global chemical industry actively participated in these negotiations. Unlike the BWC, the negotiators of a chemical weapons ban reached an understanding that this ban would be subject to international verification. To this end, trial inspections of both industrial and military facilities were undertaken, starting in late 1988.

On 3 September 1992 the ad hoc committee submitted to the Conference on Disarmament the agreed text of the Convention on the Prohibition of the Development, Production, Stockpiling, and Use of Chemical Weapons, and on Their Destruction, now commonly referred to as the Chemical Weapons Convention or CWC. The Chemical Weapons Convention was opened for signature in Paris on 13 January 1993 and it was subsequently deposited with the United Nations Secretary-General in New York.

According to the terms of the Convention, the CWC would enter into force 180 days after the 65th country ratified the treaty. To prepare for the treaty's entry into force and the implementation of the verification regime, a Preparatory Commission (PrepCom) was established in 1993. Its mission was to lay the groundwork for the establishment of the permanent implementing body for the CWC: the Organisation for the Prohibition of Chemical Weapons or OPCW. The PrepCom was housed in The Hague, which became the host city of the OPCW as well. In addition to preparing the Convention's implementation guidance, another of the PrepCom's most important tasks was training 200 inspectors to conduct inspections worldwide of both military and industrial sites in order to verify compliance with the Convention.

Hungary was the 65th country to ratify the Convention, in late 1996, and on 29 April 1997 the Chemical Weapons Convention entered into force with 87 States Parties—becoming binding international law. (An additional 22 countries had ratified the treaty in the 180 days between Hungary's ratification and entry into force.)

With the entry into force of the Convention, the OPCW immediately began its work to implement the Convention. Both the Convention and its implementing body are intended to adapt not only to shifts in the international environment and the changing needs of States Parties, but also to respond to the rapid pace of scientific and technological developments.

Every five years, the Convention foresees that the States Parties should undertake a review of the implementation process. These review conferences serve as fora for the assessment and evaluation of the CWC's implementation, and the identification of areas where change is needed. A particular focus is given to the verification regime and the changing context within which it is implemented as well as scientific and technological advances in chemistry, engineering and biotechnology. The first review conference was held from 28 April to 9 May 2003.

THE CWC AND THE OPCW

Which Chemicals are Controlled?

The chemicals, which are explicitly specified in the Convention for monitoring purposes, cover a wide range of compounds and include chemical warfare agents, as well as key and more distant precursors. These chemical compounds, or families of compounds, are listed in the three Schedules of the Convention's Annex on Chemicals. Each of these Schedules has different requirements for verification. These requirements are more stringent in the case of those chemicals that are deemed to pose a greater risk. The Verification Annex also includes restrictions on the international transfer of scheduled chemicals.

Schedule 1 chemicals include those that have been or can be easily used as chemical weapons and which have very limited, if any, uses for peaceful purposes. These chemicals are subject to very stringent restrictions, including a ceiling on the production of one tonne per annum per State Party, a ceiling on total possession at any given time of one tonne per State Party, licensing requirements, and restrictions on transfers. These restrictions apply to the relatively few industrial facilities that use Schedule 1 chemicals. Some Schedule 1 chemicals are used as ingredients in pharmaceutical preparations or as diagnostics.

The Schedule 1 chemical saxitoxin is used as a calibration standard in monitoring programmes for paralytic shellfish poisoning, and is also used in neurological research. Ricin, another Schedule 1 chemical, has been employed as a bio-medical research tool. Some Schedule 1 chemicals and/or their salts are used in medicine as anti-neoplastic agents. Other Schedule 1 chemicals are usually produced and used for protective purposes, such as for testing CW protective equipment and chemical agent alarms.

Schedule 2 chemicals include those that are precursors to, or that in some cases can themselves be used as, chemical weapons agents, but which have a number of other commercial uses (such as ingredients in resins, flame-retardants, additives, inks and dyes, insecticides, herbicides, lubricants and some raw materials for pharmaceutical products).

For example, BZ is a neurotoxic chemical listed under Schedule 2, which is also an industrial intermediate in the manufacture of pharmaceuticals such as clindinium bromide. Thiodiglycol is both a mustard gas precursor as well as an ingredient in water-based inks, dyes and some resins. Another such example is DMMP, a chemical related to certain nerve agent precursors that is used as a flame retardant in textiles and foamed plastic products.

Schedule 3 chemicals include those that can be used to produce, or can be used as, chemical weapons, but which are widely used for peaceful purposes (including plastics, resins, mining chemicals, petroleum refining fumigants, paints, coatings, anti-static agents and lubricants).

Among the toxic chemicals listed under Schedule 3 are phosgene and hydrogen cyanide, which have been used as chemical weapons, but are also utilised in the manufacture of polycarbonate resins and polyurethane plastics, as well as certain agricultural chemicals. Triethanolamine, a precursor chemical for nitrogen mustard gas, is found in a variety of detergents (including shampoos, bubble baths and household cleaners) as well as being used in the desulfurisation of fuel gas streams.

Discrete Organic Chemicals

Among those chemicals not specifically listed in the Schedules or anywhere in the Convention are discrete organic chemicals (DOCs). Manufacturing operations producing DOCs are referred to as "other chemical production facilities". These plant sites are subject to declarations and verification requirements if they produce in aggregate more than 200 tonnes of DOCs annually. They are also subject to these requirements if they comprise plants at which more than 30 tonnes of any DOCs containing the elements phosphorous, sulfur or fluorine (PSF chemicals) are produced. Thousands of plant sites have been declared to the Technical Secretariat.

ORGANISATION FOR THE PROHIBITION OF CHEMICAL WEAPONS

Article VIII of the Convention establishes the OPCW as the implementing body of the Chemical Weapons Convention. The OPCW is given a mandate, "... to achieve the object and purpose of the Convention, to ensure the implementation of its provisions, including those for international verification of compliance with it, and to provide a forum for consultation and cooperation among States Parties."

The Technical Secretariat of the OPCW is responsible for the day-to-day administration and implementation of the

Convention, including inspections, while the Executive Council and the Conference of the States Parties are decision-making organs designed primarily to determine questions of policy and resolve matters arising between the States Parties on technical issues or on interpretations of the Convention. The chairs of the Executive Council and the Conference are appointed by each body's membership. The Technical Secretariat is headed by a Director-General, who is appointed by the Conference on the recommendation of the Council.

The Convention also provides for the establishment of three subsidiary bodies to aid the three main organs of the OPCW in their work: the Scientific Advisory Board, the Advisory Body on Administrative and Financial Issues, and the Confidentiality Commission.

The Scientific Advisory Board (SAB) is a group composed of independent experts who are mandated to assess relevant scientific and technological developments and report on such subjects to the Director-General. The SAB also provides expert advice on any proposed changes to the Schedules of Chemicals and any other advice that might be required, including in relation to subjects such as verification methodologies and equipment.

As a subsidiary organ of the Conference of the States Parties, the main function of the Confidentiality Commission is to settle any disputes between States Parties related to confidentiality.

The Advisory Body on Administrative and Financial Issues (ABAF) meets regularly to advise both the Technical Secretariat and the States Parties on issues relating to the OPCW programme and budgets. The ABAF reviews draft budgets prepared by the Technical Secretariat before they are submitted to the Council and the Conference for approval.

IMPLEMENTING THE REGIME

Responsibilities of the States Parties

The CWC cannot be successfully implemented without the constant and diligent work of the OPCW Member States.

Upon becoming a party to the Convention, each State has to undertake a variety of internal measures in order to comply with the Convention and to enable the verification mechanism to function properly. Given the complexity of the treaty, this is not an easy task. The internal measures range from preparing and conducting the destruction of chemical weapons arsenals, to surveying and regulating chemical industries, to amending a number of domestic laws and administrative rules.

The first obligation a State Party must fulfil, at the time the CWC enters into force for it, is the establishment and notification of its National Authority to serve as the national focal point for effective liaison with the OPCW and other States Parties. The main tasks of the National Authority include the coordination of the submission of declarations to the Organisation, as well as the monitoring of national trade in scheduled chemicals and the oversight of any chemical weapons destruction programme.

Working with other branches of the national government or legislature on the drafting and enactment of proper implementing legislation, which codifies the CWC and its prohibitions/obligations into national law, may be another responsibility of a National Authority.

A major early obligation is the requirement to submit an initial declaration, not later than 30 days after the treaty enters into force for a given State. Other required notifications, due within 30 days, include: points of entry, standing diplomatic clearance numbers for non-scheduled aircraft, and the issuance of two-year multiple-entry visas, all to facilitate the conduct of inspections. The initial declaration serves as a declaration of any past or present chemical weapons programmes pursued by a State Party, as well as declaring the presence of any old and/or abandoned chemical weapons on its territory, or which it has abandoned on the territory of another State.

Destruction of all such chemical weapons must be completed within ten years from the entry into force of the Convention, by 2007. Any CWPFs declared by a State Party must be closed down within 90 days of the Convention entering into force for that State Party and the destruction of such facilities must also be completed by 2007. These former production facilities, following their inactivation, must be destroyed or converted to peaceful purposes. The Convention provides for the possibility of a one-time, five year extension of final destruction deadlines for chemical weapons stockpiles up to 2012. A request for extension must be made to the Executive Council and approved by the Conference of the States Parties. In special circumstances and upon approval by the other Member States, chemical production facilities may be converted for use for peaceful purposes.

An initial declaration under Article VI, or industry declaration, detailing any facilities in a State Party producing, in some cases producing or consuming, Scheduled chemicals above certain thresholds, must also be submitted to the Technical Secretariat within 30 days of the Convention entering into force for any State Party. The States Parties with chemical industry engaged in such activities must submit annual declarations on past and anticipated industrial activities and the export/import of Scheduled chemicals. States Parties with chemical weapons destruction programmes must also submit annual declarations relating to the implementation of such programmes.

Destruction / Conversion

The most important obligation under the Convention is the destruction of chemical weapons. It is also the most expensive aspect of the Convention's implementation.

Most of the destruction costs are generated by the investment in state-of-the-art technology to ensure that the risk to people and to the environment is kept to a minimum at every stage in the transportation and destruction of munitions, as well as during the removal and destruction of chemical agents. Destruction, therefore, has to be carried out at highly specialised facilities.

There are two main technological approaches to the destruction of chemical agents: the direct incineration of the agents and neutralisation by means of various chemical reactions. Research to develop other methods is continuing.

It is up to each State Party to determine which destruction method it wishes to use, provided that it meets strict environmental standards, that the destruction is complete and irreversible, and that the design of the facility allows for adequate verification.

It is important that the exploration of alternative technologies for the demilitarisation and destruction of chemical weapons continues in order to develop processes that are both cost effective and environmentally responsible.

The States Parties must submit detailed plans to the Technical Secretariat that set out the process to be used in the destruction activities and the timelines to be followed. These plans must be submitted for each chemical weapons destruction facility (CWDF)—where the chemical weapons are being destroyed—and for each CWPF that is to be destroyed as well. If a CWPF is to be converted, detailed plans of the conversion process must also be submitted. The plans for destruction and/or conversion are placed before the Executive Council for approval. If approval is not forthcoming, then destruction may commence under continuous monitoring by OPCW inspectors.

The destruction of old and/or abandoned chemical weapons is especially difficult and potentially dangerous. Old and/or abandoned chemical munitions have often become less stable with time and there is a greater risk of an explosive detonation or agent contamination. The destruction of such weapons is being undertaken in a small number of States Parties, as a matter of urgency. Thousands of tonnes of chemical agents and munitions were dumped in the North Sea and the Baltic Sea, as well as other bodies of water worldwide, in the years immediately following World War II. These weapons are not covered by the Convention, which requires only that chemical weapons dumped at sea after 1 January 1985 be declared to the OPCW.

Non-proliferation

The States Parties regulate the use of Scheduled chemicals by industry within their borders, and prepare industry to receive regular OPCW inspections designed to verify that Scheduled chemicals and "discrete organic chemicals" (DOC) are being utilised solely for peaceful purposes.

Under the terms of the Convention, the transfer of Schedule 1 chemicals is strictly controlled among Member States—only for research, medical, pharmaceutical or protective purposes, and in limited quantities—and is forbidden to States not Party. A similar ban on the transfer of Schedule 2 chemicals to States not Party came into force in April 2000. Free trade in Schedule 2 chemicals is permitted among States Parties. It is permitted to transfer Schedule 3 chemicals to both States Parties and States not Party; however, a recipient State not Party must produce an end-user certificate, which ensures that the chemicals are being used for peaceful purposes. The Convention does foresee that States Parties may consider other measures regarding the transfer of Schedule 3 chemicals to States not Party five years after the Convention enters into force.

In addition to the requirements for end-user certificates for transfers of Schedule 3 chemicals, the States Parties are required to monitor carefully exports and imports of all Scheduled chemicals and report this information to the Technical Secretariat on an annual basis.

OPCW Verification

The central role of the Technical Secretariat in CWC implementation is verification.

The Convention and its Verification Annex mandate that the Technical Secretariat verify not only the destruction of chemical weapons stockpiles and CWPFs, but also that Scheduled chemicals are being used solely for permitted purposes. The OPCW Inspectorate, a group of specially trained inspectors within the Technical Secretariat, carries out inspections of military and industrial sites.

Teams of OPCW inspectors conduct verification activities worldwide, and in some cases on a continuous basis. The verification process is conducted in an objective and transparent manner; all States Parties are treated equitably and due respect is given to each State Party's national security.

The size of an inspection team varies considerably depending on the type of facility being inspected and on the type of inspection. The composition of each team also varies according to the type of facility. A team sent to verify the destruction of chemical weapons, for example, may require specialists with expertise in fields such as chemical weapons and munitions technology, chemical production technology, analytical chemistry, and health and safety. On the other hand, a team sent to inspect a chemical industry facility may consist of specialists in the fields of chemical production technology, industrial chemistry, chemical production logistics, and analytical chemistry.

If circumstances at the inspection site do not permit the analysis of samples, the samples can be sent off site to specially designated laboratories for analysis. To acquire the status of a designated OPCW laboratory, a laboratory in a State Party must achieve a high level of performance in several OPCW proficiency tests, and participate in testing regularly to maintain this standard. If a sample must be sent for off-site analysis, stringent procedures will be followed to guarantee the chain of custody, to avoid tampering and to ensure the anonymity of the sample.

Three types of inspections or investigations are foreseen under the Convention: routine inspections, challenge inspections and investigations of alleged use.

Routine inspections are conducted at declared chemical weapons storage, production and destruction facilities (CWSFs, CWPFs, and CWDFs), as well as at declared industrial facilities that produce, process or consume in certain cases chemicals listed in the three Schedules to the Convention, or that produce the unscheduled discrete organic chemicals (DOCs), in quantities above specified thresholds.

These inspections are designed to verify the accuracy of information declared by States Parties in their initial and annual declarations, and that the activities of the States Parties are in accordance with the Convention. Challenge inspections are provided for under the Convention, which grants each State Party the right to request the Director-General to undertake at short notice an OPCW inspection on the territory of any State Party, or at any location under the jurisdiction or control of any other State Party, in order to clarify and resolve any questions of possible non-compliance.

An investigation of alleged use can be conducted by the OPCW at the request of a State Party, either to confirm the actual use or threat of use of chemical weapons, or to assess the need for assistance, or both. During all OPCW verification activities—the receipt and processing of declarations and destruction/conversion plans and on-site inspections and monitoring—stringent compliance with the OPCW confidentiality regime is maintained. The Technical Secretariat safeguards all official information in its possession in accordance with strict security regulations. The classified information submitted by the States Parties, as well as classified documents generated by the Secretariat in relation to the implementation of the verification regime, are handled electronically on a Security Critical Network, to which access is highly restricted.

Implementation Support

The Convention requires complex reporting and regulatory arrangements to be established at the national level. Moreover, each State Party must inform the Organisation of the legislative and administrative measures put in place to implement the Convention. Without the proper national controls, the Convention's object and purpose in such key areas as non-proliferation cannot be achieved in a reliable manner.

The Convention recognises that in complying with these important obligations, States Parties may require assistance from the Organisation. The Secretariat provides technical assistance and technical evaluation to States Parties in the implementation of the provisions of the Convention.

Bibliography

Ackland, Len. *Making a Real Killing: Rocky Flats and the Nuclear West*. Albuquerque: The University of New Mexico Press, 1999.

Allison, Graham: *Nuclear Terrorism: The Ultimate Preventable Catastrophe*, New York: Times Books, 2004.

Ashton, S.R.: *British Policy Towards the Indian States, 1905-1939*, London: Curzon, 1982.

Basrur, Rajesh M., and Hasan-Askari Rizvi: *Nuclear Terrorism and South Asia*, Albuquerque, NM: Sandia National Laboratories, February 2003.

Ben Wisner : *At Risk, Natural Hazards, People's Vulnerability, and Disasters*, London, Routledge, 1994.

Bradley, John. *Learning to Glow: A Nuclear Reader*. Tucson: University of Arizona Press, 2000.

Buzan, Barry & Eric Herring: *The Arms Dynamic in World Politics*, London: Lynne Rienner Publishers, 1998.

Cochran, Thomas B. *Nuclear Weapons Databook*. Cambridge, MA: Ballinger Publishing Company, 1987.

Cochran, Thomas B. *Nuclear Weapons Databook*. Cambridge, MA: Ballinger Publishing Company, 1987.

Duncan, Francis. *Rickover and the Nuclear Navy: The Discipline of Technology*. Annapolis: Naval Institute Press, 1990.

Dunn, Lewis A., *'India, Pakistan, Iran: A Nuclear Proliferation Chain'*, Colorado: Westview Press, 1977.

Fernlund, Kevin J. *The Cold War American West, 1945–1989*. Albuquerque: University of New Mexico Press, 1998.

Freedman, Lawrence. *The Evolution of Nuclear Strategy. Studies in International Security*, New York: St. Martin's Press, 1981.

Friedman, G.: *The Future of War: Power, Technology and American World Dominance in the 21st Century*, N.Y., Random House, 1996.

George Perkovich: *India's Nuclear Bomb: The Impact on Global Proliferation,* University of California Press: Berkeley, 1991.

Gerstell, Richard. *How to Survive an Atomic Bomb*. Washington, D.C.: Combat Forces Press, 1950.

Herken, Gregg. *The Winning Weapon: The Atomic Bomb in the Cold War, 1945-1950*. Princeton: Princeton University Press, 1988.

Janowitz, M.: *The Professional Soldier: A Social and Political Portrait*, N.Y., The Free Press, 1960.

Kapur, Ashok: *Pakistan's Nuclear Development,* New York: Croom Helm, 1987.

Kaufmann, Albert R. *Nuclear Reactor Fuel Elements: Metallurgy and Fabrication*. New York: Interscience Publishers, Inc., 1962.

Khan, Saira: *Nuclear Proliferation Dynamics in Protracted Conflict Regions: A Comparative Study of South Asia and the Middle East,* Vermont: Ashgate Publishing Ltd, 2002.

Leo Tansky, *US and USSR Aid to Developing Countries: A Comparative Study of India, Turkey, and the UAR,* New York, 1967.

Lifton, Robert Jay and Mitchell, Greg. *Hiroshima in America: A Half Century of Denial*. New York: Avon Books, 1995.

McPhee, John. *The Curve of Binding Energy*. New York: The Noonday Press, 1992.

Nair, A. M.: *An Indian Freedom Fighter in Japan*, Bombay, Orient Longman, 1983.

Nininger, Robert D. *Minerals for Atomic Energy*. New York: D. Van Nostrand Company, 1954.

Pash, Boris T. *The Alsos Mission*. New York: Award House, 1969.

Posen, B.R.: *The Sources of Military Doctrine*, Ithaca, 1984, Cornell Univ. Press.

Rhodes, Richard. *The Making of the Atomic Bomb*. New York: Simon and Schuster, 1986.

Rosen, P.: *Societies and Military Power: India and its Armies*, Ithaca, Cornell University Press, 1996.

Sherwin, Martin J. *A World Destroyed: The Atomic Bomb and the Grand Alliance*. New York: Vintage Books, 1977.

Spector, Leonard S., *Going Nuclear*, Cambridge, MA: Ballinger Publishing Company, 1987.

Stephen Reyna : *The Political Economy of African Famine*, Philadelphia, Gordon and Breach Science Publishers, 1991

Teller, Edward. *The Legacy of Hiroshima*. New York: Doubleday, 1962.

Winkler, Allan M. *Life Under A Cloud: American Anxiety About the Atom*. New York: Oxford University Press, 1993.

Index

❑❑❑